AAI Awards 2013

NEW IRISH ARCHITECTURE 28
AAI AWARDS 2013

Edited by John O'Regan and Nicola Dearey

© Gandon Editions, 2017. All rights reserved.

ISBN 978-1-910140-00-0

Produced by Gandon Editions for the
Architectural Association of Ireland (AAI).

design	John O'Regan
	(© Gandon Editions, 2017)
production	Nicola Dearey
	Gunther Berkus
printing	Nicholson Bass, Belfast
distribution	Gandon Distribution
	and its overseas agents
	(for back-issues, see page 179)

GANDON EDITIONS
Oysterhaven, Kinsale, Co Cork
T +353 (0)21-4770830 / E gandon@eircom.net
W www.gandon-editions.com

This is the 392nd book on Irish art + architecture
produced by Gandon Editions to date. Visit our
website, or see our colour catalogue for
information on over 200 titles in print.

front cover – SLIEVEBAWNOGUE (double-house)
(Clancy Moore Architects) (*photo: Alice Clancy*)

The AAI and Gandon Editions are not
responsible for the views expressed herein.

NEW IRISH ARCHITECTURE 28

THE AAI AWARDS

2013 + INDEX TO 28 VOLUMES

NEW IRISH ARCHITECTURE 28 – AAI AWARDS 2013

	Acknowledgements	7
Keynote Essay	BETWEEN PERMANENCE AND TRANSIENCE Elizabeth Hatz	8
	Annual Critic's Lecture	20

AAI AWARDS 2013

	ASSESSORS' REPORTS Elizabeth Hatz, Daniel Rosbottom, Shane de Blacam, Donal Hickey, Maud Cotter	22
	REGISTRAR'S REPORT	25
	Statistics, 1986-2013	26
	AAI Awards Assessors, 1986-2013	27
	FIRST IMPRESSIONS	29
Downes Bronze Medal	SLIEVEBAWNOGUE (double-house) — CLANCY MOORE ARCHITECTS	34
Awards	RECASTING — DONAGHY + DIMOND ARCHITECTS	50
	MEDICAL SCHOOL, STUDENT RESIDENCES & BUS SHELTER, University of Limerick — GRAFTON ARCHITECTS	62
	ARCHITECTURE AS NEW GEOGRAPHY (Venice Biennale) — GRAFTON ARCHITECTS	78
	SCOIL MHUIRE ÓGH, Crumlin — MARY LAHEEN ARCHITECTS	88

NEW IRISH ARCHITECTURE 28 — AAI AWARDS 2013

	HOUSE IN Co CARLOW — STEVE LARKIN ARCHITECT	102
	HOUSE 4, Firhouse — TAKA ARCHITECTS	114
Special Mentions	CARNIVAN HOUSE, Fethard-on-Sea — AUGHEY O'FLAHERTY ARCHITECTS	126
	HOUSE ON CHESTNUT LANE — BOYD CODY ARCHITECTS	134
	BORD GÁIS NETWORKS SERVICES CENTRE — DENIS BYRNE ARCHITECTS	142
	THE GARAGE, Co Fermanagh — JOHN MAGUIRE ARCHITECT	150
	VESSEL: an installation for the Venice Biennale 2012 — O'DONNELL + TUOMEY ARCHITECTS	156

ARCHITECTURAL ASSOCIATION OF IRELAND		164
MAURICE CRAIG AWARD 2013		165
Award	'Mediating Geography: Threshold Places' – Alan Hilliard (SAUL)	166
Highly Commended	'Inhabited Threshold', Brussels – Eimear Murphy, (QUB)	170
AAI DESIGN COMPETITION FOR SECOND YEAR STUDENTS 2013		172
NEW IRISH ARCHITECTURE °1-28 – AAI AWARDS 1986-2013		176
	■ back-issues	177
	■ volume by volume listings	180
	■ architects' index	200
	■ building type index	213

Acknowledgements

Gandon Editions gratefully acknowledges the support of the following bodies, companies and architectural practices for this expanded 28th volume in the annual *New Irish Architecture* series, documenting the AAI Awards 2013, and featuring a 48-page index to all 28 volumes:

Architectural Association of Ireland
Boyd Cody Architects
Carr Cotter & Naessens Architects
CCAE Cork School of Architecture
Design Strategies
Donaghy + Dimond Architects
DTA Architects
Grafton Architects
Henchion + Reuter Architects
Michael Kelly Architect
Mary Laheen Architects
John Maguire Architect
Nicholson Bass
O'Donnell + Tuomey Architects
O'Mahony Pike Architects
Jason O'Shaughnessy Architect
Queen's University Belfast
    School of Natural & Built Environment
Scott Tallon Walker Architects
Taka Architects
Tegral Building Products
UCD School of Architecture

BETWEEN PERMANENCE AND TRANSIENCE

ELIZABETH HATZ

"Action is a brief madness. Man's most precious gift is a short epilepsy. Genius contained in a tiny moment. Love is born at a glance, and a glance can be sufficient for lifelong hatred. And we have value only as we momentarily step outside ourselves. This tiny moment outside myself is a seed or is thrown like a spore. Remaining time is for developing this – or let it go wasted. There is a curiously strong tension contained in such seeds and moments. There are times that differ from others in the same way gunpowder differs from sand. Their looks are alike, their futures are incomparable.".

— Paul Valery in *Aphorisms: Waiting for the Unexpected*

You sit down against a sunlit wall to shelter from the wind and suddenly it is easier to think, pleasant to talk, and maybe even possible to start really see things. You watch people around you, the colour of the shade, passing clouds, and a car turning the street corner. After a while, you realise the wall is in fact a magnificent monument, maybe even a grave or a palace – a work of architecture [1, 2]. Let us look at this dual capacity of architecture – as figure or artefact, and as background for something more important.

A fundamental property of architecture is precisely to be the background for something that is more important, for life itself [3]. It is the tension between this property and architecture's capacity as monument, figure and artefact that begins to get problematic, and also promising. It is a tension between what I call potential architecture, or enabling architecture, and its impression as 'gestalt', as defined figure.

In his essay 'The Bread of Architecture',[1] Bernard Rudofsky talks about this property of architecture as background, the way a white wall allows us to see colour and movement, the changes of the daylight, the movement of shadows, the experience of time lived. The

opposite 1 – Architecture, reflector of transience
below 2 – Light made tangible

3 – Permanence, background for the everyday
(photos by the author, unless otherwise stated)

4 – Kodak HQ and Laboratories, Gothenburg (1983), by E Hatz for Berg Architects
(photo: ARX foto)

opposite

5 – Merrion Square, Dublin

6 – Veterinary clinic, Düsseldorf (1987), by Gabriela Seifert of Formalhaut

7 – Janna Syvänoja, *The Walls Have Eyes* (ev+a 2010, Limerick)

8 – Janna Syvänoja, *Blowing Bubbles* (1998) (photo: the artist)

wall inspiring him to these reflections was a simple patio in New York. Collected observations of this kind may become as valid design criteria as any formal programmatic requests.

In my very first job in Sweden, I can now see how the interest in architecture's dual capacity made me break almost all the rules. I was 26, two years out of the AA in London, and was given the task at Berg Architects to design Kodak's headquarters and laboratories outside Gothenburg (a 10,500m^2 project) [4]. The planning regulations said 12m over ground; I made it 18.5m. The convention for industrial buildings was a comb structure with chunky parts, easy to add to. I deliberately made it hard to add to, and very thin at 10.5m, so that all the time you had contact with both the cool light on the north side and the warm light on the south, so that you could orientate yourself with the help of the dramatic surrounding landscape. It would also require considerable effort to add to, given the landscape was both demanding and beautiful. I remember wanting it to stand like a clear figure in this landscape, in dialogue with it, and I remember cutting the windows like slots to have enough expanse of wall space for the sun and shadows to play on its surface, background for measuring time. This is where it started for me, with industrial architecture, demanding both clear and definite programs, but also capable of swift adaptation to a change of use. I thought that whatever can survive that contradiction might have something to do with architecture – something that would last even when the code was lost, when the manual was obsolete. The sphinx-like monument and the enabling background at the same time.

To become dignified, background requires something very far from complacence. The nature of that surface, the way it responds to climatic conditions, the way it relates to its context, the way it changes over time and in different lights, the physicality of its making, the way it negotiates with other materials, the joints... Georgian architecture is, through its stern and unsentimental repetition and anonymity, a sophisticated example of architectural background, but the anonymity is often broken with personalised refinements [5]. The richness lies very much in the craft of the making, how exactly these materials have been handled and transformed, the presence in the detail.

This side of architecture is again close to the observation of the transience of life itself. I don't think there are any bad materials, but there is a lot of bad handling of materials. Also, being slow to change, it takes people a very long time to develop a relationship to new materials. But we need to start trying, at least. Gabriela Seifert of the German group Formalhaut made an entrance to a veterinary clinic in a converted villa outside Düsseldorf using corrugated translucent plastic [6]. She had noted how it turns milky with age; by painting diagonal strokes across the surface, she anticipated and underlined this process and played on the capacity to create shadow, thus emphasising the temporal quality.

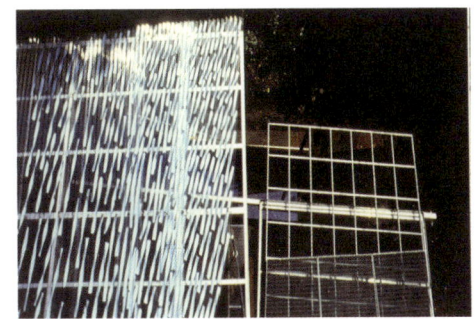

Janna Syvänoja was one of the artists I invited to exhibit at *ev+a* 2010.[2] In a time when we may begin to discover the creative potential not alone in newness and the new, but in the renewed gaze on things and matter, Syvänoja's unbelievable transformations of living materials seem highly relevant [plates 7, 8]. Materials, natural or man-made – even air or sound – undergo metamorphosis in her hands. The starting point is in an encounter, or a will to be, like the caterpillar that turns into a butterfly. Her eye on the world around us results in unbelievable transformations – paintings made of birch bark, bubbles made from spectacle glasses, walls made out of discarded sheets from a Japanese accounts office, or feather-light bowls made from the skeletons of aspen leaves. Like to someone who whispers, you stop and lend your ear. It is a rearrangement of the existing. It has surprising power. I think this opens a way also in architecture. If 80% of our future tasks will be to rearrange and alter the existing, then the existing is our new source of inventive energy. The thoughtful handling of matter and materials will be the new challenge. We have an ambiva-

9 – Unfinished shopping centre, Castletroy, Limerick

10, 11 – Nobel Industries, House 40, Stockholm (1990) by E Hatz for Berg Architects

opposite

12 – Diego Velázquez, *The Kitchen Maid with the Supper at Emmaus* (c.1617) (National Galley of Ireland)

13 – Gerhard Richter, *Stroke on Red* (1980)

lent attitude towards the half-old or half-new, and half-finished [9]. It is somehow awkwardly beyond classification, has not yet passed through our valuating filters. That's part of the reason why it interests me; the resistance these buildings present is also some kind of freedom. Maybe here we can talk more about character than beauty, as these places resist beauty or reach beauty only through character, like an aged face.

Again with Berg architects, I was asked to design two floors of laboratories and a service attic for Nobel Industries as an addition to an old chemical factory on the outskirts of Stockholm [10, 11]. The budget was as tough as the builder, and determination was required to achieve the qualities I considered fundamental to the project: large windows to allow in lots of light, brick burnt in old ovens to get the rough and raw character that could match the factory tower from the '40s, a zinc roof, and columns of projecting bricks to reflect light and add rhythm and measure. It is quite an ugly building, in fact, with the prosaic name of House 40. Just a year after its completion, I was standing at a bus-stop nearby when a man came up to me and started talking about the area, complaining about all the (in his opinion) hideous pretentious new buildings. Then he pointed at House 40, and, as I started feeling slightly uneasy, he said with some conviction: "But you see that one, that's listed, they won't be allowed to destroy that one and that's comforting to me. Because it belongs here, it's part of this place." When I had recovered and well hidden my embarrassment, I thought to myself, "I am probably walking backwards through life, and moving slowly but surely backwards in time, but also fast-forwarding, so that my buildings become listed long before I am buried and forgotten." But what that man talked about, I think, was not the value that protects buildings, but about it being part of an ordinariness that belonged, that didn't stand out, and that it was still something that deserved a permanent existence in his area – maybe architecture as background again, in a slightly different way. A sphinx of ordinariness. Can architecture be monument and background at the same time?

The theme of my practice-based research is permanence, and the transition between permanence and transience. One of my favourite works at the National Gallery of Ireland is the mysterious early painting by Velázquez, *The Kitchen Maid with the Supper at Emmaus* [12]. An important moment in religious history is portrayed through a most ordinary domestic scene, which makes it extraordinary. The two parallel situations are contrasted in scale, the actual meal being pushed to a minor element in the background, while the trivial domestic scene – life itself – occupies the foreground with its artefacts. The moment is held by the light in the domestic pots, the white cloth, the posture of the maid in her leaning forward. The painting is holding a dual moment, prolonging this second to a state of permanence on the canvas.

Gerhard Richter's 20m-long brush stroke, *Stroke on Red* (1980) [13], enlarges the actual act of painting and the material beyond recognition; it becomes a wall and a territory of its own. Only our gaze on it is rapid, while the material and physical form seem to strive towards infinite resistance, toward solidity, supported by the wall of the building where it is painted. The painting is like a theatrical performance in reverse: instead of compressing an action in the room, the space of time is abnormally expanded by the vastness of the extreme solid form. It appears as an attempt to make a temporary action permanent, retaining the occurrence, which is its own meaning – the stroke, material and action of painting. The obvious strength of the painting may be summarised in its ability to retain an ephemeral moment so it becomes all moments and more tangible that any other physical object in its surrounding, fixing time in material form. The paradox which *Stroke on Red* presents also provides the work with an impenetrable integrity as a physical artefact.

Is making permanent – in the sense of extending, postponing, retaining – a significant aspect of art? And if so, is this an aspect it shares with architecture? "Culture", writes Hannah Arendt in *The Human Condition* relates to the production of things that survive us. It is this durability which gives the things of the world their relative independence from men who produced and used them." And she continues, "because of their outstanding permanence, works of art are the most intensely worldly of all tangible things." I propose that works of architecture are potentially part of this category, and I suspect Arendt meant them to be. Architecture between enabling life and resisting time. Perhaps part of the process of architectural production is to revalue the works of art and the works of architecture.

In architecture we are sometimes surprised by the way a single building or even part of a building manages to completely change the surrounding – through its power as a singular entity – in form and intentional contraction [14, 15]. This is what I mean by the monument and artefact dimension of architecture. I am interested in its immediate relation to transience and ordinary life. The *mastaba* is one of the oldest of human constructions. Without an interior, it is like a raised platform or giant table, with petrified tablecloth, in the landscape, its burial chamber normally underground. On the side there is a blind door [16]. This is the surface where the world we know and the unknown meet. This is also where the living would celebrate the dead with a meal, and the representations of the meal in the inscriptions on the surface. The meal is one of the most basic, transient events (to keep us alive), and also the quintessence of collective occasion. The ritual of this transience is made permanent in the door niche. Monument and transience coincide and collaborate. Moreover, the door is a translation in stone of a perishable, temporary door, a rolled, pleated mat.

If architecture is primarily background for life, one wonders how to give this background the dignity to survive beyond use? How is integrity beyond function infused? In my practice-based research, I am attempting to consciously use the power of the artefact in the process of making architecture [17, 18]. The making of the thing itself, even before or beyond purpose, is a driving part of its becoming. Using simple, banal and everyday occasions and objects, I fuse them and explore their potential monumental power. Seat and sitting becomes throne; door and entering or leaving becomes porch or gate. Enlarged to huge dimensions, it resembles an enormous table where a heavenly meal may take place.

If a growing number of architectural tasks ahead have to handle not new production, but alterations of what is already produced, maybe the creative process will also have to change and adopt new strategies. The obsession with newness is, after all, a fairly recent invention. According to Paul Valéry, newness is the last aspect of a thing that we ought to bother about as it is the first to fade away. For him, an idea should be like a matured vine, not like something you found and picked up in this morning; it should be something handed down for generations. To reinterpret, revalue and rearrange the existing is, for me, the most attractive field of discovery. The attentive gaze on what is already there, however ordinary, just by the act of revisiting, seems to allow the everyday to become special and the absurd to become precious, like a new-born. What was lost is then found again and reinvented. A movement in Japan, collecting Thomassons, is one example of how the gaze on what we have already produced may tenderly transform the vision of our overbuilt condition. The term, which comes from the baseball star Gary Thomasson, who was brought to play in Japan but underused, defines things absurd and useless that occur as debris of what we build – like a staircase leading up to nowhere or a shop front without the shop, etc – and they can be both permanent or transient. Searching for Thomassons makes you sensitive to the overlooked, forgotten and discarded.

At SAUL in Limerick some years ago we ran a project called 'Inhabiting Infrastructure' (again linked to my practice-based research), where we looked at half-old places due for change, such as abandoned military camps in Sweden [19]. Whereas the buildings normally get all the attention, I noticed to my surprise how the ground itself constituted the most powerful entity of the area, the strongest architectural element, one of permanence and background for human events. Infrastructure is part of what I call potential architecture [20]. Considering how much money we spend on it and how much land it consumes, it is strange

opposite 14, 15 – Museo La Congiunta, Giornico, Switzerland (1992), by Peter Märkli

above 16 – Mastaba door, British Museum, London

17, 18 – *Permanence*, *Odd Models* (2004) by E Hatz at Fargfabriken (photos: Gunnar Smoliansky and EH)

how little architectural consideration we give to it. The process in this research was to view this ground not as void, but as physical artefact, and let this drive the analysis. As an immediate response to the site and place, the objects are made as speculative portraits, in a process that uses memory, speculation and craft, as well as precise measurement [21, 22]. These are methods I use also when I teach; practice, research, writing and teaching are really all part of the same search, all, in the end, based on close observation in the place itself.

I think it is the patient and interested gaze on the transient world that gives some kind of substance to the gradual birth of a sort of permanence. Danish painter Vilhelm Hammershi had that patience, returning again and again to the same themes, the same rooms and angles. The apparent restriction and stillness in his work feel charged with an intensity from within, like the power of a mountain, that forms a mute background to the closer events. This acts like a frame that makes the small things, the nuances, visible. If we start getting interested in the hidden and forgotten things already around us, we also soon discover the powers of things veiled [23, 24]. The veil both hides and reveals insofar as it actually emphasises certain things while obliterating others. Like clothing on a body, a unifying veil may enhance the topographic lines in a resorting of the visual order. If we want to see anew, and move beyond preconceived ideas about our architectural surrounding, we can play with these veils, like filters that selectively obliterate, in order to reveal aspects that were obscured.

As a final commentary on this theme, I should like to address this country and its architects. I love Ireland. It is rich, it is refreshingly irrational, and it persists. But this nation, just like the rest of the world, is facing a whole lot of problems. In such a situation, large and seemingly bold projects may obliterate the view of the unassuming, forgotten and ordinary as something in need of change. But perhaps what needs to be changed is our view of it and how we care for it. In Ireland we should start to embrace what may seem most awkward and embarrassing. We have a Swedish expression, *hemmablind* ('home blind') – being good at identifying qualities elsewhere but forgetting to look at what you have in front of you. Only when embracing the most ordinary, fragile and sometimes embarrassing parts of your culture can you nurture true originality and quality.

Let me start a list. For instance, the rural presence in the urban, and vice versa. This is a photo I took near Limerick city [25]. Farming is doing quite well in Ireland. It is really time to work more actively with the rural condition and stop turning our backs on it. And the villages – why are they so undervalued? Why don't villages grow denser, instead of local authorities continuing to allow isolated developments, devouring good farmland? If we as architects are concerned about our built environment, we really should care about the delicate balance and deep interrelationship in Ireland of rural and urban culture.

The sulkies and the horses, animals in the city, slowing down the traffic, irritating the drivers, showing another way of understanding communal life, outdoor life and slower time [26]. Embrace this, build stables everywhere, arrange a proud, sulkie *palio* every year in Limerick, and invite Europe!

The one-off houses. Admitted, they are often pretentious, wasteful, bad. But maybe there are also possibilities in the fact that there is habitation and a rich network of little roads never far away, so with other means of transport and work habits it could be different in the future to today's commuting, but only if people relate to the land not just as an image, as a visual commodity, but as a living thing to handle and care for.

Antiquarian, preservation – words largely taboo amongst architects in Ireland. Why? You have invaluable heritage to take care of, and it is time to act for it [27]. Who, if not architects, should take a stance, to value, defend and inform about cultural heritage? It does not

above 21, 22 – *Permanence, Recycling Space*, installation by E Hatz at Lund Art Hall, Sweden, 2006

23 – Sumerian statue

24 – Limerick back lane

opposite

19 – Abandoned military camp, Strängnäs, Sweden

20 – Quays to the south of Stockholm

17

mean that it remains completely unaltered – nothing does – but it means that you need to handle it with the utmost delicacy and with knowledge. And learn from it. I truly believe it is one of Ireland's finest assets, but one that is strangely overlooked and underestimated.

The unfinished estates and other constructions [28]. Invent events, rent them out to people with more ideas than money – for co-operatives, garden centres, local food production. Allow for more transient uses and economies, for social initiatives and businesses to emerge. And when will Dublin start trying to identify and embrace its unique and its different characters [29]? Instead of following the mainstream and importing iconic images from global style, Dublin should be beyond and ahead of the magazines and websites. *Ulysses* could be a good guide for a city-planning report.

The AAI Awards is proof that Irish architects can do all this and a lot more. Irish architects are winning international competitions, building great architecture in major world cities, and winning prestigious awards. Yes, Irish architecture and education enjoy international esteem; therefore, they should remain focussed on excellence, character, originality, pathos and ethics. In short, to copy the international mainstream would be sadly provincial. To value the provinces would support global concern.

Finally, I would just like to end with a something a little odd from *ev+a* 2010 [30]. I had to cover two very large gaps on the top floor of the Hub exhibition centre – an empty, newly built office block in Limerick city centre – and found a couple of rolls of tracing paper in an abandoned engineer's office. So I made a paper *mastaba*, an old grave for tracing paper, the paper that few architects use anymore, but my young students are starting to use again. It is thin, soft to the touch, crinkles and tears easily, but provides you the perfect surface for sketching, testing, noting, letting the hand think. The resistance of this delicate yet unassuming material, where layer upon layer of drawing anticipates past, present and future, rather like a ruin, is, in this process, revealing structures of architectural thought and form.[3] Through this repeated persistency, revealed through its transparency like a palimpsest, the sketch on tracing, for me, is at the heart of both permanence and transience.

ENDNOTES

[1] Bernard Rudofsky, 'The Bread of Architecture' in *Arts & Architecture* (Los Angeles, CA) October 1952.
[2] Janna Syvänoja was born in Finland in 1960, and has exhibited at major international exhibitions. Received the Prince Eugen Medal (Sweden) in 2012 for outstanding artistic achievement.
[3] Fred Scott, in his book *On Altering Architecture* (Routledge, London, 2008), refers to the ruin as an aspect of temporality, quoting a former student in interior design at RISD.

opposite

25 – Cows grazing in Castletroy, Limerick
26 – Sulkie near Thomond Brigde, Limerick
27 – Loughmoe Castle, Co Tipperary
28 – Unfinished shopping centre, Castletroy, Limerick
29 – David Lilburn, etching (City Hall Museum, Limerick)
30 – *Paper Mastaba* by E Hatz at *ev+a* 2010, Limerick

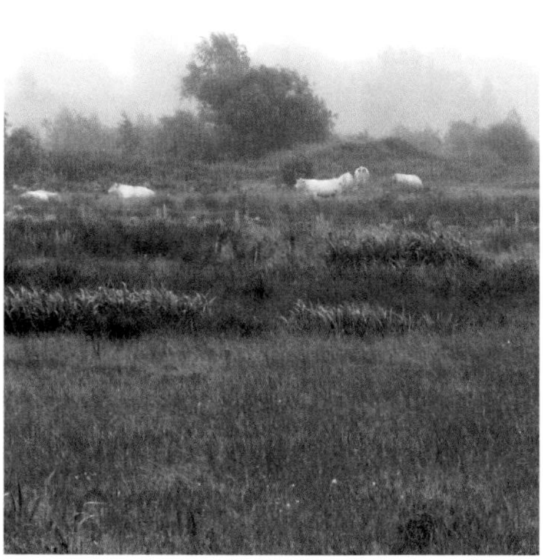
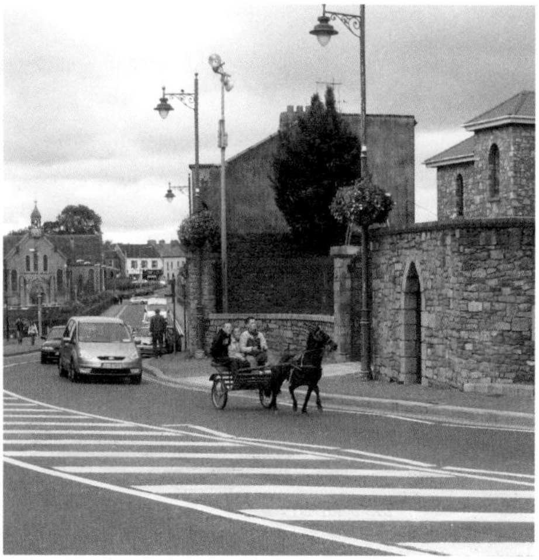
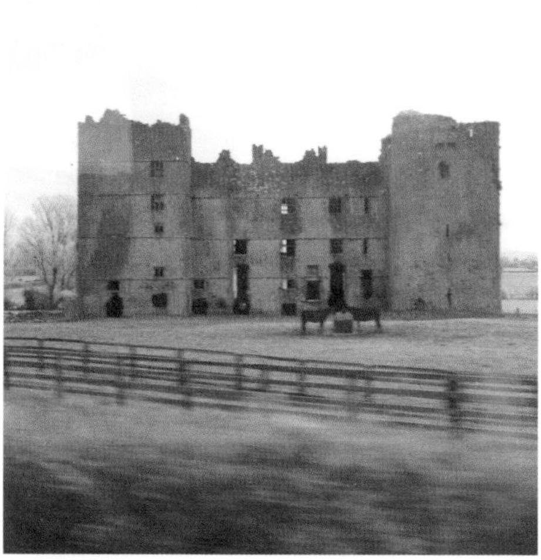
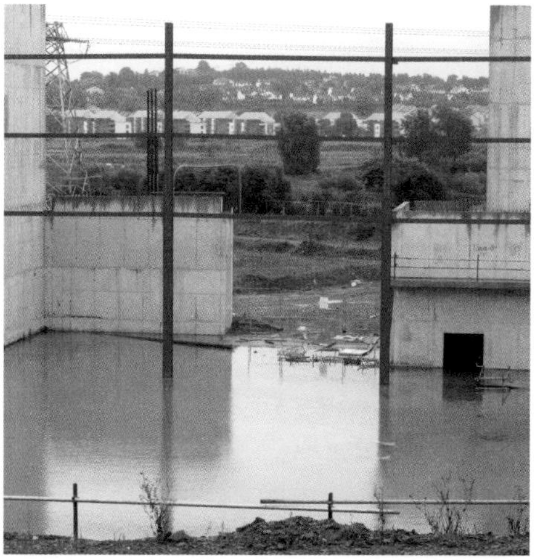
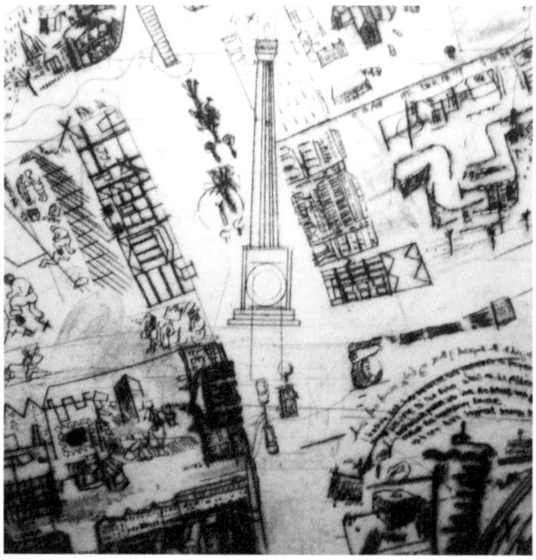
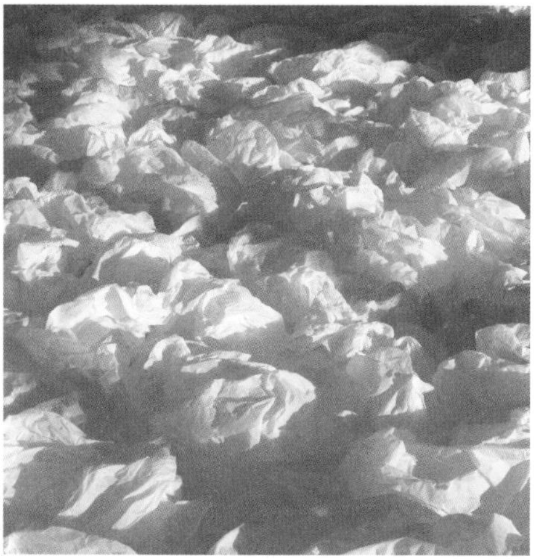

ANNUAL CRITIC'S LECTURE

Each year, the international architectural critic on the AAI Awards jury gives a lecture to the AAI. The annual Critic's Lecture was sponsored by Tegral Building Products from 1999-2008. The lectures/essays in this series have been published in *New Irish Architecture* as follows:

2012	Elizabeth Hatz	'Between Permanence and Transience'
		NIA °28 – AAI *Awards* 2013 (AAI / Gandon, 2017), pp8-19
2011	Joseph Rykwert	'Refuse and the Body Politic'
		NIA °27 – AAI *Awards* 2012 (AAI / Gandon, 2012), pp8-19
2010	William JR Curtis	'The Time of Life, the Time of Architecture'
		NIA °26 – AAI *Awards* 2011 (AAI / Gandon, 2011), pp6-13
2009	Charles Jencks	'Critical Modernism'
		NIA °25 – AAI *Awards* 2010 (AAI / Gandon, 2010), pp6-21
2008	Wilfried Wang	'Quality Matters'
		NIA °24 – AAI *Awards* 2009 (AAI / Gandon, 2009), pp6-21
2007	Francis Rambert	'New Landscapes and Fresh Attitudes'
		NIA °23 – AAI *Awards* 2008 (AAI / Gandon, 2008), pp6-18
2006	Luis Fernández-Galiano	'Dublin Duet'
		NIA °22 – AAI *Awards* 2007 (AAI / Gandon, 2007), pp6-12
2005	Andrej Hrausky	'Joze Plecnik (1872-1957), Ljubljana'
		NIA °21 – AAI *Awards* 2006 (AAI / Gandon, 2006), pp6-20
2004	Terence Riley	'This Will Kill That – A brief history of seven centuries of architecture and the media'
		NIA °20 – AAI *Awards* 2005 (AAI / Gandon, 2005), pp6-23
2003	Aaron Betsky	'Dublin from a bird's-eye view'
		NIA °19 – AAI *Awards* 2004 (AAI / Gandon, 2004), pp6-9
2002	Deyan Sudjic	'Building by Numbers – Political aspects of architecture'
		NIA °18 – AAI *Awards* 2003 (AAI / Gandon, 2003), pp6-9
2001	Dietmar Steiner	'Storm of Calm – A lecture on a theme'
		NIA °17 – AAI *Awards* 2002 (AAI / Gandon, 2002), pp6-13
2000	Jean-Louis Cohen	'Ireland's Critical Internationalism'
		NIA °16 – AAI *Awards* 2001 (AAI / Gandon, 2002), pp6-11
1999	Beatriz Colomina	'X-ray Architecture'
		published in Beatriz Colomina, *Domesticity at War* (MIT Press, 2007)

To order back-issues of *New Irish Architecture*, see page 179

NEW IRISH ARCHITECTURE 28

AAI AWARDS 2013

Assessors' Reports

ELIZABETH HATZ, *architectural critic*

I was honoured and delighted to act as architectural critic for the AAI Awards 2013. Ireland, on the edge of Europe and with a population of 4.5 million people, has some of the best architects in the world and enjoys an architectural culture of deep engagement. Considering the harshness of the economic downturn, with architecture at the vanguard, the display of high-quality, thoughtful design work this year is worth an award in itself, and carrying through with the assessment process in the economic climate is equally laudable.

On a general note, my impression is that projects with a low budget, an odd or pragmatic programme, or a particularly difficult site are sometimes the strongest, as if the challenge triggers an outstanding performance. The best contemporary Irish architecture, in my view, stands out internationally through its strong material presence and singular connection to the complex particularities of site and culture. There are tones and certain colours, in the sense of character and mood, that you find nowhere else. There is boldness and wit, a solemn timelessness and sometimes elegance, often in negotiation with contradictory surroundings. The connection and dialogue with what is already there is the key to whether a project works or doesn't. This, however, is difficult to convey in conventional presentations; it needs to be seen in the flesh.

When we look at project presentations in drawings, texts and images, we are in laboratory conditions where geometries and ideas may be scrutinised in an uncontaminated state, and the crispness of thought stands out in all its purity. As Alois Riegl would have put it, we are in the optic realm of understanding the work rather than the haptic. But the optic needs be informed by the haptic. The image of architecture is always part of a dream; the precision of drawings reveal a level of competence and insight. This, however, is never the way with architecture when built; it is why it requires the test of translation between real and ideal, between the haptic and the optic. In the end, it has to deal with the complexity of its location. Even with projects that consciously and directly grapple with the unglamorous reality, there is always a difference when truly experiencing what they actually do to a place. For this reason, the AAI Awards process offers a challenge for the assessors as the buildings are never visited. The risk is that important work gets overlooked. The AAI Awards remains an amazing opportunity for architectural inspiration and discussion, but I believe many would greatly welcome a change in the assessment process, one that is fairer to the projects as well as to assessors, with a selected shortlist that is actually visited, particularly as Ireland is so manageable geographically. The amplified graphic sophistication in manipulating computer rendering, ironically, further increases the need to confront project presentation with scrutinising the physical reality of the building in its surrounding. Irish architecture is of such quality and the Awards so prestigious that they both deserve this commitment and rigour.

ELIZABETH B HATZ is an architect, senior lecturer in architecture, assistant professor, architectural critic and art curator in Sweden and Ireland. As chairman of SAR (Swedish Association of Architects), she founded Färgfabriken, the centre for art and architecture in Stockholm. In 1999 she became Professor of Architecture at KTH Stockholm. She has acted as an external examiner and guest lecturer and critic at UCD, Copenhagen Academy, AHO/Oslo, ETH, The Cooper Union, Mendrisio, London Metropolitan, amongst others, and curated *ev+a* 2010 – *Matters* in Limerick. She is currently a studio teacher at KTH, and a year master at SAUL, Limerick. She runs her own office in Stockholm. Recent writings include texts on Peter Märkli and Hans Josephson.

DANIEL ROSBOTTOM, *foreign assessor*

It was an honour to be invited as a critic for the AAI Awards, a concentrated day alleviated and made pleasurable through its atmosphere of conviviality and generous hospitality. Arriving from another place and with only a little knowledge of Irish architecture, the range of work offered a realisation of the extent to which the country's architectural milieu is European in its outlook whilst maintaining, in the best cases, an absolute particularity. Although in some cases architects had evidently succumbed to the temptation to stretch ambition beyond what a given circumstance could comfortably accommodate, the best works I saw, regardless of their scale or programme, felt both situated within their place and responsive to broader concerns of architecture, culture and society, demonstrating an economy of means that allowed them to transcend the extreme constraint of prevalent economic conditions. The winner of the Medal was not alone in making a genuine contribution to the history and experience of our discipline.

DANIEL ROSBOTTOM is Professor of Architecture and Interiors at TU Delft, The Netherlands, and was formerly head of the School of Architecture and Landscape at Kingston University, London. He is also a founding director of the internationally acclaimed practice DRDH Architects, London. Their recently completed Stormen Konserthus and Bibliothek in Bodø, Norway, was named Building of the Year for 2014 by the *Architects Journal* and the *Daily Telegraph* in the UK, and was awarded the 2015 Norwegian State Architecture Prize. Alongside practice and academia, Rosbottom writes regularly on both architecture and art.

DONAL HICKEY, *Irish assessor*

The luxury of spending a day amongst peers and the work of colleagues is a rare and rewarding one. The covenant to assess the works presented for awards on the basis of architectural quality and agency is what sets the AAI Awards apart, the explicit intention being to identify works which advance the progress of architecture in Ireland. The range of works submitted for the Awards has narrowed substantially in recent years. There were few, if any, unbuilt propositions or speculative projects, while public housing has virtually disappeared. The increased number of pavilions may be indicative of the attrition of the scope of the architect, but also the confidence to agitate and make propositions beyond architecture as disconnected artefact.

The demonstration of skill and architectural rigour, while present, was predictably restricted to domestic or small-scale projects, many of which were a delight. Why such care and attention is lavished on such projects is often due to the lack of access to commissions for projects of a greater scale. The two notable exceptions were University of Limerick and Bord Gáis, both of which demonstrate the commitment of those commissioning the works in collaboration with their architects. That said, the public faces of major institutions have increasingly migrated to the urban margins, leaving only a digital imprint and interface, while these new headquarters struggle for identity in the diluted infrastructural margins.

My disappointment expressed during the judging is that the progress of Irish architecture relies heavily on the output of a minority of privately commissioned works. One questions the architectural policies and politics of good intentions when publicly commissioned works do not register a greater responsibility to spearhead architectural culture.

It is easy to understand Grafton Architects' attraction to the South American modernists in their speculation on a 'new geography'. One is aware of a position of ethical and social responsibility, of humanity, but above all we can learn from its realised conspicuous generosity.

DONAL HICKEY studied architecture in Ireland and France, graduating from the Dublin Institute of Technology and Trinity College Dublin in 1996. He is a lecturer at the Dublin School of Architecture, DIT, where he has taught since 1999. Donal Hickey Architects was established in 1999. It has won a number of awards, and work has been published and exhibited in Ireland and internationally. It was premiated in the international competition for an Atlantic City Boardwalk Holocaust Memorial in 2011. Hickey is a founding member of the Irish Architecture Foundation, and past president and honorary member of the Architectural Association of Ireland.

MAUD COTTER, *distinguished non-architect*

Art and architecture occupy a shared territory of matter. It is in this territory that my appreciation and interest in architecture, as a practicing artist, lies. Reciprocal and singular moments in each discipline open new spatial possibilities and material behaviours. Aesthetically charged amalgams, the quicksilver moments of exchange between disciplines, deepen understandings in each, releasing a more vital investigative practice. Add to this a perceptual shift that acknowledges the innate agency in all previously understood as dead matter, and the game changes.

MAUD COTTER is a graduate and Adjunct Faculty Member of the Crawford Municipal College of Art & Design, Cork. She is co-founder of the National Sculpture Factory, Cork, and a member of Aosdána. Recent exhibitions include *Matter of Fact*, DOMOBAAL, London (2016); *Compression*, Ormston House Gallery, Limerick (2015); *Fourth Space*, Uillinn – West Cork Arts Centre, Skibbereen (2015); *From Point A to Point B and Back Again*, Point B, Williamsburg, NY (2015); *The Air They Capture is Different*, MAC, Belfast (2013); *A Solution is in the Room* (solo), CIT Wandesford Quay, Cork (2013). She has lectured in art and architecture colleges in Europe and America. She lives and works in Cork.

Registrar's Report

The Architectural Association of Ireland (AAI) was founded in 1896 "to promote and afford facilities for the study of architecture and the allied sciences and arts and to provide a medium of friendly communication between members and others interested in the progress of architecture."

The AAI Awards were established in 1986 as "an annual award scheme for excellence in architectural design". The intentions of the Awards are:
– to encourage higher standards of architecture throughout the country
– to recognise projects which make a contribution to Irish architecture
– to inform the public of emerging directions in contemporary architecture

The Awards scheme is open to architects practising in Ireland and Irish architects practising in their own right abroad, submitting current projects and buildings.

A panel of five distinguished assessors is invited to make a broad selection of schemes which they feel would make a contribution to Irish architecture. The assessors comprise an architectural critic; a foreign architect; two Irish architects; and a distinguished non-architect. The intention behind the composition of the jury is that the two foreign assessors offer an international perspective, while the two Irish architects ensure that due consideration is given to the particular context in which Irish architects work.

The assessors for the AAI Awards 2013 were: ELIZABETH HATZ (*architectural critic*, Sweden), DANIEL ROSBOTTOM (UK), SHANE DE BLACAM and DONAL HICKEY (Ireland), and MAUD COTTER (*distinguished non-architect*). They awarded the Downes Bronze Medal and made six Awards and five Special Mentions.

This is the twenty-eighth exhibition and publication in the series since 1986. The AAI Awards 2013 attracted 68 applications, with 65 valid entries. In the 28 years to 2013, the AAI Awards has assessed 1,991 projects. The Medal has been awarded in 19 of these years (with a joint medal in 1996). There have been a further 147 Award-winners, and 288 Special Mentions. The annual AAI Awards exhibitions and books have featured a total of 455 buildings and projects by over 100 architectural practices. (All 455 projects are listed in the 48-page index included in this volume.)

The AAI Awards have been published annually as *New Irish Architecture*. The series represents the most comprehensive documentation available of the best of contemporary Irish architecture. Previous volumes in the series are available from good bookshops, or can be ordered from Gandon Editions (see page 179).

Statistics

year	published as	applied	valid entries	Medals	Awards	Special Mentions	total exhibits
1986	NIA °1	69	51	0	5	11	16
1987	NIA °2	58	39	1	3	11	15
1988	NIA °3	89	71	1	7	13	21
1989	NIA °4	85	68	1	4	8	13
1990	NIA °5	97	80	1	6	15	22
1991	NIA °6	60	40	0	4	9	13
1992	NIA °7	81	75	1	4	11	16
1993	NIA °8	47	47	1	3	1	5
1994	NIA °9	66	61	0	4	6	10
1995	NIA °10	61	51	1	6	14	21
1996	NIA °11	58	50	(joint) 2	4	9	15
1997	NIA °12	54	54	1	4	14	19
1998	NIA °13	61	61	0	4	8	12
1999	NIA °14	55	51	1	(incl 1 SA) 7	12	20
2000	NIA °15	81	66	0	(incl 3 SA) 6	12	18
2001	NIA °16	94	83	0	8	15	23
2002	NIA °17	122	121	1	3	9	13
2003	NIA °18	82	73	1	6	8	15
2004	NIA °19	103	91	1	7	13	21
2005	NIA °20	74	69	1	3	9	13
2006	NIA °21	73	71	1	7	8	16
2007	NIA °22	102	96	0	6	6	12
2008	NIA °23	92	88	1	(incl 2 SA) 5	7	13
2009	NIA °24	128	118	1	(incl 2 SA) 7	19	27
2010	NIA °25	116	105	1	(incl 2 SA) 6	14	21
2011	NIA °26	71	70	0	(incl 4 SA) 7	15	22
2012	NIA °27	81	76	0	(incl 1 SA) 5	6	11
2013	NIA °28	68	65	1	6	5	12
		2,228	1,991	20	(incl 13 SA) 147	288	455
					SA = Special Award		
highest number		128	121	2	8	19	27
lowest number		47	39	0	3	1	5
annual averages		79.6	71.1	0.7	5.3	10.3	16.3

Assessors

From 1986 to 1990, the three-member AAI Awards jury comprised a foreign assessor and two Irish assessors (including the previous year's Medal-winner). From 1991 to 1999, the five-member jury comprised a foreign assessor, three Irish assessors (including the previous year's Medal-winner), and a distinguished non-architect. Since then, with the introduction of an architectural critic programme, the five-member jury has comprised an international architectural critic, a foreign assessor, two Irish assessors, and a distinguished non-architect.

Each year, the international architectural critic on the AAI Awards jury gives a lecture to the AAI. The lectures/essays in this series are published annually in *New Irish Architecture* as the keynote essay (see page 20).

Wiel Arets	(Netherlands)	1996
Ivana Bacik	(professor of law / senator)	2011
James Barrett		1995
Florian Beigel	(Germany / UK)	2000
Ciarán Benson	(psychologist)	1996 / 2006
Aaron Betsky *	(Netherlands)	2004
Esteve Bonell	(Spain)	1990
Angela Brady		2003
Noel Brady		2012
Merritt Bucholz		2011
Denis Byrne		2005
Gerry Cahill		1996
Ross Cahill-O'Brien		1992
Alberto Campo Baeza	(Spain)	1998
Gerard Carty		1992
David Chipperfield	(UK)	1989
Shay Cleary		1990
Jean-Louis Cohen *	(France)	2001
Beatriz Colomina	(Spain / USA)	2000
Eddie Conroy		2004
Peter Cook	(UK)	1993
Maud Cotter	(artist)	2013
Dorothy Cross	(artist)	1997
Edward Cullinan	(UK)	1987
Michael Cullinan		1995
William JR Curtis *	(UK)	2011
Shane de Blacam		1994, 2013
Tom de Paor		1994
Andrea Deplazes	(Switzerland)	2010
Julien De Smedt	(Denmark)	2008
Mary Donohoe		1993
Theo Dorgan	(poet)	1999
Noel Dowley		1993
Mary Doyle		1999
Peter Doyle		1990
Felim Egan	(artist)	1995
Michelle Fagan		1996
Yvonne Farrell		1987 / 2010
Luis Fernández-Galiano *	(Spain)	2007
Marian Finucane	(broadcaster)	2004
Sheila Foley		2001
Kenneth Frampton	(USA)	1997
Tony Fretton	(UK)	2011
John Gerrard	(artist / photographer)	2008

Arthur Gibney		1986	Ruairí Ó Cuív	(arts consultant)	2012
Michael Gold	(UK)	1988	Michael O'Doherty		2001
Gráinne Hassett		2009	Sheila O'Donnell		1989, 1998
Elizabeth Hatz *	(Sweden)	2013	Seán Ó Laoire		1993
Neil Hegarty		1988	Prof Cathal O'Neill		1996
John Hejduk	(USA)	1994	Antoinette O'Neill		2004
Martin Henchion		2008	Fintan O'Toole	(journalist)	1993
Róisín Heneghan		2002	Dominic Papa	(UK)	2009
Donal Hickey		2013	Robert Payne		2007
James Horan		1992	James Pike		2000
Andrej Hrausky *	(Slovenia)	2006	Carmé Piños	(Spain)	2006
David Hughes		1997	Francis Rambert *	(France)	2008
Michael Hussey		1997	Terence Riley *	(USA)	2005
John Hutchinson	(gallery director)	2002	Paul Robbrecht	(Belgium)	2004
Louisa Hutton	(Germany)	2003	Tim Robinson	(artist, writer)	2009
Garry Hynes	(theatre director)	2000	Vivienne Roche	(artist)	1994
Charles Jencks *	(USA / UK)	2010	Angela Rolfe		2008
Jan Olav Jensen	(Norway)	2002	Daniel Rosbottom	(UK)	2013
Kees Kaan	(Netherlands)	2005	Joseph Rykwert *	(UK)	2012
Richard Kearney	(philosopher)	1991	Jonathan Sergison	(UK)	2001
Raymond Keaveney	(gallery director)	2010	Dietmar Steiner *	(Austria)	2002
Kevin Kieran		1998	Sam Stephenson		1997
Eero Koivisto	(Sweden)	2009	Dominic Stevens		2006
Yves Lion	(France)	1999	Deyan Sudjic *	(Italy / UK)	2003
Mary McCarthy	(arts administrator)	2007	Jo Taillieu	(Belgium)	2011
Tarla Mac Gabhann		2000	Ronald Tallon		1991
Michael McGarry		2012	Peter Tansey		1999
Peter McGovern		2007	Barrie Todd		2002
John McLaughlin		2010	John Tuomey		1991
Des McMahon		1989	Mark Turpin		2003
Shelley McNamara		1999	Derek Tynan		1987
Edward McParland			Corban Walker	(artist)	2003
	(architectural historian)	1998	Dorothy Walker	(art writer)	1992
Manuel Aires Mateus	(Portugal)	2005	Wilfried Wang *	(UK / Germany)	2009
John Meagher		1986	Keith Williams	(UK)	2012
John Miller	(UK)	1986	Peter Wilson	(UK)	1992
Gerry Mitchell		1988	Kevin Woods		1995
Rafael Moneo	(Spain)	1991	Jonathan Woolf	(UK)	2007
Patrick T Murphy	(gallery director)	2005			
David Naessens		1991	* architectural critic programme, 2000-		
Willem Jan Neutelings					
	(Netherlands)	1995			
Esmonde O'Briain		1998			
Joan O'Connor		1994			

First Impressions

ASSESSORS' COMMENTS, Assessment Day, 8th November 2012

DANIEL ROSBOTTOM – Coming from the UK, I was really taken with the examples of public infrastructure being built here. Some of the educational projects feel like they have a real sense of purpose and quality and care, which I think is symptomatic of a fundamentally strong profession, but also a strong social sensibility in a country. In England, where lots of money has recently been spent on schools, their architectural qualities are often variable, to say the least. I think there's a sense of care and an understanding here that these things are pivotal for a community.

ELIZABETH HATZ – You have some outstanding ideas in these projects about architecture and its current position. There are very few larger projects, but there are a lot of residential projects showing delicacy and refinement and a local dialogue. That's the predominant impression I have.

ROSBOTTOM – I think another thing that's interesting about a lot of those projects is what they say about the aspirations of the architects. There's a lot of material complexity, but one of the things I would like to understand more is what they do to the things around them? There are some intriguing relationships to context, but some of the projects are quite hermetic. Overall, the projects are symptomatic of the time we're in: they're about architects trying to play their best card in whatever circumstance they are in.

HATZ – Maybe I have a selective memory, because I only recall those who are actually quite original in their way of addressing the existing. There are a few of these kind of neutral, sleek projects, but the ones that really jump out at you are either sensitive to their contexts, or even bold! There are some really original ones there.

ROSBOTTOM – Another thing to immediately strike me was the scale of some of the new-build houses; actually the scale of houses in general. Coming from England, I was interested by the size of domestic space and the number of quite large villas being built on large plots in interesting places.

SHANE DE BLACAM – I made a summary of the projects entered. Half of them are houses or house extensions. There are ten pavilions, detached pavilions which are independent of anything; three manifestos, which are sort of statements of intent of architects; and then twelve public buildings, which can be broken down into four schools, three university buildings, three offices, one public housing project and one hospital. Then there are other buildings which are environmental experiments in one form or another, both in space and building construction terms and/or also manipulating the natural environment in one form or another.

It has always seemed to me in relation to the AAI Awards that an issue arises in relation to what is represented in drawings and photographs as against what the reality of the building is, and this is the case particularly with the university building in Limerick. It's very clear to me that to discuss that building it needs to be visited. I have great difficulty because I would want to see that building. And that's something that goes to the core of this form of assessment.

But overall, the level to which professional activity in this country has been reduced by the recession is terrifying.

DONAL HICKEY – I notice that there are a number of generations' work here. Even with the pavilions, there are ones that are clearly being done by young architects whose only hope is to make something themselves to show they have sufficient skill to do something else, which is kind of depressing. And then there are the Venice ones that are very similar to what the architects are actually doing in practice. They're a kind of propaganda, maybe. When I look at the small-scale residential work, there are some that are clearly by established architects, and then there are others clearly by younger practitioners. They all seem to be bunched in the same territory.

As a society, I think it's really worrying that the school, the second home for children, is so poorly represented in the projects here. I found it disappointing that there is such skill being exercised at a microscopic, insular scale in small-scale residential projects, and then at the scale of society the same thing isn't happening.

ROSBOTTOM – That's interesting, because I think one of those schools is a really strong work of architecture, and I think the standard here is much stronger than in England.

There's something interesting in the conversation about material that goes on in the work here. I don't like the word "materiality" very much because it seems like it's about the idea of material as a kind of representation rather than a tectonic idea. There's a lot of wrapping of material across surfaces – material as a wash – and things that don't really understand the way that material actually operates and the way that making actually happens. There are a lot of themes that get replayed, but sometimes they are played articulately and they're about a sense of material.

MAUD COTTER – There are some moments that I am very taken with – the sort of tailored piece in space, where there's a real critical sense of something having arrived. In those instances I am looking at quite a sparse and very economic use of materials. Also, the relationship of architecture with nature is interesting, in particular when it really takes on a site geologically. I love some of those elements in the projects.

I'm also interested to find that there are a number of propositions around communal acts, which have a democratic feel to them. Groups of people are getting together to make something very tentative with architectural structures, and are beginning to attribute new values, new questions, beginning to enter into that terrain. There are some civic pieces, and it's interesting for me to see how some of those commissioned works take on new values, like the integration of the planting, translucence, how that begins to open up the cores of buildings and stuff. I like that.

But generally speaking, I find a lot of the domestic extensions very introspective. In actual fact, sometimes they create their own spatial field, which presupposes that it's not in a total environment, that it's in a completely hermetic condition, especially in quite tight spaces. I like the pieces that use hybrids of architecture – say, on a roofscape in some instances – opening up new architectural languages within an old fabric. I like this idea that you go into an old fabric and you invent aesthetics of reuse. That's something I would be looking out for in terms of examining what real shifts or changes are there in architectural practice that accommodate the position we are in at the moment. And those concerns are there.

HATZ – In a country of four million that's in an economic crisis, I am still surprised by the level of quality in many of these projects. But what I'm worried about is that with the originality and sensitivity and wit and edge seen in many of these projects, even the house extensions, why don't these architects get commissions to actually shape the environment and to shape society? Architects maybe need to go out there and mix with decision-makers. Why is architecture and planning so severed in this country? I find that really disturbing. I also find it worrying that those commissions that have the capacity to deal with civic space are often of quite poor quality generally, despite being very important projects. The authorities and the architectural community should realise that architecture is also about how to strategically place a particular building, how to actually build these environments on a strategic level, on a planning level.

ROSBOTTOM – I was looking to the projects for a sensibility about the wider condition. I always refer back to Diener & Diener, who will draw a city in order to place their building in it. I think too often the projects here aren't arriving with that sensibility of a wider condition. There is a kind of hermeticism, this idea that the house is turned in on itself – which is not just in this country; it's everywhere – the idea that the back has become the front and that these kind of extraordinary statements happen at the back of people's houses, disregarding the fact that you are in a 4- or 5m-wide plot with a neighbour who also has one. I think there's something quite neurotic about that. That is a concern.

I think that compression that you're talking about, Donal, between established, highly skilled architects and young architects, which you're seeing as result of the crisis, has never not been there. I remember Tony Fretton writing about Jonathan Woolf, saying that this person ought to be planning a city, so why is he working on refurbishments? We are all working with an incredibly compressed field. The mass of architecture that's going on in England is almost entirely prescribed by commercial practice. You see very little interest in quality or urbanity, or any of those conversations. So when I look around the walls here, it feels like there is a lot of underlying strength and quality to this. We would struggle to produce this breadth of quality in England. So I wouldn't be quite as depressed about it as you are. Or maybe I should be really depressed about where I am!

COTTER – When you think of it, the corporate grip on values in architecture and the power politics that go on here have really asphyxiated aesthetic potential in this country. What we have now, hopefully, is an ebb in the tide, and what we're seeing is a real potential for embracing new values. Not just new values for the sake of it, but also a recognition of ones that are actually already there, and confirming them, like the exquisite sense of placement of one material with another, and how weights are played out in the built world, how one builds on uncertain ground, how one takes on these territories. I think that Irish architects have a great sensitivity to material.

I am very concerned also with schools, because a school is such an important environment, where you're teaching children how to live in a space, how to be intimate with a space. They're in a position of observing light in a building for five or six years. It should be a drama, it should be providing an experience of intimacy with the building that will stay with them for the rest of their lives.

ROSBOTTOM – Actually a school is the first moment when you have an unaccompanied experience of public life. You arrive in a school, and it's the first time you are away from your parents, and you're in a public domain where you have to establish your own relationship with the things around you. So they are critical, because they become a place where you establish the kinds of behaviours and relationships that people then take into a wider understanding of public life. So I think you're absolutely right to be concerned. But I think in the best cases here, there is really some strength and quality.

COTTER – I think the whole public realm thing is depressing to be honest, really very bad. What is it? Why can't we deal with civic space? I think it is to do with history, that it is the realm of...

HATZ – The British? It's the same problem with planning. The attitude is that planning is authority and authority is bad. The focus has to switch from private interest to collective interest. It has to!

COTTER – But do you find that the best public work brings a sort of intimacy into it? One of the schools here – the national school in Crumlin – creates a beautiful intimacy of light and space.

HICKEY – The one that steps out onto the street? And actually there's a bunch of houses opposite it, which is so untypical of just about every school you see being built now, which tend to be isolated in a field somewhere. So it's interesting to have something that's stitched in, knitted into its surroundings.

COTTER – But I believe the constraints the architects work under – spatially and in terms of budget – are terrible when it comes to building a school.

DE BLACAM – Paul Keogh was talking in yesterday's paper about how the profession has been driven to a point where it's actually not possible to do the work for the fees that are being offered or that are being taken up. The point I'm trying to make is that traditionally in Irish architecture, an architect like the one for this school [in Crumlin] would get this project, which is ten times bigger than any other project they would have in their office. And they would get that because there would be individuals in the Department of Education who would recognise that this work will be conducted at the highest level and they will produce a building with the kind of care and energy that it deserves. And yet, because of the new restrictions, these type of architects will never get another school again.

COTTER – Such a waste.

HICKEY – It's interesting what you say. By virtue of being small, these architects can really put their guts into it to actually deliver something that's worthwhile for the people that are commissioning it. Whereas if the same project went to a practice who is delivering numerous PPP schools, and this is just one of a number of them, it actually doesn't really matter: it's just a kind of conveyor belt, out the door, absence of risk. They're not really interested in the project in the first place. It's just to keep the show on the road. And that's an interesting distinction when you consider it.

ROSBOTTOM – It's very sad if that's the case. One of the things that seems interesting looking at that project [Crumlin] is that there is an inherent level of articulation in the plan and in the section and in the way that it's operating relative to its size that tells you someone has taken a lot of time and care over it. In Switzerland or Belgium or Portugal, where practices are small, they're allowed to collaborate, and the infrastructure of procurement allows them to do that. What's troubling is that a system we in the UK imported from America we are now exporting to other parts of Europe. It's all public private partnership; it's all based on pre-qualification questionnaires. And then that criteria [in the AAI Awards], which is about the future of Irish architecture... If what you're wanting to give is a message that these are the things that have value, that actually the way one procures buildings is fundamental to the quality of architecture, then that's something we ought to be thinking about.

HICKEY – It can't be about an absence of risk, which is what it's about at the moment.

ROSBOTTOM – The problem is to ask the question of what risk means. The perception of what risk is in the wider sense is not determined, is it? Risk is only about finance.

COTTER – I feel there's an aesthetic crisis in the country. When I was growing up, there was always an aspiration that we were evolving a visual language, we were evolving an architectural language. I really felt this. And then we just got blinded with money, and what did people do? Buy crap! Go out and just engage fulsomely in the most corporate of cultures, without question. Have we forgotten what good aesthetic values are? And where's the memory? Where is that kind of learned curve? Somebody who evolves a language for a school should be able to continue with that, and be acknowledged and recognised for that, for those hard-won values that take years of maturation. I'm a bit disillusioned about that. It's across the board in lots of things.

DE BLACAM – And in architecture it stopped dead. It just stopped to the point that official policy is inimical to it.

ROSBOTTOM – I don't think you can ascribe the kind of tightening up of things to economic downturn. I'm working in Norway at the moment, which is in economic boom, and they're implementing exactly the same systems. A Norwegian architect said to me, "We've spent all this money, and all we've achieved from doing it is to make sure that nothing is ever really bad, but nothing is ever really good either. We have just arrived at a terrible middle ground." It does come down to this question of what risk means. And coming back to Shane's point about whether this architect would ever get another school... I mean it's not necessarily important that they get another school; it's that they get other challenging buildings to work on. I think there's something quite interesting in people not becoming specialists. The culture of specialisation in contemporary architecture is a really big issue. Practices, by default, end up doing ten or twenty schools.

DE BLACAM – It seems to me that the selection of architects is far too complicated, whereas it's really extremely simple.

SLIEVEBAWNOGUE (double-house)

CLANCY MOORE ARCHITECTS

This project involved the construction of two dwellings for a brother and sister, whose family have lived in the area for generations. A 19th-century reservoir dominates the valley floor, and has led to the area being designated an area of outstanding natural beauty. In this context, the approach was to site the houses in the scar of a disused phyllite quarry. Within this fractured landscape of discarded spoil and outcrops of bedrock, the houses act as an inhabited bridge. Touching the uncertain ground in just three places, they span both natural and manmade outcrops (i.e. service structures and shared entrance staircase). Constructed in timber, the architectural language derives from the structure required to achieve these spans. The exposed vertical fins which bind the structure together also act to protect the more fragile cladding-boards set deep between them – a language developed through an interest in early Irish timber henges and in Nordic stave construction.

Constrained by the shadow cast by the quarry wall to the south and a planning-line which restricted construction to the north (due to proximity to the potable water reservoir), the project is urban or 'infill' in a rural condition. Within the given form between these two lines, living spaces and bedrooms are arranged to provide well-proportioned spaces, deep views and contained rooms. This exercise in *poché* extends to the section, which is modelled to present a variety of scales of spaces. More intimate living spaces and bedrooms occur in a lower, north-east-facing wing, while taller living spaces address the south-west.

Striking the one horizontal line in this dramatically varied topography, the houses offer the only manicured spaces in the form of rooms, indoor and outdoor, covered terraces and a roof garden. The form of the two dwellings closes the quarry to create a shared communal garden-room overlooked by a long verandah and the tall living rooms. This 'room in the landscape' was the primary ambition of the project. The rest of the site is left as found. The houses are fully integrated with the natural resources of their site: rainwater is harvested, and timber from the forest is chopped, left to dry in the external areas below the house, and burnt in stoves and gasification boilers, while extensive solar collectors heat the water. Due to the nature of their timber construction, the fabric of the houses acts to sequester 250 tonnes of CO_2.

The structure and plan of the houses allow them to grow and contract over the lifetime of the family, from two houses with two apartments, to two four-bedroom dwellings, and with the possibility of combining both houses into one.

address – Bohernabreena, Co Dublin
client – private
photography – Alice Clancy

design to completion – 2007-2012
site area – 1.6ha / floor area – 420m^2
budget – n/a

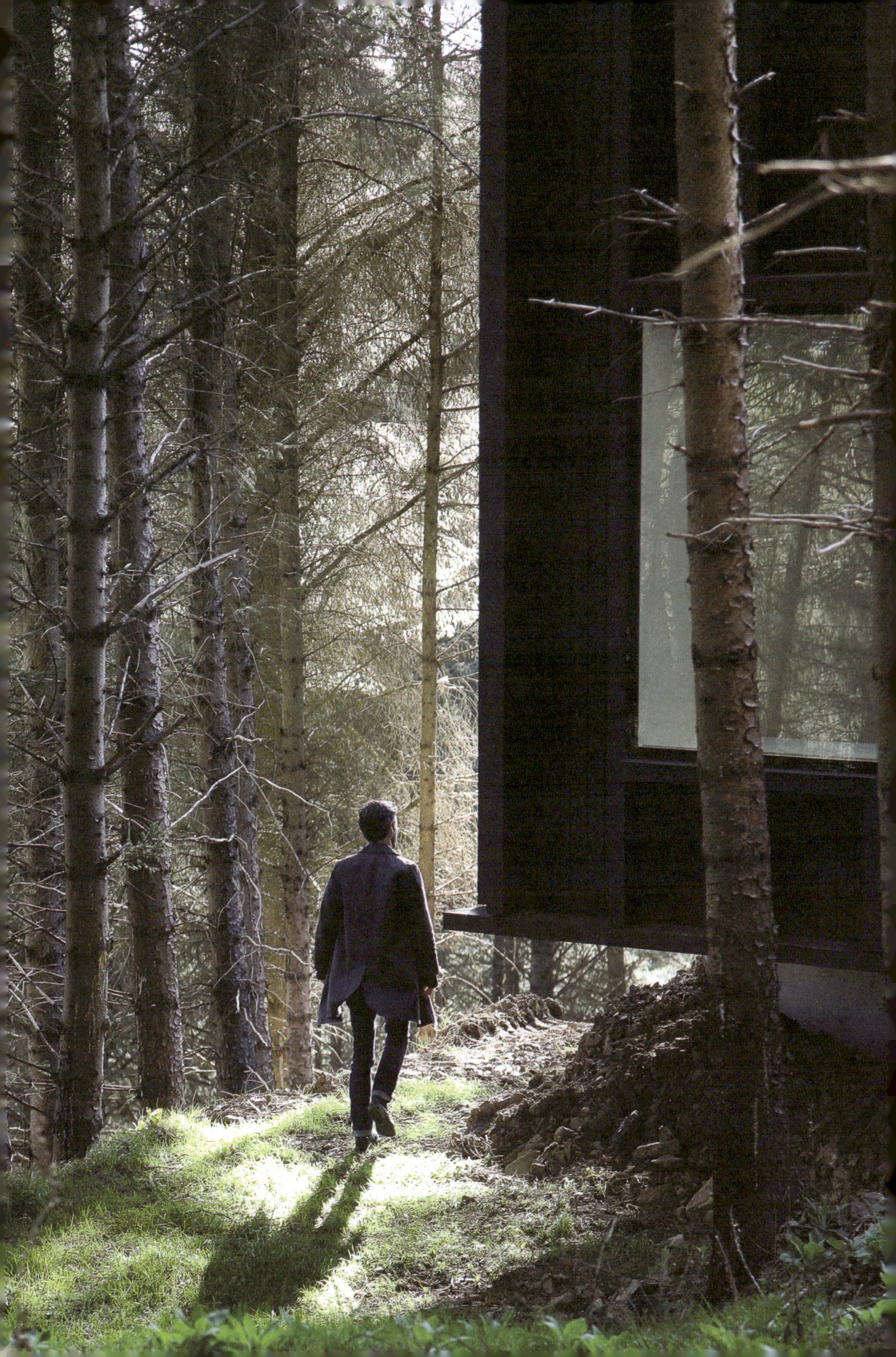

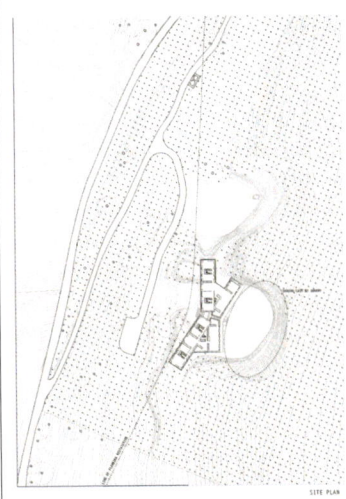

SLIEVEBAWNOGUE

This project involves the construction of two dwellings for a brother and a sister. Situated in a disused quarry with uncertain ground conditions of discarded spoil, the houses act as an inhabited bridge, spanning between natural and man made outcrops of service structures and a shared entrance staircase. The houses language derives from the structure necessary to achieve these spans.

Constrained by the shadow cast by the quarry wall to the south and a planning line which restricts construction to the north (due to proximity to a potable water reservoir) the project is paradoxically urban or 'infill' in this otherwise rural condition. Within the given form between these two lines living spaces and bedrooms are arranged to give well proportioned spaces, deep views and contained rooms. This exercise in poché extends to the section which is modelled in present a variety of scales of spaces. More intimate living spaces and bedrooms occur in a lower, north-east facing wing. Taller living spaces address the south west. The form of the two dwellings closes the quarry to create a shared communal garden room overlooked by a long verandah and the tall living rooms.

The houses are fully integrated with the natural resources of their site. Rainwater is harvested, timber from the forest is chopped, left to dry in the external areas below the house and burnt in stoves and gassification boilers. While extensive solar collectors heat the water. Due to the nature of their timber construction the fabric of the houses acts to sequester 250 tonnes of CO2. The structure & plan of the houses allows them to grow and contract over the lifetime of the family from two houses with two apartments devisable to two four bedroom dwellings. While the possibility of combining both houses into one residence is preserved.

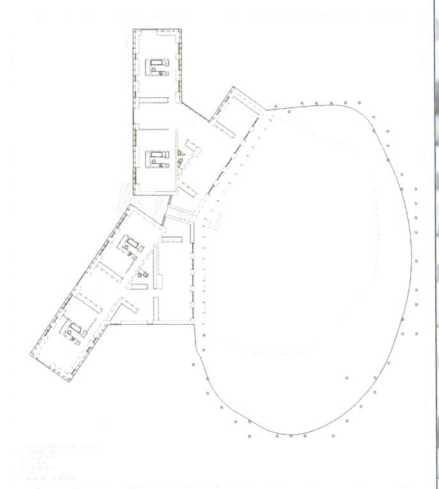

VERANDAH TO UPPER QUARRY  · HOUSE 2 VIEW FROM KITCHEN TO LIVING ROOM  · VIEW FOREST

SHORT SECTION

HOUSE 2 OVERLOOKING LOWER QUARRY

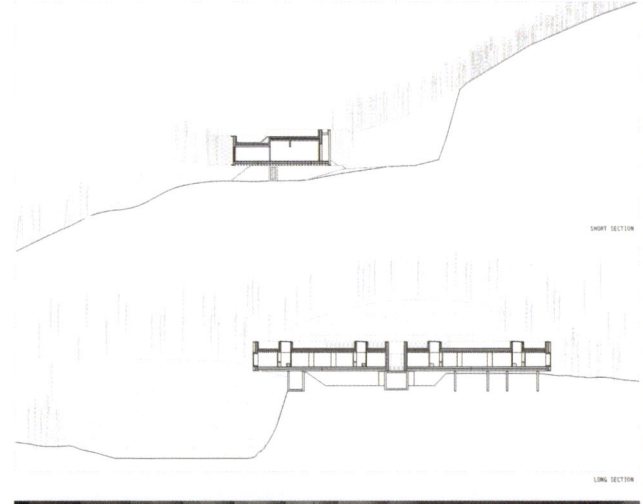

LONG SECTION

VERANDAH OVERLOOKING QUARRY

LIVING ROOM HOUSE 1  · VIEW TOWARDS SEA HOUSE 2

37

N

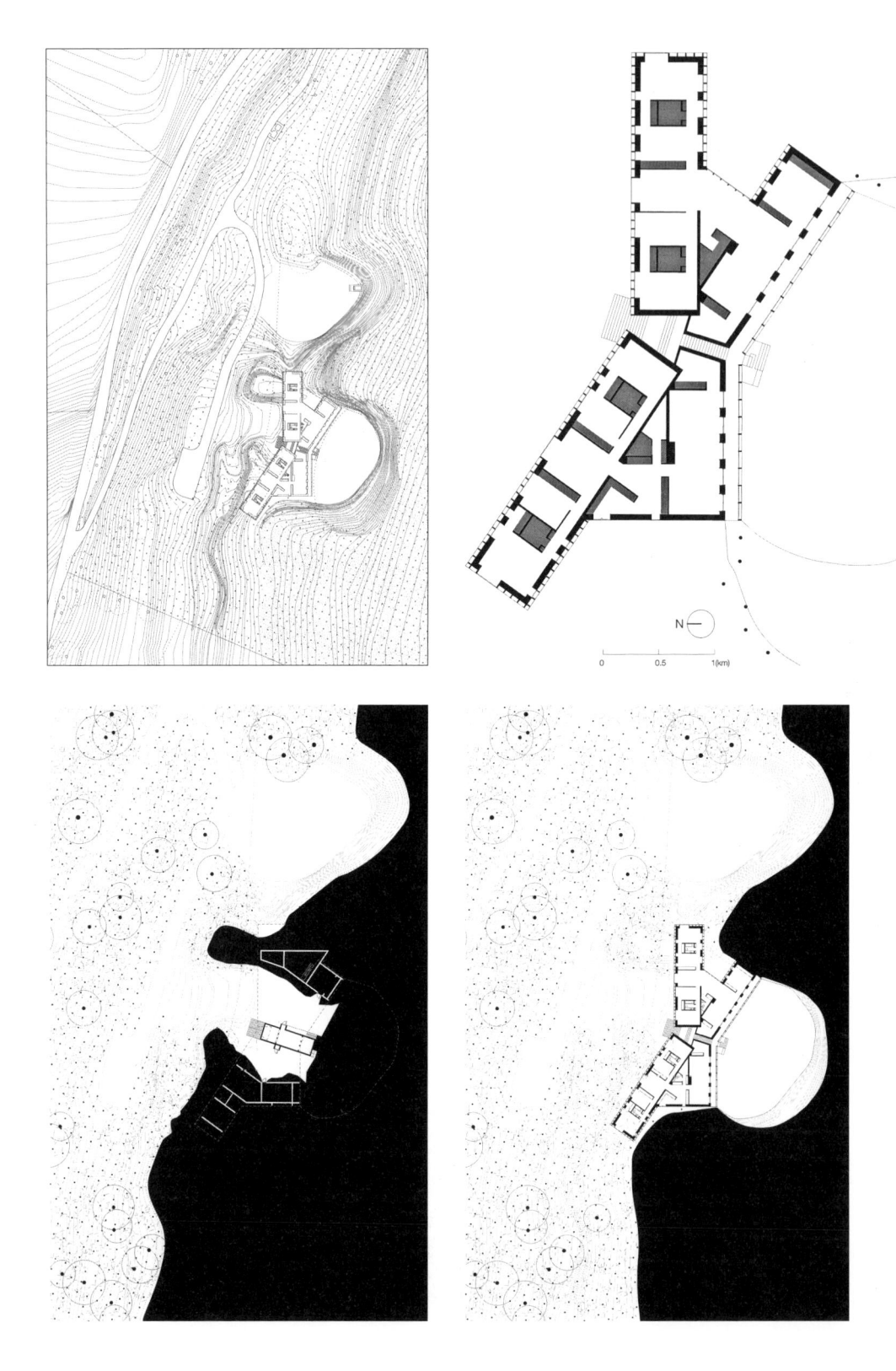

0   0.5   1(km)

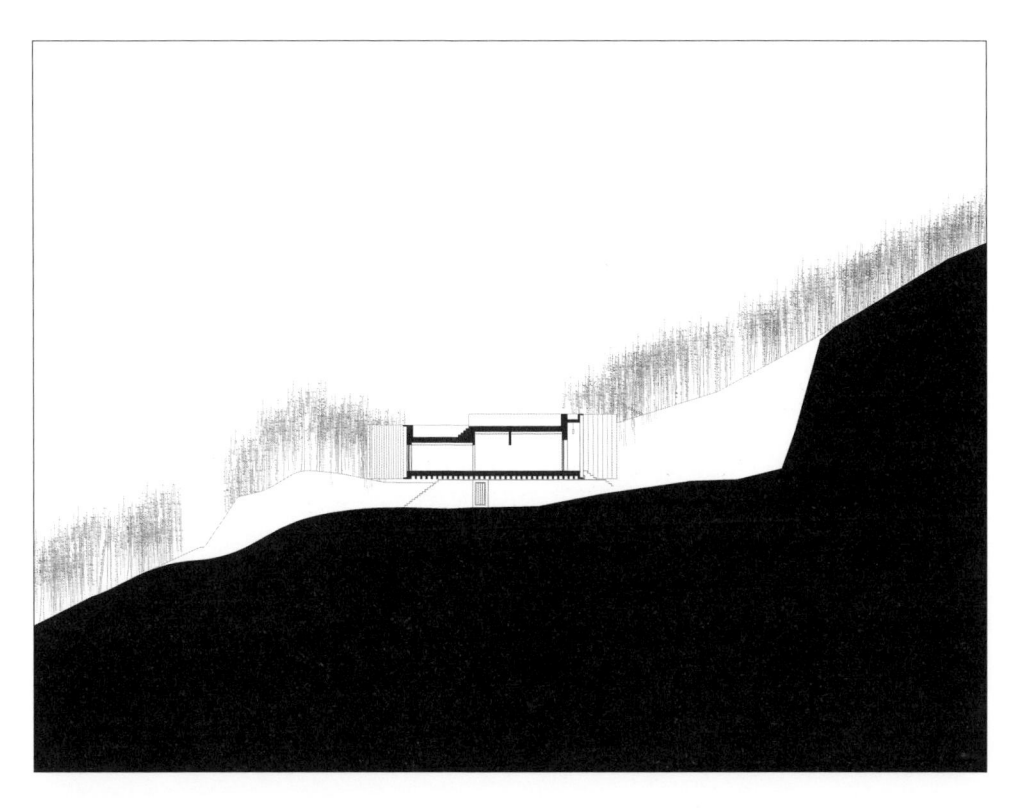

SLIEVEBAWNOGUE (DOUBLE-HOUSE)

Cross section
Longitudinal section

opposite – Plans – site, basement and ground-floor plans in context, ground-floor

pages 36-37 – AAI Awards entry panels

overleaf – View to house
A shared garden room between house and quarry
The form of the house in the forest

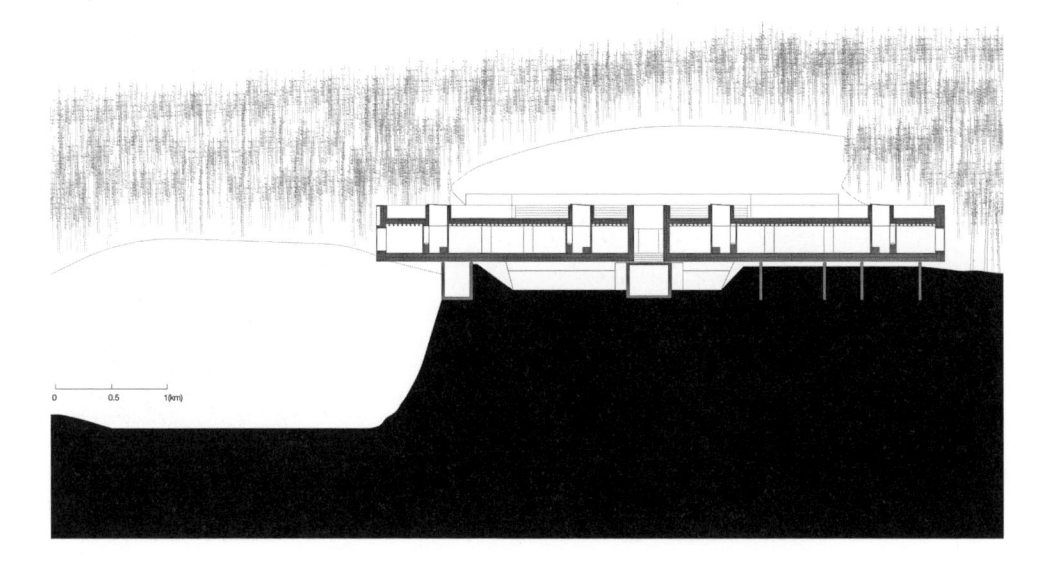

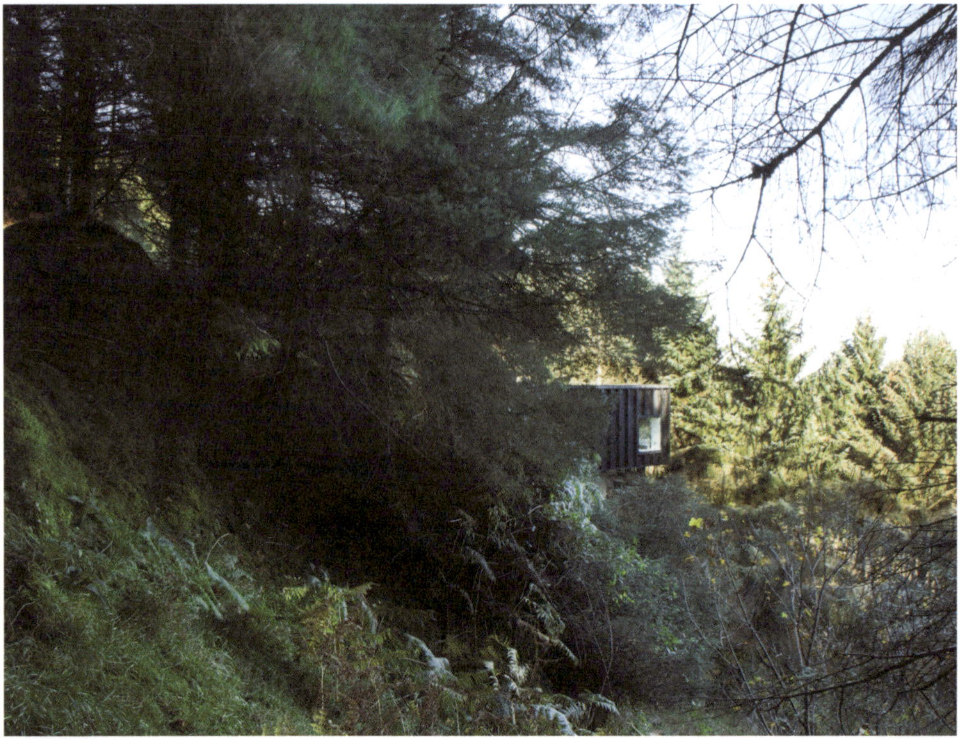

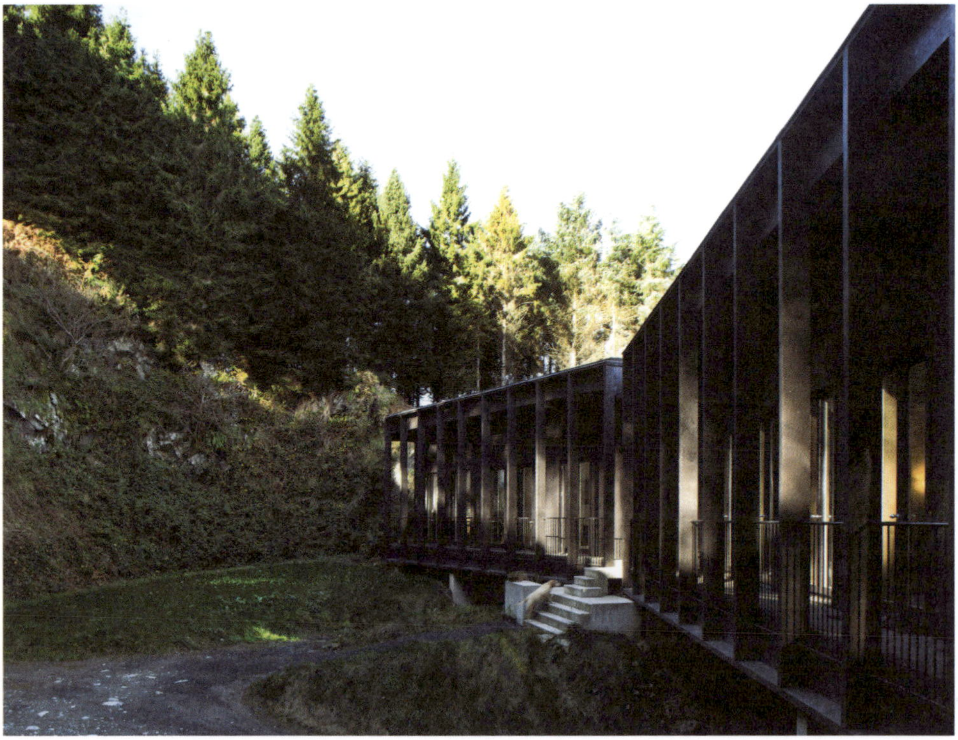

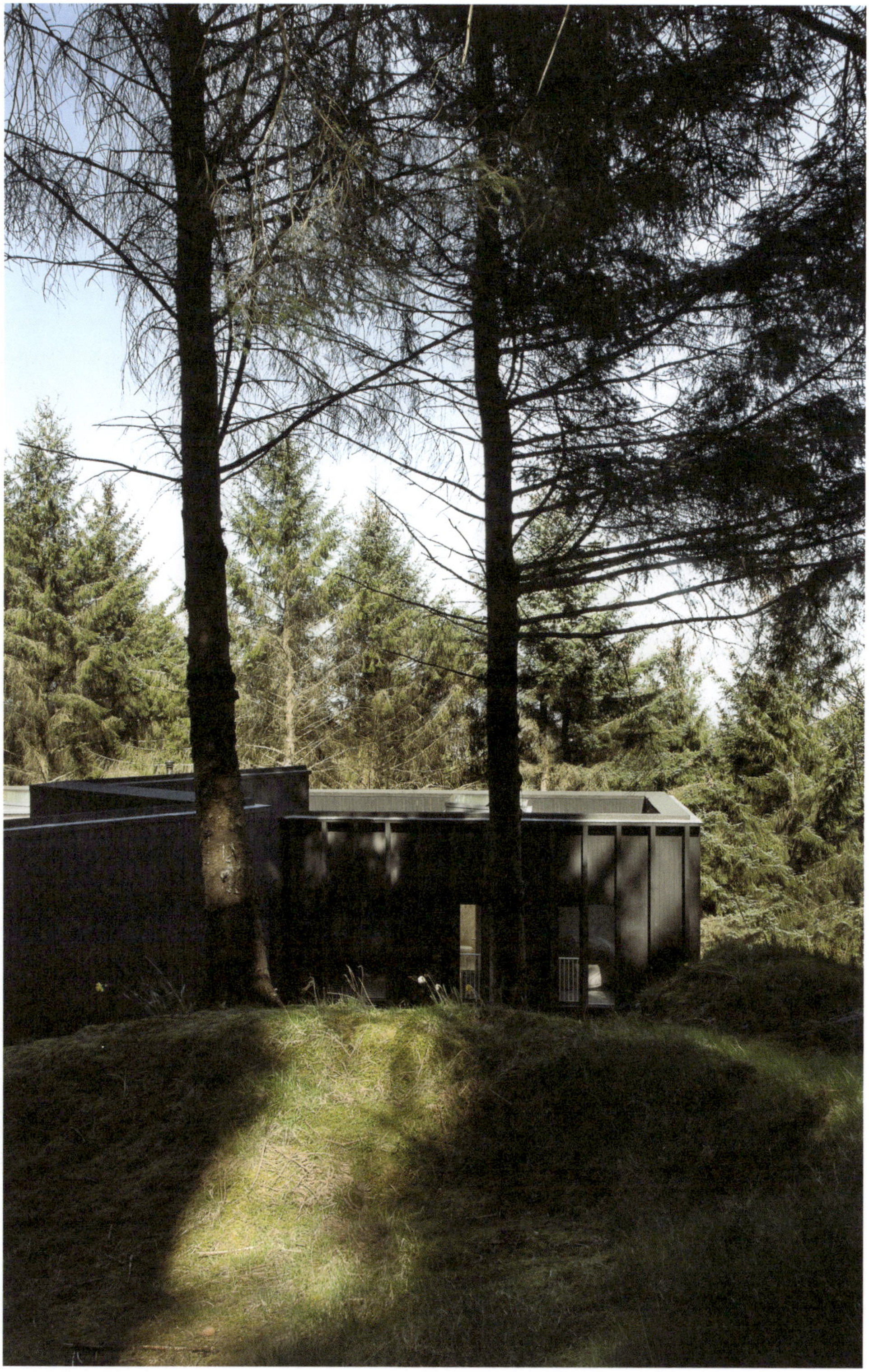

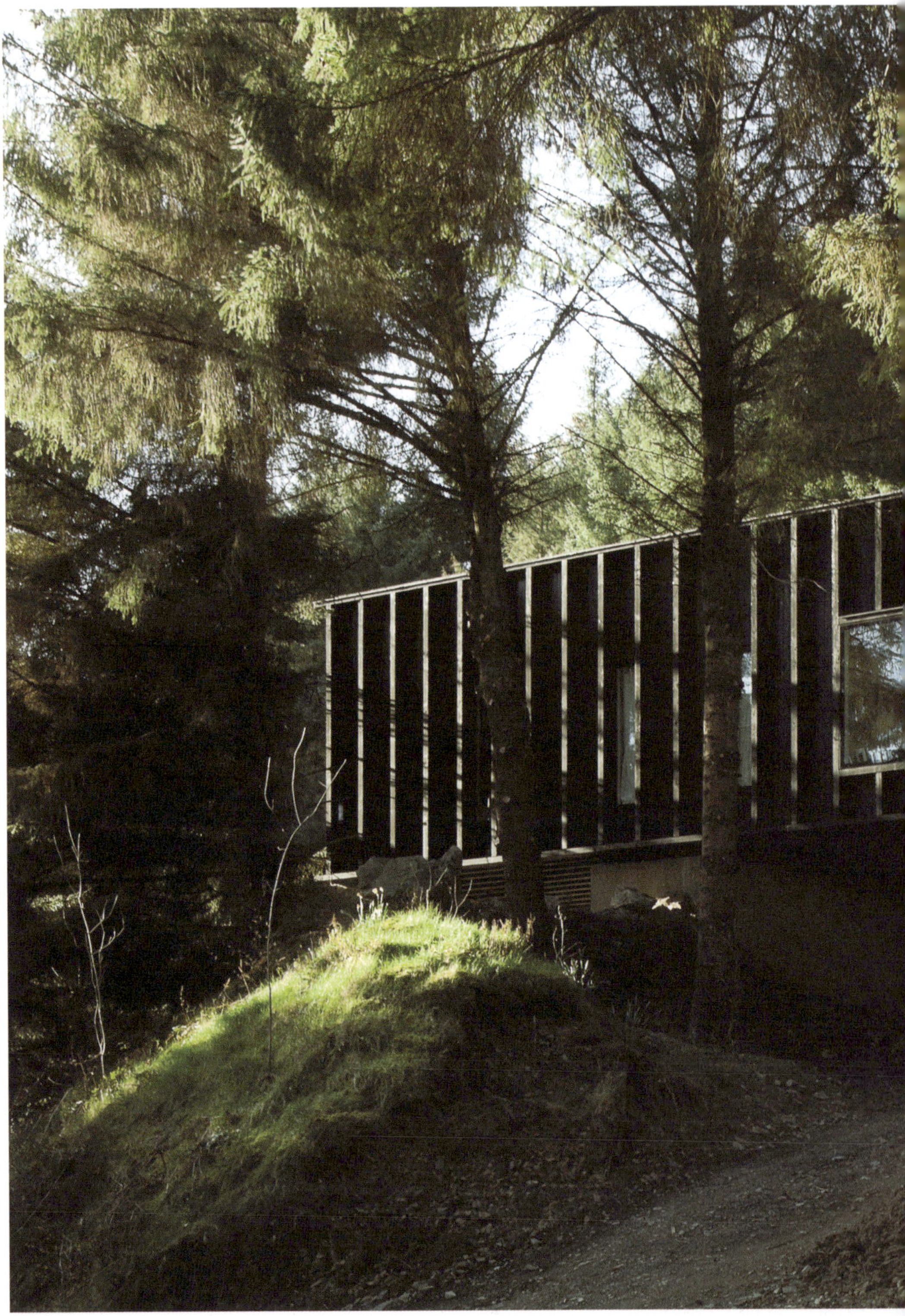

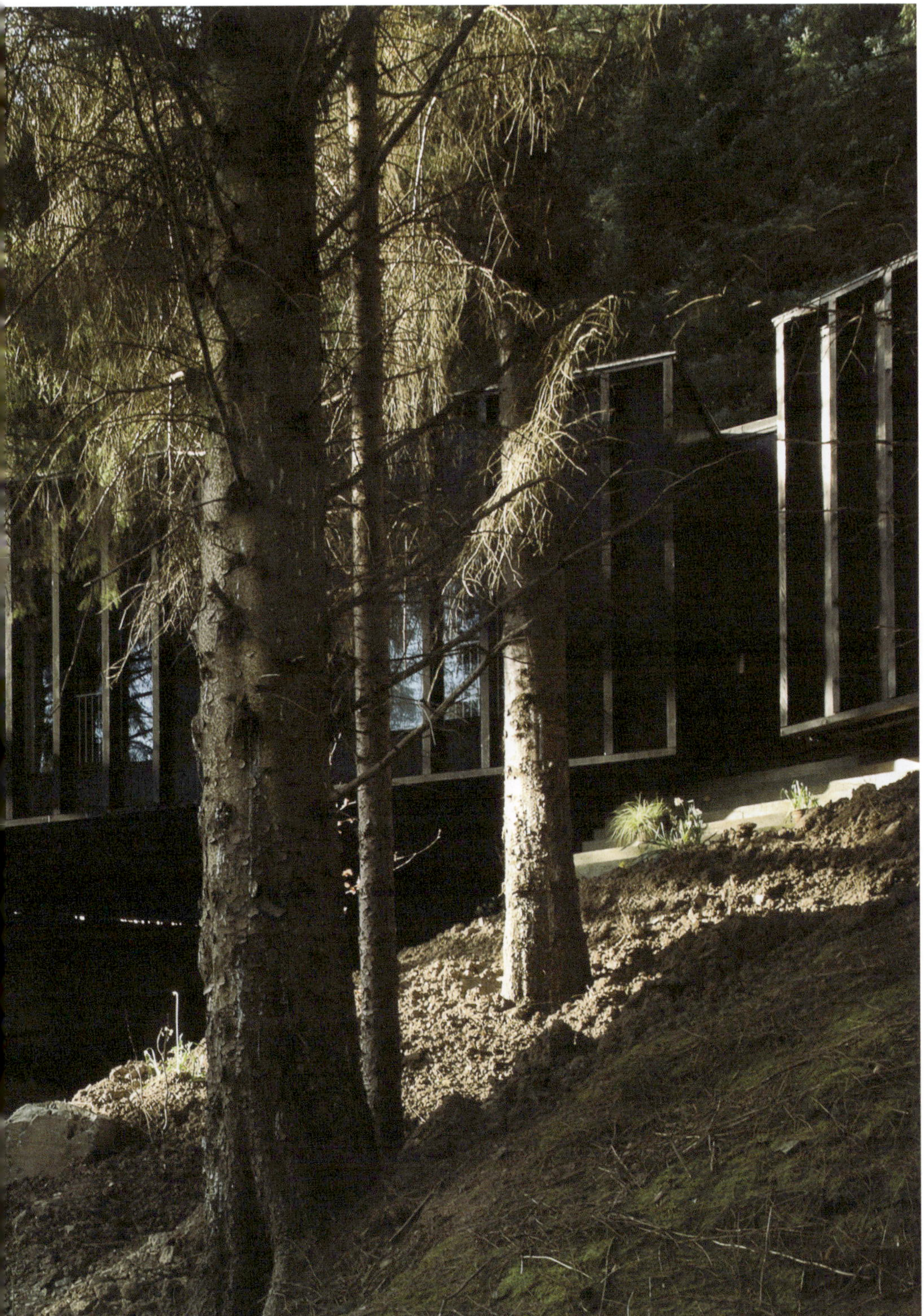

SLIEVEBAWNOGUE (DOUBLE-HOUSE)

pages 42-43 – *A bridge through the forest*

View towards entrance
Picture window
Steps to verandah overlooking the garden

ASSESSORS' COMMENTS

DE BLACAM – I think this is serious.

HATZ – It's so intriguing and so mysterious. And well after the sister and brother for whom it was built have left this place, it will still be this incredible, mysterious bridge.

ROSBOTTOM – I also think this is good. It has an interesting ambivalence about what it is. At one level, it is like the *barchessa* [open barns] of a Palladian villa, orchestrating a landscape beyond it. But then it also has a very direct engagement with its immediate landscape: you can read it as a bridge. There's something interesting about the quiet rhythmical quality of it, of its façade and the depth of shadow.

HICKEY – And it's on both sides, which is particularly nice. I like this piece; the way the two wings create a pinch point at entry, open to the sky, is fantastic.

ROSBOTTOM – I think you could have had a bit more tension in the symmetry. In the UK, the architect Jonathan Woolf has done a series of houses for extended families, and one of the things I enjoy about his Brick Leaf House is that it starts as a kind of double, and then you start to understand character within the doubleness. On initial reading, I think I find the symmetry in the plan here a bit over-emphatic. But I think it's a really serious piece of work.

HATZ – It looks temporary, like a wooden bridge, but then by holding on through sheer oddity, it has a kind of remoteness at the same time, like a bridge leading nowhere, and then you occupy the bridge in this gap.

HICKEY – But it doesn't lead nowhere, because it makes the space behind with the shadow of the wall.

HATZ – Sure, it leads underneath, but as a bridge it leads nowhere. You inhabit that gap. It really has so many layers... It works in section and in plan.

COTTER – At the heart of it, I love the uncertainty of the ground conditions, that it was built in this tentative terrain, and then that it cradles the air in the quarry itself very gently by closing that space. I love those kind of sculptural moments within it. And then it creates this almost inky shadow, its own drawing and atmosphere underneath it.

ROSBOTTOM – And I think there's something powerful about moving from the brooding forest to the lightness of the domestic interior in a way that somehow maintains the tectonic language.

COTTER – And of course, then, it's a bridge. I love the fact that it's in suspension up there. There are all these tentative concepts at the heart of the building.

HICKEY – It kind of tells you what to expect. It gives you a language when you meet it on this side and travel underneath it, and then on the opposite side it breathes out, and allows you to filter back into it, and I think that's a very beautiful thing to do.

COTTER – I have a sense of the poetry of the life lived in this building. There's something about the vegetation, the way the building sits into it, not just the volume and emptiness of the quarry, but also the verticality of the vegetation and the elevation.

DE BLACAM – You talk about the vertical. A veranda is what they call it in the description, which is very wonderful. You can see someone sitting on it in the photograph, which is really, really lovely to see.

ROSBOTTOM – There are these extraordinary moments as well within this overarching

46

symmetry where you get a window that opens to a view of the bark of a tree, and on the other side you get the hill on the opposite side of the valley.

HATZ – It's full of surprises.

DE BLACAM – Imagine the nightmares of the planning officer faced with this proposal! Anyway, this is a definite. It's wonderful.

COTTER – I love the ease with which it reflects on its surroundings. It's like the building itself has a psychological potential to interpret because it presents you with moves and views.

ROSBOTTOM – It has an incredible atmospheric quality whilst being a very precise measure of its place.

HATZ – I find the plan very clever because it's so consistent and strict in its geometry, but spatially it's not strict. You know, we sometimes read plans as figures, which is so wrong. We should always translate them into space. Because here it's the hinge, and what is happening in these connections is very sophisticated. It's like a Scharoun plan in a way, like the project for an art gallery where he makes a spatial loop, and that works very well.

ROSBOTTOM – The entrance stair in the middle is a piece of mannerism, isn't it?

HICKEY – That's the bit I like least, to be honest.

HATZ – I love that!

DE BLACAM – Scharoun wouldn't make a symmetrical plan.

HATZ – No, he wouldn't. But this is not symmetrical either; it's almost symmetrical, but not quite. This piece is not equal to that piece. There are a lot of things, and every one of these moves has an impact on the space. It's extremely sophisticated.

ROSBOTTOM – The plan actually gets less and less symmetrical as you study it.

DE BLACAM – Well, there's one room extra on the north side.

HICKEY – Yes, the little blip at the end. That actually makes the space behind it. It needs that. We don't really see the ends though; we don't see any images of this side and this side. I wonder what they are like actually.

COTTER – It's an amazingly brave gesture because it takes on a natural environment, and it slips architecture into the theatre of nature.

HICKEY – It does justice to the place it's situated, and I think that's as good a commendation as you can give it.

ROSBOTTOM – The other thing to note is the transcendental nature of the material. If you look at what the timber is like from the exterior, and you look at the joinery indoors, there's this idea that timber moves from something that's of the forest to something that's of incredible refinement, and classical in its understanding. It's very good.

HICKEY – I think this is the best project in the room; there's a level of sophistication in it that deserves consideration for the Medal. There are things about it that I'm not completely happy with, but overall I think it's an extremely accomplished piece of work.

DE BLACAM – The way this is photographed, in the half-light, makes it difficult to read. Everything about this house would give you confidence and makes you feel very well about it, but I have some small worry about the way it's photographed. If you went to see it, you might see it's all hollow or it's very lightweight or insubstantial.

HICKEY – You don't think that though. You're just worried about it.

DE BLACAM – I think it's possible. There's no doubt, there's a risk in this form of assessment in relation to what is represented in drawings and photographs as against what the reality of the building is, and this is the case here and particularly with the university building in Limerick, although less so with other projects. I really have difficulty because I would want to see these buildings.

ROSBOTTOM – That is the nature of judging awards from a set of photographs and drawings. But I think this feels compelling – and that might be something to do with this representation, I agree – but it feels compelling in a way that the others don't. And it feels like it stands up in a context of the villa as a type internationally. I think it could sit in a discussion with other great houses of the past.

And, of course, there's always a wariness. I can totally agree with Shane. You know, when you start saying this is the best project in Ireland in the last year, and you're doing that from photographs and drawings, and I don't even know who the architect is so I have no knowledge about whether it's someone who does make things beautifully, it makes you nervous. But I feel like there's a level of control and understanding, and a compulsion about that building in that place, which makes me able to believe that its the best project here.

COTTER – There is sufficient stability in the vertical. The trees are vertical and they are solid. The vacuum of air in the quarry is there. And the tension with the nature of the site here, that's there. And to me, they are all functioning beautifully. So I don't see the problem with the photography at all. I would put this project above all the others, and give it the Medal.

HICKEY – I think this is deserving of the Medal.

CLANCY MOORE ARCHITECTS – Andrew Clancy and Colm Moore studied architecture at University College Dublin, and established Clancy Moore Architects in 2007. Both partners teach at the School of Architecture, Queen's University, Belfast. DESIGN TEAM – Andrew Clancy, Colm Moore, Colm Dunbar, Rae Moore, Billy Mooney

CLANCY MOORE ARCHITECTS
33-34 Vicar Street, Dublin 8 – T 01-7093005 / E info@clancymoore.com / W www.clancymoore.com

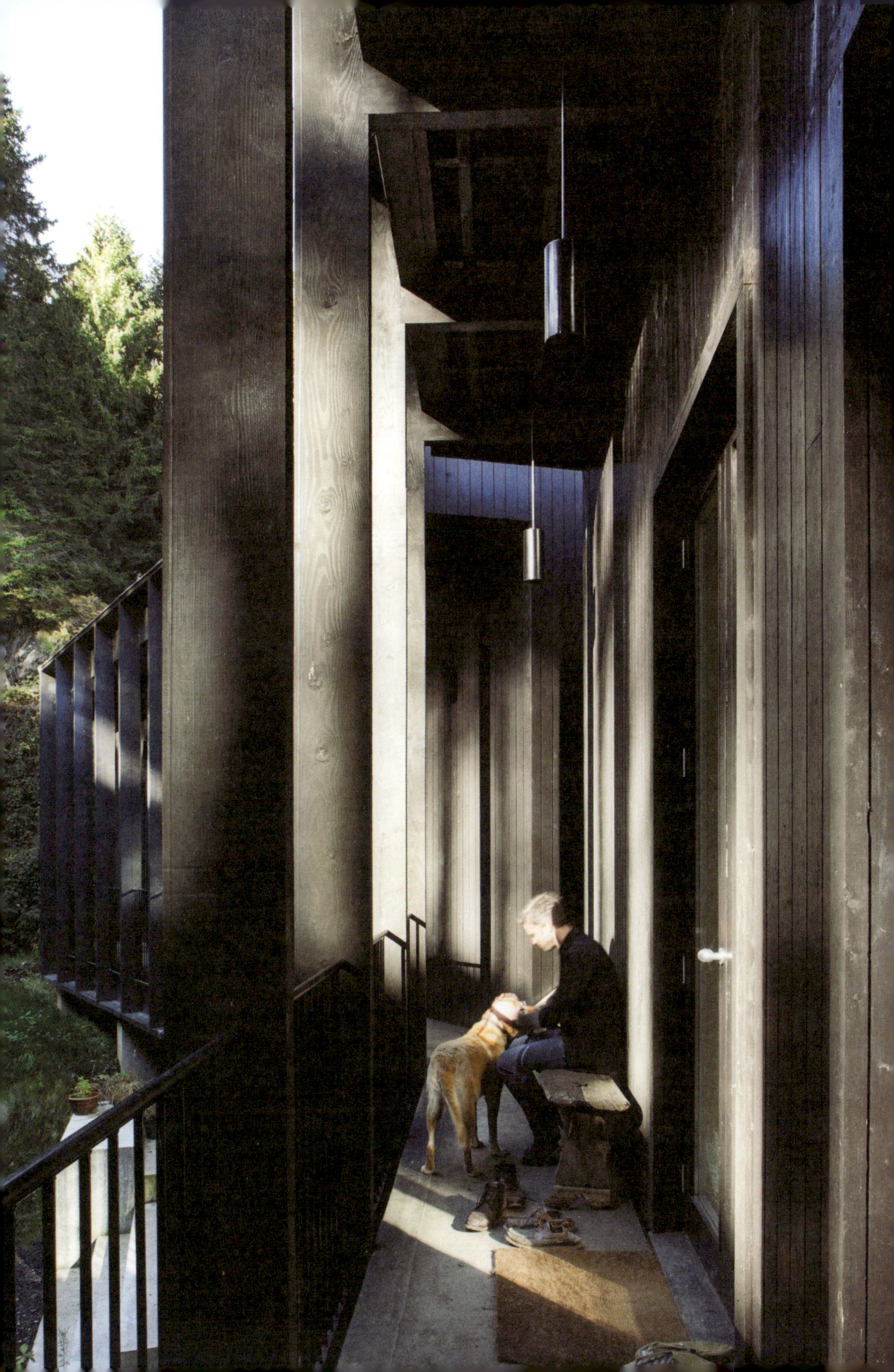

AWARD

RECASTING

DONAGHY + DIMOND ARCHITECTS

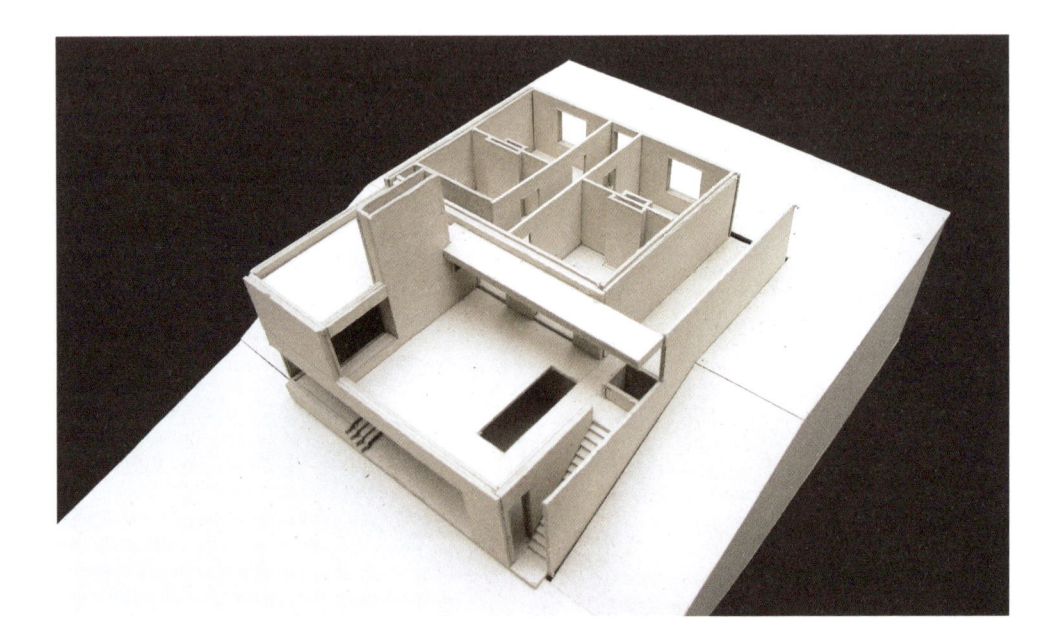

The project was to extend and remodel a 1920s bungalow by the edge of a busy road. The ground falls away steeply behind the house, which formerly stood aloof from its garden. The design draws the living quarters down the hill into a new relationship with the garden. The rooms of the bungalow are given over to entrance, bedrooms and bathroom. The new concrete structure bridges and binds the house to the garden, and its chimney anchors above and below. The span of the extension houses a double-height living-room, kitchen and utility spaces, stepping down and out through a terraced plinth to the garden below. The form of the casting springs and rotates to draw one down into the south and west light. The living room is floored with end-grain woodblock and the kitchen with polished concrete. Walls surfaces are rough and smooth bush-hammered concrete and painted timber sheeting. The kitchen/dining room opens up as a terrace to the garden, and a sunlit deck is carried on its back.

address – Dundrum, Co Dublin
client – private
photography – D+D

design to completion – 2005-2012
site area – 675m^2 / floor area – 120m^2
(existing 65m^2 / new 55m^2)
budget – n/a

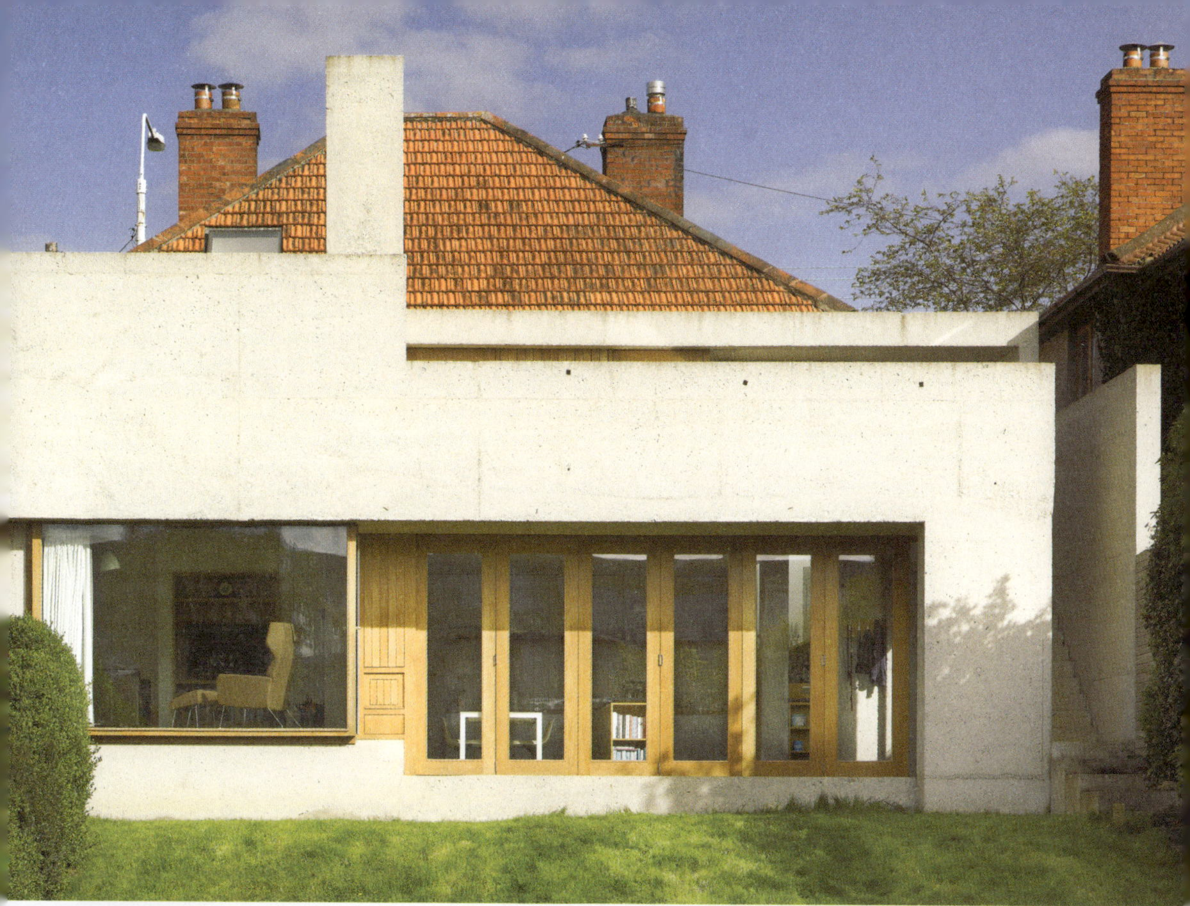
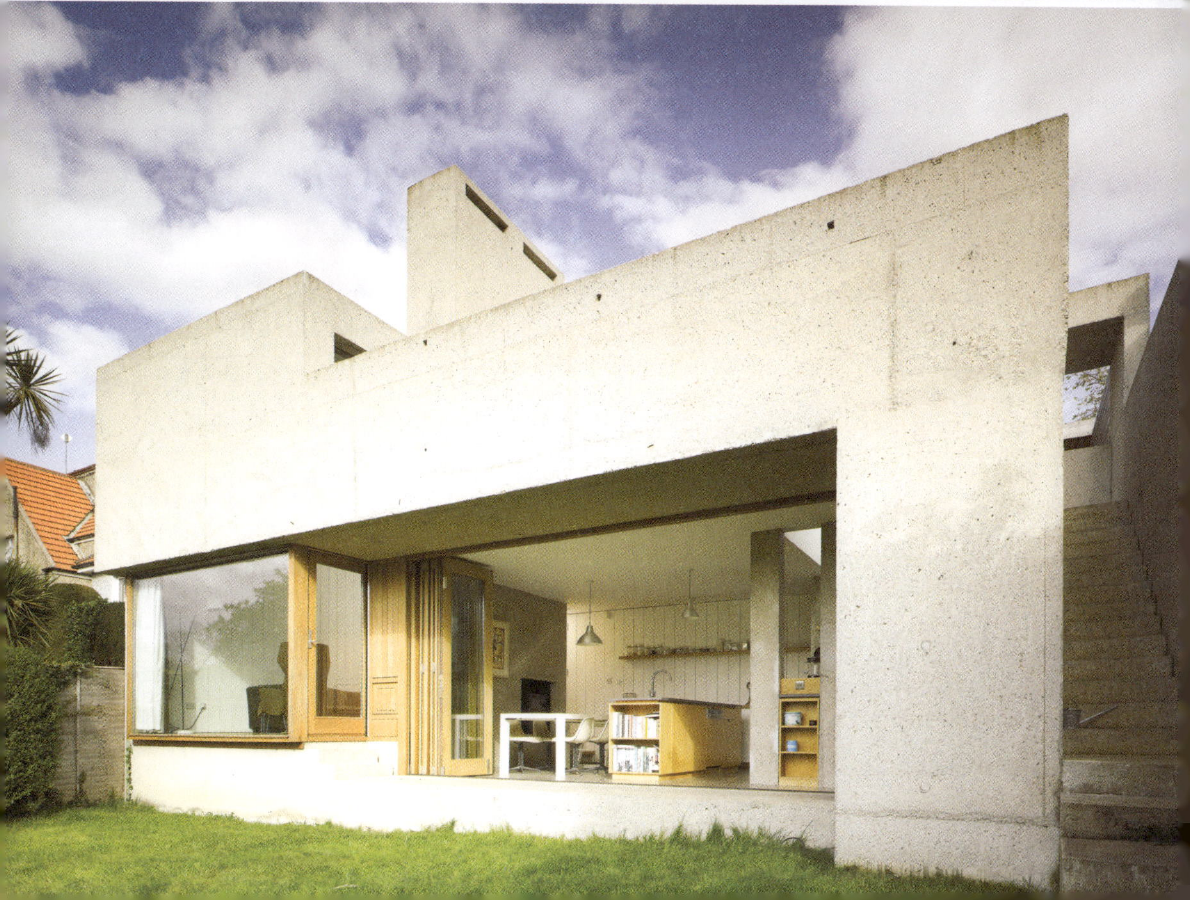

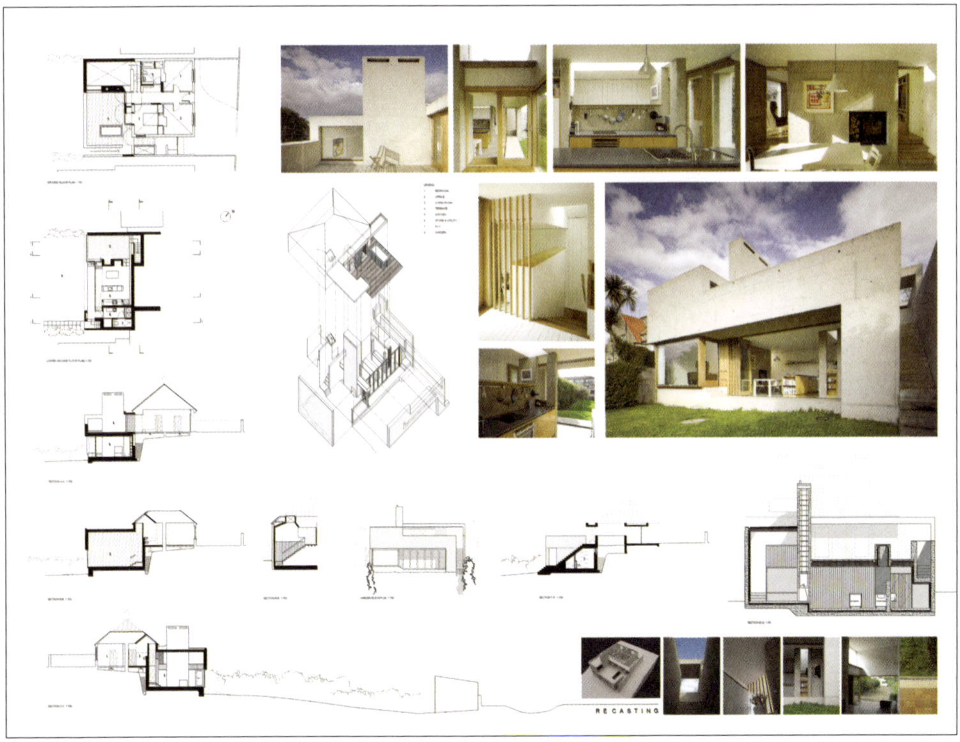
RECASTING

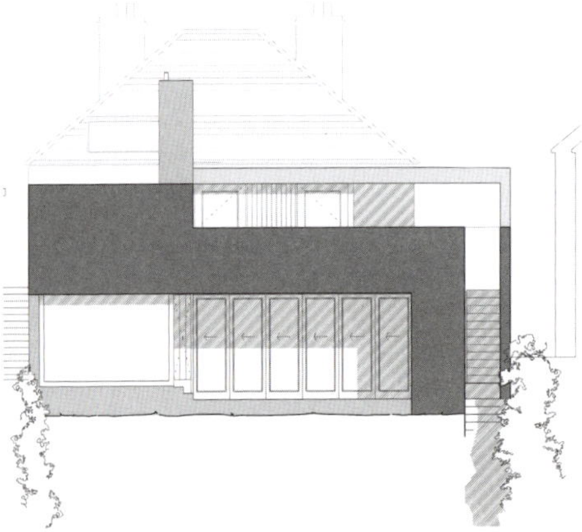

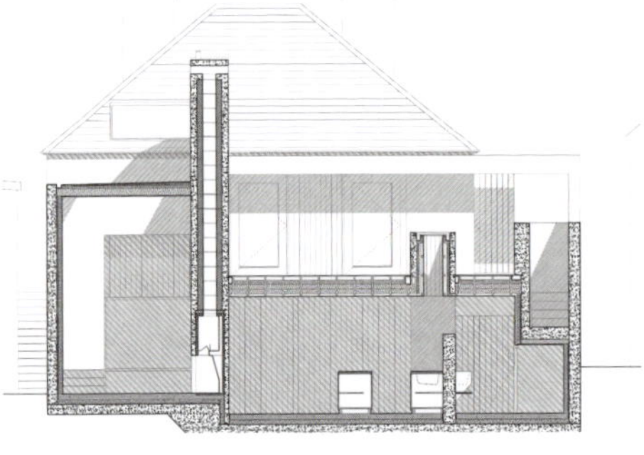

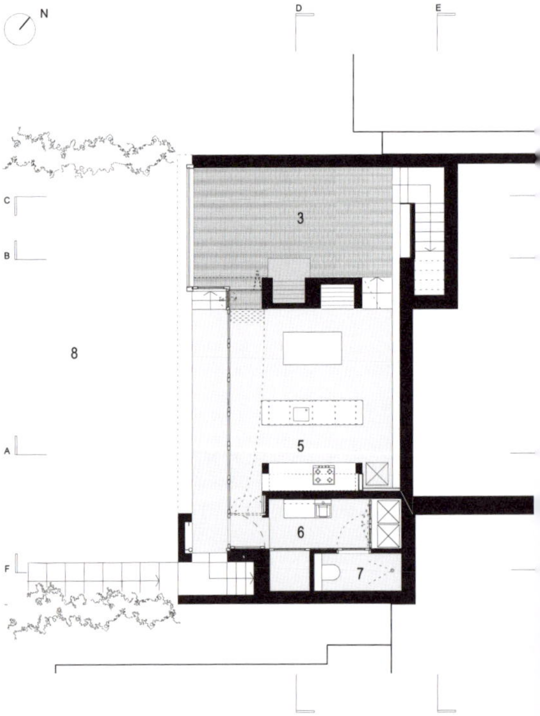
N
D
E
C
B
A
F
3
8
5
6
7

RECASTING

View of upper deck
Upper ground-level plan

opposite

AAI Awards entry panel
West elevation / Detail section DD
Lower ground-level plan

page 53

Garden elevation
View of kitchen/dining terrace and stairs from garden to deck

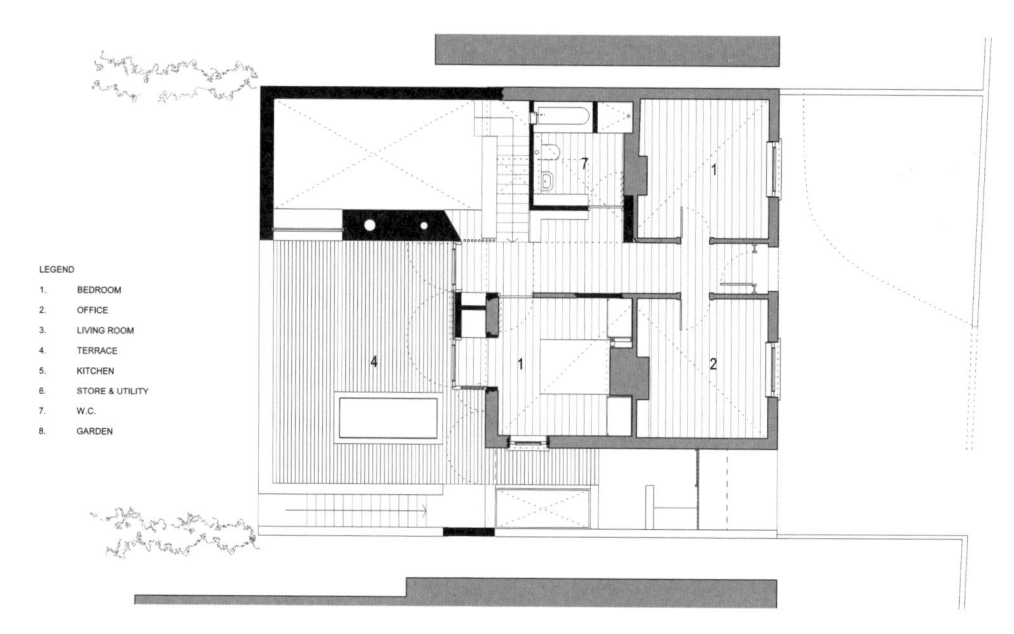

LEGEND
1. BEDROOM
2. OFFICE
3. LIVING ROOM
4. TERRACE
5. KITCHEN
6. STORE & UTILITY
7. W.C.
8. GARDEN

53

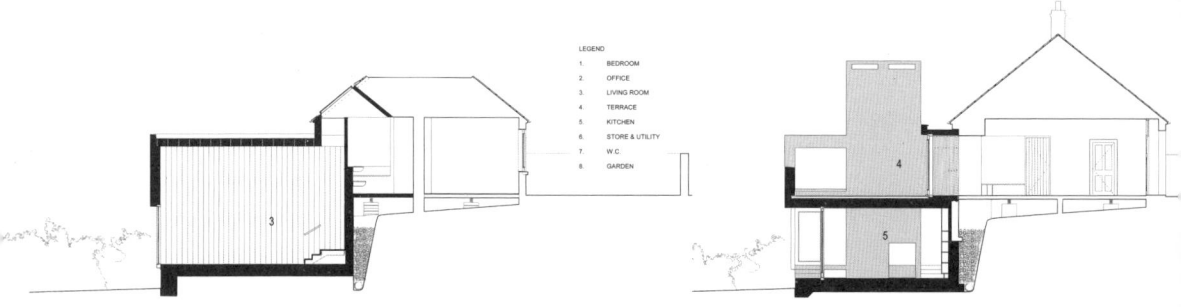

LEGEND
1. BEDROOM
2. OFFICE
3. LIVING ROOM
4. TERRACE
5. KITCHEN
6. STORE & UTILITY
7. W.C.
8. GARDEN

RECASTING

View of kitchen/dining terrace to garden, and stairs to upper deck
Exploded axonometric
Cross-sections – BB AA, FF looking north, and CC looking south

overleaf – Views of kitchen/dining area (p56) / Interior views (pp58-59)
Detail of garden elevation (p61)

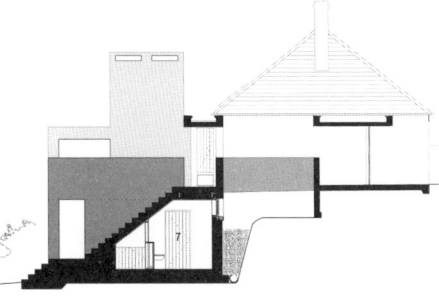

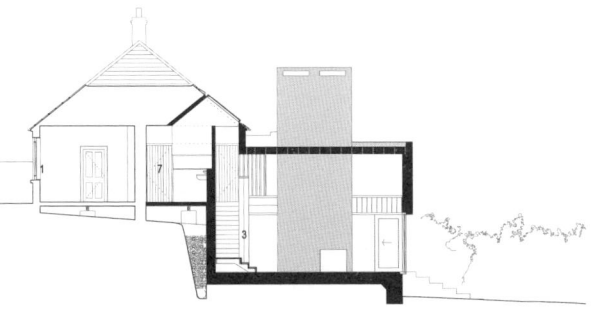

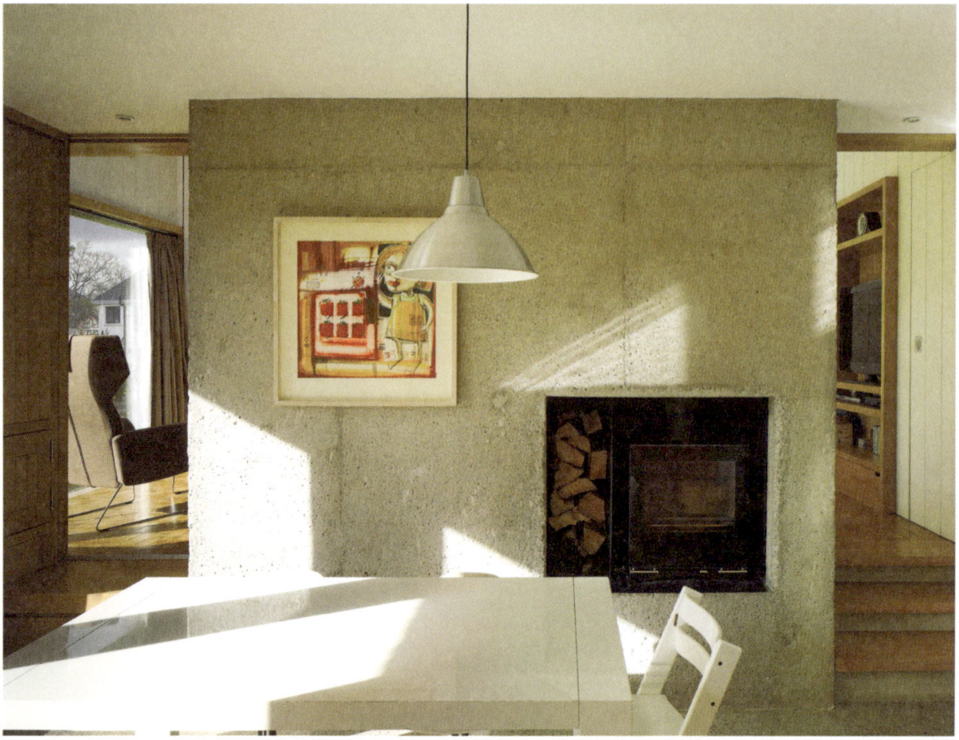

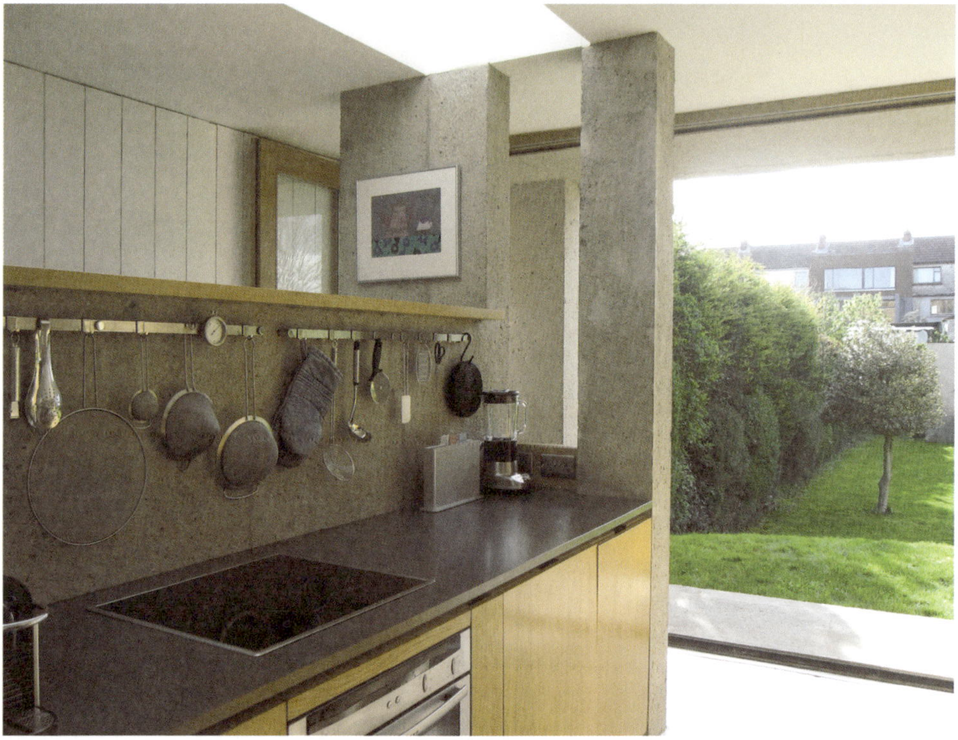

ASSESSORS' COMMENTS

HICKEY – I like this project. It's quite sophisticated in two or three different places.

ROSBOTTOM – This level of external articulation is quite good. It reminds me of Schindler.

COTTER – I like the way it steps down and engages with a different architectural language. It's in a suburban context, but it opens up. It's without the pressure of enclosure we have in some such developments.

ROSBOTTOM – It sets out a very straightforward and sensible premise about a house which doesn't connect to its garden, and it makes the connection to the garden in an intriguing and spatially sophisticated way. It also looks well made.

HICKEY – I like the over-the-wall moments – this one over the living room, on the left, and then the one on the other side, from the upper terrace to the living room.

HATZ – It's like a piece of infrastructure really. It's house and infrastructure and it completes the plan at the same time. It's not very beautifully proportioned, but in a funny way that's okay because it's still disciplined. You have the feeling that it was already there and they just moved into it.

HICKEY – Do you mean they built it as a piece of infrastructure and then they inhabited it?

HATZ – Yes. It looks like that.

ROSBOTTOM – It's a slightly awkward neighbour, isn't it? I know it's very secondary, but I quite like the relationships with the existing roofs and gables in the photography. It definitely has something.

HATZ – Also, it's not just spreading out. It's quite disciplined. It reminds me of that house by Peter Märkli, where you have all these sliding panels which are sometimes open, sometimes half-open, because it's robust and it's kept within its perimeter.

HICKEY – And it's not overblown either.

COTTER – No. It's not trying to be anything it isn't. The fact that proportionally speaking these concrete forms are not dissimilar, I find satisfying sculpturally; they are stepped to make an extension very simply.

ROSBOTTOM – It's not brittle. I mean, some of the things that you see, you get the feeling that domesticity will undermine them. This feels like it will take on domestic life and be added to through time.

HICKEY – The two routes down are very nice. They come down around the outside with a little space on top, with a chimney that you can sit against, and the chimney faces south. It's a big element. I really like that. And then you move down to a series of rooms. It's quite a nice way of getting from a higher level to a whole storey down.

DE BLACAM – Can I talk about the concrete for a second? As somebody who has made this mistake, I think the rule "do not touch" in relation to concrete is all-commanding. This concrete here has all been sandblasted, both internally and externally, and so, therefore, they'll have to go on washing it, which maybe is not a bad thing.

HICKEY – Or will it just get very dirty and grow moss and lichen and stuff?

DE BLACAM – I think it's curious to have the concrete as the outer leaf. If you look at the sandwich of the construction, here in the section, it's thin enough in terms of what it might be giving them in U-values, or whatever. I suppose the point I'm making is about their confidence in the concrete. And this is concrete poured with plywood.

HICKEY – It's a kind of hard master though, isn't it?

DE BLACAM – It's terribly difficult, and I almost think it's impossible in Ireland.

ROSBOTTOM – You do it a lot, though.

HICKEY – Well, we try it. But you need the concrete to hold the space up, or else this doesn't work as a building.

DE BLACAM – The reason I'm dwelling on this is because it's to do with Elizabeth's remarks about the awkwardness of it. Ultimately it's an argument about the form, about the choice of material, and the intent and the geometry. That is the argument that is at play, and I suppose you can describe it simply as stepping down from the house into the garden, and so on. But it's a fairly interesting piece of work.

HICKEY – Despite your reservations about the nature of the surface after it's been cast, I don't think you can do something like this in any other way. You can only use concrete to make a step down like this in the way the spaces are articulated.

HATZ – I would like it to have some moss and stuff on it. It looks a bit too new now!

HICKEY – It will have it pretty quickly, won't it Shane?

DE BLACAM – Well, I think to put a sandblast machine on concrete is ultimately flawed. The day that is done on site, really, everyone can walk away. But we've all failed in that regard.

HICKEY – Requiem for the surface concrete! Ultimately, though, I agree with you.

DE BLACAM – You have to ask the question, Why?

COTTER – Why can't they leave the imperfections, the oxidisation and the film that's on it?

59

I mean, it's all about this expectation of the modernist façade. And actually the patination of the mould, the mistakes, the slightly glazed bits, the kitschy bits, the changes in tone hold the aesthetics that make the difference. Why does it have to be the same tone – tidy-mindedness? I think we have to accept the way materials behave. It's one of my bugbears about architecture.

ROSBOTTOM – It's about imageability, isn't it? That actually these things live to some extent as images and the material becomes about its image rather than its character. But I think there's a bigger question, and it comes out in a lot of these projects. I would really like to understand is how this concrete piece engages with the existing house, because I think you could actually have made it in other ways. I'm not sure this material is necessary, that the heroism of this material is necessary.

DE BLACAM – It's perfectly clear. What one does in small jobs like this is you work it all out. I mean, the architect has made it now, they have learnt all about it, and they have done it, and that's the advantage, I suppose, in making projects like that. It's their laboratory. They have worked it out, found out what they can do.

HICKEY – It's not easy to do this. Concrete is just not easy.

DE BLACAM – No, it's not.

HATZ – You look at La Congiunta in Giornico by Märkli, and think that they built it themselves. And it's got all the faults, but it's using the flaws of concrete as part of the building. Without that roughness and memory of the shutter-work, you would not have the same presence, or even the same sense of scale. You can work that way too.

ROSBOTTOM – But there you walk across to the storm-drain at the edge of the field, and it's exactly the same construction. And there's something fantastic about the fact that this thing is almost part of the infrastructure of the valley that has emerged as art gallery. But this here is a domestic project, and someone, who's not an architect, is living with their idea of what concrete is.

COTTER – Concrete is open to as many disguises or surfaces you care to use. It's a very mercurial medium, like plastic.

ROSBOTTOM – Concrete can now be anything it wants to be. And actually all of these projects are quite nostalgic about concrete – it's a particular idea of concrete. But it's interesting, when you think about these things as material, where an architect's heroic understanding of concrete meets a domestic client. So there's an inherent compromise that happens. Of all the domestic extensions we looked at, this one feels like a different order. I think it's an Award. It feels to me like a serious architect who's at the beginning of their career and testing a load of stuff out, seeing if it works. To do this in such circumstances feels like someone who's got real potential.

DONAGHY + DIMOND ARCHITECTS was formed by Marcus Donaghy and Will Dimond in 2001. Practice ranges from furniture design to houses and gardens to public space and buildings in urban and rural conditions. MARCUS DONAGHY (b.1968) graduated from UCD in 1993 and worked as a graduate architect in New York and with Paul Keogh Architects in Dublin. WILL DIMOND (b.1961) holds a BA in modern languages from Bristol University (1980-84), and graduated from UCD in 1992. He worked with O'Donnell + Tuomey Architects from 1992-2001. Both have been part-time lecturers at UCD School of Architecture since 1999. DESIGN TEAM – Marcus Donaghy, Will Dimond, Conal Ryan (project architect).

DONAGHY + DIMOND ARCHITECTS
41 Francis Street, Dublin 8 – T 01-4168132 / F 01-4169730 / E info@donaghydimond.ie / W www.donaghydimond.ie

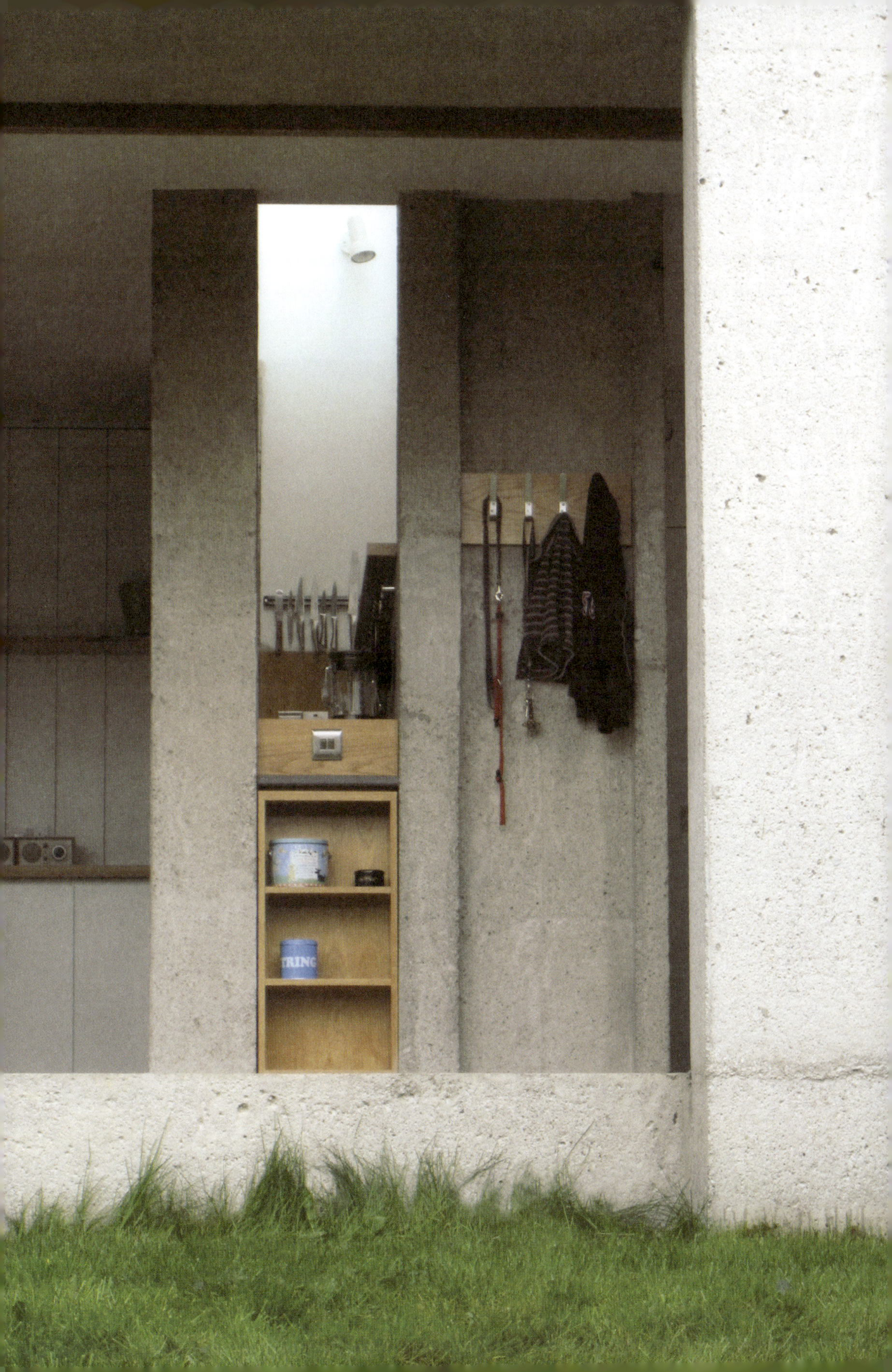

AWARD

MEDICAL SCHOOL, STUDENT RESIDENCES & BUS SHELTER, University of Limerick

GRAFTON ARCHITECTS

Siteplan 1:500

01 Student Residences - House 01
02 Student Residences - House 02
03 Student Residences - House 03
04 Graduate Entry Medical School
05 Bus Shelter
06 Plazza
07 Health Sciences Building
08 World Music Academy of Music and Dance
09 Sports Pavilion Building
10 Foyer
11 Café
12 Auditorium
13 Seminar Room
14 Plant

The aspiration is to combine faculty buildings and residences in a manner which encourages overlap and contributes to the life of the public spaces at the university. Aspects of the formal character are derived from an interpretation of the campus master plan, which requires an organic approach to the making of public spaces on the north side of the River Shannon. Here the ground is sloping, and remnants of the agrarian landscape are still evident in the form of old field-patterns and hedgerows. This new suite of buildings combines with three existing, neighbouring institutions – the Sports Pavilion, the Irish World Academy of Music & Dance and the Health Sciences Building – to make a new public space.

The new buildings consist of a medical school, three blocks of student housing and a canopy/pergola forming a bus and bicycle shelter. The Medical School, the last in a series of set pieces, acts as an anchor around which the other buildings now loosely rotate. The

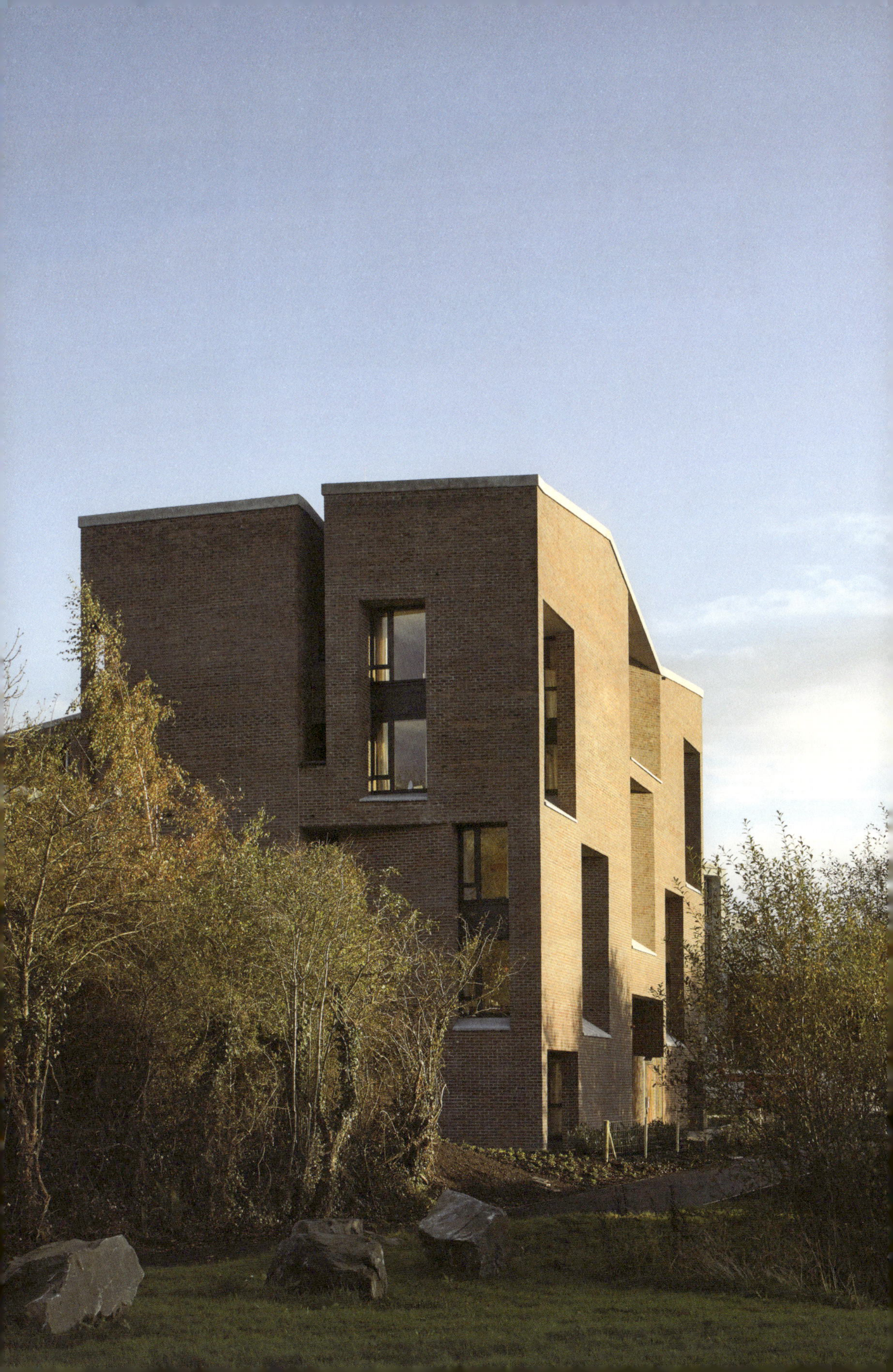

language of the Medical School is that of an educational institution, while the student residences appear like three large houses. The concrete bus shelter, together with the residences, combine with the Medical School to form a loose edge to the public space. The bus shelter canopy, steps and ramps negotiate the level change to the Sports Pavilion beyond.

The central space slopes gently to the west. Three oak trees, stone seats and steps occupy a central level platform, subtly providing a focal point before the space moves out, fracturing at the edges to connect to the residences, car-parking and other faculty buildings. The surfaces of the public space move from hard to soft, south-sloping grassed spaces, designed with and without furniture to provide for leisure and lingering. The buildings stand guard, facing the public space, distinguished by their material.

Limestone is used to represent the 'formal' central Medical School, making reference to the limestone territory of Co Clare, where this side of the campus is located. The stone wall is folded, profiled and layered in response to orientation, sun, wind, rain and public activity. A colonnade to the south and west corner acts as a gathering and entrance space. In contrast, the north and east walls are more mute.

In response to the deep plan, the roof form is modulated to light multiple spaces, including the central circulation space, the clinical skills labs, the corridors, and a small roof terrace. An open central stair connecting the primary spaces threads through all levels of the interior, designed as a social space with enough room to stop and chat or lean on a balustrade or shelf and view the activity of the entrance and spaces above and below.

Brick follows through to the Student Residences from the existing accommodation buildings behind. Here the material is given depth and the façades are deeply carved to provide a form of threshold between the domestic interior and the public space that they overlook. All living spaces address the public space to the south-east, with the more private study bedrooms facing north-east or north-west.

The undercroft of the residences is carved away, providing archways, which allows for pedestrian movement from the car park and bus park to the north, as well as forming sheltered social spaces for students. Large gateways open into the entrance courts of the housing blocks, where stairs, lift, bicycles, bins and communal laundry facilities are.

address – Clare Campus, University of Limerick
client – Plassey Campus Developments
photography – Dennis Gilbert/VIEW

design to completion – 2007-2012
site area – 1.2ha / *floor area* – 8,080m^2
    (*school* 4,300m^2, *housing* 3,600m^2)
budget – €14.54m

Second Floor

12	Clinical Skills
13	Anatomical Skills
14	Computer Lab
15	Clinical Skills Video
16	Self Directed Learning
17	Hot Desks
18	Offices
19	Store

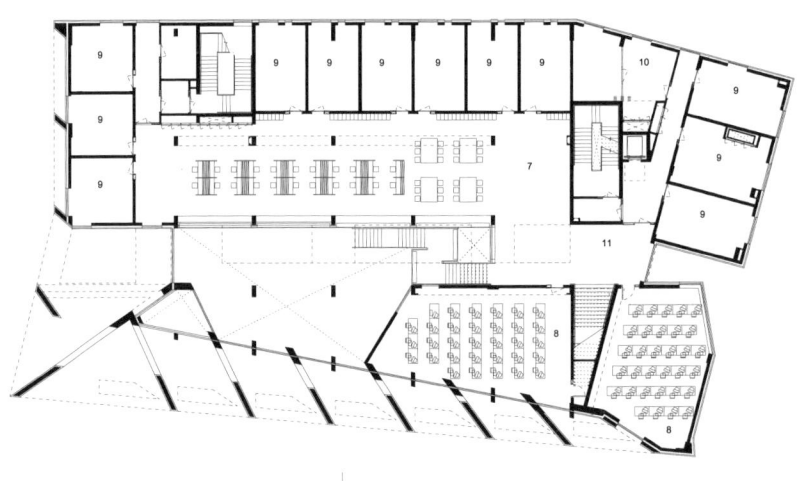

First Floor

07	Self Directed Learning
08	Computer Room
09	Problem Base Learning
10	GP Core
11	Circulation

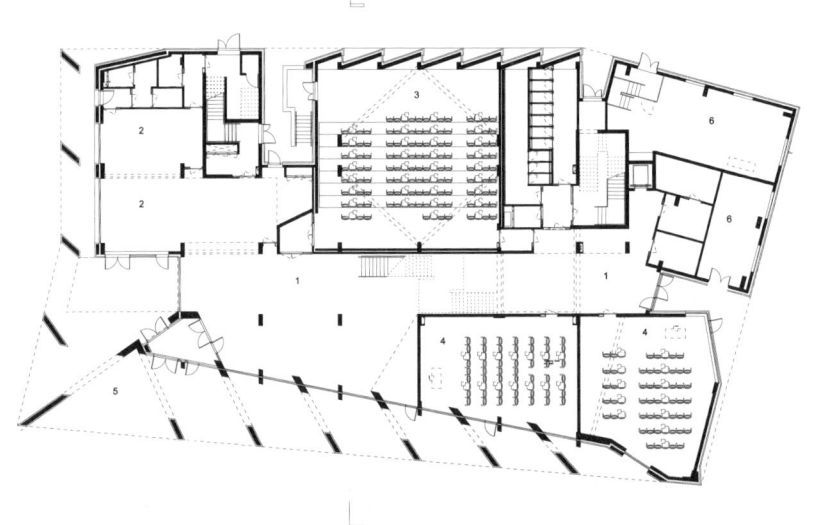

Medical School
Ground Floor

01	Foyer
02	Café
03	Auditorium
04	Seminar Room
05	Colonnade
06	Store/Plant

Third Floor

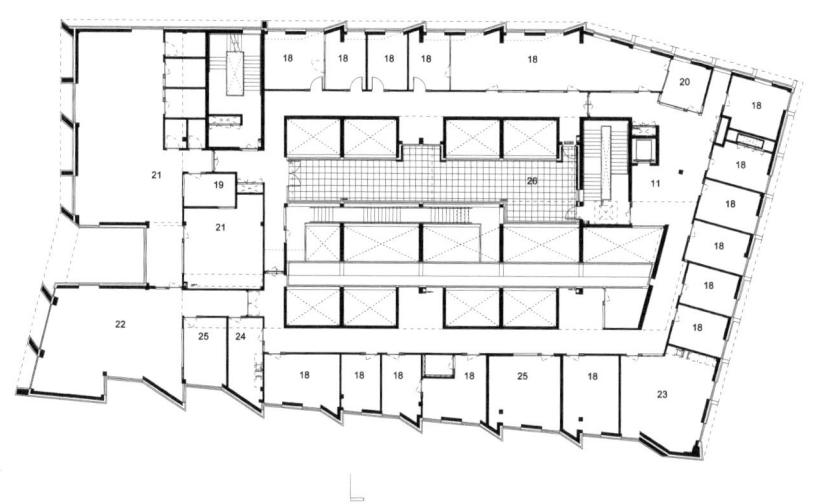

18	Offices
19	Store
20	School Reception
21	Research Laboratory
22	Research Write-Up A
23	Staff Room
24	Kitchen
25	Meeting Room
26	Courtyard

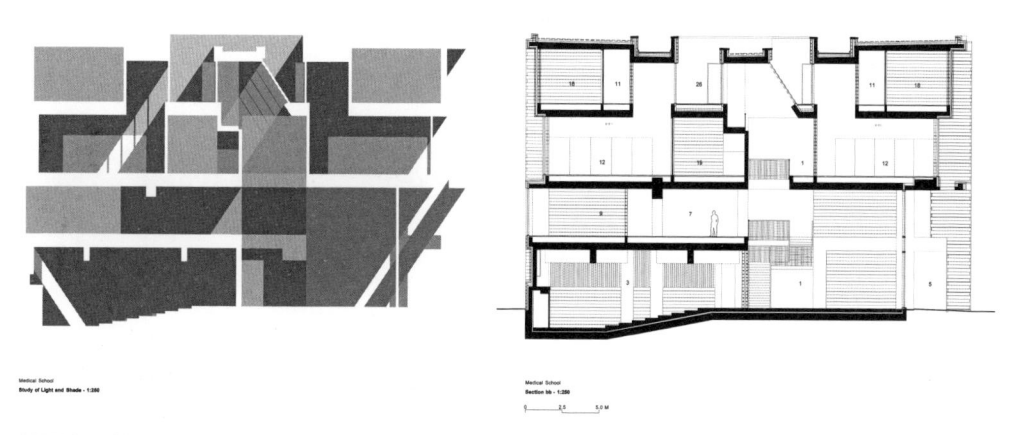

Medical School
Study of Light and Shade - 1:350

Medical School
Section hh - 1:350

MEDICAL SCHOOL, UL

Plans – ground, 1st, 2nd, 3rd floor overleaf page 70

Study of light and shade View through colonnade View of central space from first floor
Cross-section West elevation Central space
Elevations – south, west The south colonnade in the rain View of colonnade from within

Medical School
South Elevation

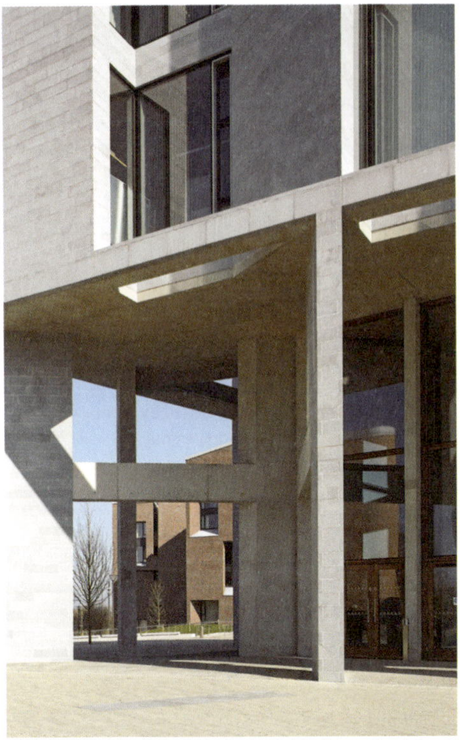

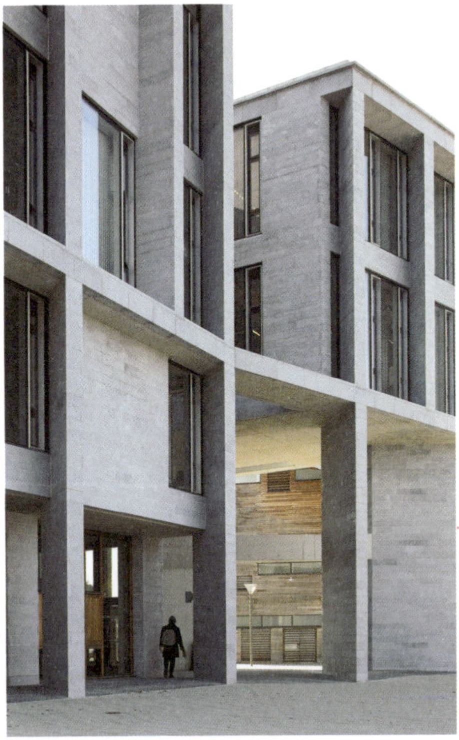

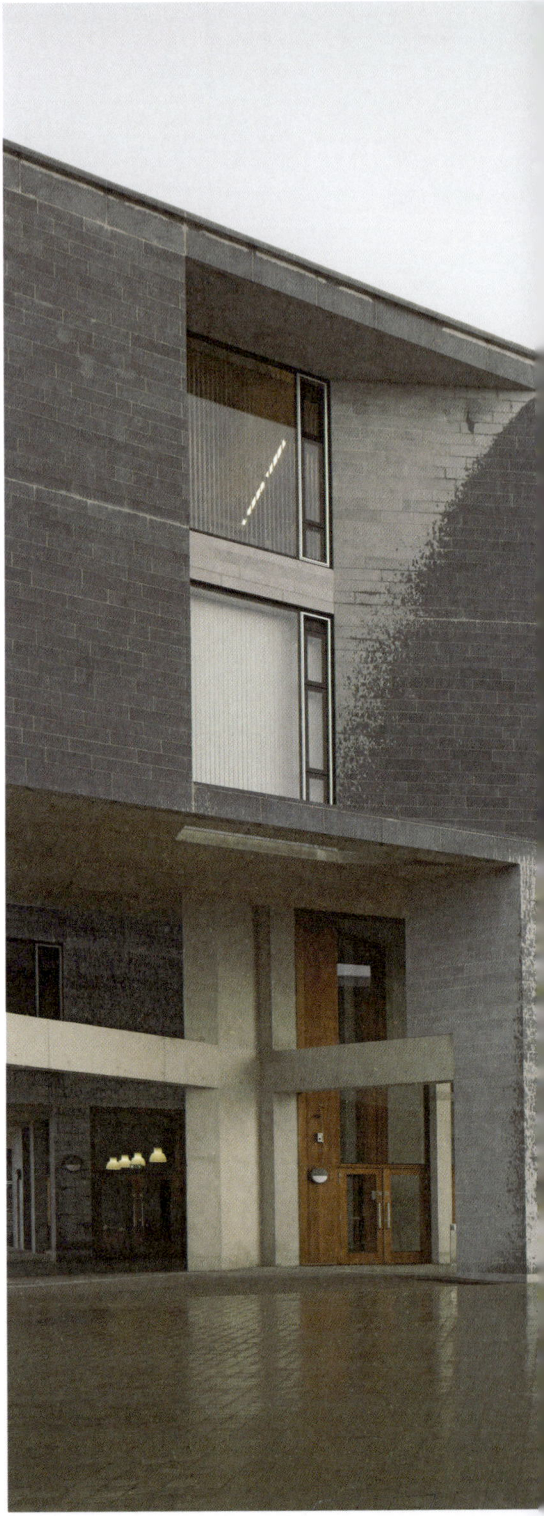

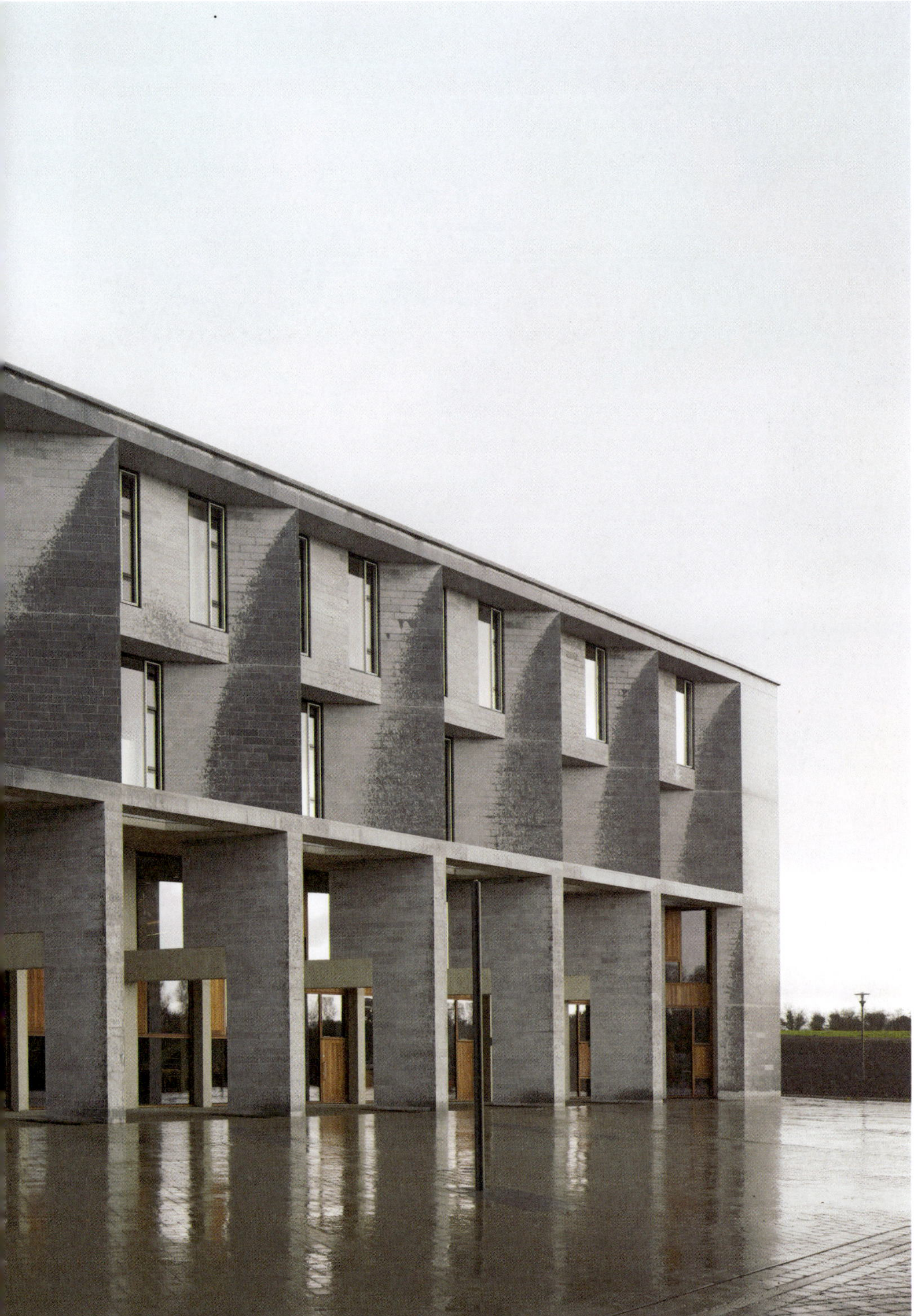

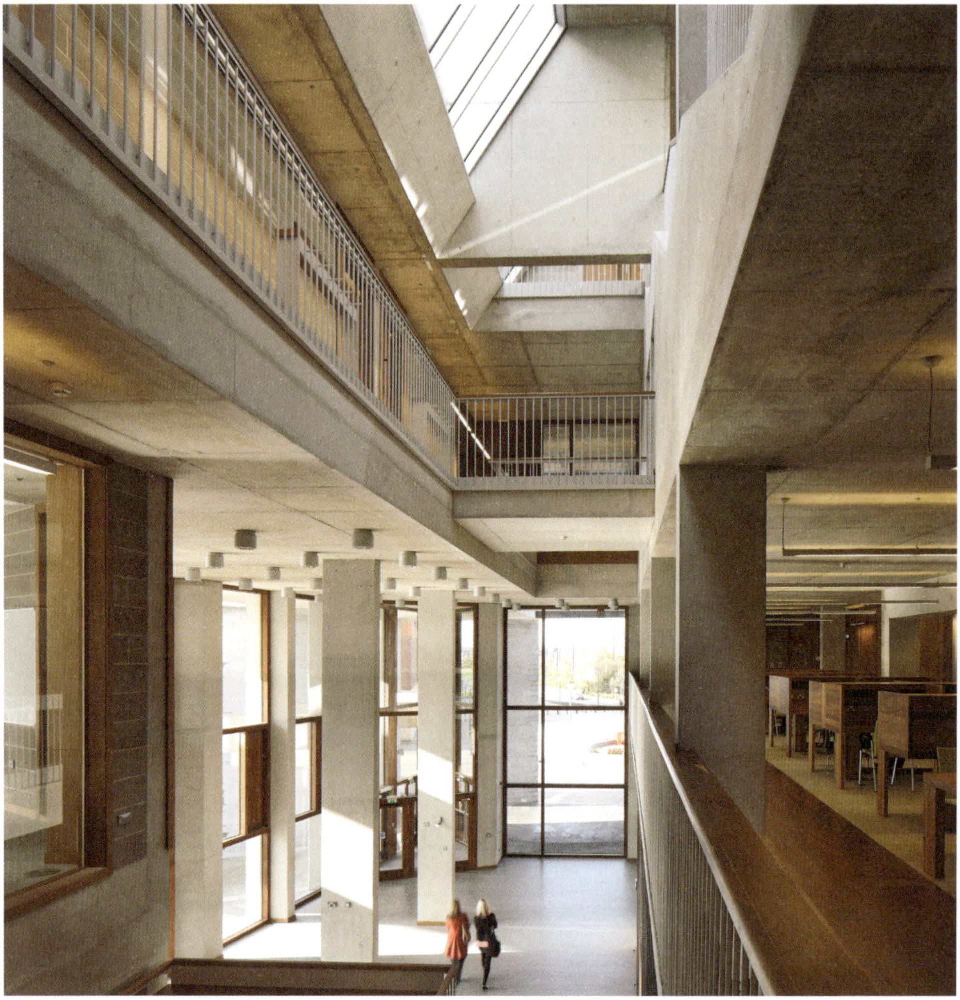

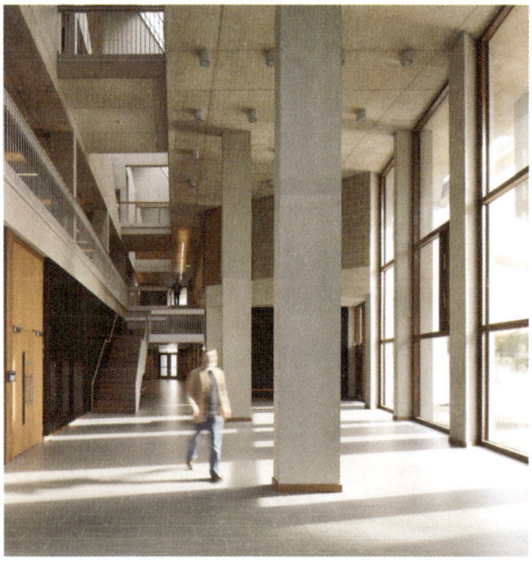

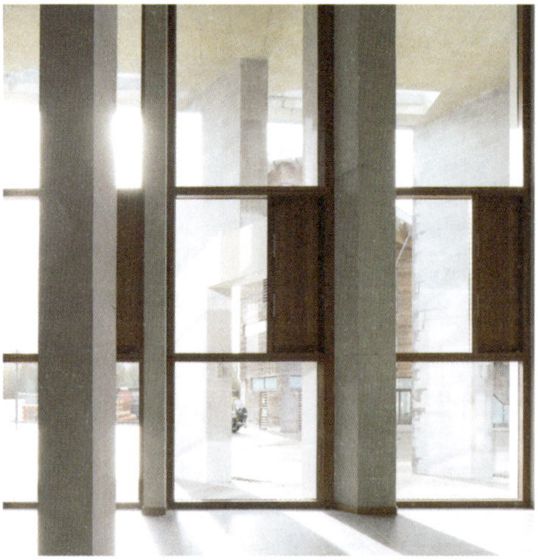

ASSESSORS' COMMENTS

HATZ – I have seen this, but not completed. It's an incredibly difficult site, because there are two absolutely horrible buildings confronting them. But this set of new buildings has a dialogue and a dignity, and they suddenly just anchor everything in a very clever way. The Medical School is like an inhabited massive structure, and then the Student Housing is actually like an enclosing wall. And also you don't get the feeling of housing really because they tie the openings to each other so they are much more dignified in scale. It's really a very, very clever project.

ROSBOTTOM – I was trying to understand what the buildings do as an ensemble. It feels like it's potentially very powerful, but I think it's a pity that we don't have a clearer understanding of its spatial consequence: what's the space that these pieces make? I think the pieces themselves are formally very compelling. The west elevation of the Medical School is a kind of palazzo. It feels like Terragni, it's really powerful. But it would be really interesting to understand it more clearly in its landscape.

HATZ – The handling of the section in the Medical School is really interesting, and the use of the construction to lead light through the spaces is very strong. The three brick bodies are the Student Housing, and what they do is restore a scale that is missing at the university, almost a monumental scale, which is good. They are quite big buildings, and with their big openings they are acknowledging the scale of the campus, and also taking it down to a more human scale. It's an interesting play of scales.

ROSBOTTOM – Do you get to see these buildings from a distance? From the interior, it seems like you are looking at a fairly distant landscape horizon, but do you get to look back at them from somewhere, as an ensemble of things?

HATZ – You would, but I've only seen them from when you come across that curved bridge, and you come between these two overly designed buildings, which make you feel like you've been in a tumble-dryer because there's so much going on. And because there's also a kind of broken-ness in this set of new buildings, they have some kind of dialogue, but they are, in fact, anchored here, and the three brick bodies almost read like one. They're very beautiful in scale. I have rarely seen such powerful, yet balanced and nuanced university buildings anywhere.

HICKEY – The Student Residences look much tighter in this photo. They actually look like they nearly touch each other, whereas in the site plan there seems to be much more space between them.

HATZ – The impression when you're there is that they're very close.

ROSBOTTOM – That's because, I think, the plan is overhanging. That is partly the problem with the drawing: it's hard to judge what the sense of enclosure in that space is. I'm really interested in the idea of institutional housing, and that these things operate at a scale that's somehow between the domestic and the institutional. The reason I ask about the distant view is that one can imagine they become quite ambiguous: how big is that when seen on the horizon from afar?

COTTER – In the Medical School, the quirkiness is increasing with the scale, and even though they have a confidence in handling the volume, I think they're also very benevolent in character. I like the way that benevolence on the exterior extends and

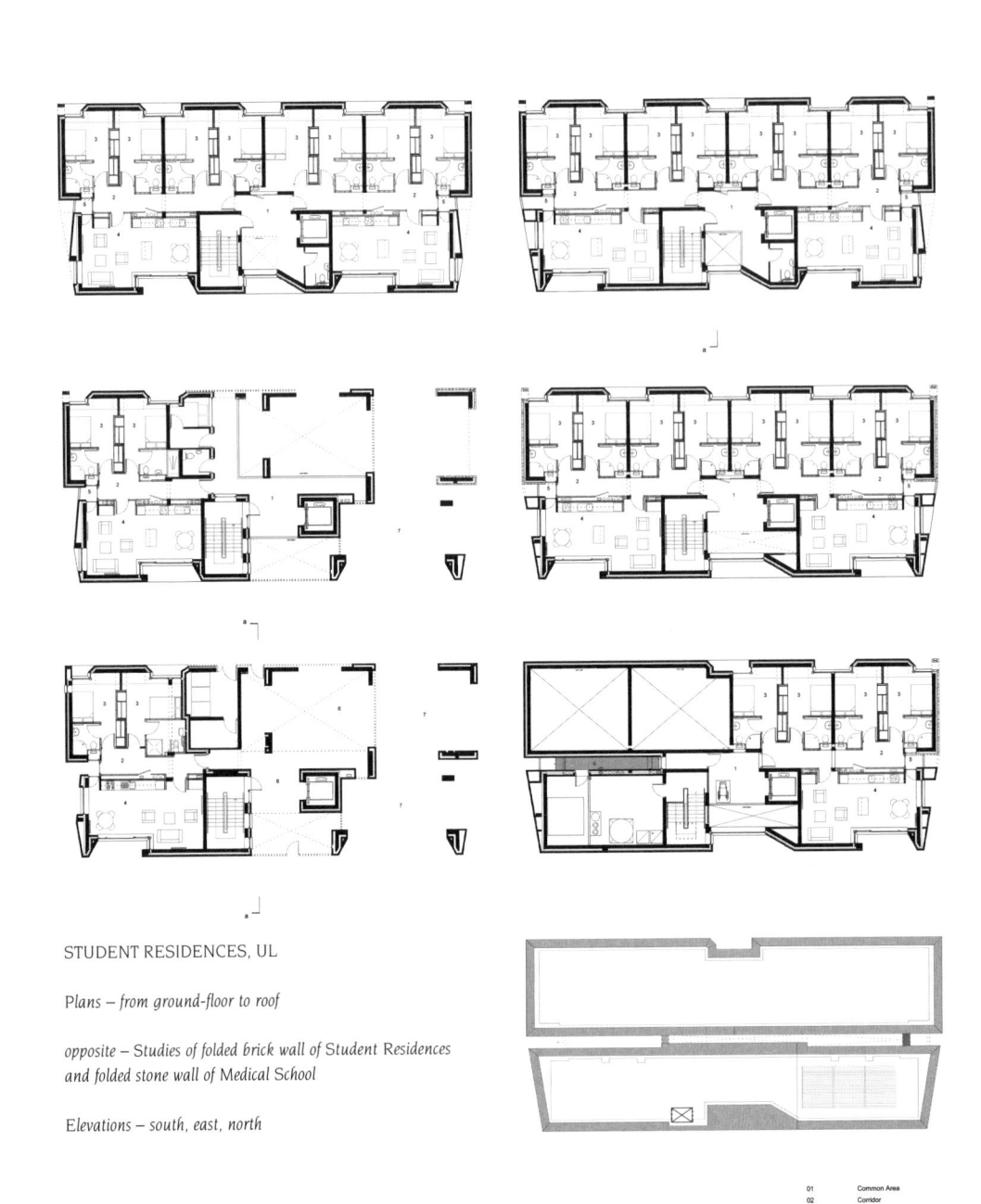

STUDENT RESIDENCES, UL

Plans – from ground-floor to roof

opposite – Studies of folded brick wall of Student Residences and folded stone wall of Medical School

Elevations – south, east, north

01	Common Area
02	Corridor
03	Study Bedroom
04	Kitchen/Living
05	Balcony
06	Entrance Forecourt
07	Archway

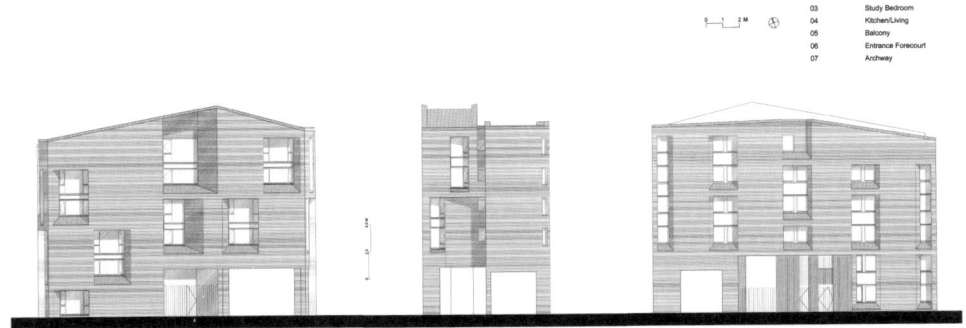

has a comparable language in the interior. When you go in, it isn't disappointing.

HATZ – What I also like with the Student Housing is the kind of warmth and the community feeling that you get. I always wanted to go to Ahmedabad, the Indian Institute of Management by Louis Kahn, because there's this kind of monumentality, but it makes sense because it creates these kind of enclaves of microclimates, which can create a new reality. In an institutionalised dwelling you can feel a kind of institutionalised coldness, but I don't feel that here. And also, they are like little communities, the way they are managed as spaces... They have thicknesses to walls and there are passages into each unit – it's not just a corridor and door.

The stone piers in the Medical School stand like fins, and when you're in here they let the light in, but they actually obliterate a little bit of the other buildings, which is a blessing.

ROSBOTTOM – It's a very interesting plan. The ground-floor plan, where the glazing pulls away from those fins, creates a really mannerist space. I mean that as a compliment.

HICKEY – The end of the Medical School reminds me of the end of the Salk Institute by Kahn. And this piece, the break down the middle of the plan, reminds me of that kind of canyon between the offices, the laboratories. One of the things that bothers me about this is it just seems to be foreshortened. It seems too short to feel right.

HATZ – That it should need more extent to have that kind of language? That's interesting.

ROSBOTTOM – It's a really intriguing and powerful section, isn't it? And it's an interesting plan the way that you build from this kind of mezzanine around a double-height space with this portico or *loggia*, and then you arrive in something more atrium-like, and then you arrive at a series of what almost feel like patios, or slots for light at the top, which deal with the grain of the plan, getting finer on each level. It's a kind of filter as you move up through the plan. I find it quite a fascinating relationship between the complexity of the plan and the controlled repetition of the façade.

DE BLACAM – I think it's difficult because of the presentation to adequately respond to this. I'm sort of perplexed. There's an awful lot going on in section and in elevation and even on the roof. So I'm completely handicapped in the absence of seeing these buildings and being able to comment adequately on it. I mean, I see wonderful things in the drawings, but I find it hard to read what is going on. What's the relationship between these pair of rooms in the Student Housing section, or are they completely separate?

HATZ – Here's a good section of the housing. Four apartments are brought together, stacked two floors high, around a double-height common room. And then they are stacked on top of each other.

ROSBOTTOM – They look like very pleasant places, they are very nicely planned, and they

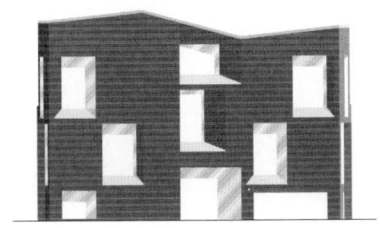

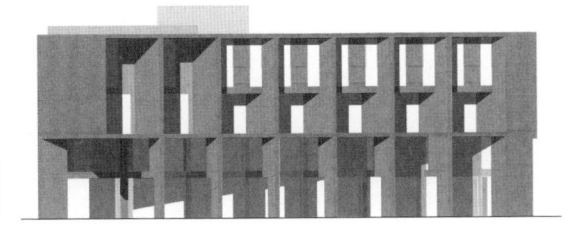

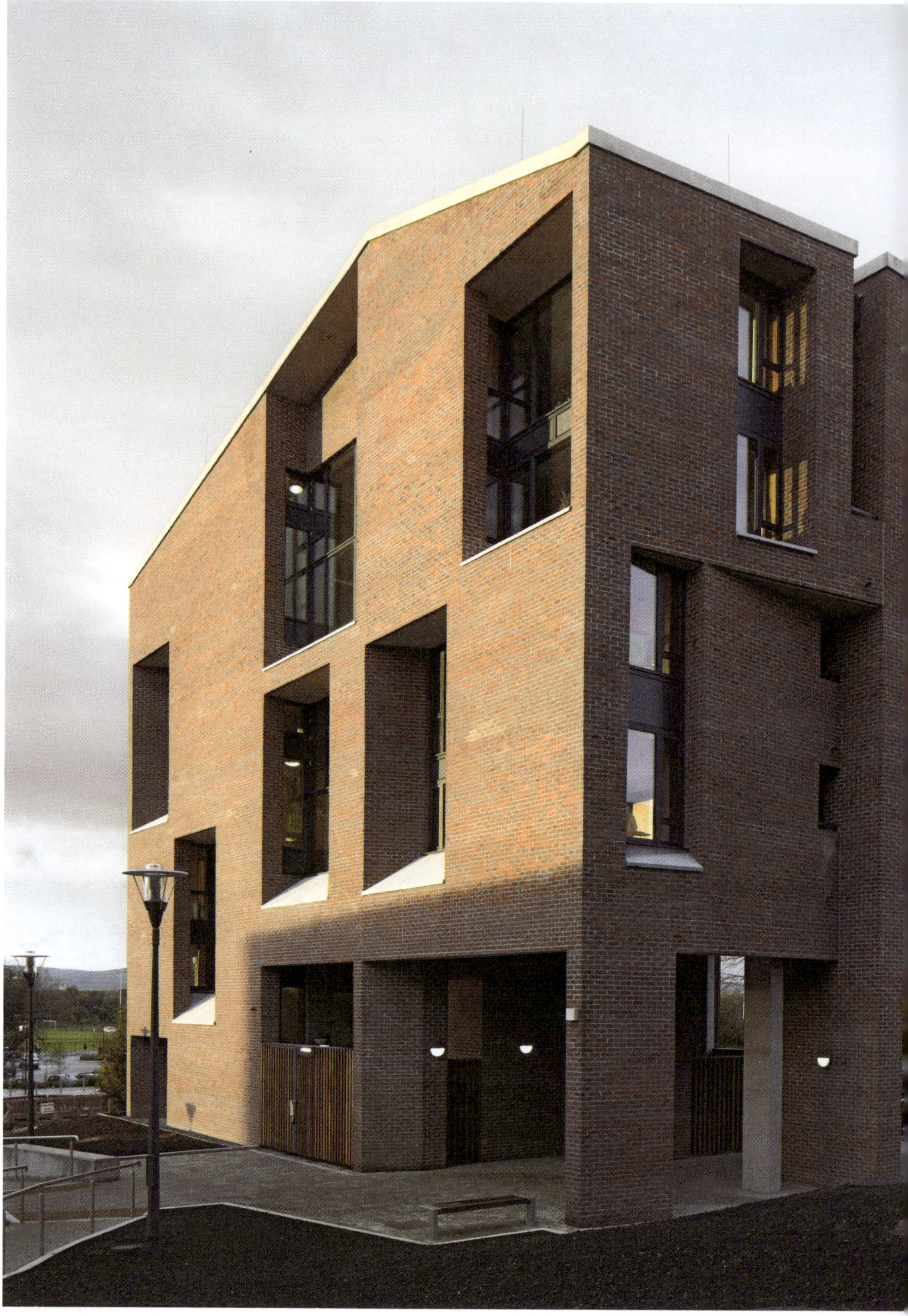

STUDENT RESIDENCES,
University of Limerick

*Student Residences 2-3
Entrance to Residences 2-3
Study of light and shade
Cross-section*

*page 77 – Medical School
colonnade*

Student Residences - House 02
Section aa - Light and Shade

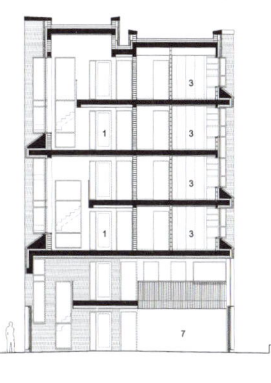

Student Residences - House 02
Section aa - 1:250

0   2.5   5.0 M

01	Common Area
02	Corridor
03	Study Bedroom
04	Kitchen/Living
05	Balcony
06	Entrance Forecourt
07	Archway

look like good places to live. And the other thing worth mentioning is the heroism of the bus stop, which I enjoy, this big canopy.

HICKEY – I'm not so sure about as an Award. I can't make my mind up as to whether it does some of the things I expect it to do, or not. The way those two housing blocks sit together infer that they are actually making quite a generous space, but in an altogether relaxed way, which I find extremely compelling. But when I look at some of the images, I'm not sure whether it does that, and there's nothing to confirm that that is absolutely the case. So that's the only reason I'm a bit concerned about it.

ROSBOTTOM – I would like to know more about the intermediate spaces and the complex spatial condition that it sets up in terms of the relation between things. But if I just look at the buildings as they stand, I think they have real qualities. There are really eloquent moments in the plans, and a generosity in the planning, and the section is very interesting, and for all of those reasons, for me, it's an Award.

DE BLACAM – I am unable to come to a conclusion whether it's an Award or the Medal.

HICKEY – I wonder about that top floor [of the Medical School]. I really want to know what that's like and I don't get it from the panels. Or these vertical fins, which I think look very interesting, but I'm not sure what it means in terms of that plan.

HATZ – It's a way of leading light from above and from the side. It's a very complex, sophisticated and strong building on a very unforgiving site. I think it's a definite Award.

ROSBOTTOM – I think this project is really strong. They feel like very powerful buildings. I find the west façade of the Medical School, and this moment where the piers turn the corner very sophisticated. But it is very difficult to appreciate the ensemble.

COTTER – It would worry me if we don't acknowledge the scale of ambition in this project.

HICKEY – I think the Medical School has an internal character that is wholly compelling, though I still have reservations about it as an ensemble, like Daniel. But on the balance of probability, I think it is a Special Award.

ROSBOTTOM – There is a history of universities being patrons of bodies of great architectural work, and that has been lost in the UK. It has passed over into a kind of procurement process that leads almost entirely to mediocrity. With the exception of maybe a Cambridge college or two, most universities have reneged on their responsibility. And it's great in a difficult economic climate to see the University of Limerick investing in its infrastructure with very powerful architecture. I think that's the sort of message you want to be giving to the country.

GRAFTON ARCHITECTS was established in 1978. Directors YVONNE FARRELL and SHELLEY McNAMARA are graduates of University College Dublin. Teachers at UCD from 1976 to 2002, they have been visiting professors at European and American schools of architecture. Grafton Architects has won numerous international awards, including World Building of the Year Award 2008 for Universita Luigi Bocconi in Milan. Recent projects include a new school of economics for l'Université Toulouse 1 Capitole, and a new university campus for UTEC Lima in Peru.

DESIGN TEAM – Shelley McNamara, Yvonne Farrell, Ger Carty, Philippe O'Sullivan, Kieran O'Brien, Matt McCullagh, Abi Hudson, David Healy, Simona Castelli, Kate O'Daly, Ciara Reddy, Paul O'Brien, Nina Alberg Arge, Eibhlin Ní Chathasaigh.

GRAFTON ARCHITECTS
12-14 College Green, Dublin 2 – T 01-6713365 / E info@graftonarchitects.ie / W www.graftonarchitects.ie.

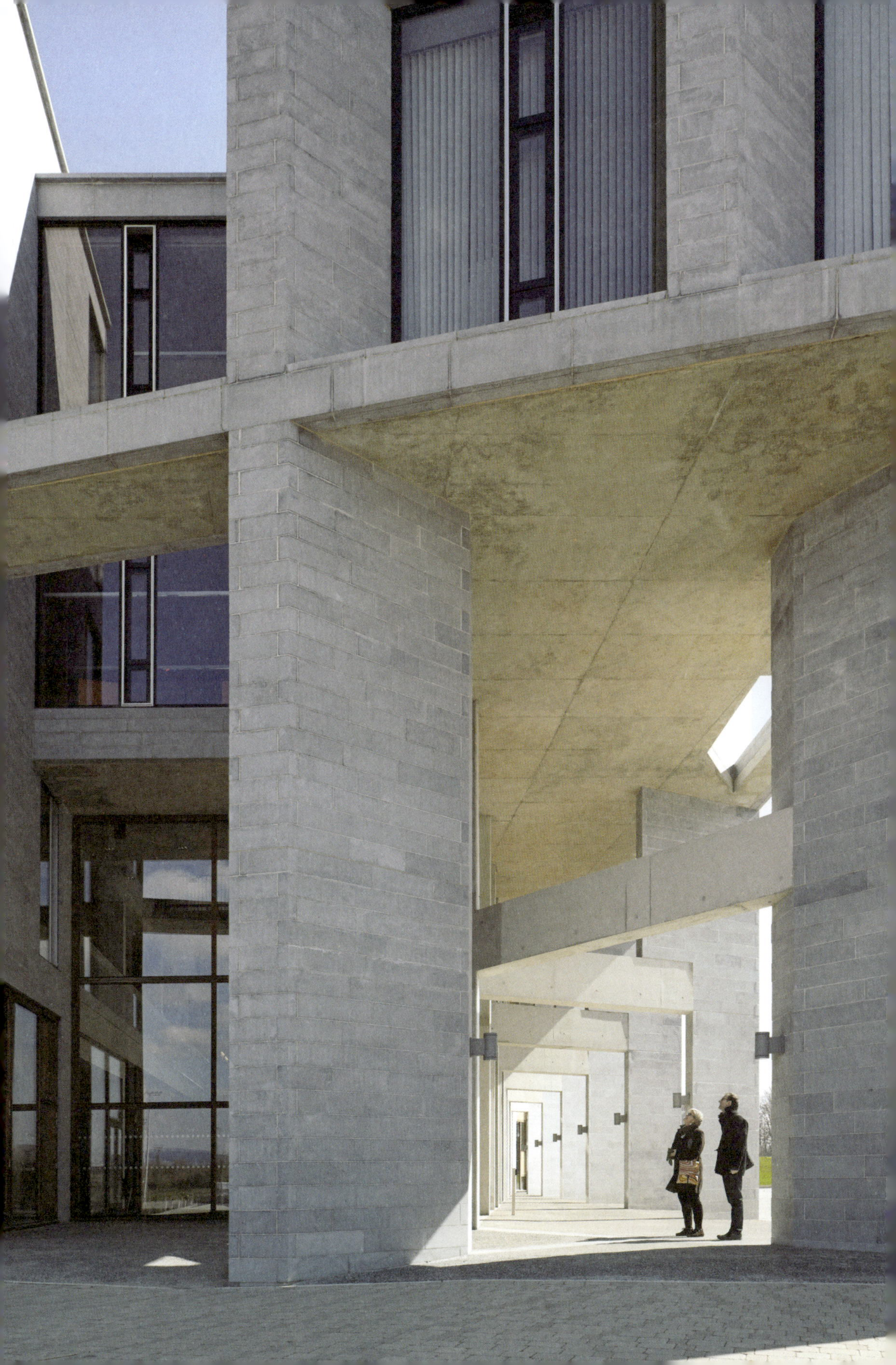

AWARD

ARCHITECTURE AS NEW GEOGRAPHY
La Biennale di Venezia

GRAFTON ARCHITECTS

The making of this exhibition was an exploration of influences and ideas. We used the opportunity to analyse in more depth the "effect" the work of Paulo Mendes da Rocha has had on the development of our own work. In trying to find a fresh insight into this work, which was familiar to us, we also gained insight into our own, very new and as yet undeveloped university project in Lima, Peru. The collaboration with a sculptor gave us the technique of making large-scale rudimentary models which have a sense of weight and materiality. Papier mâché, watercolour paper and stone models were made in order to explore space, weight and lightness. Fragments, like ruins, leave space for the imagination, both our own and that of the audience.

Arena of Learning – The exhibition proposes two "figures" forming a sense of common ground – Paulo Mendes da Rocha's Serra Dourada Stadium in Goiânia, Brazil, and our new university campus project in Lima, Peru. Like silent actors on a stage, the figures face each other across the primal space of a circle. We are investigating the idea of the university as an "arena of learning". The monumental undercroft of the Serra Dourada Stadium forms a

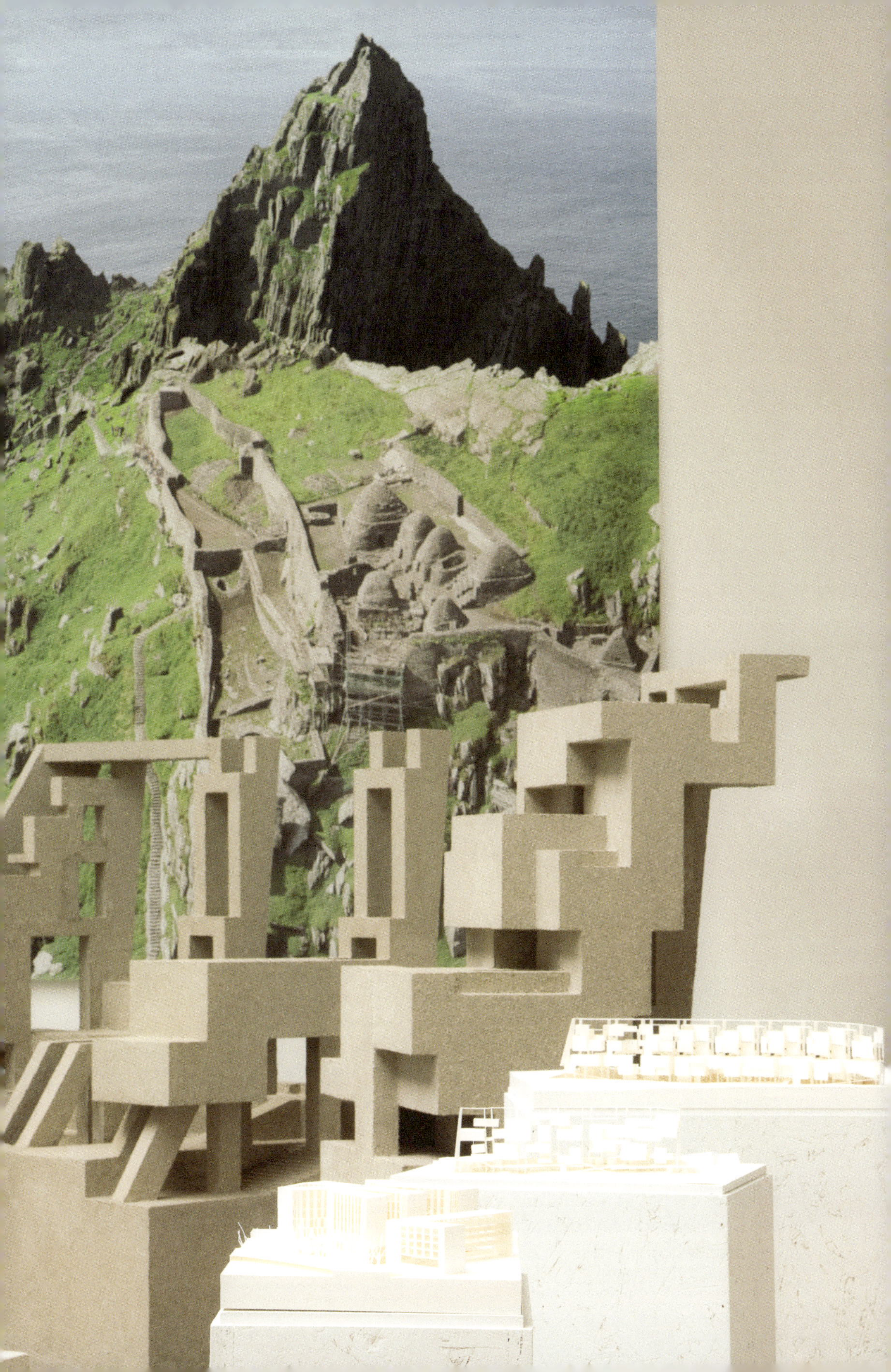

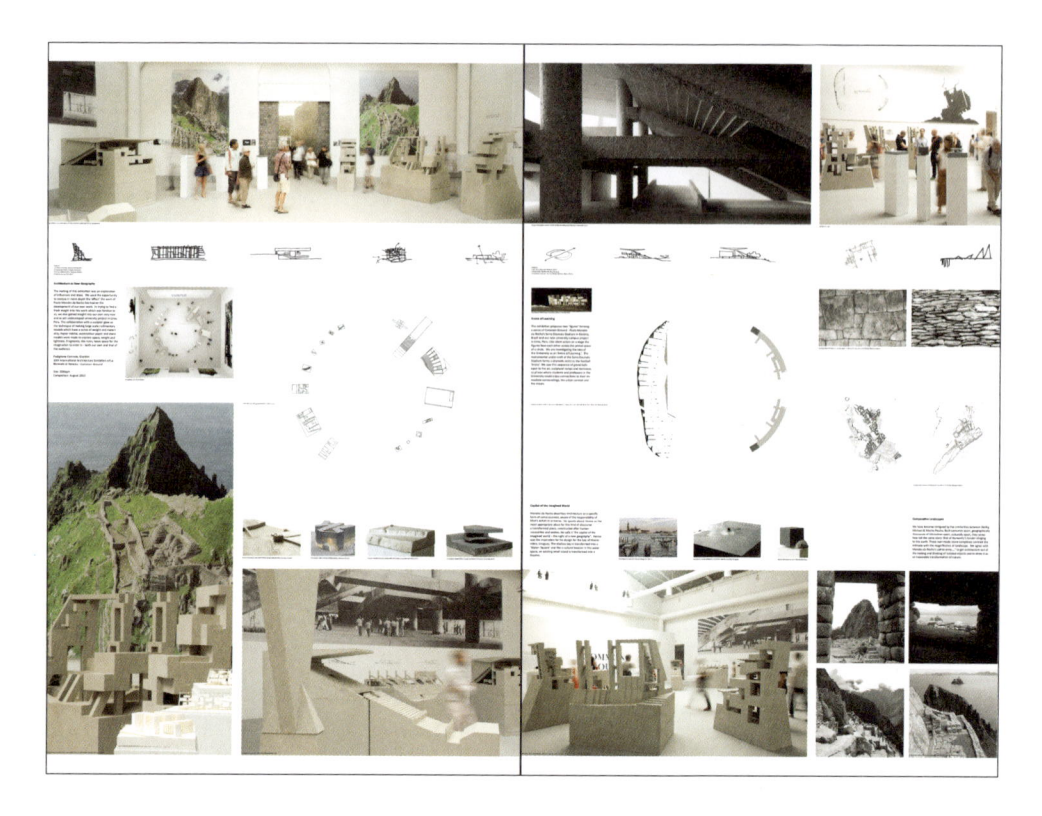

dramatic entry to the football "arena". We saw this sequence of grand halls open to the air, sculptural ramps and staircases, as places where students and teachers at the university could enjoy connections to their immediate surroundings, the urban context and the ocean.

Capital of the Imagined World – Mendes da Rocha describes architecture as a specific form of consciousness, aware of the responsibility of man's action in the universe. He speaks about Venice as the most appropriate place for this kind of discourse – a transformed place, constructed after human necessities and wishes. He calls it "the capital of the imagined world – the sight of a new geography". Venice was the inspiration for his design for the bay of Montevideo, Uruguay. The shallow bay is transformed into a "water square", and like a cultural beacon in this water space, an existing small island is transformed into a theatre.

Comparative Landscapes – We are intrigued by the similarities between Skellig Michael and Machu Picchu. Built centuries apart, thousands of kilometres apart, culturally apart, they somehow tell the same story – that of humanity's tender clinging to this earth. These man-made stone complexes contrast the intimate with the magnificence of landscape. We agree with Mendes da Rocha's call-to-arms "to get architecture out of the making and thinking of isolated objects and to show it as an inexorable transformation of nature".

Common Ground, 13th International Architecture Exhibition of La Biennale di Venezia, Italy

address – Padiglione Centrale, Giardini, Venice
client – La Biennale di Venezia
photography – Alice Clancy

design to completion – 2012
site area – n/a / *floor area* – n/a
budget – n/a

ARCHITECTURE
AS NEW GEOGRAPHY

Juxtaposition of plans and photos of
Machu Picchu (left) and Skellig Michael

opposite – AAI Awards entry panels

ARCHITECTURE AS NEW GEOGRAPHY

Plan of circle of fragment models (not to scale)

Sketches (top) – 1, 2. New university campus in Lima, Peru / 3. Capela San Pedro, Campus do Jordao / 4. School of Economics, Toulouse, France / 5. Goiania Jockey Club, Brazil

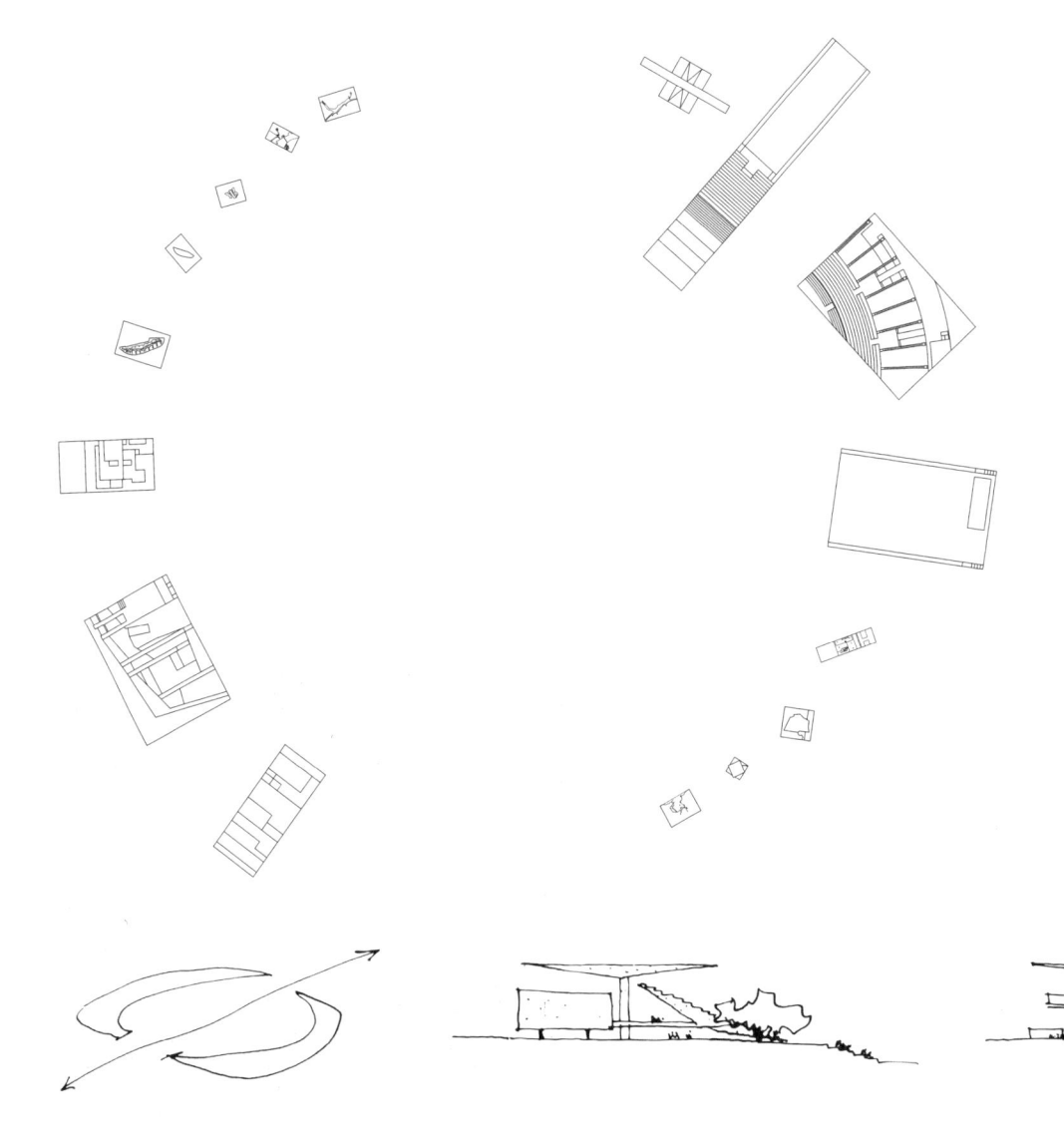

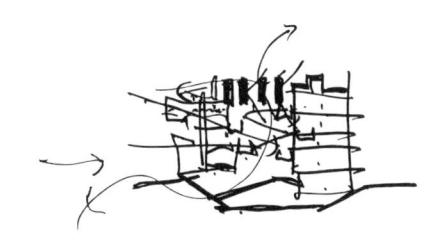

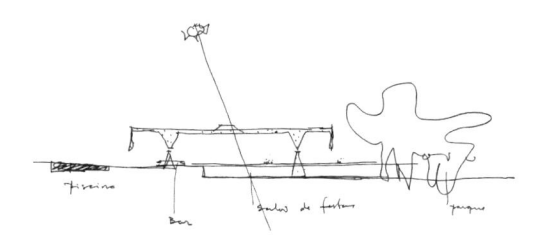

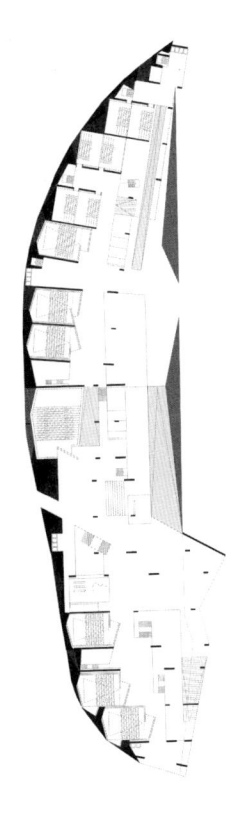

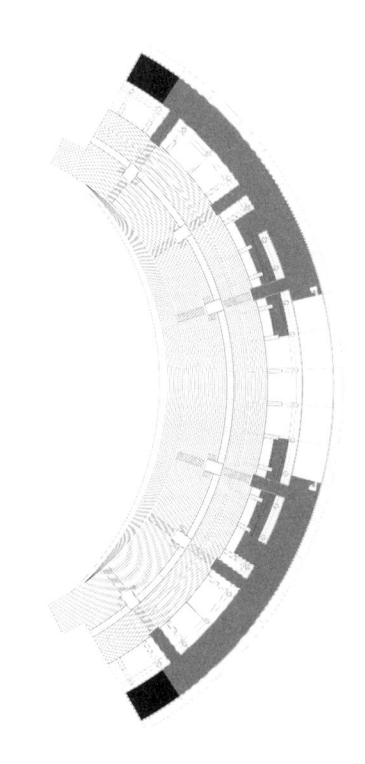

Juxtaposed plans of one half of the new university campus in Lima, Peru (left) and one half of the Serra Dourada Stadium in Brazil

Sketches (bottom) – 1, 2, 3. Serra Dourada Stadium, Brazil / 4. Project for Montevideo Bay, Uruguay / 5. Common Ground – Venice, Skellig Michael, Machu Picchu

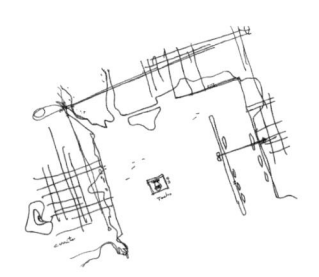

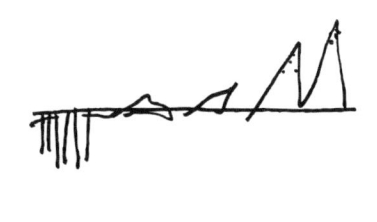

ARCHITECTURE AS NEW GEOGRAPHY

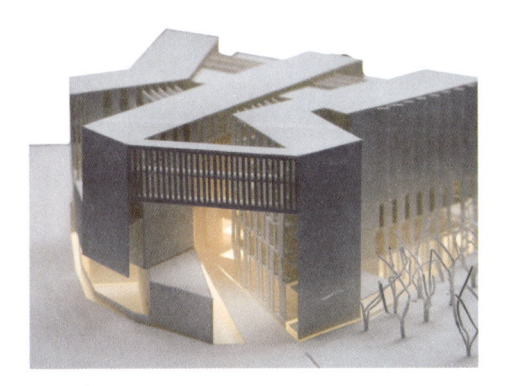

*Large-scale papier-maché model of the
Serra Dourada Stadium undercroft space*

*French limestone site model of the School of Economics,
Toulouse, France
Card model of the School of Economics, Toulouse
French limestone model of the cliffs of the Barranco district in
Lima, Peru*

Card model of the new university campus in Lima
Limestone model of PMdR's project for Montevideo Bay
Limestone model of the Capela San Pedro in Campus do Jordao
Model of theatre island in Montevideo Bay

ASSESSORS' COMMENTS

ROSBOTTOM – I saw this at Venice, and I thought it was a really fantastic exhibit. It was a real highlight. Those models were incredible, when you actually saw them. They look like the chewed paper that swallows make, the texture of them. They're characters, and then you see people through them. They were just really fantastically spatial and material, and also rudimentary. And these stone models with the polished pieces are completely exquisite things, although it doesn't really come across in the presentation.

COTTER – Are the large models made from MDF?

HICKEY – I think they're made out of formwork, and they are covered in this skin of stone.

COTTER – Oh, maybe it's been sprayed onto it.

ROSBOTTOM – Anyway, they're really amazing. I would propose it for an Award.

HATZ – I agree. I think it's stunning. I am really taken by this.

HICKEY – If we take this project, and consider it with the other installations or objects, I think this is the most generous of all of them, both in spirit and in content. I think it's a very beautiful thing.

HATZ – And it does something for our understanding of architecture.

COTTER – It's installation as a means of opening a process of thinking in architecture. I feel it reaches a sufficient sculptural abstraction that leads you to think about architecture in the context of a very evolved and simple terrain, like the Inca site of Machu Picchu and the Skelligs. Judging just on that, I think it's an interesting way of investigating architectural things now without a building being built.

ROSBOTTOM – If you read these two plans that they've made, placed in opposition, and then read the series of fragments, it's really clever without being demonstrably so.

HICKEY – That's what being clever is though, isn't it?

HATZ – It's extremely architectural, and kind of tying Irish architecture to a lot of other countries and to landscape, which I think is very clever as well.

COTTER – It embeds architecture in the land of a simple geological event: in a way, it's remembering some of the simplicity of those sites and contexts.

ROSBOTTOM – It exists somewhere between a speculation and a ruin; it's a construction and a speculation and a ruin all at once. And it's archaeology and it's modernity. It deals with many things and places them in dialogue with each other in a very sophisticated way. I think it's very eloquent.

DE BLACAM – I'm okay with this.

GRAFTON ARCHITECTS – for biog and contact details see page 76

DESIGN TEAM – Shelley McNamara, Yvonne Farrell, Ger Carty, Philippe O'Sullivan, Simona Castelli, Kieran O'Brien, Matt McCullough, James Rossa O'Hare, Donal O'Herlihy, David Healy, Joanne Lyons, Ivan O'Connell and Edwin Jebb. SCULPTOR – Eileen MacDonagh. CREDITS – exhibition made with the help of Denis Forrest, Conor Maguire, Philip McGlade and Albert Tobin at UCD, and kindly facilitated by Prof Hugh Campbell. Thanks also to Marta Moreira / MMBB, Dermot Foley Landscape Architects, Klaus Bode of BDSP, and the Photographic Unit of the National Monuments Service, Dept of Arts, Heritage and the Gaeltacht.

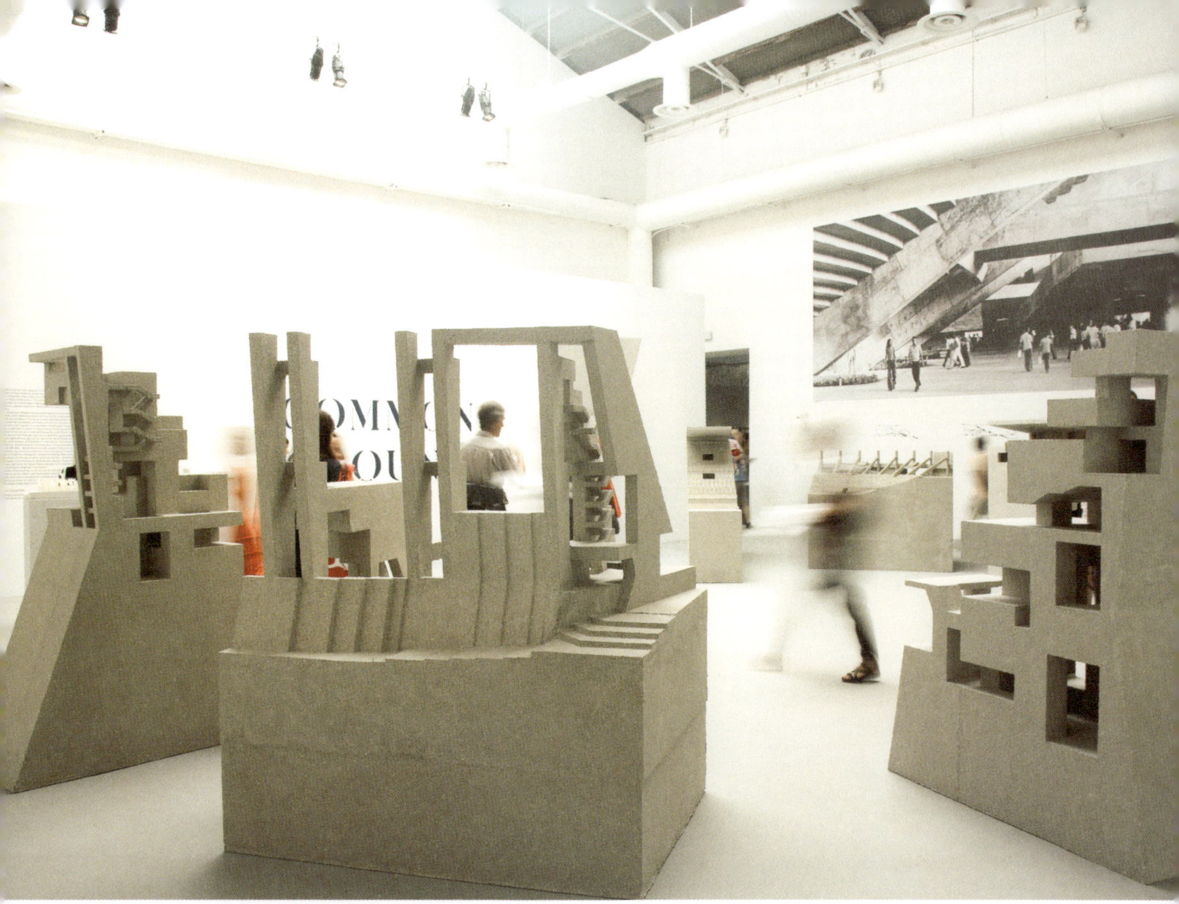

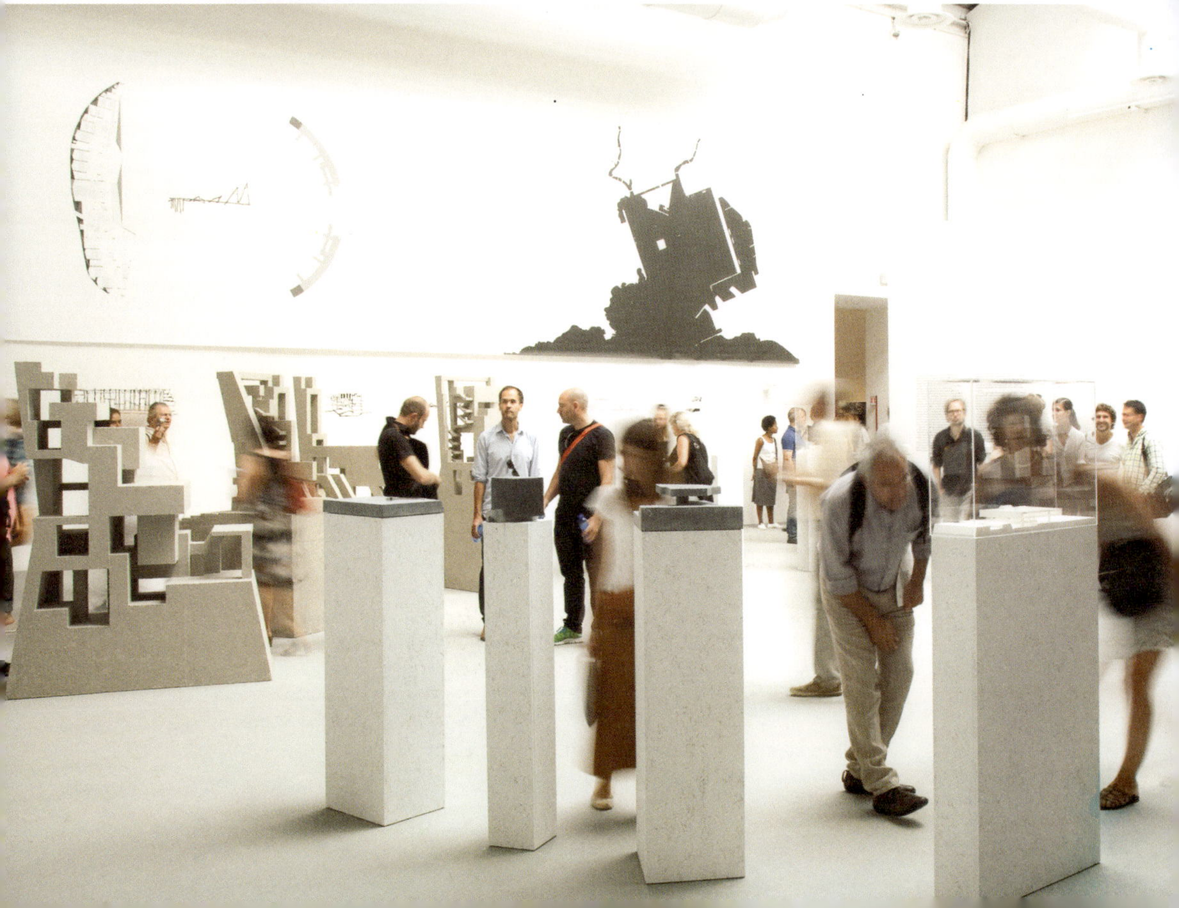

AWARD

SCOIL MHUIRE ÓGH, CRUMLIN

MARY LAHEEN ARCHITECTS

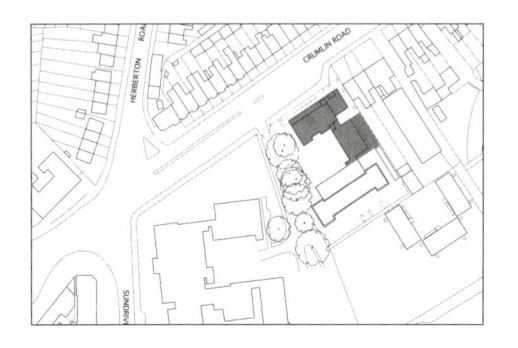

Scoil Mhuire Ógh is a national school for girls between the ages of 8 and 12. The new extension is located at the street edge of the site on Crumlin Road, giving the school a civic presence in the local community. The civic-scale spaces behind the street façade include the library, entrance hall and foyer; as well as staff and administration rooms. The large general-purpose room, which will occasionally be used by the community, is also at this level. Five new classrooms are on the upper levels of the building.

The new threshold of entry to the school follows a series of turns on axis, from the gateway at the street, up the steps to the undercroft (which is lined in hardwood and provides a bench for waiting parents), through the opening in the concrete cross-wall to the reception/administration desk. Here, the visitor turns again to arrive at a circulation axis parallel to the street, which is marked by a series of tall openings in the concrete. To the west is a view outwards to the mature trees of the boundary, to the east is the entrance to the library – a double-height space connected at gallery level to the staff floor. Diagonally adjacent to this arrival point is the double-height entrance hall or meeting space – the focal point around which the school rotates. Held by the fairfaced concrete walls of the cross-wall system, the room looks out to the playground through the infill wall of timber panels and glass, protected by sliding and folding timber shutters. This space will act as a foyer to the general-purpose hall for a community event. At mezzanine level, staff accommodation and circulation weaves around and through the space. The general-purpose hall, a large room floored in solid oak boards, looks onto the playground and mature trees beyond through a screen wall of tall, attenuated windows. The classrooms, located on the upper floors, face away from the busy street towards the mountains.

The constructional system of fairfaced, reinforced-concrete cross-walls is expressed externally, in particular to the front where the concrete fin-walls emerge at the face of the building, and are joined by infill walls of sheeted timber.

address – Loreto Senior Primary School,
  Crumlin Road, Dublin 12
client – Board of Management, Scoil Mhuire Ógh
photography – Ros Kavanagh

design to completion – 2000-2011
site area – 3,030m^2 / *floor area* – 1,332m^2
budget – €3m

scoil mhuire

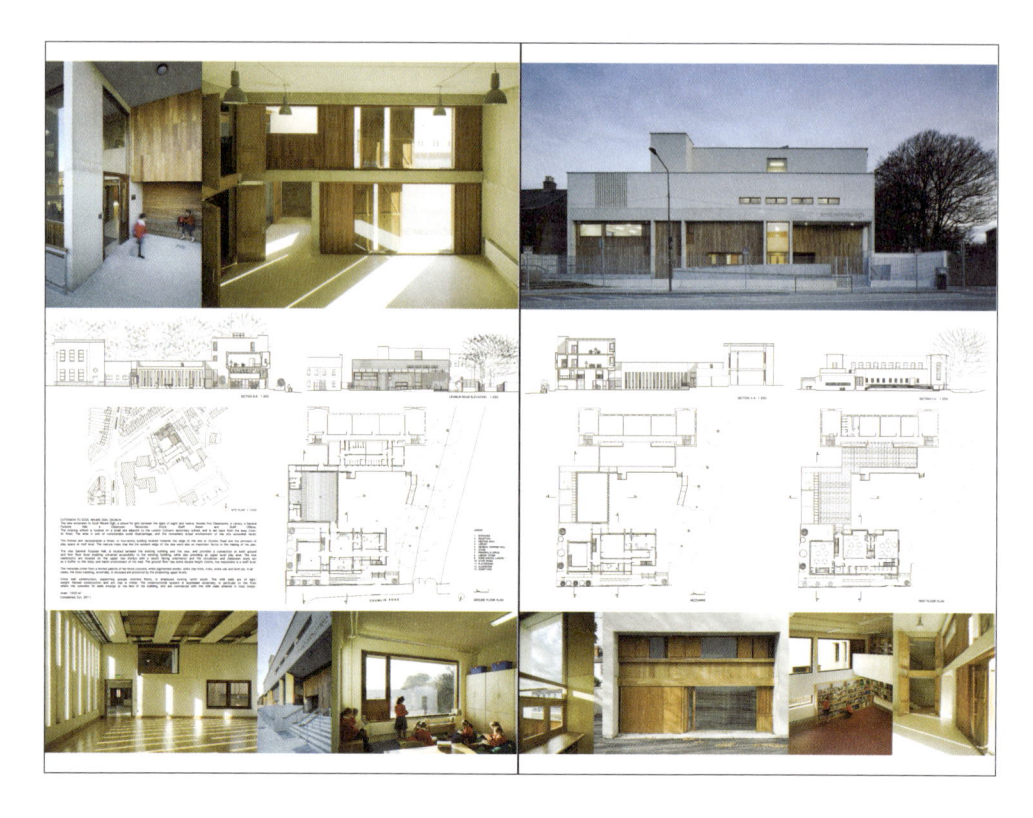

SCOIL MHUIRE ÓGH, CRUMLIN

AAI Awards entry panels
Street view from Crumlin Road, evening

page 88 – Site plan
page 89 – Front entrance, looking east

opposite

North elevation to Crumlin Road
Elevations – south, west
Section AA through foyer, playground and existing school
Section BB through general-purpose hall and library

91

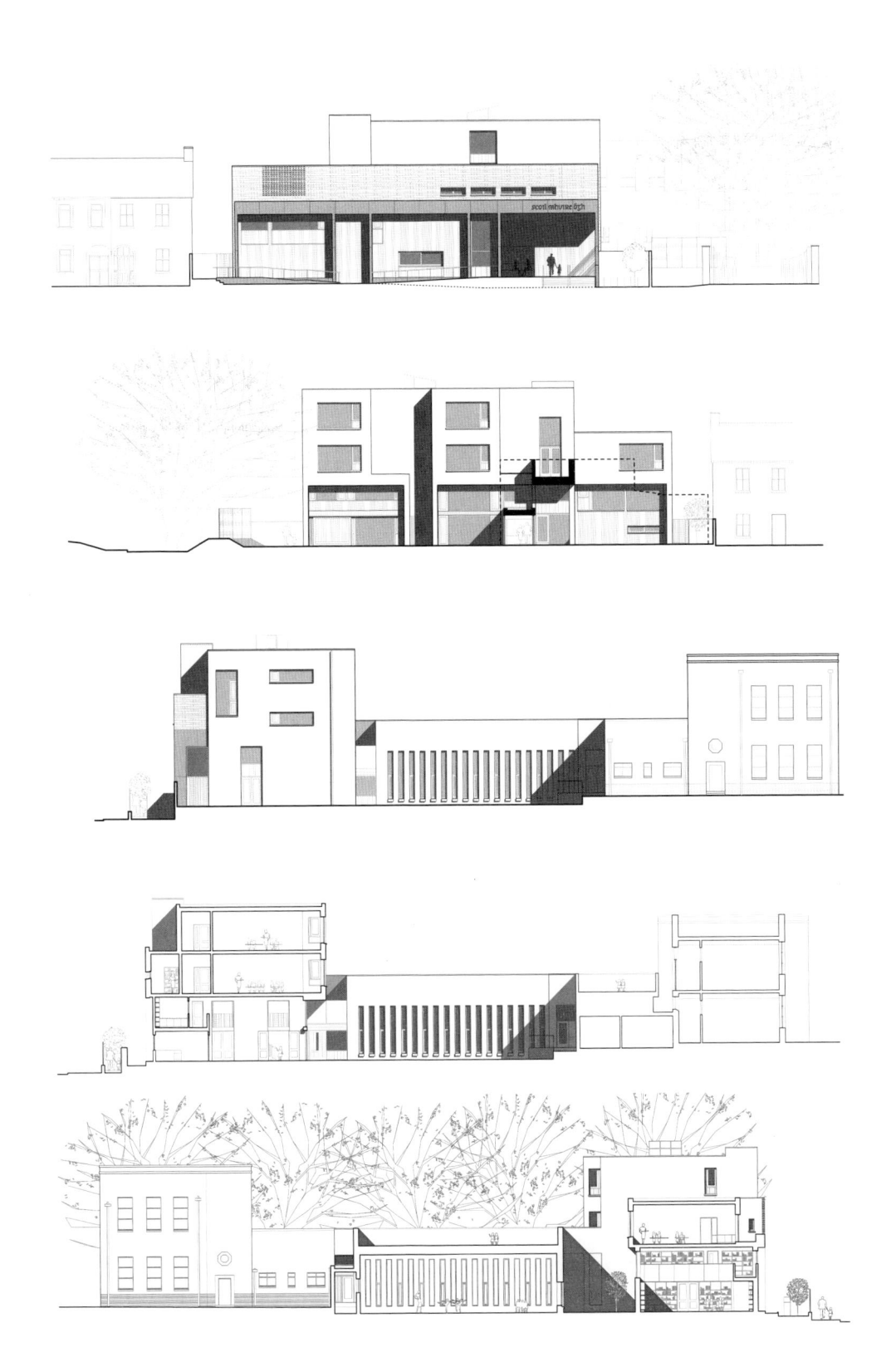

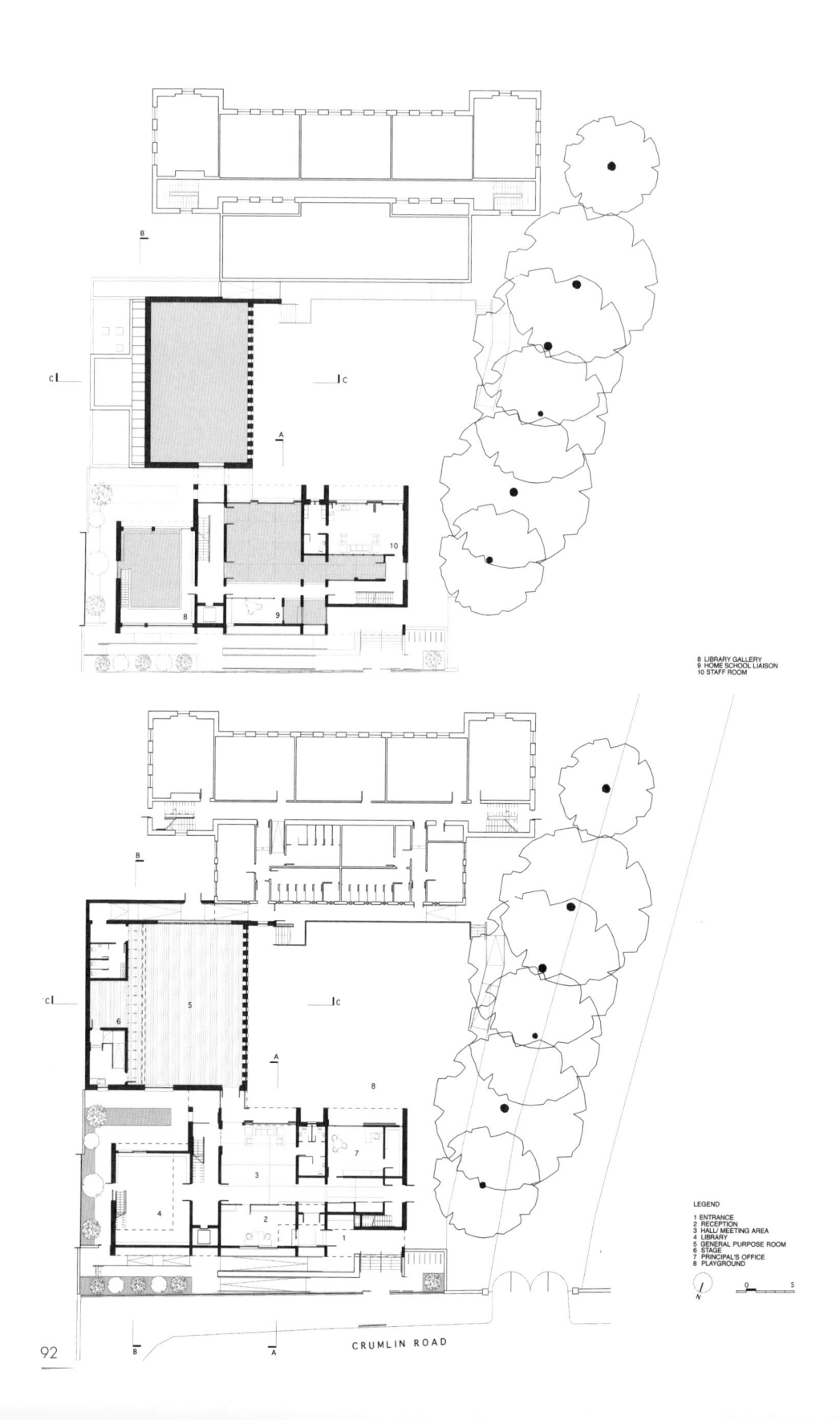

8 LIBRARY GALLERY
9 HOME SCHOOL LIAISON
10 STAFF ROOM

LEGEND
1 ENTRANCE
2 RECEPTION
3 HALL/ MEETING AREA
4 LIBRARY
5 GENERAL PURPOSE ROOM
6 STAGE
7 PRINCIPAL'S OFFICE
8 PLAYGROUND

CRUMLIN ROAD

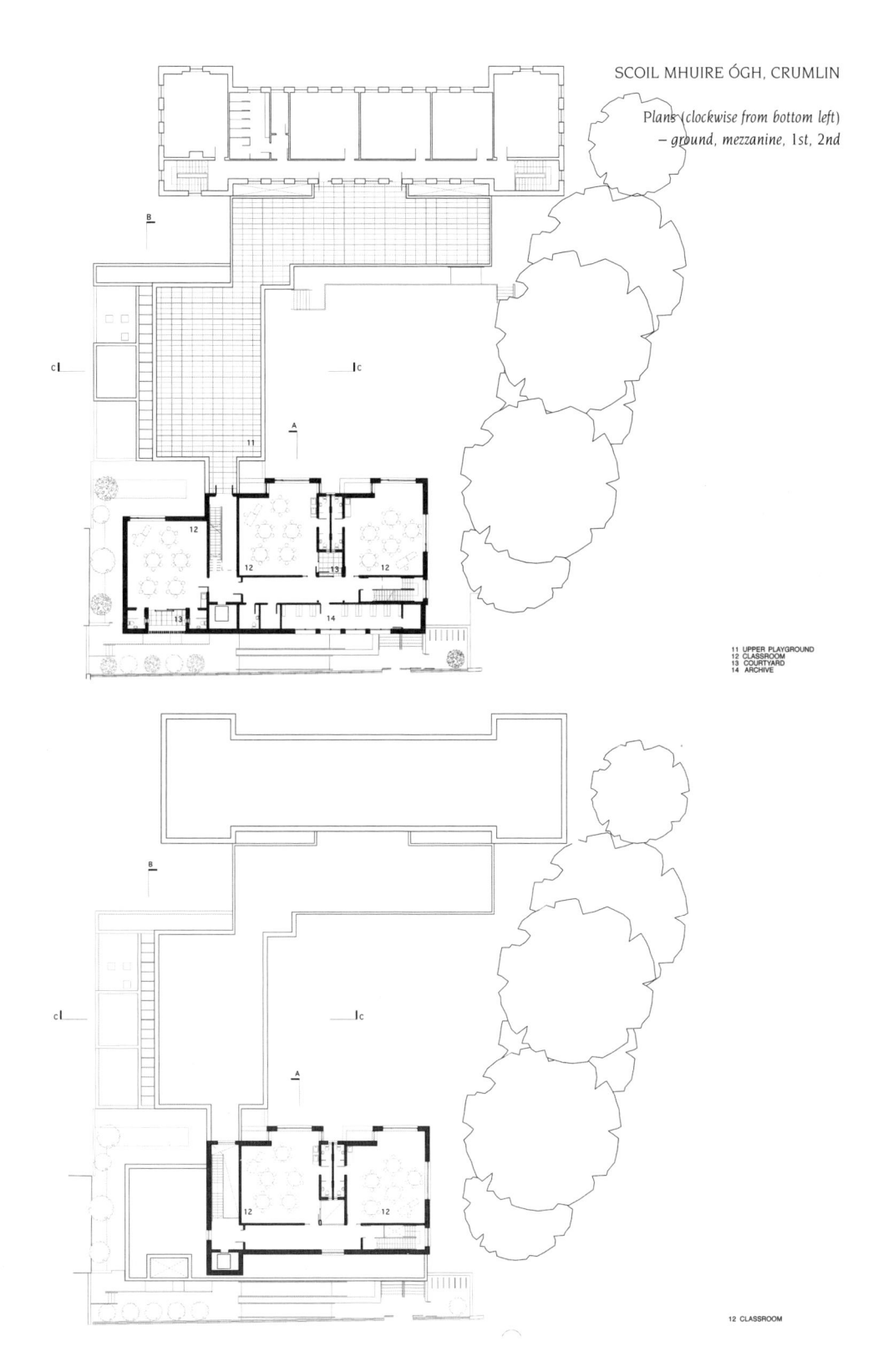

SCOIL MHUIRE ÓGH, CRUMLIN

*Plans (clockwise from bottom left)
— ground, mezzanine, 1st, 2nd*

11 UPPER PLAYGROUND
12 CLASSROOM
13 COURTYARD
14 ARCHIVE

12 CLASSROOM

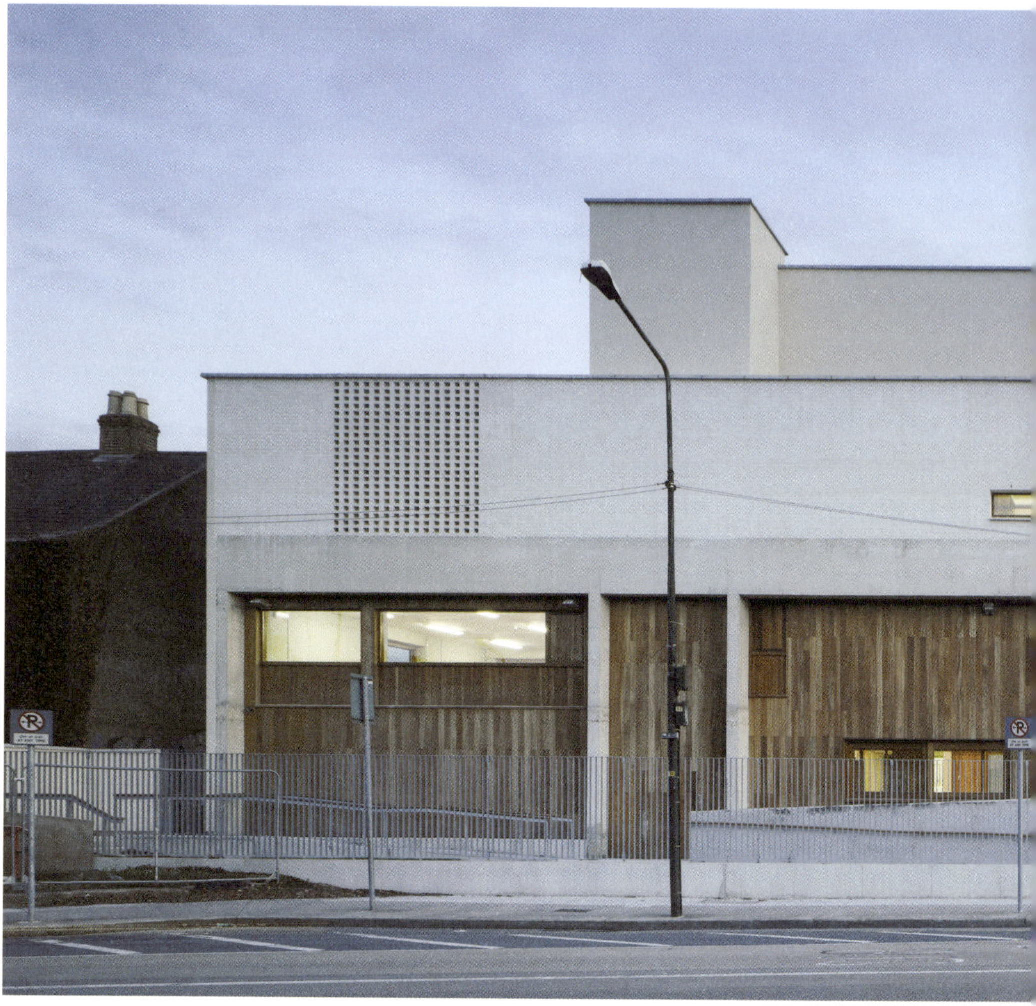

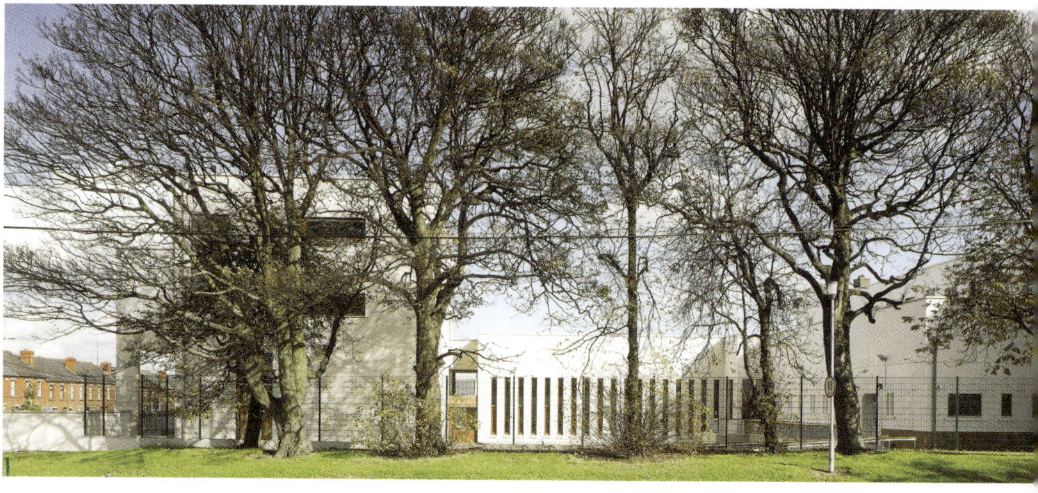

SCOIL MHUIRE ÓGH, CRUMLIN

opposite – View of new three-storey block, general-purpose hall and playground from west

View from Crumlin Road

Exterior view of shuttered windows on south elevation
Double-height library exterior

SCOIL MHUIRE ÓGH, CRUMLIN

Double-height entrance hall / meeting place

opposite – View from entrance hall / meeting place towards stairs

General-purpose hall, with screen wall of tall windows

overleaf
Classroom window
Library from mezzanine
View from admin / reception desk

page 101 – Children at school entrance

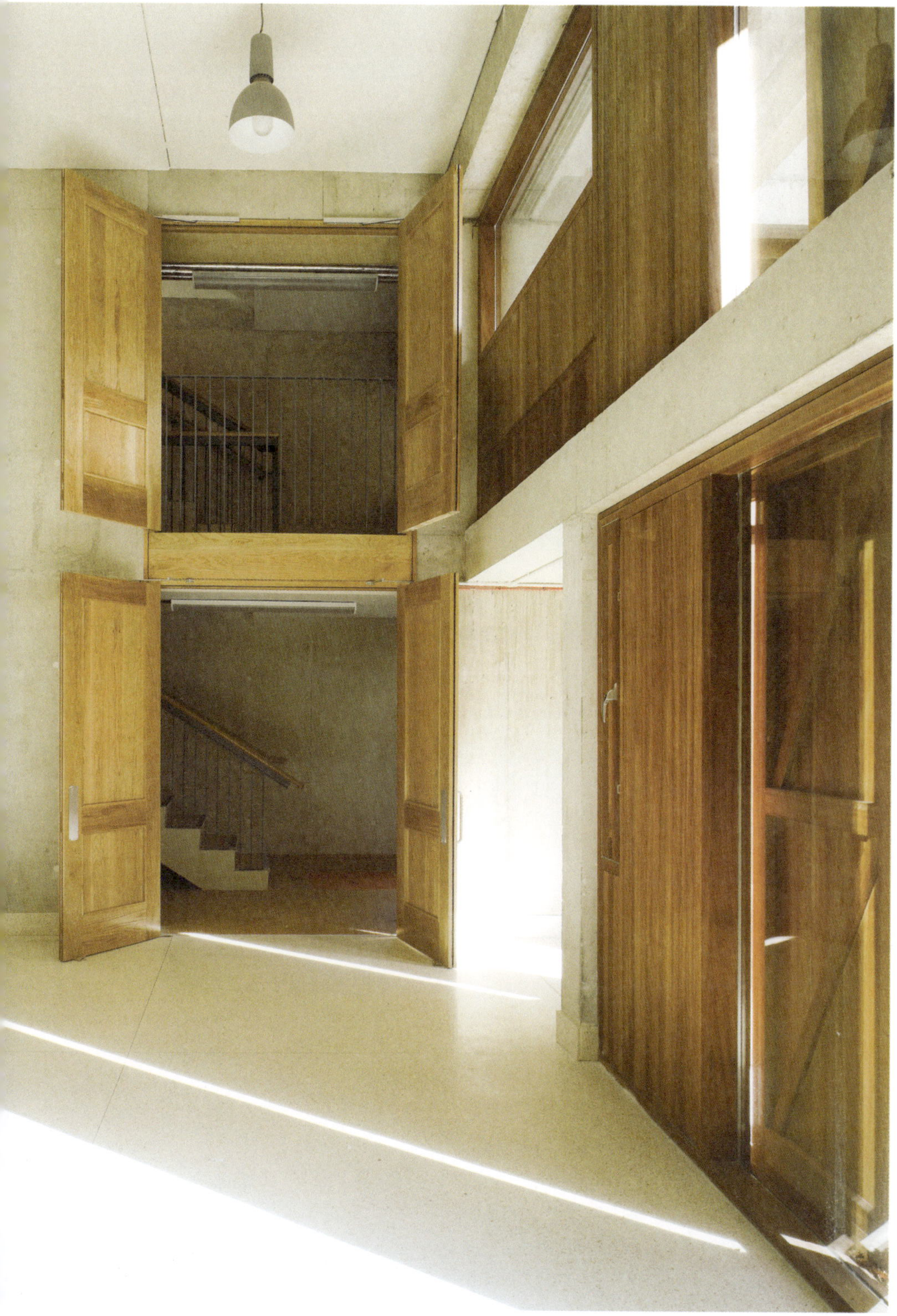

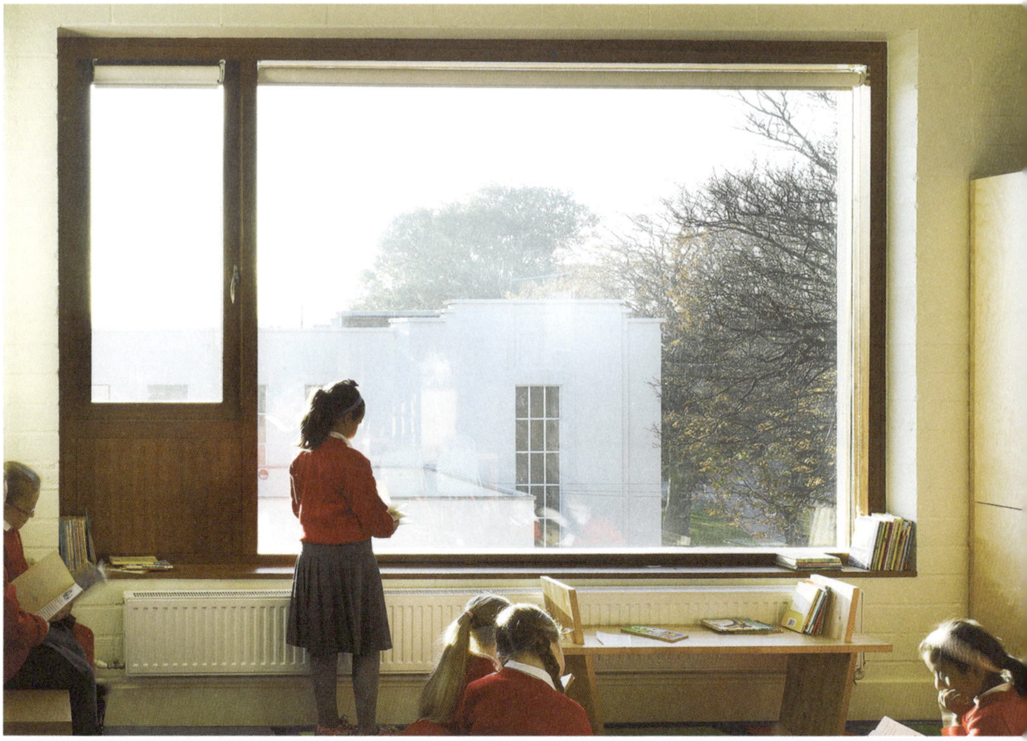

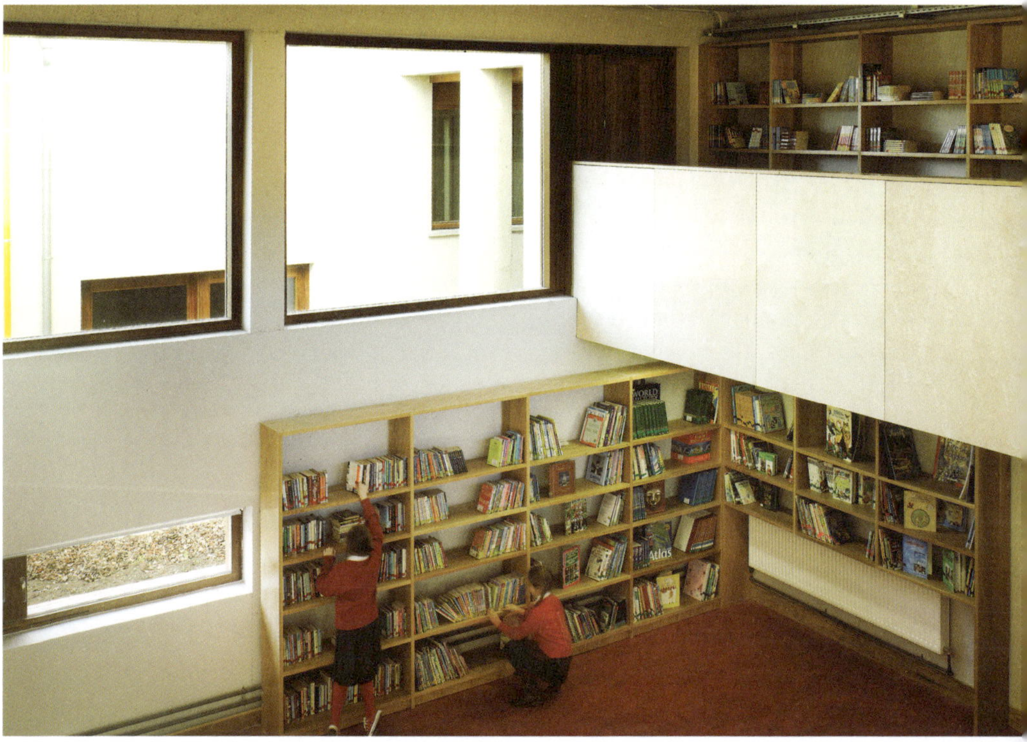

ASSESSORS' COMMENTS

ROSBOTTOM – This is really good. I think the plan is very interesting – the idea of a school which has the character of a generous house. It does some very nice things. It's also one of the few projects that really tells you about where it is, and I think the scale relationships between the new and old school buildings, separated by the trees and the GP hall, is powerful. In fact, the one pity for me is that you didn't get a sort of Nolli plan, where you understand these big rooms within this sequence of exterior rooms.

COTTER – I love the use of light, the handling of light, and the tonality. I love the fact that it brings in these very gentle tones into the interior.

HICKEY – And even the way it talks to the rest of the street. There's a kind of rhythm in this that speaks of domesticity on the one hand, but then it's not doing that at all once you move past the threshold, which I think is very comforting. This is for small children. This is their first experience of being part of society, and I think this is a very nice introduction to society.

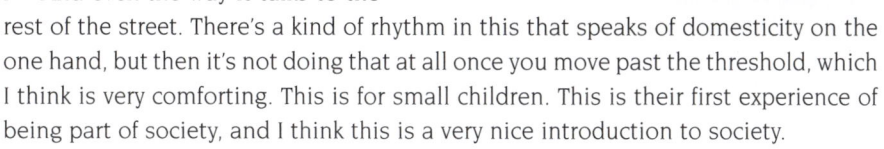

ROSBOTTOM – I think that's really, really important. Civic-ness in school buildings is really important because this is the moment when people learn what it is to be public. And this building really offers that sensibility. It also manages to mediate very successfully. It's like a grand house in a way, a house with public rooms. It's very nice.

HICKEY – And describing it as a house has that sense of ownership which is so fundamental to that first introduction.

COTTER – I think it gently gathers the students into a daily routine. You can already feel that sense of presence in it, whereas some of the other schools here are quite cold, I thought. You didn't feel there was any ambiance.

HATZ – And it's quite funny that it looks like a 1970s fire station, at the same time. I like that actually. It's kind of quirky.

HICKEY – Thanks be to God it doesn't look like a conventional school, or like any of the other schools we've seen today.

ROSBOTTOM – The new building is very well judged, but I wish there were more external images of it because I want to understand it relative to the scale of the existing building. I don't get much sense of what that middle space is like, and those trees feel like a series of quite important characters in that relationship.

HICKEY – The old school is one of these really nice schools, really good schools, that were built in the 1950s. There's something about them that's quite generous, and there's something about this new building that adds to that in a way that makes sense. Like, the fact that there's these little places like this [first-floor courtyard], where I can imagine children being very protected. That's a very generous thing to do.

DE BLACAM – It's a bit unexpected in this location – the white brick and the concrete and the amount of timber on the front of it, and the ramp and the gate and the steps. Where do you actually go to get beyond that, in the plan, how you negotiate your way through it. I would prefer if it was in red-brick and if the access to it was clearer than it is, or that it was simpler. And all this unfinished iroko, which will weather and will not always be quite as beautiful as it appears in the photograph. I assume this is all for child safety, all these railings and stuff, and I presume that the door is in there beyond.

HICKEY – But I think this is the problem with lots of primary schools. They don't want you to see the activity that's happening in the life of the school. So you're shut off from the school, and then they double that by putting railings in front of it, and actually closing it down so it's not public anymore.

COTTER – The windows are set very high with the light coming in at a very high angle.

HICKEY – And I'd love to know the story behind this, whether that's part of the reasoning.

ROSBOTTOM – Looking at it originally, I wondered why they hadn't used the central court as the space of entry, and I was guessing it was for precisely that reason. You're not allowed to. If the entrance was somewhere here, rather than having all this negotiation, you could have come up the side and gone in.

DE BLACAM – You see, in relation to schools, those kind of conversations never take place. You're set adrift by the Department, and the school is terrified to open its mouth to the architect in case there's any hesitation in the progressing of the project.

HATZ – I think it's very good. I like the perception of what a school is, and its relationship with the street as a public building. I don't mind the entrance at all. I think it's lovely. It's very direct and it's very welcoming.

COTTER – Yes, it is warm and intimate. I think it's important to say that this is a kind of culture of school that the Award should support.

ROSBOTTOM – Well, I think it says something about public building and the standards that one ought to expect in public buildings. Coming from outside your context and looking in, I think this is extraordinary for a contemporary school, and especially compared to what happens in England in terms of school-making. But I also think it stands up as a piece of architecture. I would propose it for an Award.

MARY LAHEEN ARCHITECTS – established in 1995, the practice engages with architecture through the design of contemporary buildings, conservation of existing buildings and landscapes of cultural and historical interest, and through writing and teaching. The contemporary building design has an emphasis on constructional and spatial legibility and the integration of buildings with their site context and with the natural world. The work ranges from small domestic and commercial projects to education and cultural buildings. DESIGN TEAM – Mary Laheen, Eoin McCarthy

MARY LAHEEN ARCHITECTS
1 Upper Gardiner Street, Mountjoy Square, Dublin 1 – T 01-8730784
E mlaheenarchitects@eircom.net / W www.mlaheenarchitects.ie

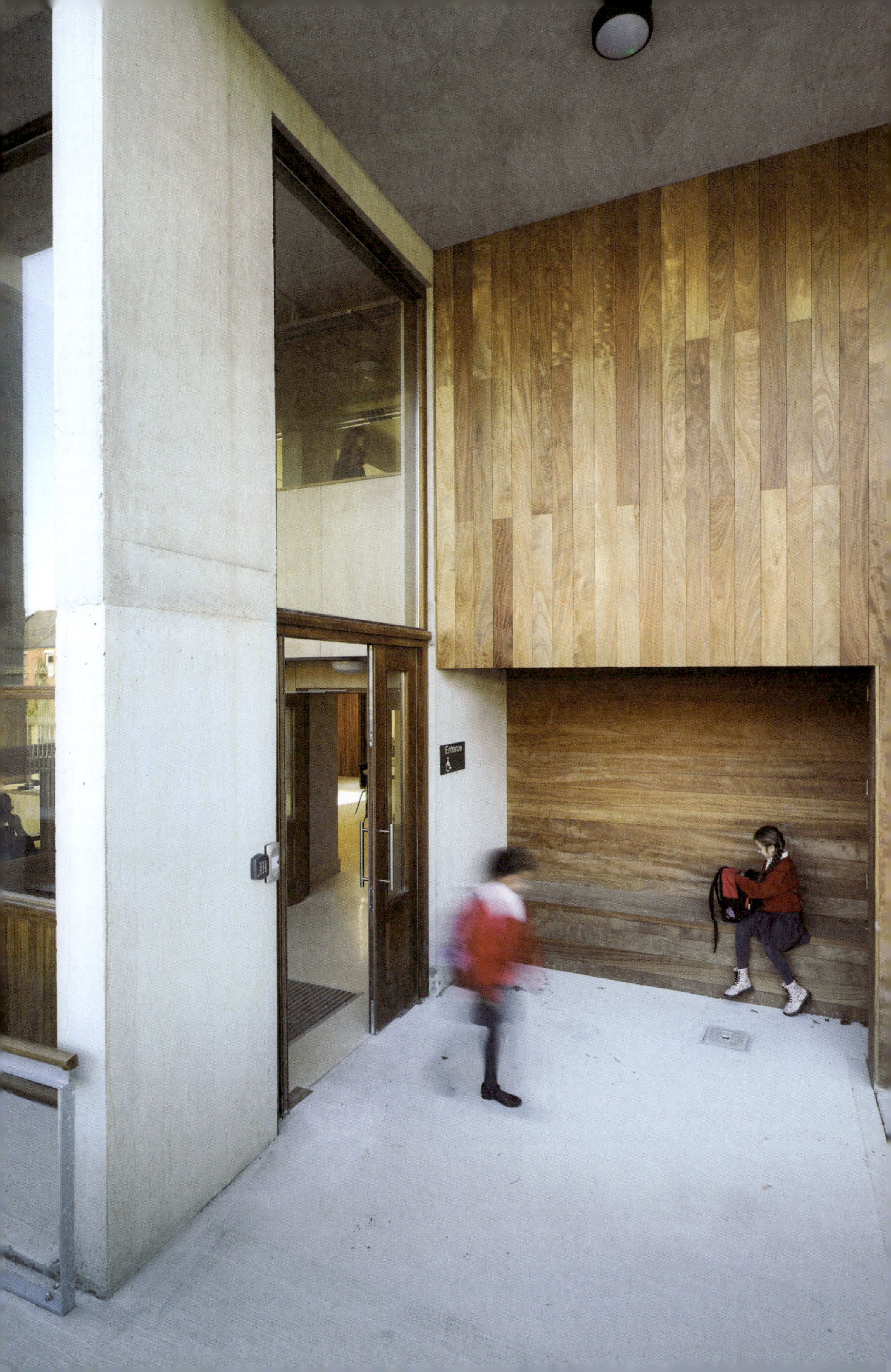
Entrance

TEACH NUA, Co CARLOW

AWARD

STEVE LARKIN ARCHITECT

Planned with an unbuilt gatehouse, this project explores the long farmhouse typology characteristic of this area in Co Carlow. This house type works successfully at a number of scales, such as an ability to make intimate building clusters while also reading as a clear object in the wider landscape. The house is organised around an entrance courtyard and two gardens. An orchard is planted to the south-east and a kitchen garden to the south-west. The house is seen as a place to live between these gardens, to be opened up in the summer months. Walls extending into the landscape frame the gardens and provide for vertical planting.

The plans are efficient while supporting the different relationships to landscape from the various rooms. The plan orientates landscape views and relationships to the gardens while modulating between layers of interiority. It also establishes a collection of room proportions loosely open to each other, exploring the edges of closed and open plans.

The ground-floor plan is organised in simple enfilade, allowing liner and diagonal axes through the house. This exaggerates the layering of colonnade and structure. The sitting room is double height, providing a point of congregation of the various spaces in the house. The accommodation in the extending walls is used to frame the gardens.

A long library with intimate study overlooking the living area organises the first-floor plan. Access to the bedrooms is through the bookshelves, which provide personal and acoustic privacy. Bedrooms are organised efficiently with relationships to the landscape.

New vertical, sliding sash-windows run along the SE and NW elevation at ground-floor level to form colonnades. These colonnades orientate entry and circulation. The windows can recede to first-floor level to provide access to both gardens in summer months. This window type allows elegant detailing by eliminating visible frames and door leafs in order to maximise threshold and views to gardens. The windows develop a relationship between opening and wall, characteristic of many houses in the area. It also provides for vertical planting as required. Attention to detail is carried through all parts of the project.

address – Baile Eamoinn, Baile Haicéid,
   Co Ceatharlach
client – private

design to completion – 2009-2012
site area – 0.35ha / *floor area* – 200m^2
photography – Alice Clancy

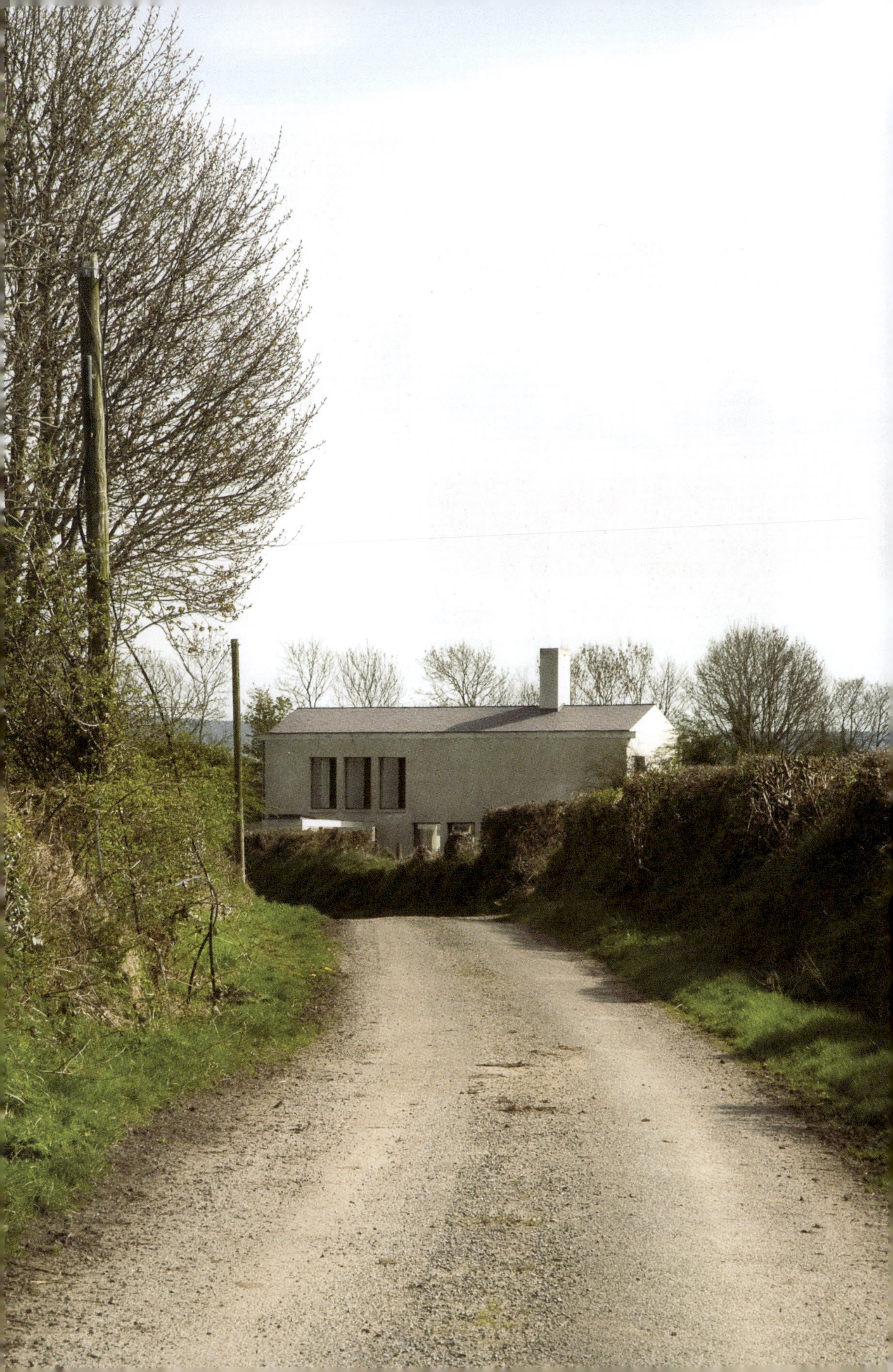

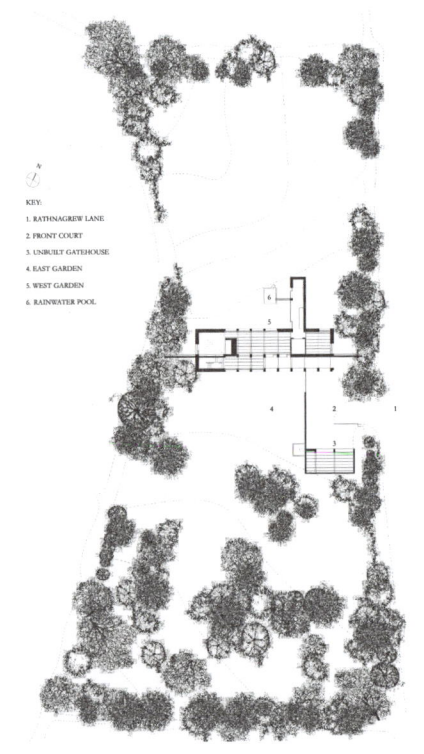

TEACH NUA, Co CARLOW

AAI Awards entry panels

Site plan
Cross-section

opposite – Plans – ground, 1st floor

page 103 – View of house from the lane

overleaf – House in the landscape

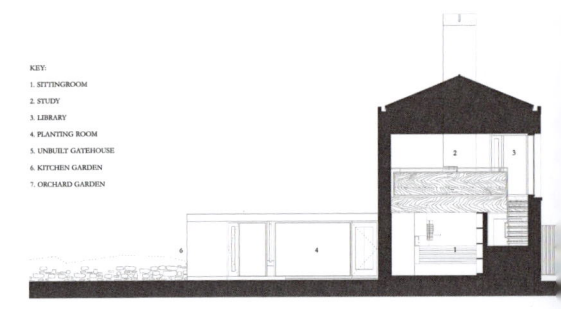

KEY:
1. RATHNAGREW LANE
2. FRONT COURT
3. UNBUILT GATEHOUSE
4. EAST GARDEN
5. WEST GARDEN
6. RAINWATER POOL

KEY:
1. SITTINGROOM
2. STUDY
3. LIBRARY
4. PLANTING ROOM
5. UNBUILT GATEHOUSE
6. KITCHEN GARDEN
7. ORCHARD GARDEN

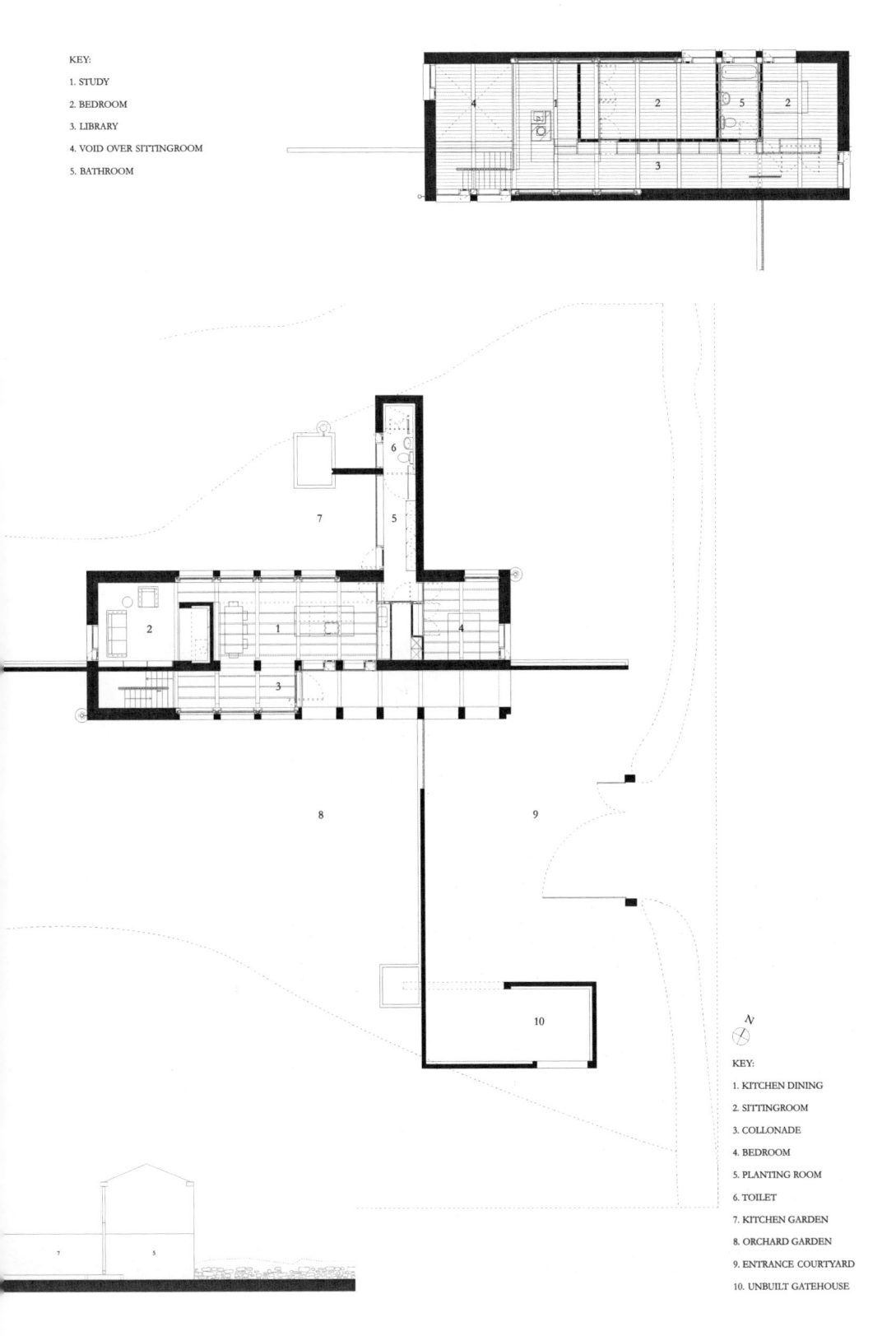

KEY:
1. STUDY
2. BEDROOM
3. LIBRARY
4. VOID OVER SITTINGROOM
5. BATHROOM

KEY:
1. KITCHEN DINING
2. SITTINGROOM
3. COLLONADE
4. BEDROOM
5. PLANTING ROOM
6. TOILET
7. KITCHEN GARDEN
8. ORCHARD GARDEN
9. ENTRANCE COURTYARD
10. UNBUILT GATEHOUSE

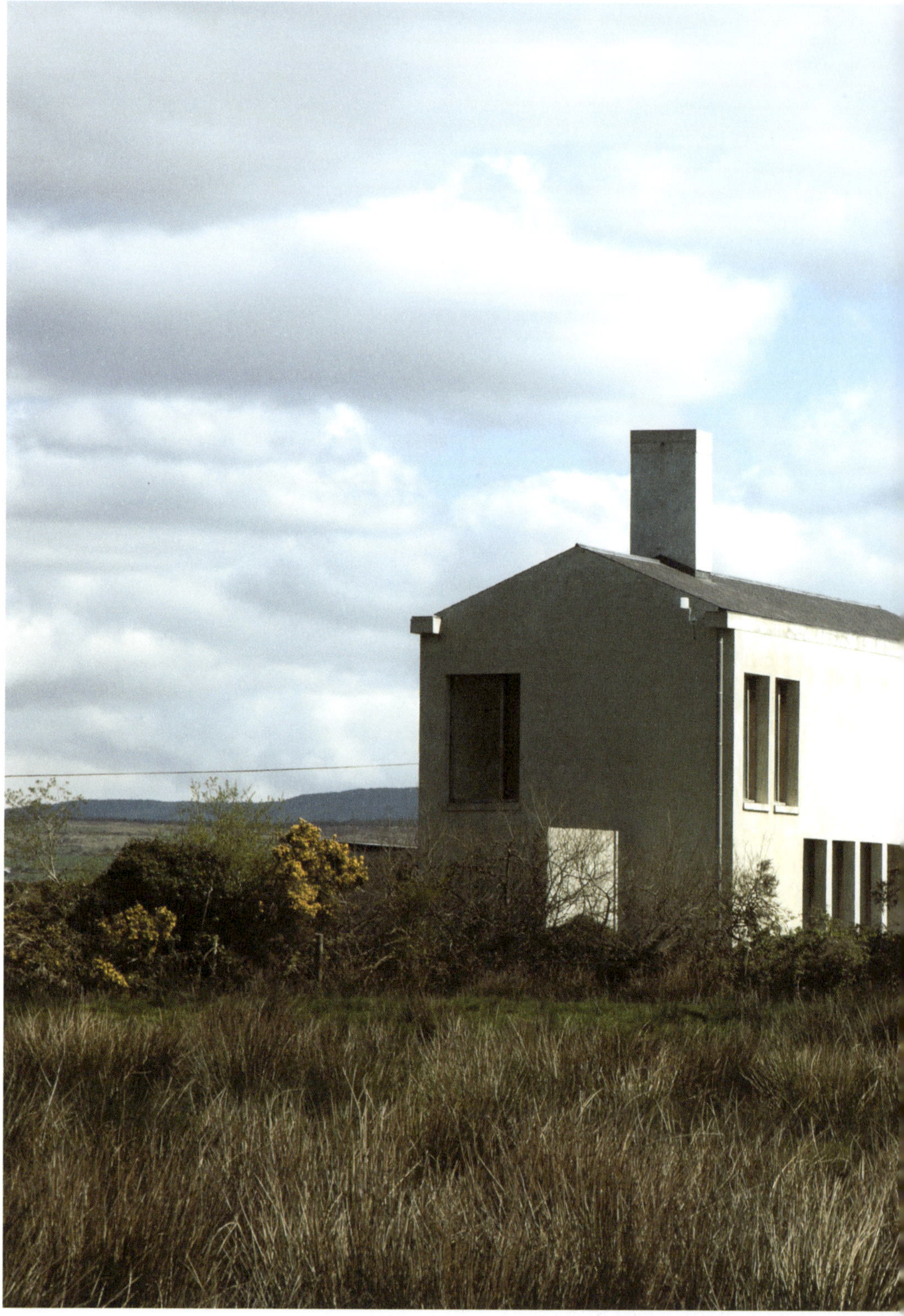

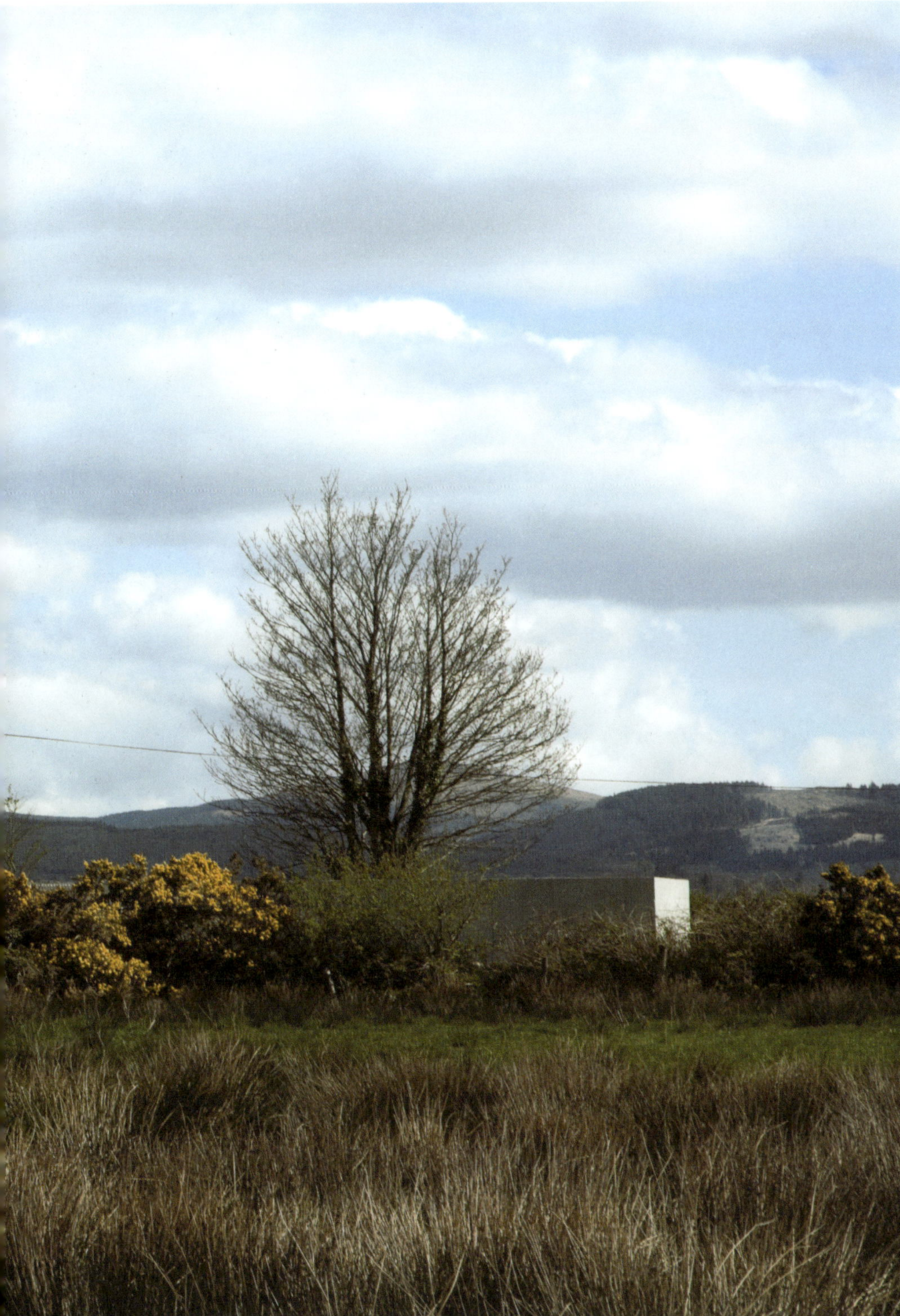

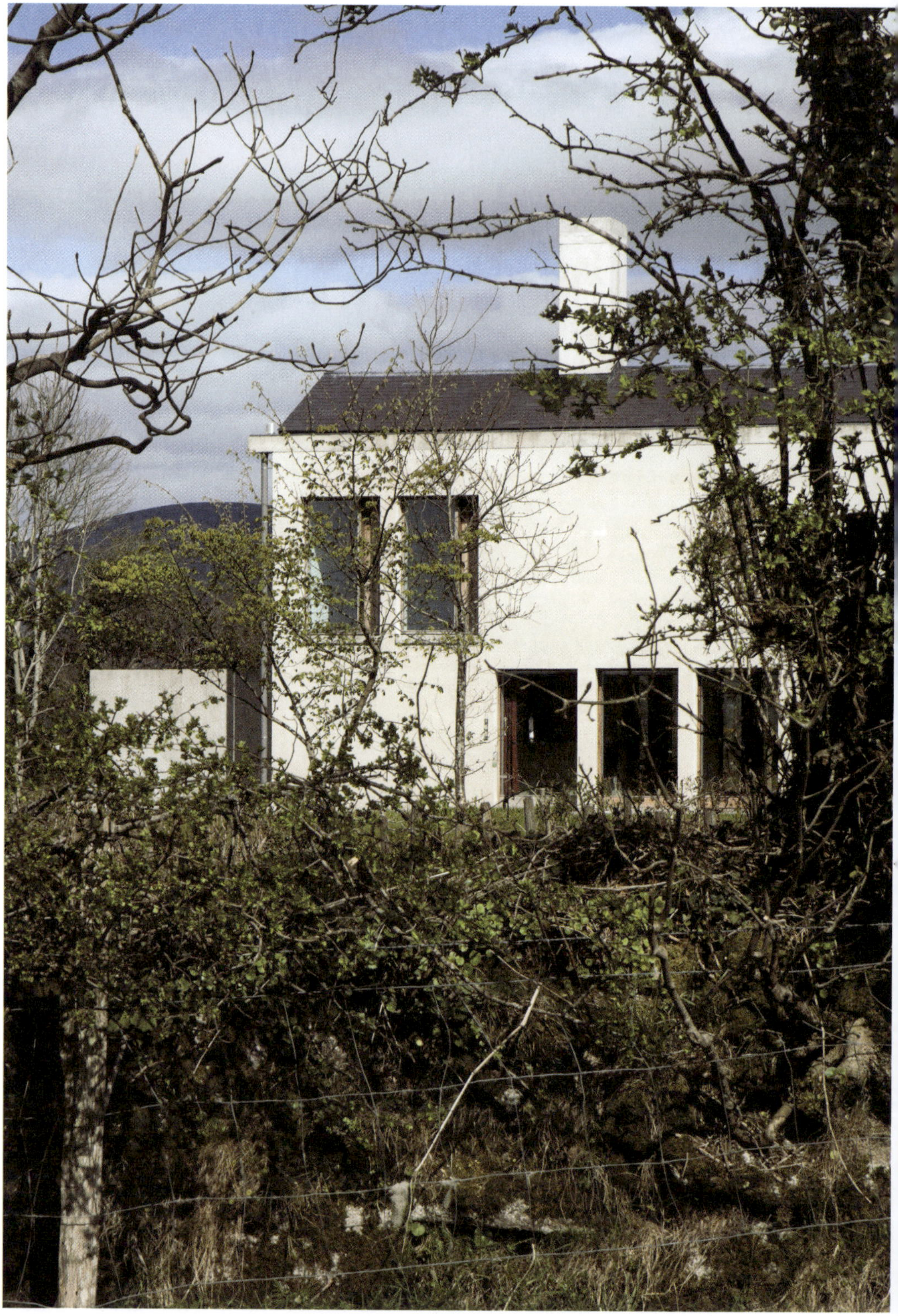

ASSESSORS' COMMENTS

HATZ – There's a quietness and robustness to this that appeals. It's well detailed without being precious. It's proud and simple, and I like the thin, crisp meeting of roof and wall. It's an Edward Hopper with a hint of Walter Pichler, but distinctly Irish. I like it. It's very good. And I like the plan as well.

ROSBOTTOM – I was interested in this Rossi-esque type, this thing standing in the landscape that's something distinct from it, but also part of it. And I quite like the way it stretches what feel like familiar things to make them strange: the chimney is taller than it needs to be, becoming kind of monumental, and it's in a slightly strange place. This over-extended kitchen offshoot stretches out into the garden. So the plan almost feels like Mies's Brick Country House plan. It's very eloquent in these conversations. And within the austerity, you get these moments of intricacy, which feel like they're accreted. They're happening because decisions are being made and things are being enjoyed as they arrive.

HATZ – The openings are both destabilising the building and stabilising it, because they're actually sliding horizontally in elevation. So it's somewhere between being very robust and stable, and actually sliding, which is again like the Brick House; it's a good reference.

COTTER – In the complete acceptance and the utilitarian culture of it, it's kind of quasi-urban industrial, but still rural farmhouse building, but a lovely hybrid of those elements. I love this detailing, where you almost have a Pythagorean kind of thing here, where the line splits on the column. And I love the ease and stretch in the spaces.

HICKEY – I think the stretch is one of the things I particularly enjoy about it, like that long return that stretches back behind. It kind of recognises that it's sitting somewhere; you know, it's not an object. And the way you slide into it is particularly successful.

ROSBOTTOM – Its site plan is really good, and makes you think that it sits within a mature landscape with trees, and it's making rooms of those. And when you see it you realise, actually, that's probably a future idea, that those things will grow and evolve, and it will make a series of rooms in the landscape. So I think it oscillates between being an object and being something that will, in time, become rooted as a series of spaces.

HICKEY – But even the height of the large sash windows on the ground floor, that go up and down, and the horizon that the window heads set up... There's a scale to the way it hits the ground that's really very nice. And I don't know if it relies on having trees that will happen in the future. I think it just recognises quite a subtle scale. And you see that the scale of the hedgerow does the same thing.

DE BLACAM – I think that [country lane] image is troublesome when you come to the Brick Country House reference. I wonder if Sandy Wilson's concrete block houses in Cambridge are not a more urban reference for this. I agree though that it's a very interesting and serious piece of work.

COTTER – I love the way that it doesn't induce any overreaction on the part of the landscape. It sits simply in the terrain as given. There's no excessive domestication of plantation or anything. There's a sparseness to it. With a lot of country houses

TEACH NUA, Co CARLOW

page 108 – House and ditch

Column / Hall / Sash windows

overleaf – Kitchen windows / Dining sash / Dining area

there's an assumption that you've got to upscale nature to meet the architectural luxury of the building.

HATZ – Well, this is why I imagine Hopper because it's resisting that. It has a certain urbanity about it – it could be a lonely petrol station. And that contradicts the kind of Quaker thing inside. The inside and outside are a nice contradiction of each other.

COTTER – It is very confidently painted, in terms of the tone, the fenestration – the way that the windows are just simply slipped into the façade. I like the economy of line, the unromanticisation of any of the junctures; they're very simply met, all the materials.

ROSBOTTOM – I don't really know the Irish landscape, but I enjoy your point, Donal, about the fact that a kind of horizon exists within the building, which is perhaps dealing with what is quite stunted growth. There is something quite compelling in that image [across the field] about the idea that a deep façade, or a sort of space within the façade, holds the darkness of that horizon of the hills in the background. It deals with the landscape at different scales.

COTTER – And it's not rich land – it isn't like Tipperary or Munster. It's somewhere where there's a bog, and there's a nice ordinariness to that, the building captures that.

ROSBOTTOM – I think the one disappointment is that there isn't any image that describes what it's like to be there, closer to the building, where these two scales come together. You either see it as a distant object, or you're very close in. And what you don't get is the middle ground.

HICKEY – I think you're right – you can't really tell what that middle ground is like. You're either seeing is from sufficiently distant so you can't actually read the scale of how intimate it is in terms of the ground…

HATZ – I'm not very worried about that.

DE BLACAM – I don't know if you noticed it, but it says that this guesthouse at the entrance is unbuilt, this whole leg here is unbuilt. So that's a truck on the road, is it not?

HICKEY – Get away! How did they get that to stay there? It's exactly where the gatehouse should be.

COTTER – I'm not sure if I prefer it without that, because I like the tenacity of the building, the way it sits there. It's vernacular. It's a beautiful hybrid of the ordinariness of Irish rural functioning buildings, so I think it's enriching a language that's already there in rural Ireland. I love that, because I just think it's so indigenous an aesthetic.

ROSBOTTOM – Does it really feel indigenous? I'm interested that you use that word.

COTTER – It does, totally, to me. I've been in places that carry little spores of that. But it's also evolving a language

ROSBOTTOM – Perhaps it can be read both as something that has a kind of indigenous quality, and also something that's definitely an import.

HATZ – From the plans and the sections, there are four quite different outdoor rooms, potentially, and with the planting and landscape and orientation, they could be very different. It's quite a high wall there, making a distinction between two spaces. I really like that actually. It's very rich.

ROSBOTTOM – It would have been useful to have seen more about the quality of those outdoor rooms. Maybe it it's too emphatic about always having to extend an arm into the landscape, but I really enjoy this thing that the kitchen offshoot does.

HICKEY – This front piece is very extravagant. There's a blue Noel Moffett house in Sutton [Dublin], that has a big sloped pitched roof – it's Yves Klein blue – and it has this corridor that goes across the full width of the plan, and it's extravagant.

HATZ – I think it's hovering between being very simple and very calm, and between being very silent and very proud at the same time. I think that's very clever. It's very sophisticated the way it establishes that front entrance, but then there's the gallery or library that is connecting the upper rooms. It gets better the more we look at it.

HICKEY – I think this project is probably an Award. This is a much more mature project to me.

DE BLACAM – I sort of agree. I think that in a sort of intellectual way, yes, in an architectural way, this is certainly an Award.

ROSBOTTOM – It's a very strong figure in the landscape, although it concerns me that we don't know what it's like at that point where the fingers are attached. I find this stretched chimney and gable and the deep reveals against the mountain very, very strong as an image. It's a very beautiful house.

———

STEVE LARKIN is a musician and architect. He graduated from UCD School of Architecture in 2002 and established his practice in 2007. He is involved in many collaborative and research initiatives and is co-founder of Strand Studio, a shared studio for young architects in Dublin. He is a studio tutor at QUB and DIT schools of architecture. STEVE LARKIN ARCHITECTS is interested in the simple poetic of architecture. It seeks to balance the metaphysical aspects of light, weight and timelessness with the practical art of building. Embedded in this is a respect for the longstanding craft of assembly and detail. The practice has received national and international awards, including an AAI Award in 2012 for House in Bogwest, Co Wexford. DESIGN TEAM – Steve Larkin, Daire Bracken.

STEVE LARKIN ARCHITECTS
33-34 Vicar Street, Dublin 8 – T 01-7093019 / E stevelarkinarchitects@gmail.com / W www.stevelarkinarchitects.ie

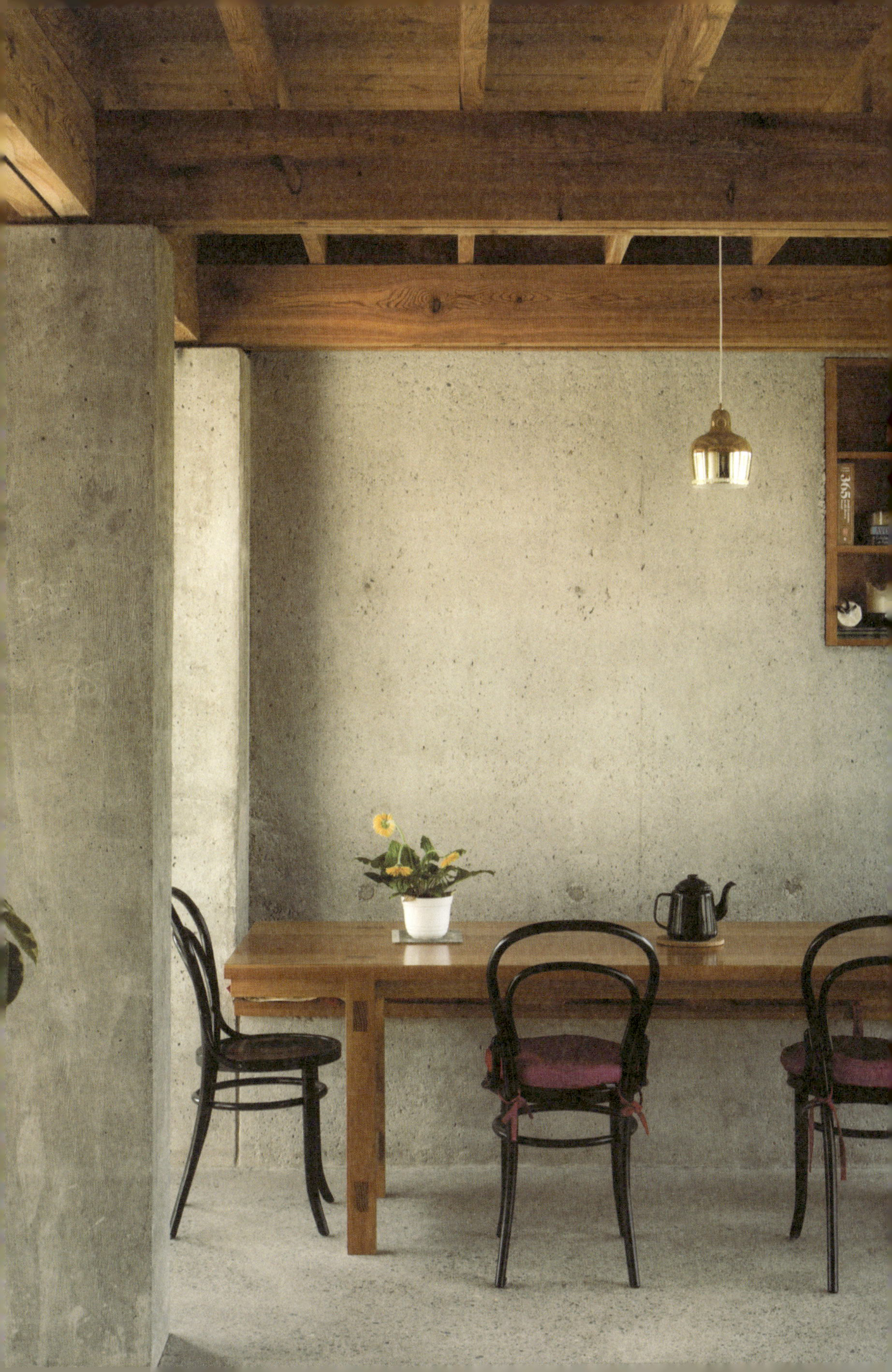
365

AWARD

HOUSE 4, Firhouse

TAKA ARCHITECTS

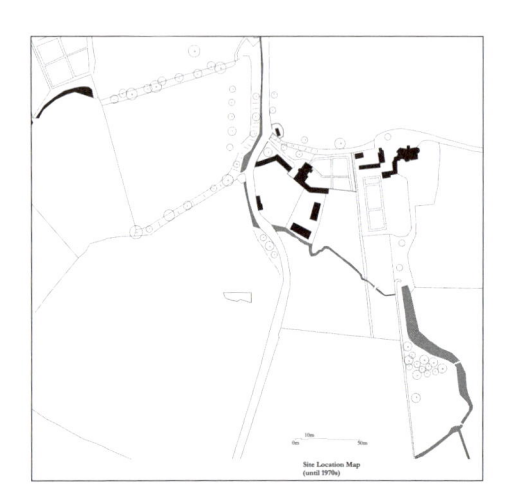

This newly built house is located in a semi-mature housing estate typical of Dublin's outer suburbs. The layout of the 1970s housing estate, which consists of a series of similar housing types, creates a coherent and robust architectural context. Prior to the arrival of the housing estates, Knocklyon Castle (a couple of hundred metres from the site) was the only building in the vicinity, which now appears somewhat out of time with the general context. House 4 seeks to establish a similar relationship with the suburban context, to be viewed as an 'erratic' – something both alike and unlike its neighbours. The design aims to balance the desire to engage with suburbia while also differentiating itself from the surrounding typologies by being specific to its place and time.

The site for the house is the side garden of an existing corner house. The plan form is generated by the largest two-storey footprint allowable within planning restrictions and the site layout. Internally, the plan is largely based around the requirement for four rooms upstairs within the compact form. To achieve this, the stairs arrives in the centre of the plan at first floor. The first-floor structure, in turn, splits to accommodate the stairs. On the ground floor, the location of the stairs separates the spaces into kitchen, living and dining spaces in an otherwise open plan.

The external materials and form take their cue from the neighbouring buildings – concrete-tile pitched roof and rough-cast pebbledash walls. However, the house differentiates itself at the level of detail: there are no overhanging eaves and the window cills and frames are suppressed to give the form a taut, abstract quality. The rough-cast is of larger aggregate and left unpainted so that it can weather naturally over time. This approach

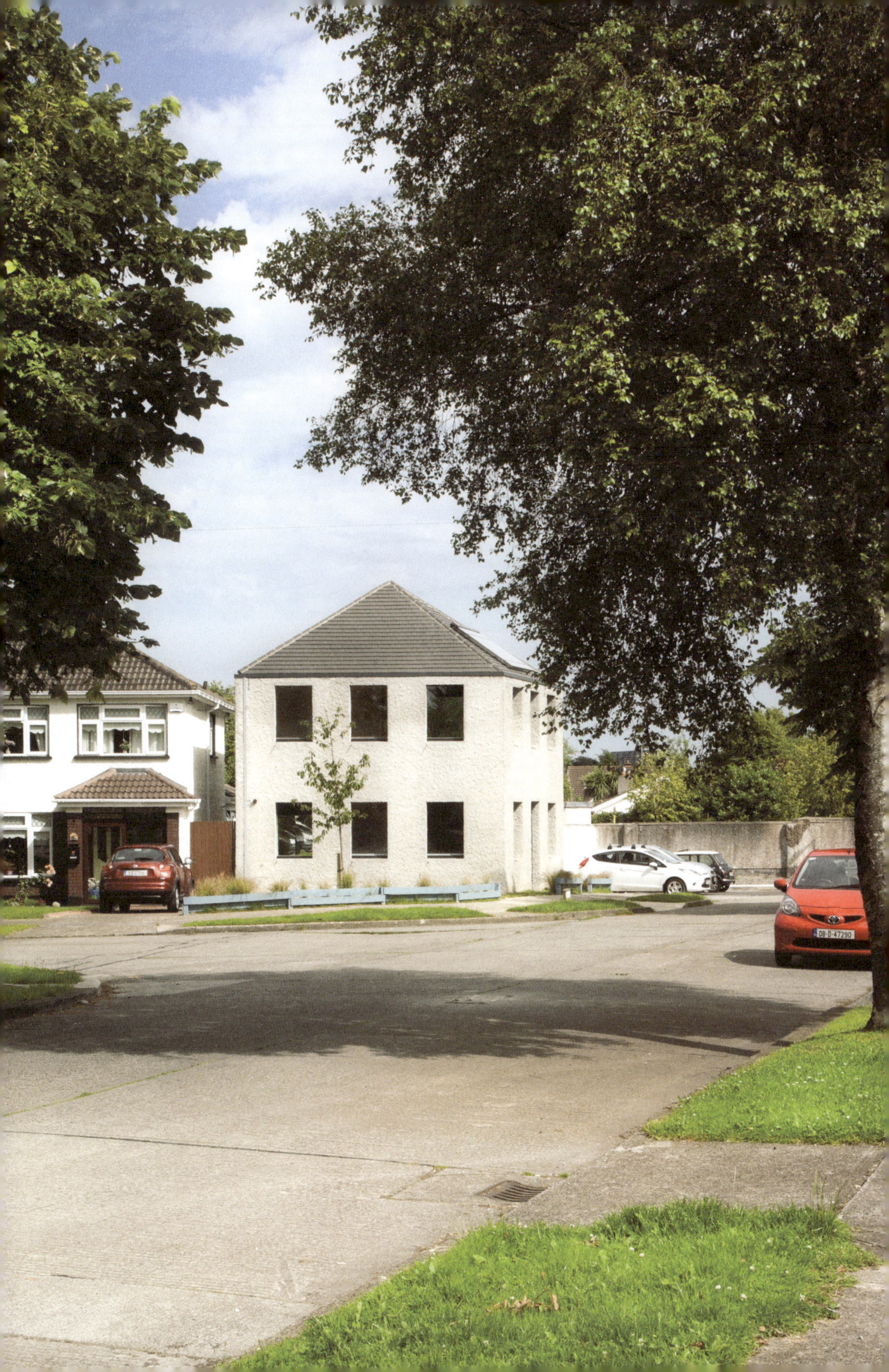

HOUSE 4 , FIRHOUSE

AAI Awards entry panel
Cross-section
Site section

opposite – Site plan / Ground floor / 1st floor and elevations
pages 114-115 – Location maps / View of house in context

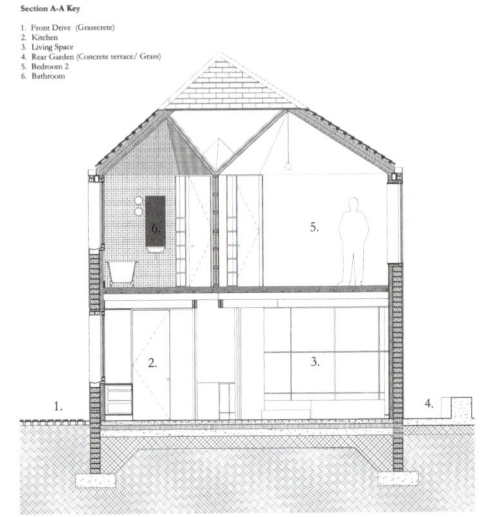

Section A-A Key
1. Front Drive (Grasscrete)
2. Kitchen
3. Living Space
4. Rear Garden (Concrete terrace/ Grass)
5. Bedroom 2
6. Bathroom

seeks to connect the house with the older rural buildings dotted around the suburban landscape.

Internally, the ground-floor communal spaces are lined with birch-ply fitted furniture which varies in depth to hold anything from shallow shelves to window seats to a fitted kitchen. The first floor is broken into four rooms, each with individually tented roofs. Three bedrooms and a bathroom (the typical requirement of a suburban house) are accessed from a central, mirrored landing space. Through this approach of 'lining' individual spaces, the interior world of the home can be freed from a direct reflection of the external form and its contextual obligations.

address – Monalea Grove, Firhouse, Dublin 24
client – private
photography – Alice Clancy

design to completion – 2008-2011
site area – 220m^2 / *floor area* – 95m^2
(plus 25m^2 shed and utility)
budget – n/a

Site section looking north
1. New House
2. Knocklyon Castle

Site Plan Key:
1. Original corner house
2. Driveway
3. Entrance
4. New house
5. Rear garden
6. Utility
7. Binstore
8. Shed

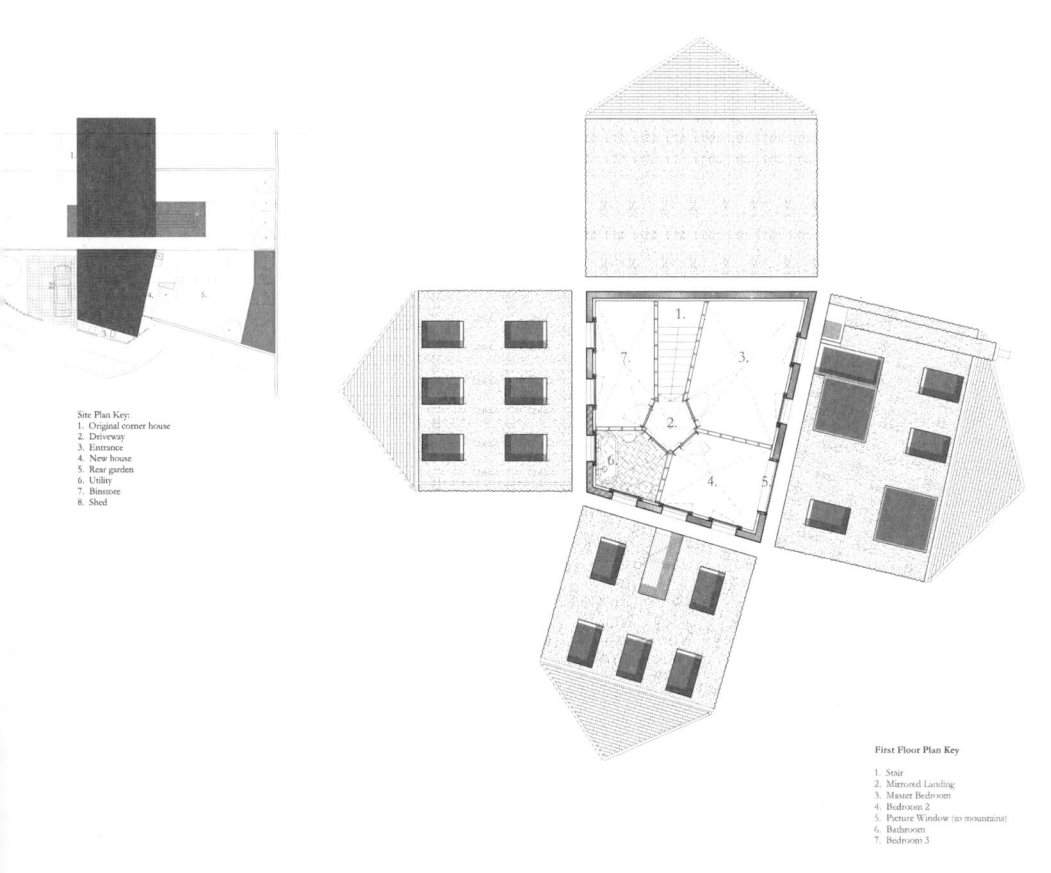

First Floor Plan Key
1. Stair
2. Mirrored Landing
3. Master Bedroom
4. Bedroom 2
5. Picture Window (to mountains)
6. Bathroom
7. Bedroom 3

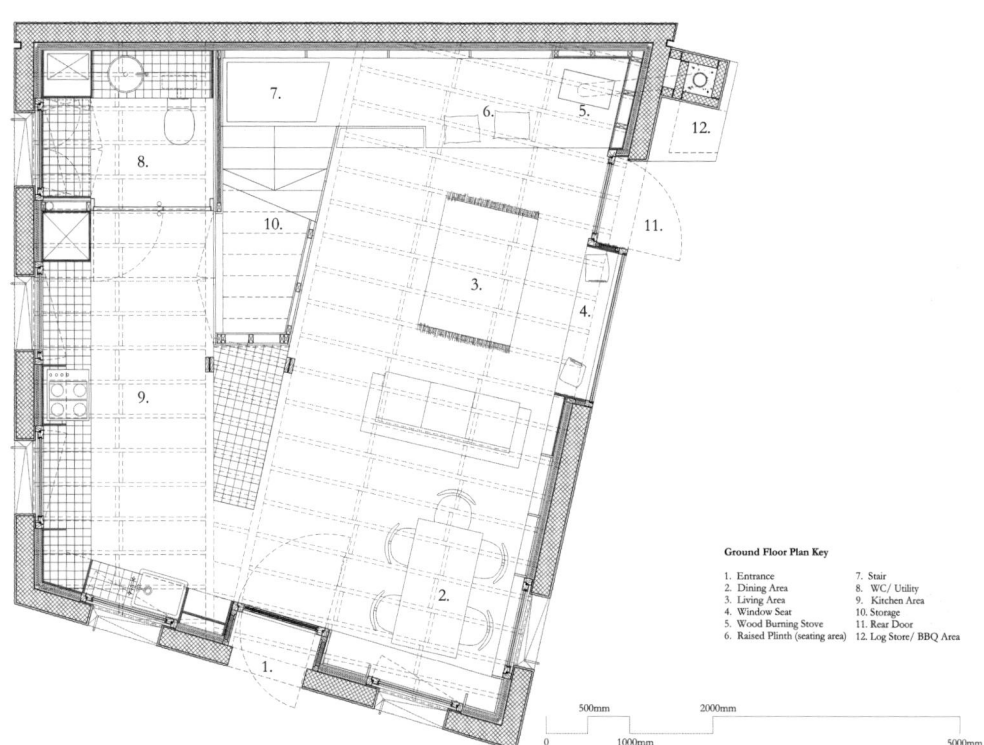

Ground Floor Plan Key
1. Entrance
2. Dining Area
3. Living Area
4. Window Seat
5. Wood Burning Stove
6. Raised Plinth (seating area)
7. Stair
8. WC/ Utility
9. Kitchen Area
10. Storage
11. Rear Door
12. Log Store/ BBQ Area

117

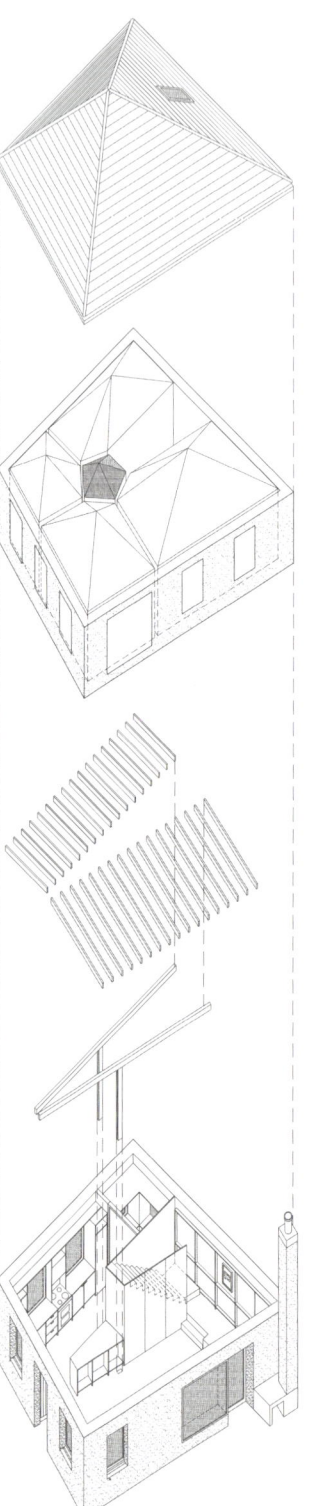

Concrete tiled pitched roo

First Floor
- individually roofed priva

First Floor Structure
- flitch 'T' columns and ex

Ground Floor
- timber lined communal

Exploded Axonometric

118

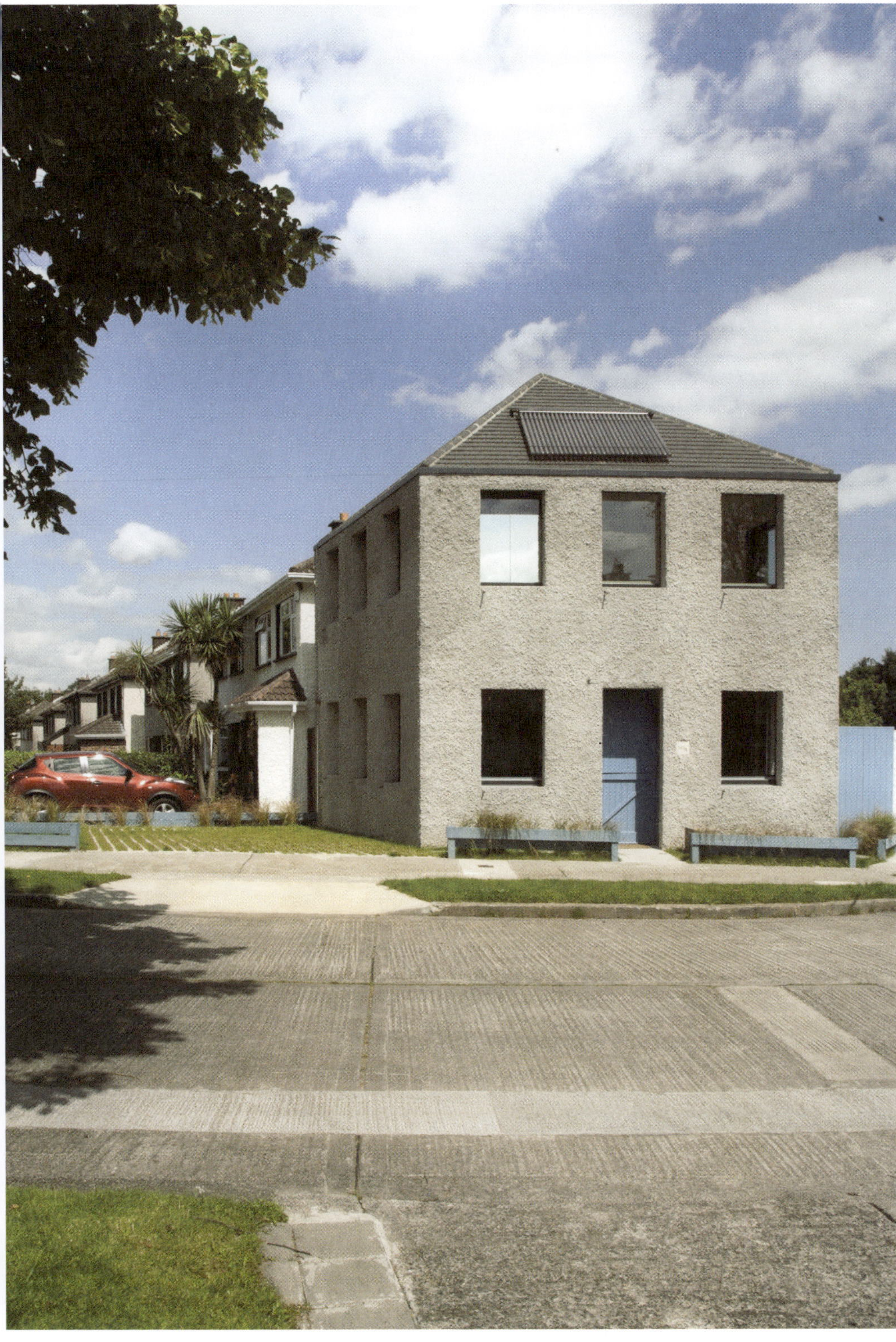

Detail Key

1- Unpainted rough-cast render to external walls. 20mm river rounded aggregate

2- Unpainted rough-cast render to reveals. 10mm river rounded aggregate

3- Proprietary concrete lintels over openings

4- Flashing lapped up under render at edges and sealed to concrete cill

5- 15mm diameter copper spout

6- Painted hardwood inward opening tilt-and-turn window

7- Custom precast window cill (cill overflows at front should spout be blocked)

8- Steel angle to support window

9- Birch-plywood lining to interior spaces

10- 100mm solid insulation

11- 215mm blockwork external leaf with DPM

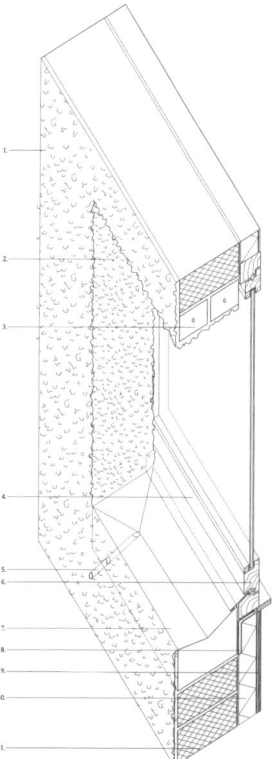

Axonometric Detail of Typical Window

120

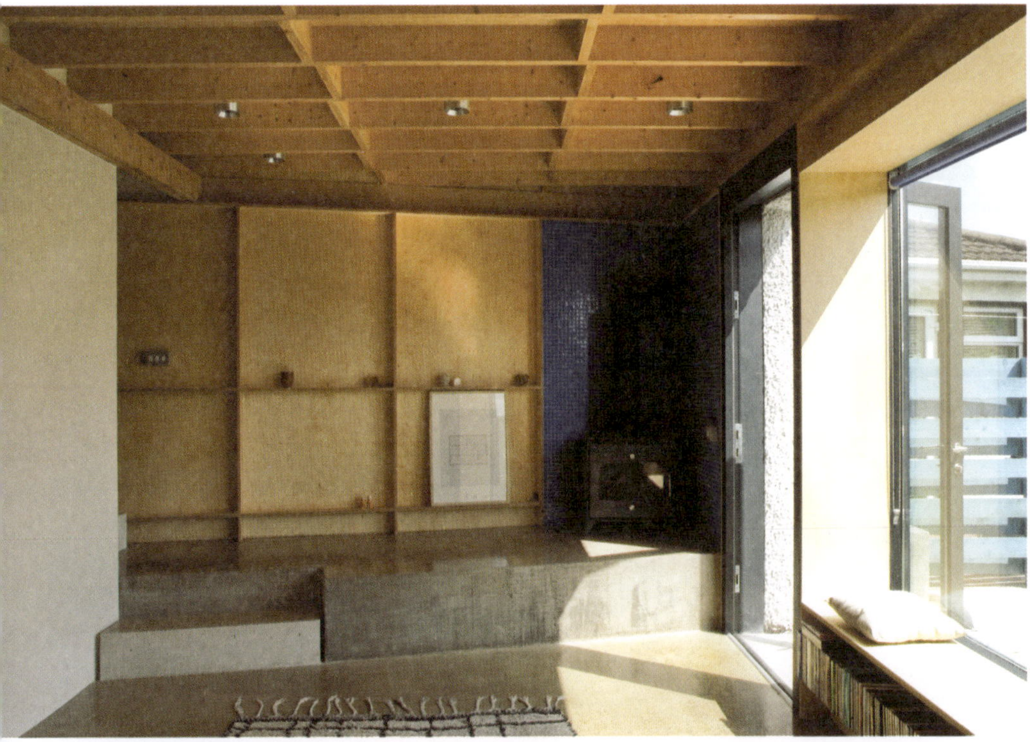

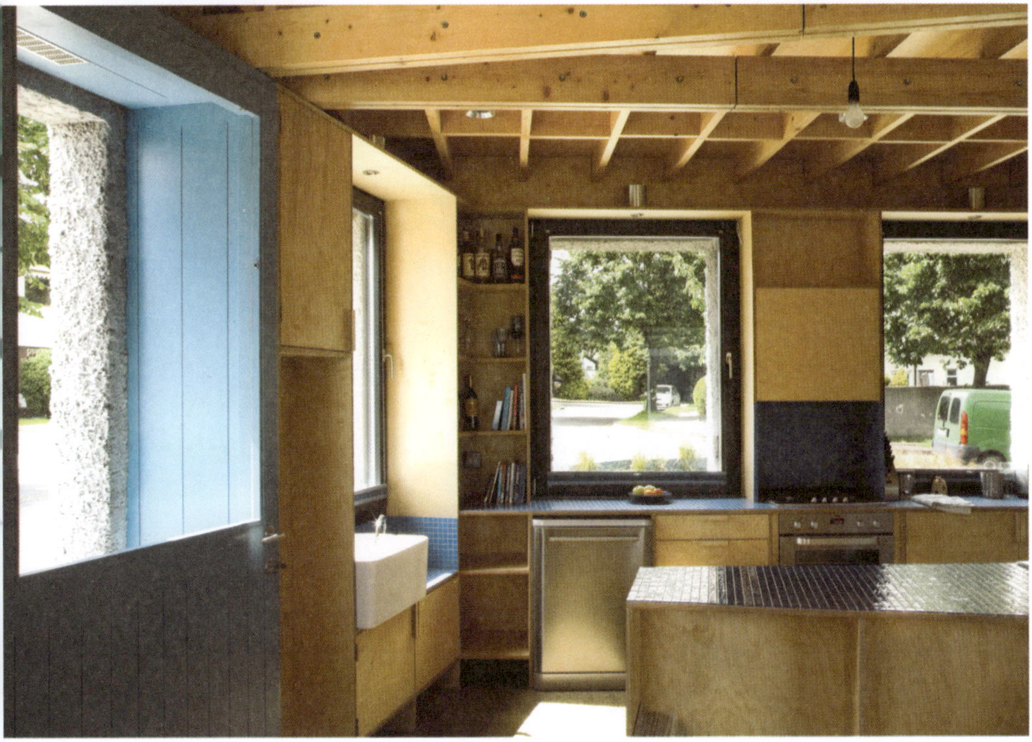

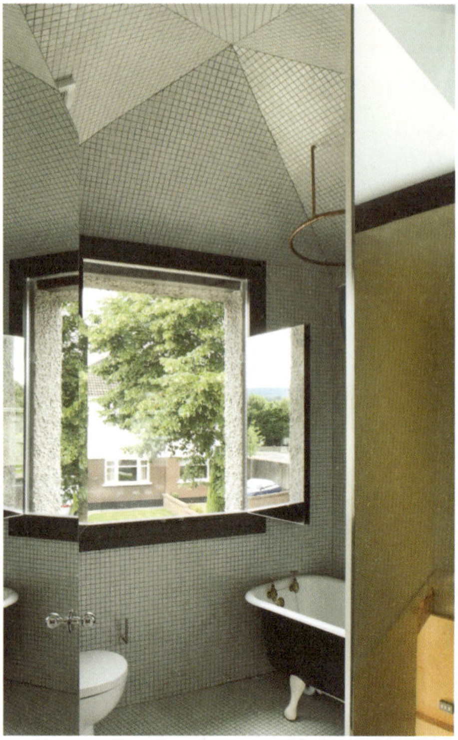
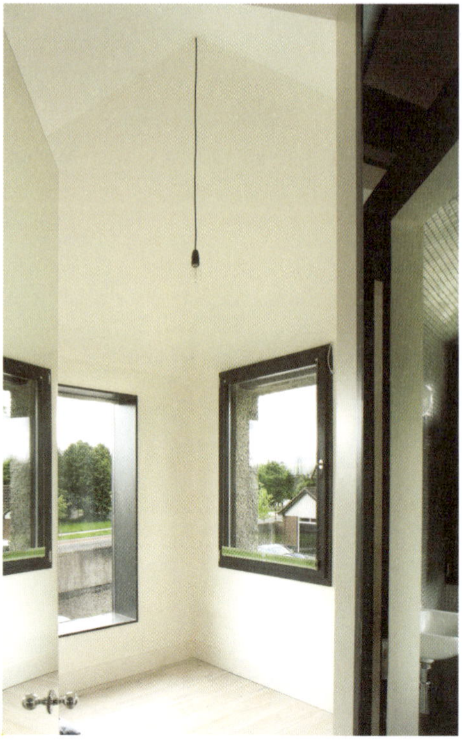
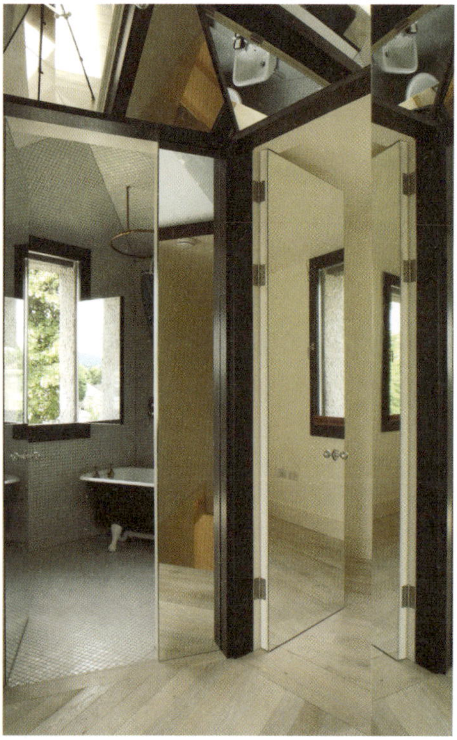
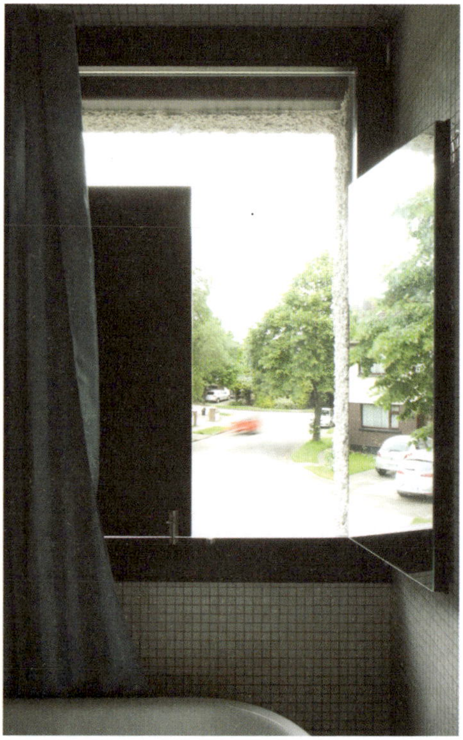

ASSESSORS' COMMENTS

COTTER – I like this. I like the tight, tailored, textured feel to the actual building and the fact that the windows are set back. There's an anonymity to it. But while the exterior is quite stern, it's extraordinary how the architect uses mirror on the inside to unlock some of the spaces.

ROSBOTTOM – The movement from surrealism to austerity is quite intriguing. I'm even more intrigued that it's on the edge of a 1970s council estate, on the side of a street. I find it incredible that people are building these extraordinary things at the back of ex-council houses on estates. That I find amazing.

DE BLACAM – I'm sort of afraid of being predictable in this, saying that because it's architecturally interesting, we're going along with it... The half-door is...

COTTER – A bit irritating?

DE BLACAM – Ah Jesus, I mean...

HICKEY – It's like that early Smithson house. It's doing something other.

HATZ – It's as good as Adolf Loos in some senses.

HICKEY – What?!

HATZ – Yes. It's a bloody good building actually.

DE BLACAM – Have you examined the plan? The concept of a kitchen and dining, that sort of relationship, on either side of the half-door is bizarre. In concept, I mean, anybody with an idea of a modern house... I mean, that arrangement is so extraordinary as to be unreal.

COTTER – But it's a very full and developed culture within quite a stern exterior. And I like it because it flaunts the choices in the rest of the estate. I like the fact that it's critical of the buildings around it. It's provocative.

ROSBOTTOM – I think the Viennese thing is really accurate, but it reminds me of Herman Czech more than Adolf Loos. You know those Herman Czech interiors? The odd placement of the door... I quite enjoy it.

HATZ – I enjoy it. It's very austere at one level, but you can also imagine people moving around with their radio outside this house. It's very contained and it's really relating at the same time. I find it absolutely charming and really clever. And I love the proportions. I would live there.

ROSBOTTOM – I also think there are bits of early Venturi in it. It's very knowing about its references. Somewhere between Magritte and a Calvanist.

HICKEY – And then you expect Mon Oncle to live in it. It's a kind of parody.

HATZ – It's like a good film. It can be understood by someone who hasn't a clue about architecture, and it can be lived in.

HICKEY – That's because it has all the bits that you'd kind of recognise.

COTTER – But it offers a very unique culture within something that's usually delivered in a very banal, generic way.

HATZ – I love this building. I think it's beautiful.

HICKEY – I don't think it's beautiful, unfortunately, though I do like it. Do you really think that's beautiful?

HATZ – Beauty comes in many forms.

ROSBOTTOM – I think what's clever about it is that it looks ordinary until you see it next to the ordinary house, and then it really doesn't look ordinary. I think it's a potential Award.

DE BLACAM – I would be worried about giving this an Award.

COTTER – I think it's particularly important to include this because it subverts the norm. And we have to find new forms of expression for this particular form.

HICKEY – It's certainly sufficiently provocative for it to be in. It is a very knowing project. Despite reservations we might have about it, it has to be included as an Award.

HATZ – Absolutely. It's really knowing. I think it's one of the stronger projects here. It is very well thought through. It has an edge and it has humour.

COTTER – It's an act of agitation, even though it's very still. I like that implied movement within the stillness of it. And it has a sort of cretaceous edge; it's kind of abrasive in the air. I think it's important that we put a sting in the tail of that particular agenda in Ireland, and that one does it for me. So I'm very happy that we send that out there with an Award.

ROSBOTTOM – In the context of what we've seen today, what's interesting about it for me is its ability to manipulate and be playful with its own reference material. There's something very provocative about placing something that could be understood as a villa, but also as something that's on a housing estate. It manages to be multiple things at the same time, and I guess it's got an extraordinary interior.

DE BLACAM – The interior is very small.

HATZ – Yes, but it's amplified by the form of the roof. It really is quite astute. This building knows what it's doing.

ROSBOTTOM – I think there are things that are unnerving about it, but I find its unnervingness compelling, for very different reasons. Someone is taking note of in a suburban context and finding it of value and deciding to build something of that quality amongst it. And I suppose that's another interesting context for Ireland, as it is for England, this idea of the value of these estates which were built in the 20th century, and how do we add to them? How do we appropriate them?

HATZ – This is actually making something dignified, almost a little monument, out of something quite mundane.

ROSBOTTOM – It manages to go between Venturi and Herman Czech and the Smithsons, and that's nearly Ledoux down there – that moment where you see it without any window. And I think anybody who can do that, and make all those interiors, and do a bit of Magritte in the shutters... It's full of imagination and verve, and I think there's a place for that in architecture.

TAKA ARCHITECTS was founded by Alice Casey and Cian Deegan. TAKA exhibited at the Venice Architectural Biennale in 2008 and co-curated the Irish Pavilion in 2010. As well as numerous national and international awards, the practice has been nominated for the Mies Van der Rohe Award, and was a finalist in the 2014 BD Young Architect of the Year Award. The practice is concerned with the communicative potential of architecture, with tectonic expression and with place-making. DESIGN TEAM – Alice Casey, Cian Deegan

TAKA ARCHITECTS
33-34 Vicar Street, Dublin 8 – T 01-7093004 / E office@taka.ie / W www.taka.ie

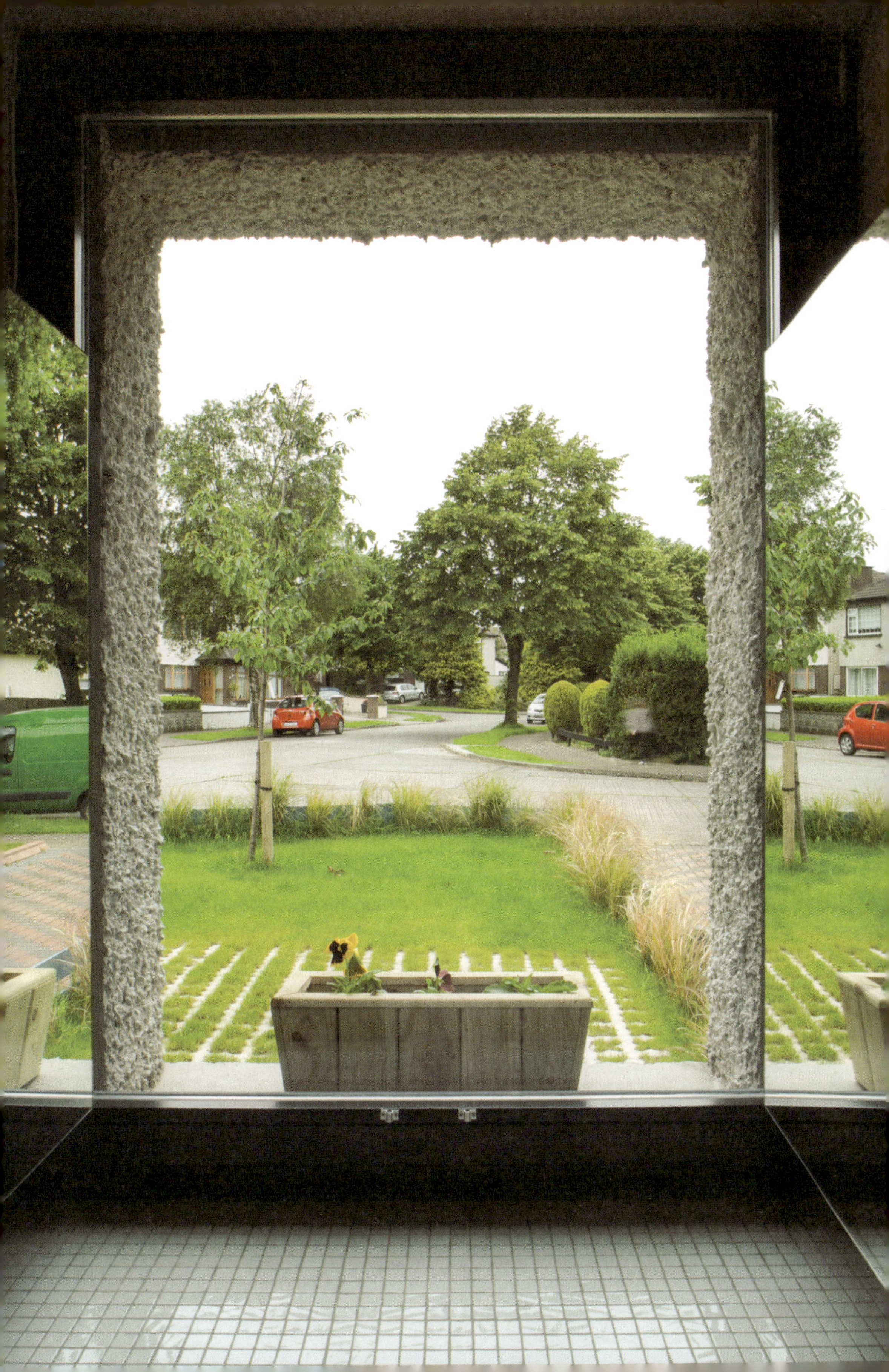

Special Mention

CARNIVAN HOUSE, Fethard-on-sea

AUGHEY O'FLAHERTY ARCHITECTS

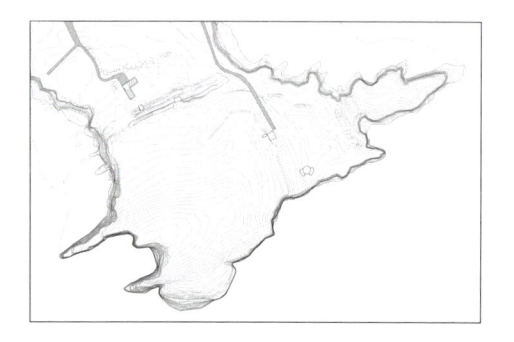

The site for this house is on a headland, Bangui Head, a protected scenic amenity area containing a Norman wall and bounded on three sides by cliffs and sea. The challenge was to deal with the potentially conflicting objectives of creating a home that was sensitive to this beautiful landscape and also made the most of it.

The form of the house is a simple L-shape in response to function, the path of the sun throughout the day, and to the wind. The dual-aspect living accommodation is located in one wing and avails of the east-west orientation. The bedroom accommodation is located in the other wing and avails of the north-south orientation. The entrance and services are located at the intersection of the two wings. This square intersection has a low ceiling height to allow for a roof terrace above, open to the sky and concealed within the roof profile.

The building is kept low, and the L-shaped plan is rotated to avoid the prevailing (regularly wild) winds from the sea. The two wings shelter a south-facing garden, which completes the square. Three external covered spaces are cut into the L in the form of niches of varying depth. The entrance porch is located in a recess on the more public, northern side. A south-facing terrace opens the bedroom wing to the garden. A long west-facing covered porch opens the living room wing to the wonderful landscape and views of sea and sunset to the west.

The house is a combination of new and traditional construction technologies, designed to be energy-efficient and cheap to run. It is a super-insulated, air-tight, prefabricated timber structure, wrapped in a local random rubble, sitting on a polished concrete base. Its layout and detail were guided by the principles of sustainable design: the use of natural light is integral; tall ceiling-heights and large areas of full-height glazing and sliding screens maximize solar gain; east, west and north façades are exceptionally thermally efficient; and a marsh grass roof increases thermal efficiency and links it with the ground. The house is 260m² in size.

Address – Fethard-on-sea, Co Wexford
Client – private
photography – Marie-Louise Halpenny

design to completion – 2008-2012
site area – 0.8ha / floor area – 260m²
budget – n/a

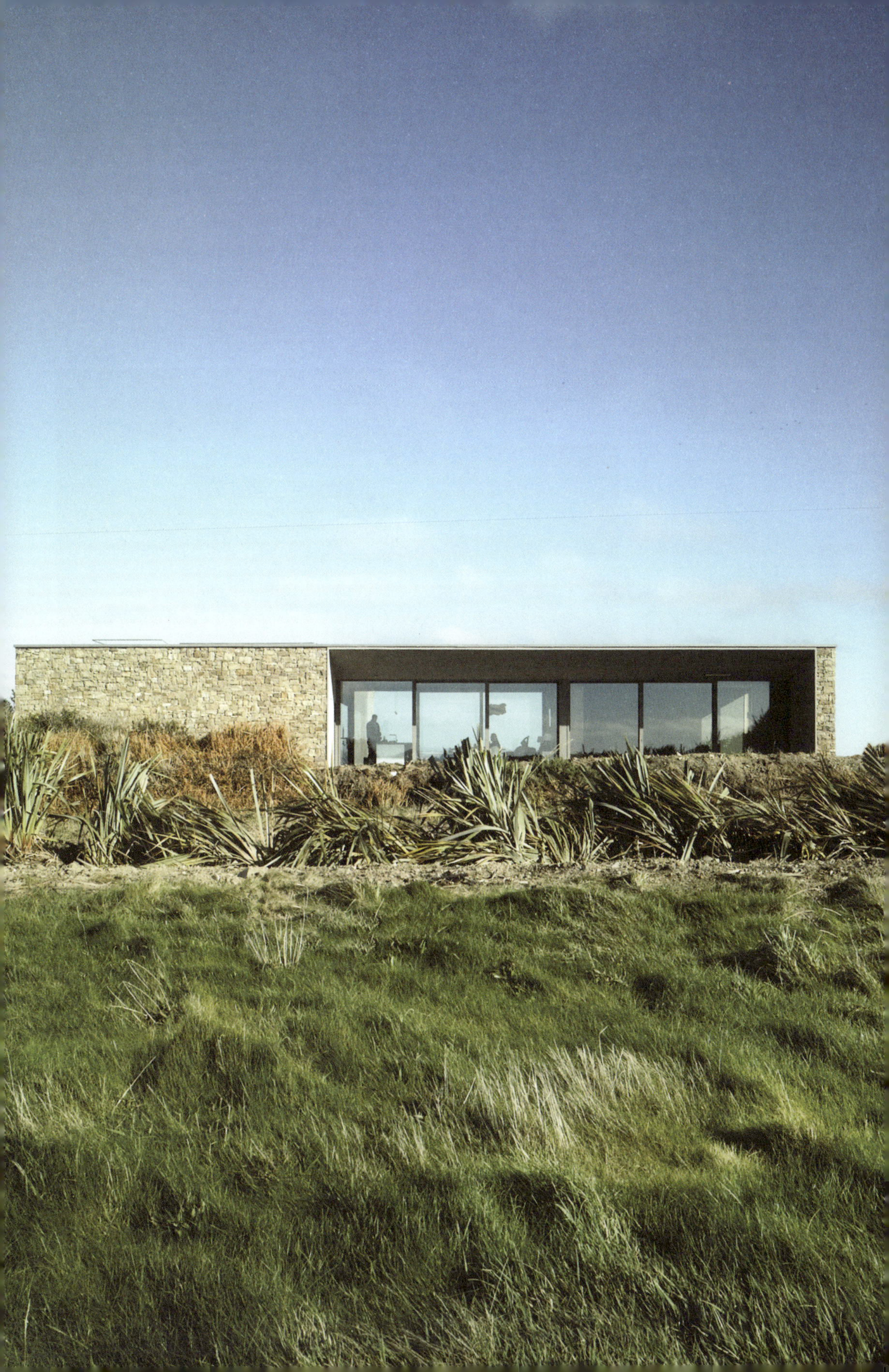

section A-A

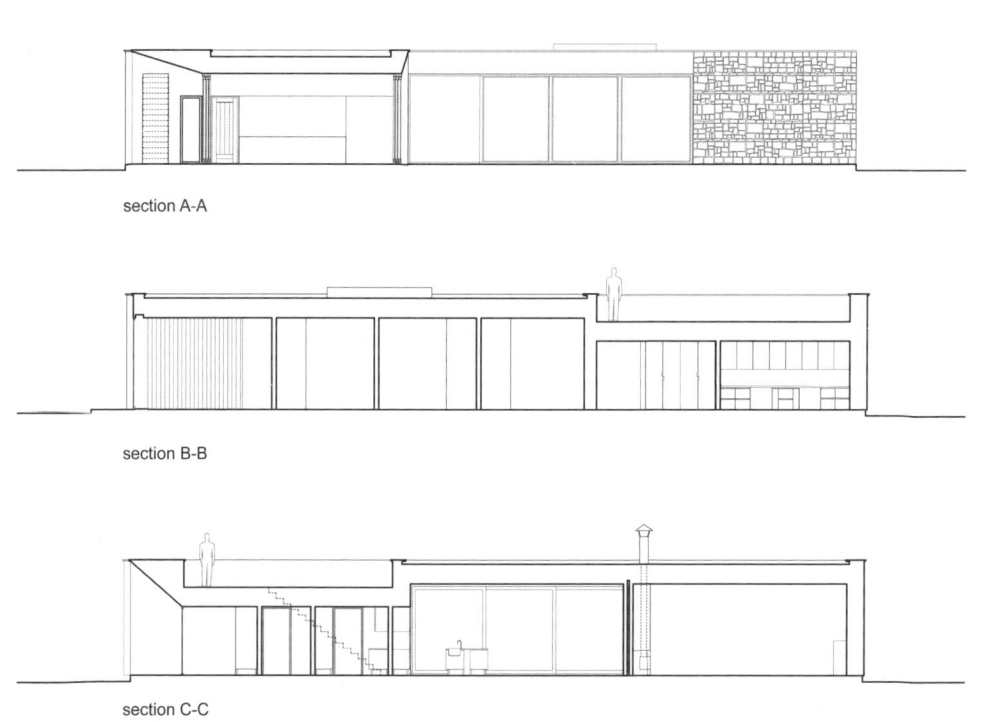

section B-B

section C-C

CARNIVAN HOUSE

Axonometric / Plan

opposite

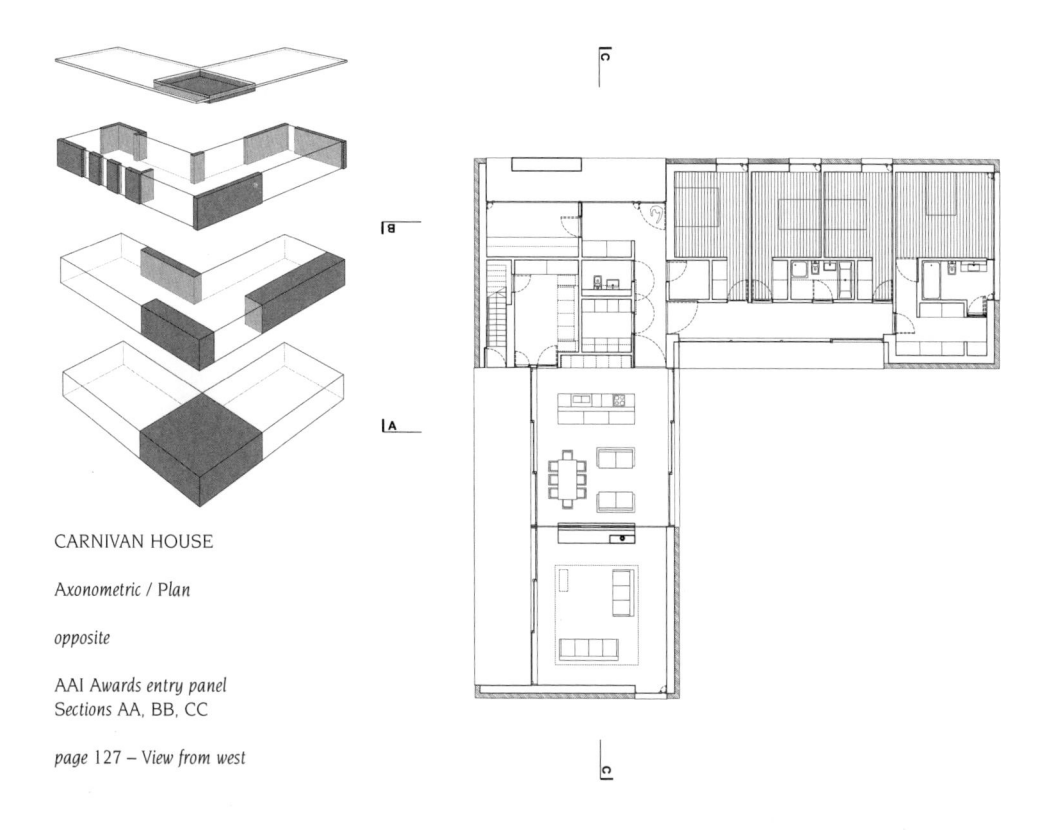

AAI Awards entry panel
Sections AA, BB, CC

page 127 – View from west

ASSESSORS' COMMENTS

ROSBOTTOM – There are a series of large houses here, of which this is one, and I like it better than many of the others. I quite like these deep threshold spaces, made by these cuts into the façade. And it's an interesting thing that they do in terms of making moments of tension in the plan, but it's quite hard to see how they play themselves out, and how they might frame a piece of landscape.

COTTER – As a house in rural Ireland, one thing I like about it is the fact that it respects the landscape. It sits into the land. As against some of the abominations you come across, I like the way it discreetly sits in there. It seems to be saying things I've seen before, but it's sharper. It's an amazing site, and it's a sharper way of articulating those particular ideas.

HATZ – I'm a bit disappointed because I think it promised something to me, that it would be not just another cool and elegant house, but that it would have another dimension. If the openings had been sharper, so that it became more of a monument. But it's very capable.

HICKEY – I suppose one thing is you've got to raise the bar quite high on private houses for rich clients, because where's the constraint? I like your idea about sharpening. The thing I find the most irritating is the coping. Once you have this idea that you carve these voids into the coping with this shadow line, it isn't quite strong enough as a way of dealing with it within the horizon. And I want each of these cuts into the

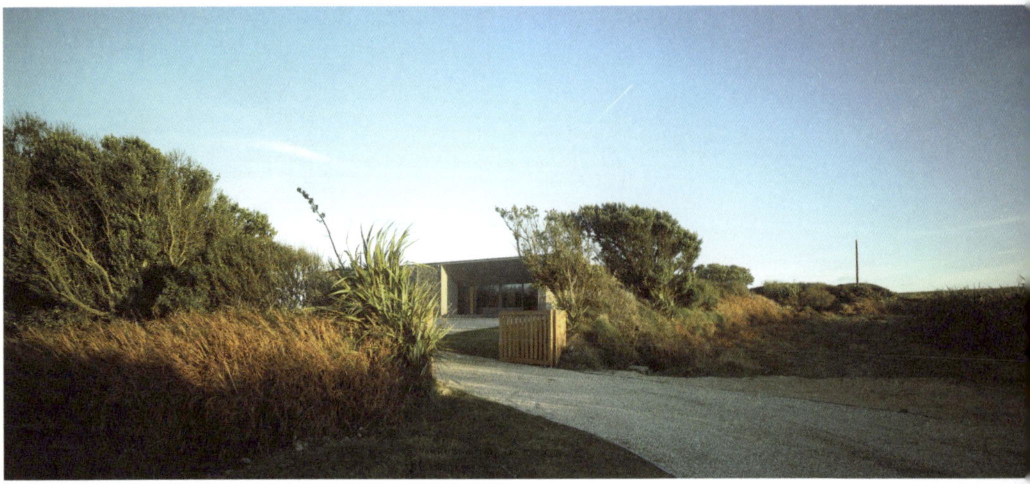

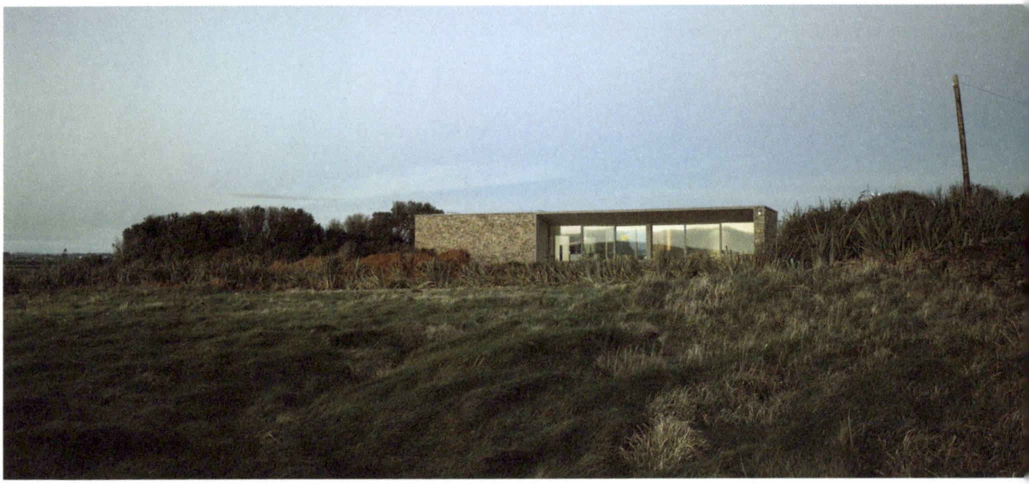

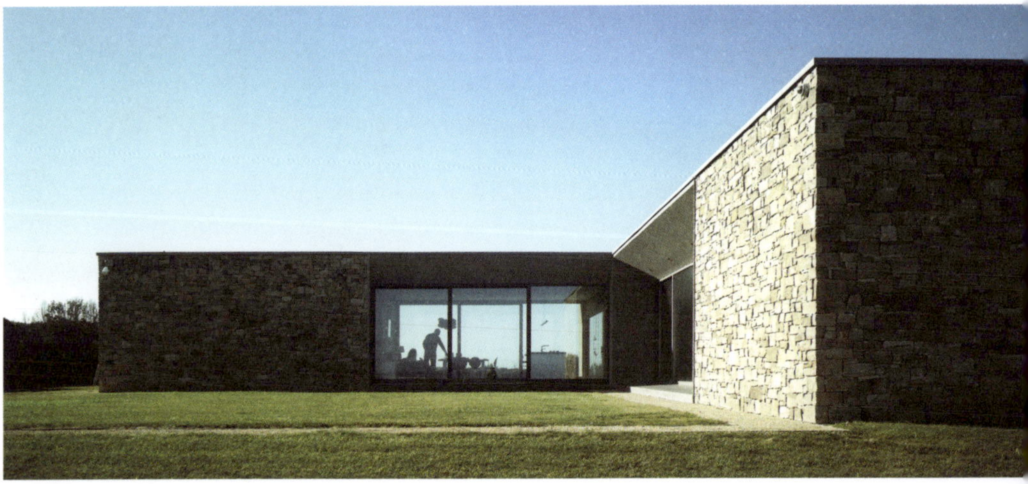

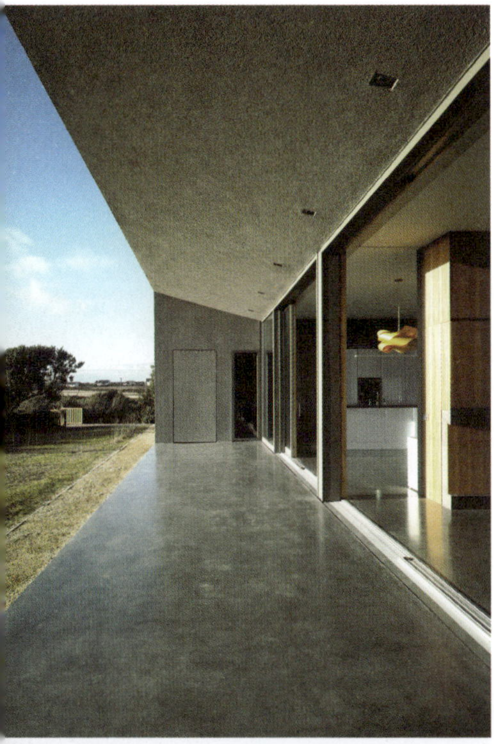

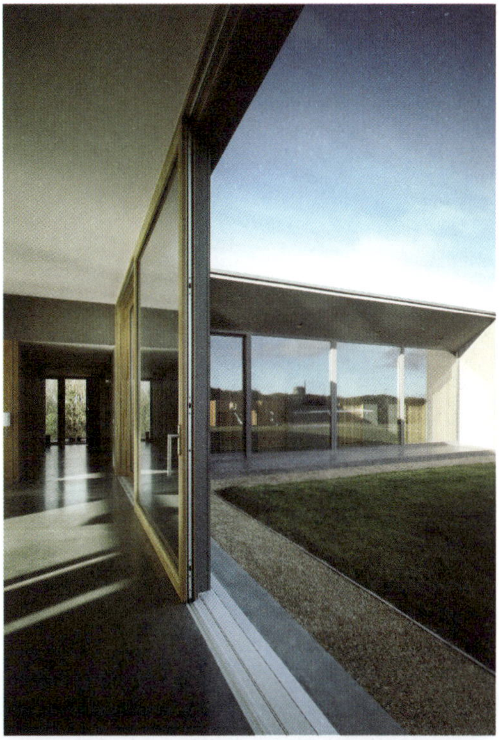

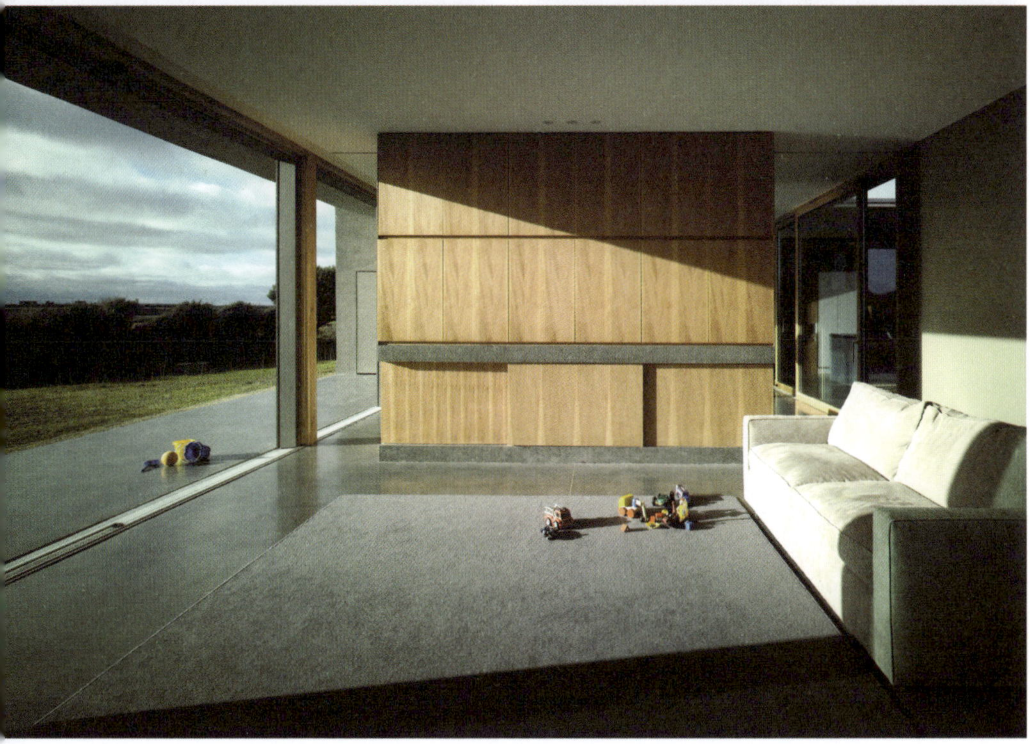

façade to have a conversation with the other one, as they ought to do. Somehow, spatially, there should be a dialogue between each one, or at least between two every time. So, although the plan is very competent, it doesn't quite work itself through. But I think it's pretty good.

COTTER – The tension between the solid and the ope here, I think, is compromised by this pier. It's almost like it needs to be treated more like a piece of sculpture, it needs to be more restrained.

ROSBOTTOM – I think that's probably right. That's actually the question, isn't it? When you arrive at that as your *parti*, how do you then deal with making windows in it?

COTTER – Because the whole dramatic palette there is this inhalation of light, in a way, creating these internal spaces, which are external. And the façades then just absorb the light.

ROSBOTTOM – You're absolutely right, because if you take those three windows away, it becomes much stronger. And I don't quite believe it when the glazing turns the corner, like that does.

HICKEY – Does it, at the beginning, promise that it's going to define the way that you might live in a different way? And then when you read it, actually it's pretty ordinary in terms of how it's organised, and that for me is the most disappointing part about it.

DE BLACAM – This house I would have substantial objections to.

HATZ – Once again in a presentation, there's this over-emphasis on the views. It sits quite elegantly in the landscape, but there's no real relationship, is there, with these terraces, which are the feature of the building?

COTTER – I prefer it when it is working with this kind of landscape and texture here. It works well when you see it across the field.

ROSBOTTOM – It has a perfectly respectable historic attitude to the landscape. I wouldn't damn if for that.

AUGHEY O'FLAHERTY ARCHITECTS was established by Lora Aughey and Max O'Flaherty in 1999. Starting with small domestic extension work, the practice has slowly grown and developed an expertise in the design of homes, old and new. It has won many national and international awards. MAX O'FLAHERTY is director of Aughey O'Flaherty. He has taught design at UCD and DIT. DESIGN TEAM – Max O'Flaherty, Joseph MacMahon.

AUGHEY O'FLAHERTY ARCHITECTS
32 Nassau Street, Dublin 6 – T 01-6729932 / E hello@aof.ie / W www.aof.ie

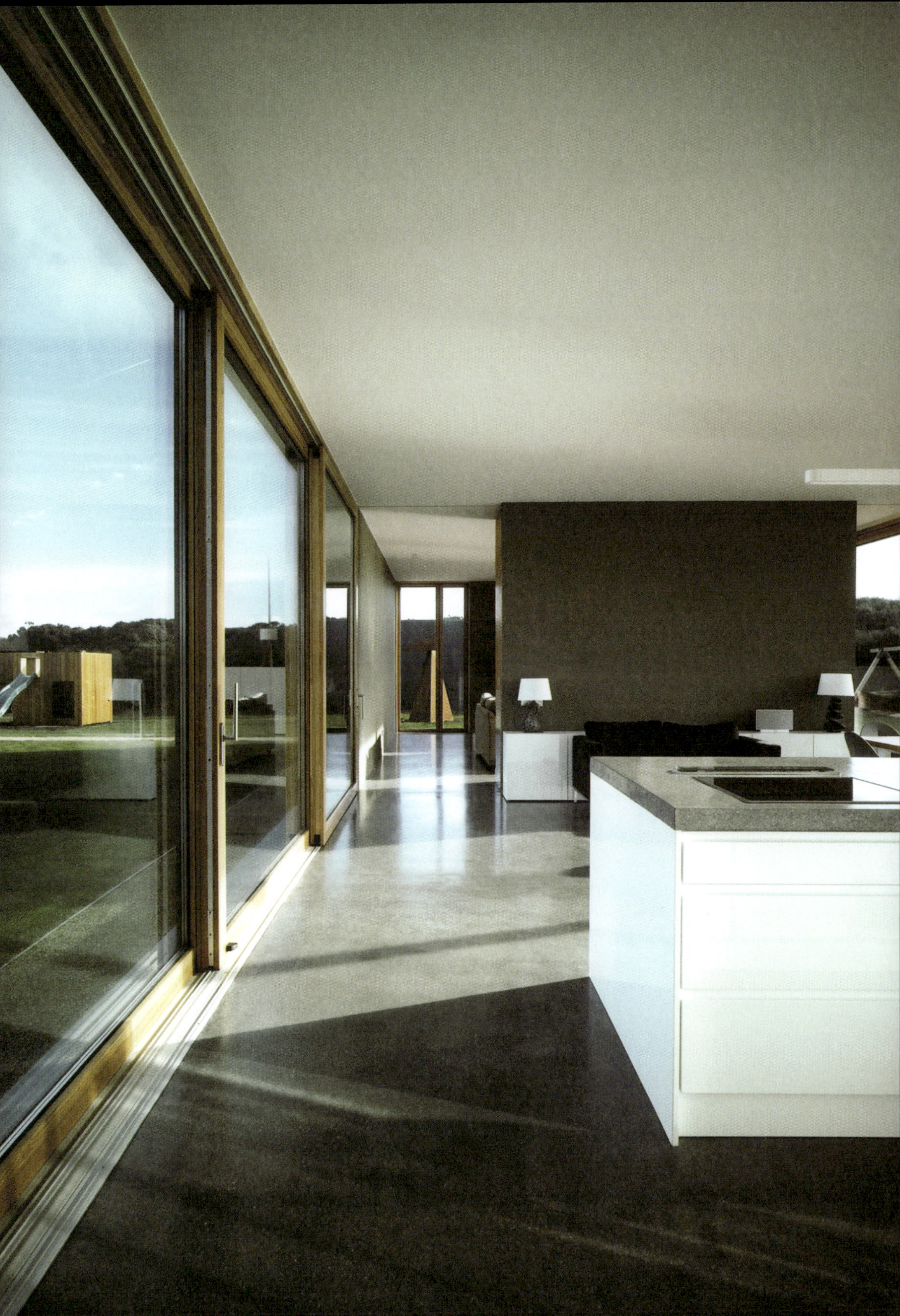

HOUSE ON CHESTNUT LANE, Galway

BOYD CODY ARCHITECTS

This modernist villa sits on a north-eastern sloping site in a leafy suburb of Galway on the existing footprint of a demolished house. It is designed around a central void, and the established planting and landscaping on site was not unduly disturbed. To further preserve the site, all the activities of the house are consolidated within its square plan and the form eroded where necessary with vertical and horizontal voids. Accommodated within the plan is a car port and entrance at the upper-ground floor; a covered utility area at lower-ground floor; master bedroom, study, ensuite and terrace at first floor, and, most importantly, a double-height courtyard or void at the centre of the plan which brings natural light deep into the house throughout the day.

The main living, dining and kitchen space runs around the northern and eastern side of the void to give the primary living spaces expansive views of the garden and the surrounding mature woodland. As this room is dual-aspect, it is always light-filled, the various zones of domestic activity demarcated within a stepped ceiling above. The service zone for the house is provided at the lower-ground floor, containing utility, gymnasium, workshop and garden storage areas. The master-bedroom suite is located at first-floor level.

Externally, a silver birch tree is surrounded by the granite gravel of the central courtyard. This gravel, taken from the underlying bedrock of the site, is also used in the forecourt. Selected pigmented concrete paviors are used on the external voids within the footprint of the building. In-situ brushed white concrete is used to form a floating terrace to the south side of the house and steps to the west side.

The house is a timber-frame construction, with steel Keystone lintels and columns forming the ribbon windows, while the larger spans over the horizontal voids are formed with I-beams. The external skin is a self-coloured rendered blockwork. Silver satin-anodised aluminium panels and large glazed screens give a horizontal emphasis to view and form. The corners of the dark grey volume are eroded by window and panel, radically altering the perception of the house in the round as it negotiates the sloping site.

address – 2 Chestnut Lane, Lower Dangan, Galway
client – private
photography – Paul Tierney

design to completion – 2008-2012
floor area – 320m^2
budget – n/a

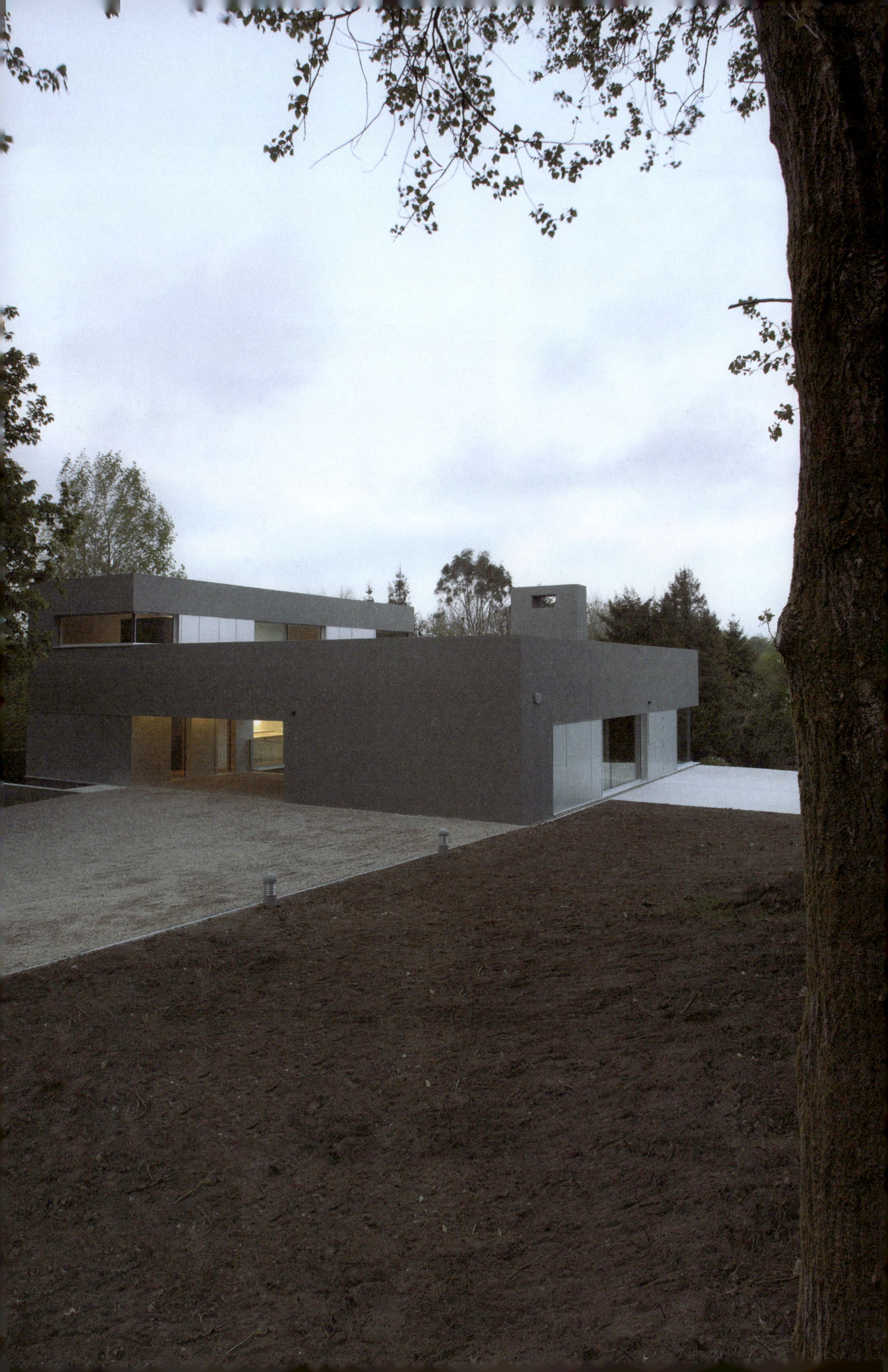

1. ENTRANCE
2. CLOAK RM
3. KITCHEN
4. LIVING
5. DINING
6. BEDROOM
7. BATHROOM
8. COURTYARD
9. STUDY
10. WARDROBE
11. ROOF TERRACE
12. GYM
13. WINE STORE
14. UTILITY
15. GARDEN STORE

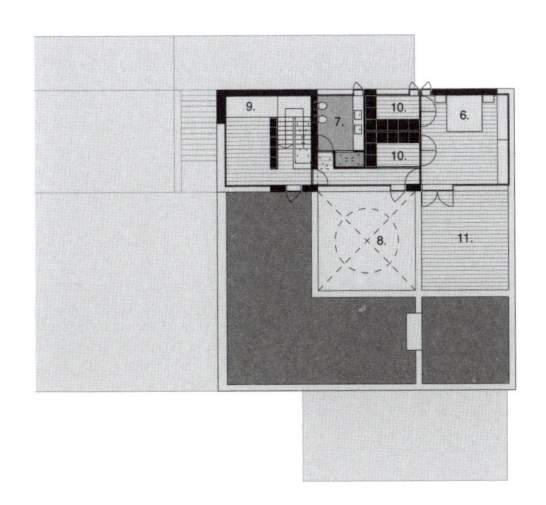

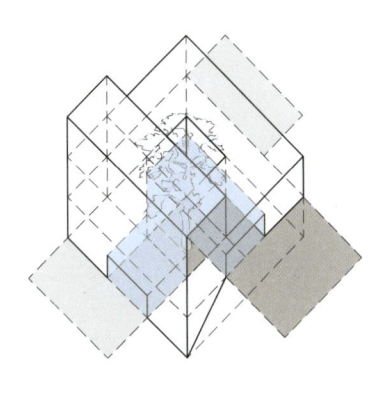

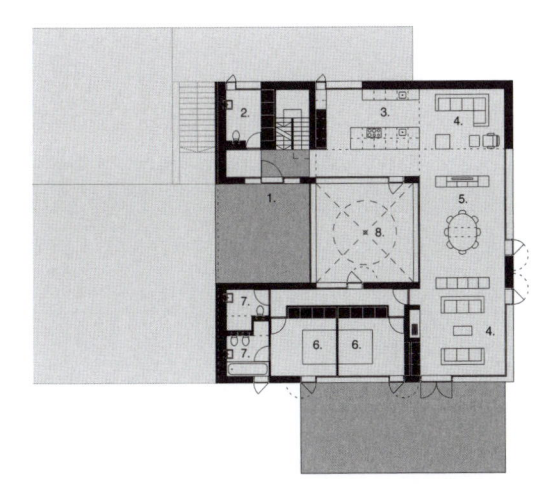

HOUSE ON CHESTNUT LANE

Plans – lower ground floor, ground floor, 1st floor

opposite

AAI Awards entry panel 1/2

Cross-section through courtyard, looking east

page 135 – View from south-west of entrance and south-facing terrace

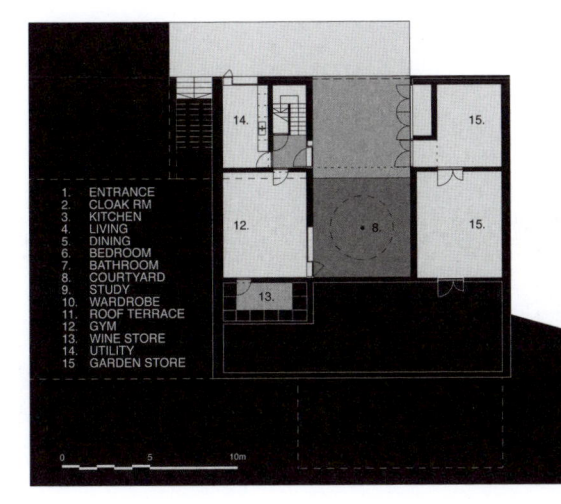

1. ENTRANCE
2. CLOAK RM
3. KITCHEN
4. LIVING
5. DINING
6. BEDROOM
7. BATHROOM
8. COURTYARD
9. STUDY
10. WARDROBE
11. ROOF TERRACE
12. GYM
13. WINE STORE
14. UTILITY
15. GARDEN STORE

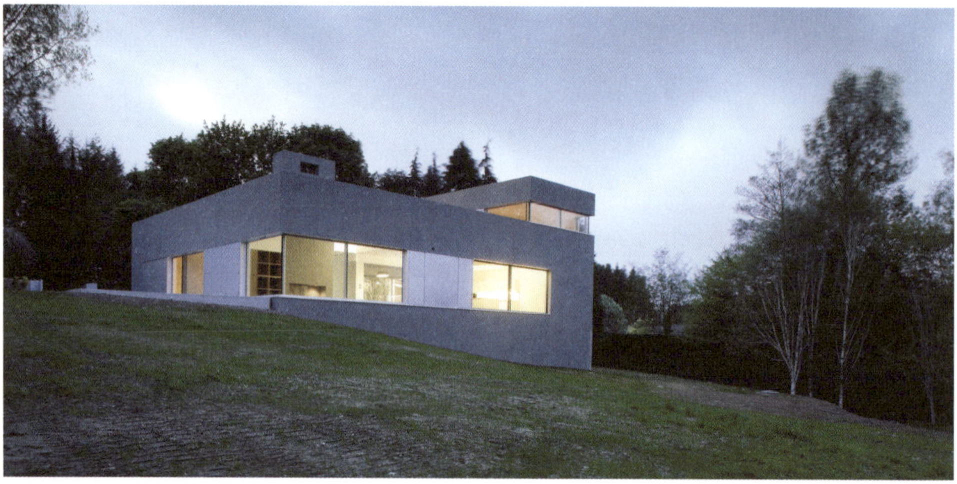

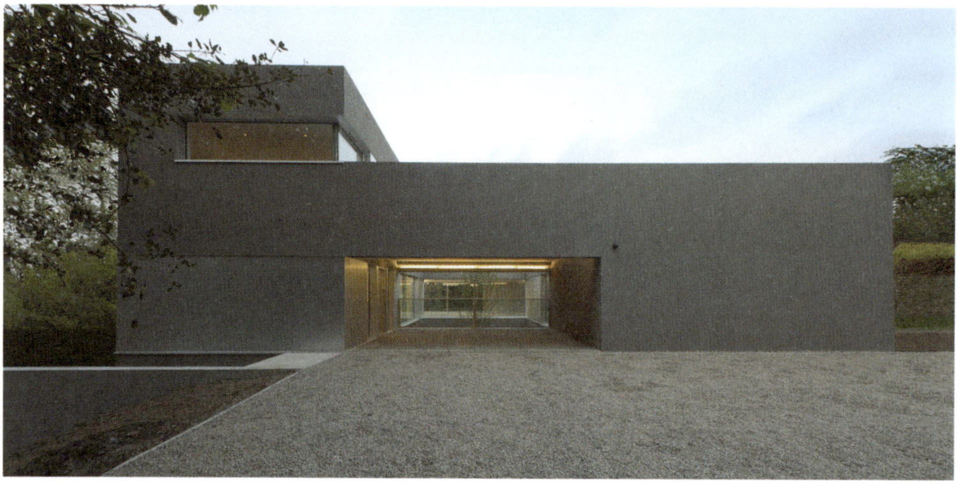

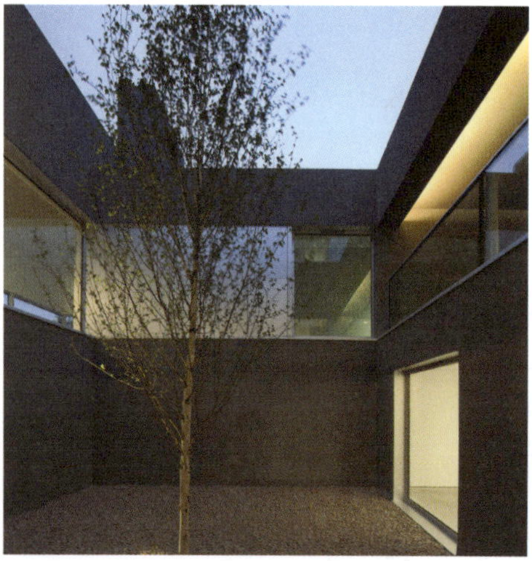

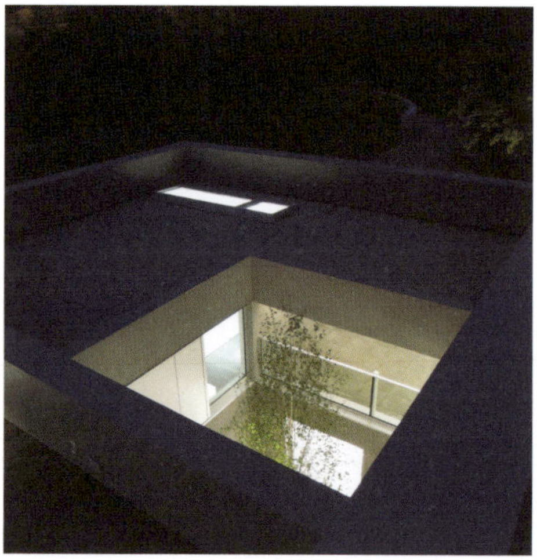

ASSESSORS' COMMENTS

HATZ – I'm dreaming of this house becoming other things in the future, like a school or a crèche or a workplace. I'm just testing other uses for this particular kind of architecture.

HICKEY – Is this the problem that we were talking about earlier, that we have people exercising themselves to distraction on domestic projects that become unnecessarily problematic? And the whole approach may well be more appropriate for something completely different?

ROSBOTTOM – What I find odd is this language of stretched tautness in relation to a language of burying and cutting. So you're making this thing that's kind of dug into the ground, and then you're making a skin which is all about stretching, and you never really get to understand what happens when the two meet.

HATZ – It's so elegant, in a way, like a sleek object, and yet that interior courtyard is going to be so windy and cold. And yet I find it a beautiful object...

COTTER – I find that any dramatic content that was built up on the approach has been completely depressed by the proportion of the entrance opening. What goes on on the inside would have to be especially interesting for me to overcome the exterior.

ROSBOTTOM – But that's an aesthetic sensibility.

COTTER – It is, yes.

ROSBOTTOM – If you are going to make houses for individual clients on sites, in a way you're setting up your own conditions for working. Unlike some of the other projects where you can see that there are lots of constraints, this one is actually solving a set of problems that it set up for itself. It's an object placed in a landscape, so its constraints are self-imposed. And then the question is how well does it deal with those things? And that sets the bar quite high. I find these buildings feel like they probably reached their epiphany in the computer-render. You know, everything after that is a degradation from the render into reality. And so I get troubled by these kinds of buildings.

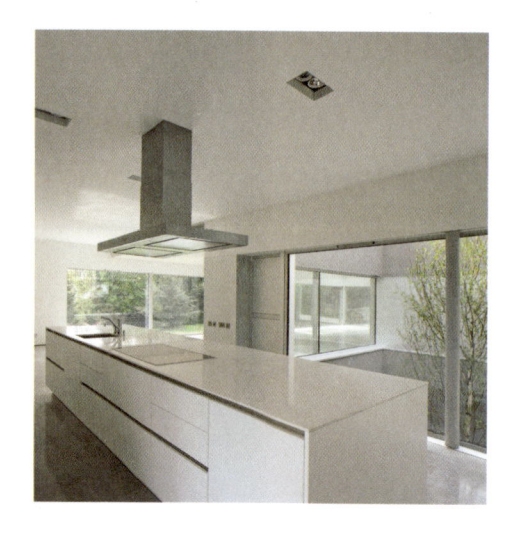

HATZ – It's so contained in its multiple squares. It's compact, and it's playing with that, with the plan and then the section set into the topography. And then you have the idea that a building, which is a house, becomes something else besides a house, and by actually manipulating this contained space with solids and voids, allows the house to become something else that is not just a home. I think there is competence in that plan, and I like that it's contained within a square.

HICKEY – There's competence in lots of places, but it kind of lacks soul for me. It says it's a house, but it doesn't ever really appear to be a house. It's like it's running away from that question about how you dwell somewhere, and the centre of it is gone. But someone worked awfully hard to do this.

DE BLACAM – The presentation does it no favours. It's very difficult to know exactly what's going on.

ROSBOTTOM – My worry about it is it doesn't deal with the realities of being a house in a landscape, cut into a hill, with some trees overhanging it.

HICKEY – In Belgium, Stéphane Beel has done a house that's a bit like this, with voids in it, but it's altogether better handled in the way it structures itself.

HATZ – I think it has quite a sophisticated plan, and I like the way that this solid is offering so much transparency. The interior feels larger than the exterior.

ROSBOTTOM – It's a very conceptually driven project. As an architect, I recognise the level of attention in it, which has value.

BOYD CODY ARCHITECTS is a design-led practice established in 2000. Its directors, Dermot Boyd and Peter Cody, graduated from Dublin Institute of Technology in 1990. They teach at DIT and UCD schools of architecture respectively. Boyd Cody has received numerous awards including first place in the Monaghan Civic Offices competition in 2002 and the AAI Downes Medal in 2005. Their work has been widely published and exhibited, including the Venice Architectural Biennale (2006), Lisbon Triennale (2007), *Rebuilding the Republic*, Leuven (2010), and *Nine Architects, Nine Propositions to Live* in Heyères, France (2012). DESIGN TEAM – Dermot Boyd, Peter Cody, John Maguire, Oran Ó Síocháin.

BOYD CODY ARCHITECTS
36 College Green, Dublin 2 – T 01-6330042 / F 01-6330041 / E info@boydcodyarch.com / W www.boydcodyarch.com

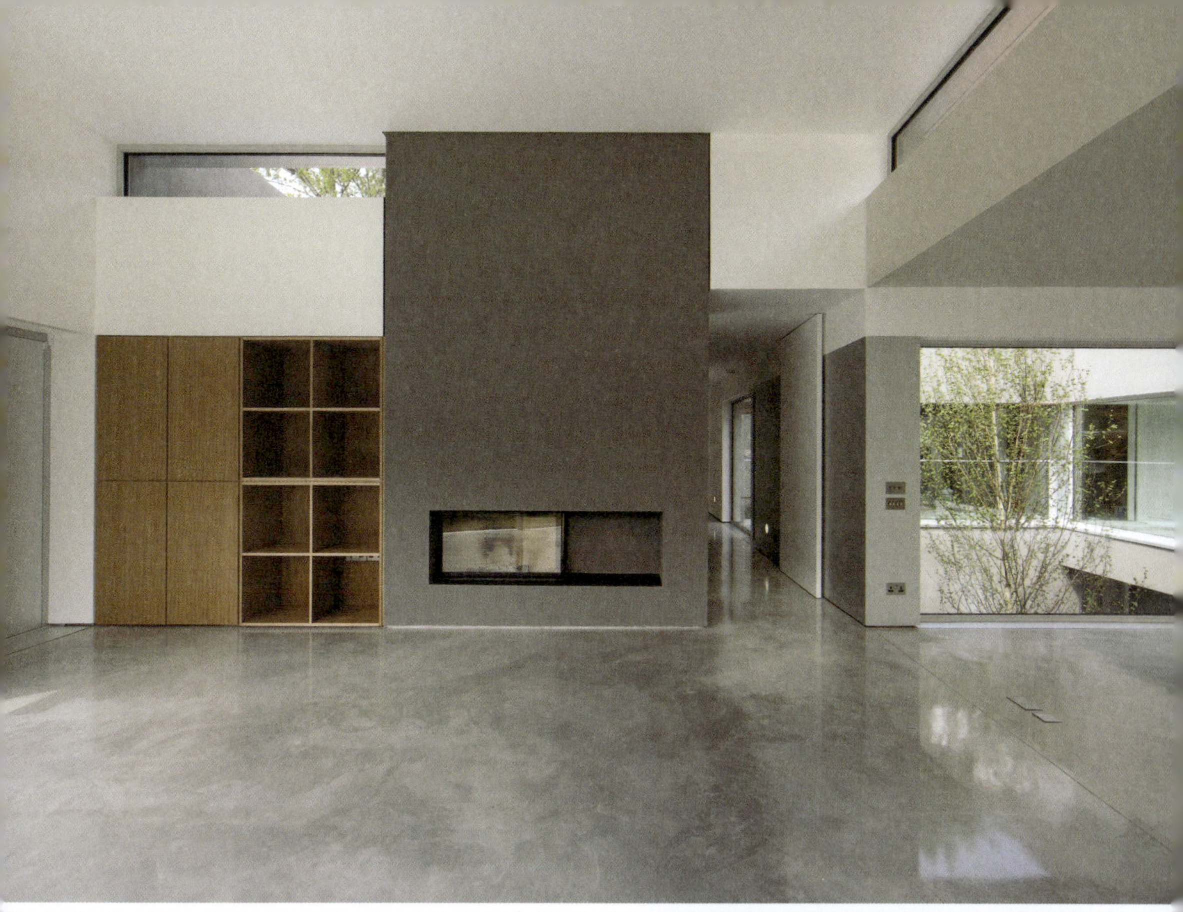

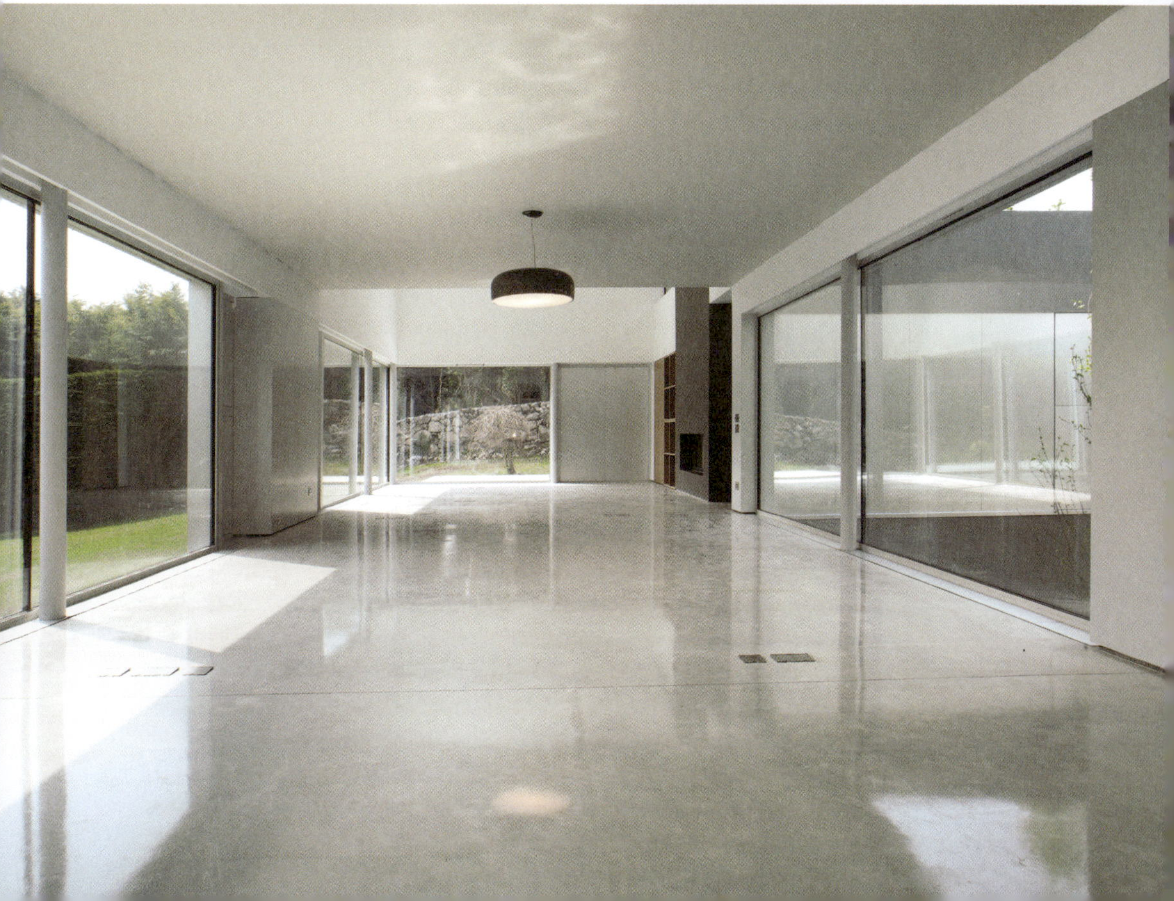

Special Mention

BORD GÁIS NETWORKS SERVICES CENTRE

DENIS BYRNE ARCHITECTS

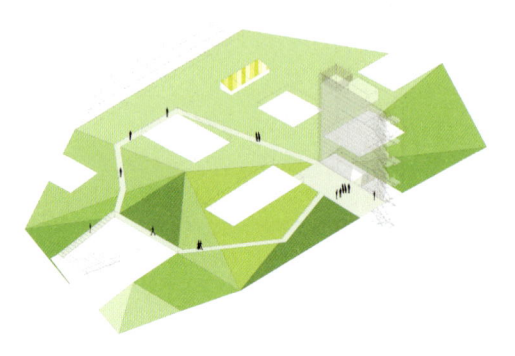

The design of the new Networks Services Centre reflects the commitment of Bord Gáis Networks to sustainable development, environmental protection and energy-conservation. It focuses their Dublin operations in a single location on a 5-acre site, including 24/7 operation of Ireland's natural-gas distribution network and 24/7 emergency response for Dublin and surrounding counties, the National Technical Training Centre and the Health, Safety, Quality & Environment Unit.

The design team defined sustainability targets early on in the design process, formulating an integrated sustainable-design approach. This approach combines microclimate, biodiversity and landscape, water management and use of renewable energy technologies to establish a service facility with a high-quality and permeable work environment. In terms of energy-use and environmental control, the building is responsive to user needs, employing a system based on the principles of high thermal mass, natural and displacement ventilation, maximised natural daylight, and radiant cooling and heating supplied by a ground-source heat pump and chilling device. The superstructure of the building is formed using an exposed concrete flat-slab-and-column construction. Along with the highly insulated and compact volume of the building, the high thermal mass of the exposed concrete ceilings is used as a passive space-conditioning system. The building is wrapped with a perforated screen of silver anodised aluminium, which changes its appearance from solid to transparent according to the weather and position of the sun.

Taking its inspiration from industrial and infrastructure buildings, and combining it with a sophisticated office environment, the building expresses its diverse operational programme as a utilitarian landmark. Organised over two levels with sheltered gardens, office areas, operational facilities and circulation woven to an informal fabric, the building promotes an inter-departmental, multidisciplinary work environment. A new landscape integrates car-parking and loading areas, and connects the existing site and the anonymous green along St Margaret's Road to an extended parkland – a green interface to the city.

address – St Margaret's Road, Finglas, Dublin 11
client – Bord Gáis Networks
photography – Paul Tierney

design to completion – 2008-2011
site area – 2.06 ha / *floor area* – 5,200m^2
budget – €17.5m

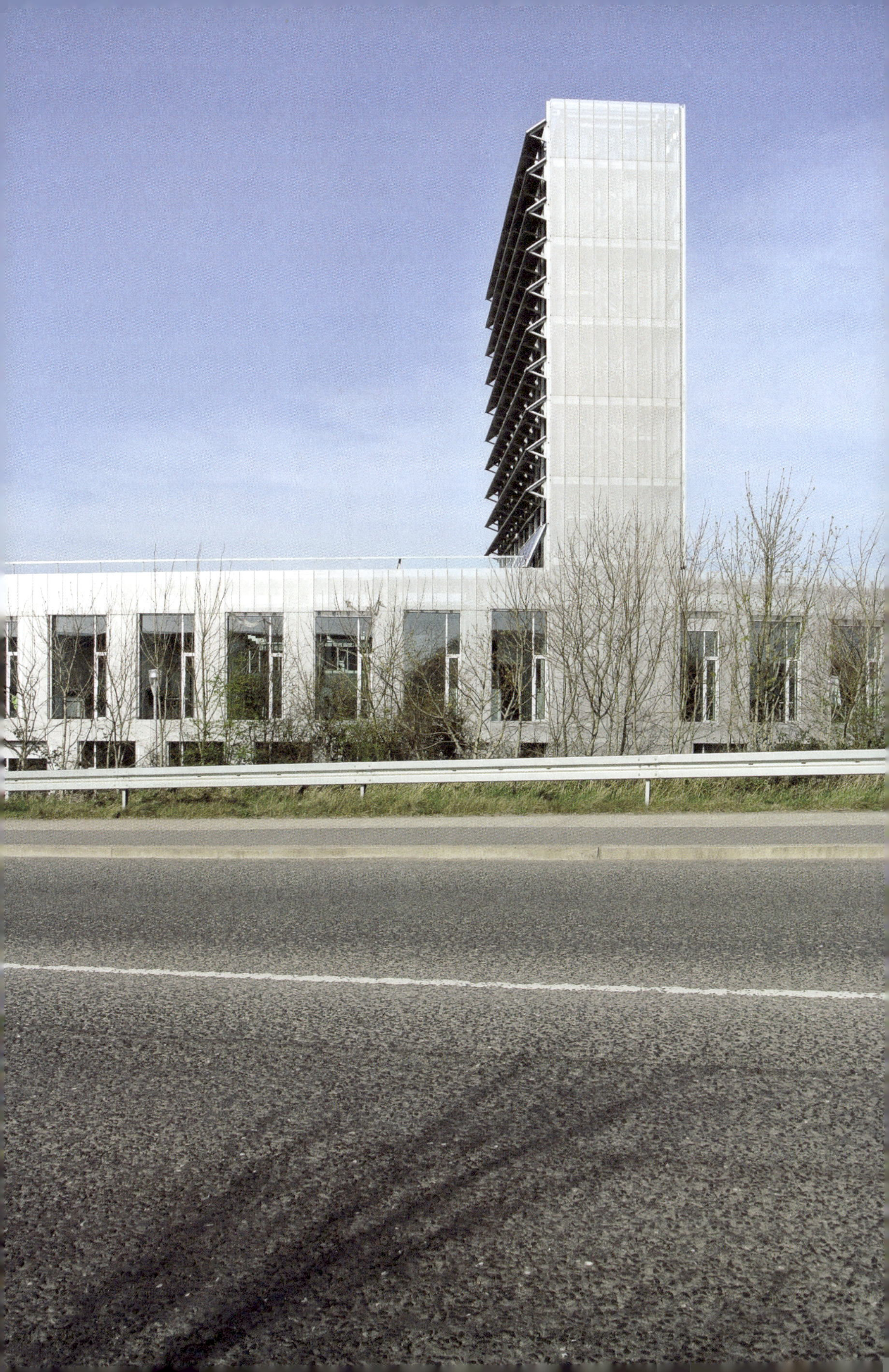

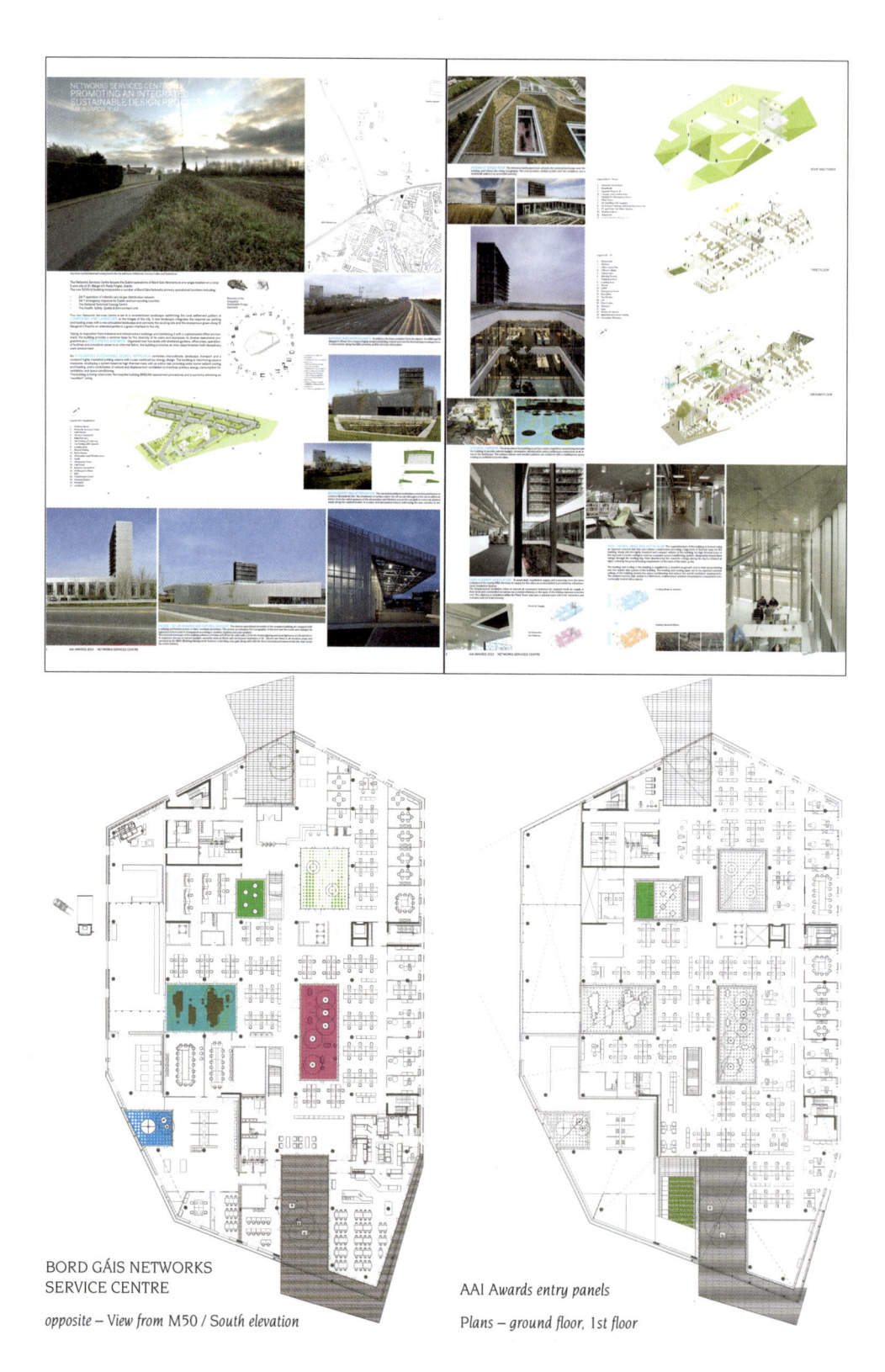

BORD GÁIS NETWORKS
SERVICE CENTRE

opposite – View from M50 / South elevation

AAI Awards entry panels

Plans – ground floor, 1st floor

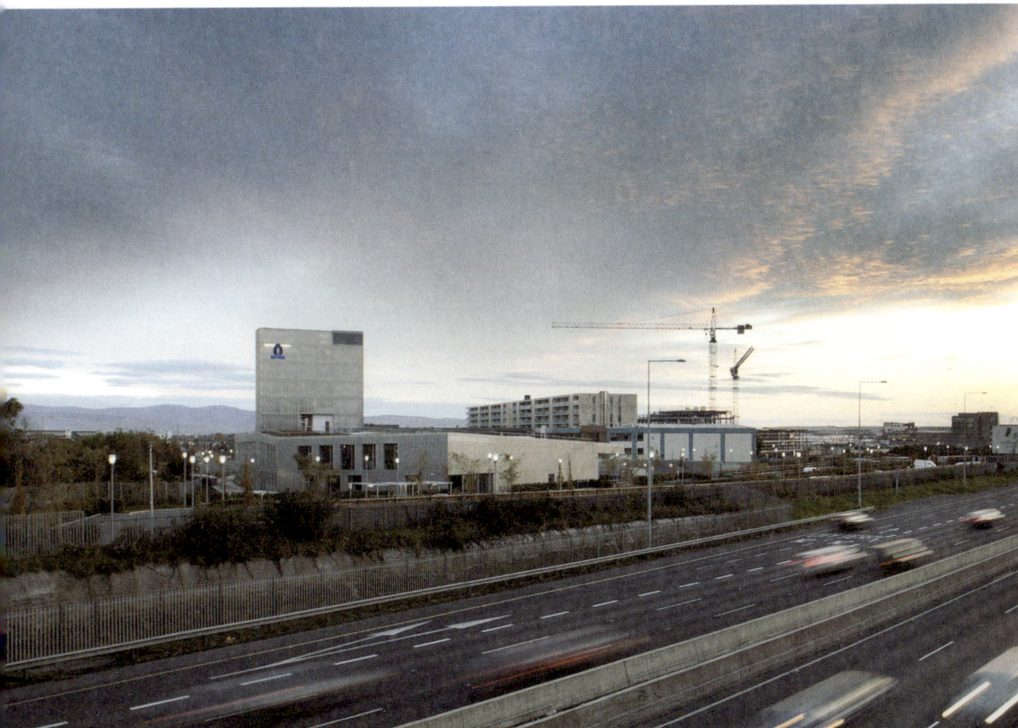

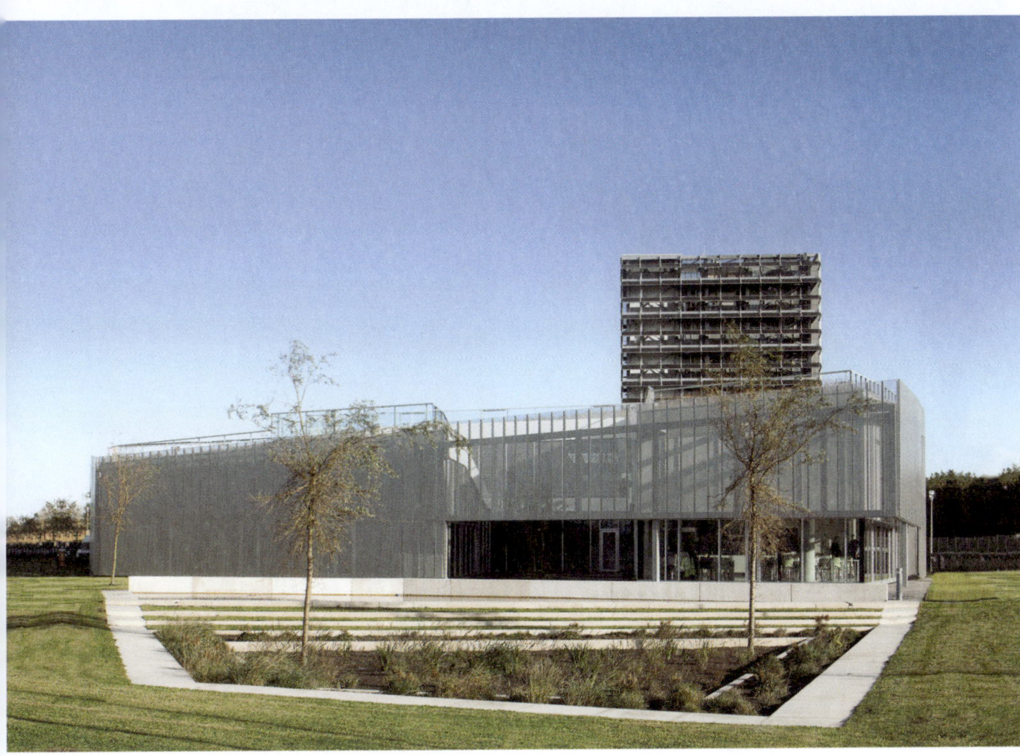

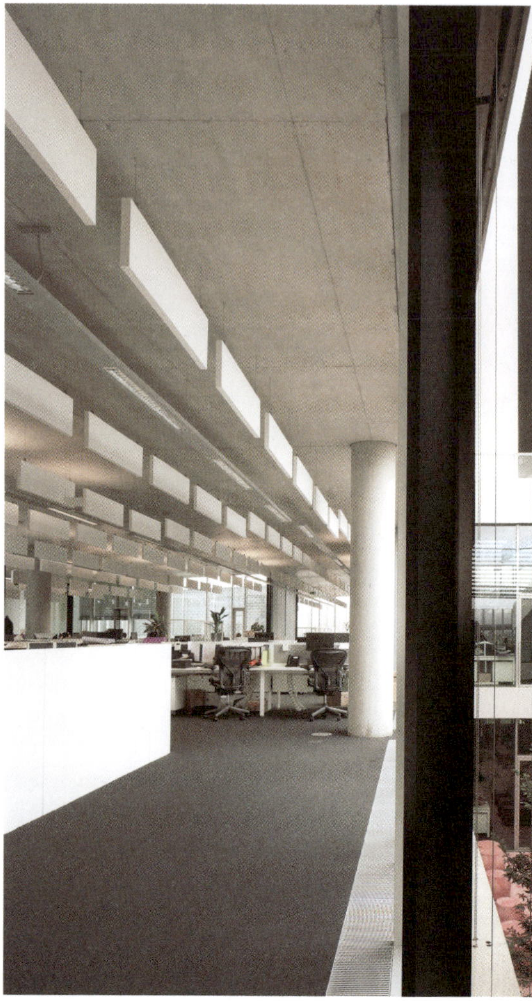

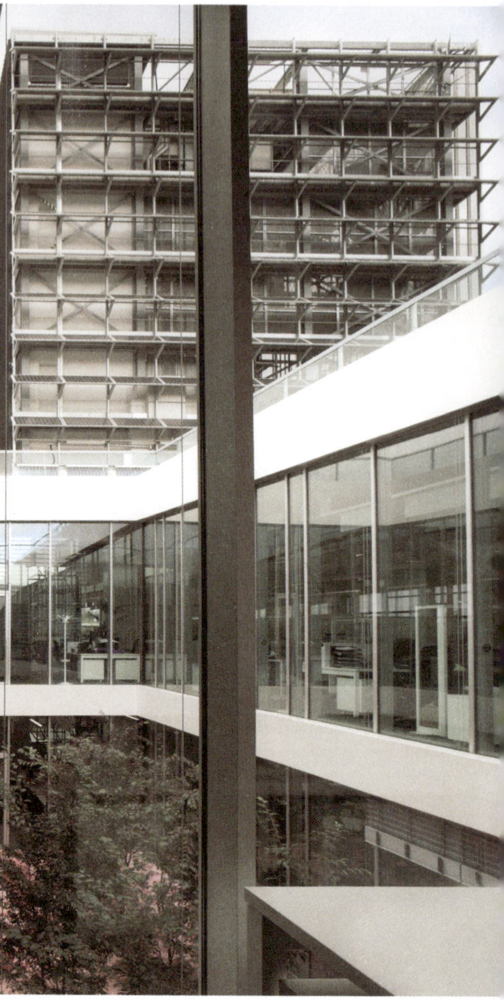

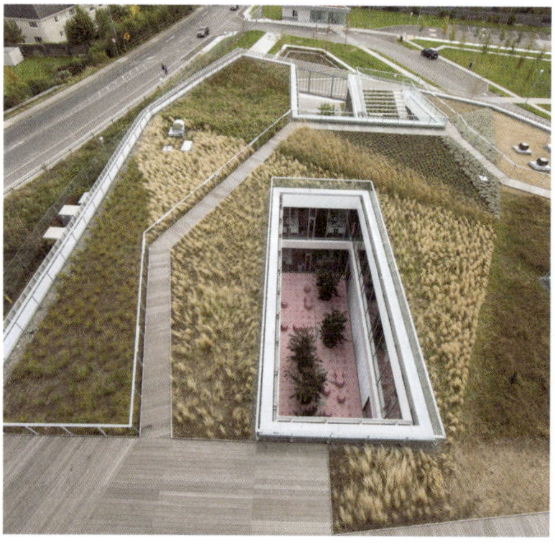

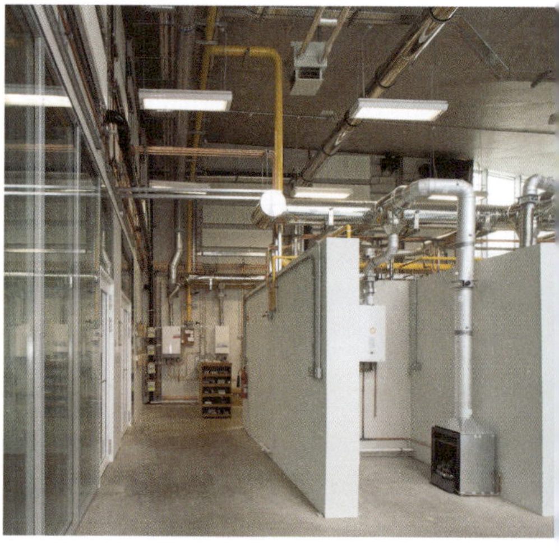

ASSESSORS' COMMENTS

ROSBOTTOM – This is one of those big infrastructural objects that float around on the edge of a city. In this case, however, you can get up on the roof, can't you? And the roof is planted with a kind of prairie. Given that it's not the kind of thing that I normally like, I am quite compelled by some aspects of what this does in the context of being a big scaleless object next to a motorway.

HATZ – I think it's elegant. But it has a bigger agenda of energy management which I can't quite understand.

ROSBOTTOM – Yes, it's elegant, but I don't know how to judge that bigger agenda.

COTTER – I like the fact that this commercial entity has somehow decided it needs to include a sustainable culture. It has a lot of garden integrated into the building, whether or not that's successful… It's interesting that a gas company should begin to involve itself with that – green roof, solar panels, internal gardens.

HATZ – I have some doubts about this project. It seems like a very expensive manifestation of something, but will it work? I mean, the architecture is elegant, but it relies on actually being what it says it is. There's a huge tower for services, so it has to work, but it looks like a lot of building for ventilation and solar panelling.

DE BLACAM – There's also two extensive floors of bürolandschaft office landscape, and it's naturally ventilated because of the stack effect that comes through that courtyard.

HATZ – Overall I find it elegant, and great with these huge ceiling heights for the floors. But then it must be expensive and rather difficult to maintain. I don't understand the courtyards because they seem only made to look good; there is little engagement with them as spaces to use and relate to. If we are to understand this as sustainable design, the solutions seem a bit over-elaborate. I understand the ambitions, and it shows competence, but as an industrial architect of old I wonder could it have been made simpler, easier to maintain, basic and durable over time, possible to alter and add to, yet a good place to work in?

DE BLACAM – It's another one of these projects that is obviously very, very serious, and it needs an architect of considerable ability. It's arising out of a competition, and that's laudable. But we are relying on photographs and drawings here, and that always makes me uneasy.

HICKEY – But this is what we've got, and I'm sympathetic to it, I must say.

COTTER – It pulls a lot of functions that are disparate into a complete whole. But I agree with Elizabeth – I find it a sense of disconnect with this interior garden.

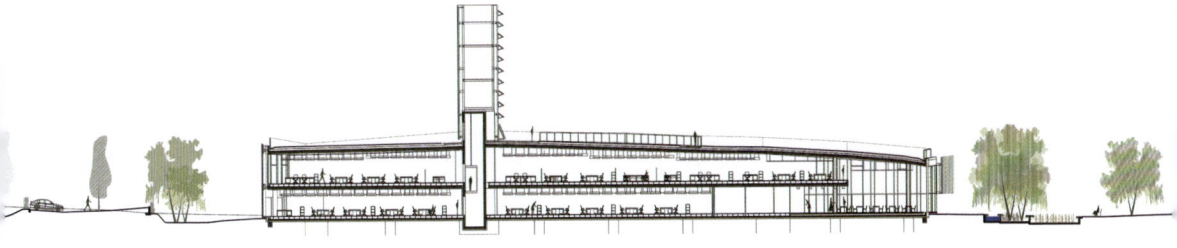

HATZ – You know, there are a lot of serious projects by well-known architects that actually don't work, because the projects themselves lack common sense and the programmes are not thought through. Then the project becomes its own reality and no-one stops to say "Wait a minute; what is actually the task here? Which are the most relevant responses to this, in the long term?"

DE BLACAM – There could be a worry about the environment, that you really are confined to these courtyards, and that it's a sort of prison.

COTTER – There are security aspects to this as well. It reminds me of the new Department of Defence building in Newbridge by Murray O'Laoire, where there are integrated gardens, a notion of softening the interior culture of the building. And this is, in fact, high-risk. It requires a security brief that's not mentioned here. I would imagine that a lot of the candy of the building is disguising the security remit.

DE BLACAM – What security remit could there possibly be working for a gas company?

ROSBOTTOM – I think this is an interesting type – big buildings next to motorways – and although I hear people's reservations about it, it feels to me like it does a reasonably good job. If you actually think about this as being something which is trying to deal with raising aspirations…

HICKEY – …for an unloved condition.

ROSBOTTOM – For a really, really difficult condition or one that people will generally overlook. This is trying quite hard to do something with that as a type, and do it with conviction.

DENIS BYRNE ARCHITECTS was founded in 1998. The practice profile includes master-planning, landscape design, urban design, and furniture and interior design, all pursued within the parameters of larger environmental and social concerns. In all projects, of fundamental importance is the proper placement of the new construction within the character of a given context and the careful consideration of the art and craft of its making. The practice has won awards for 'House in the Field' in Co Westmeath, and the 'Cigar Box' apartments and offices, in Dublin. DESIGN TEAM – Sean Attley, Serena Bastianelli, Roland Bosbach (project architect), Denis Byrne, Louise Clavin, Dave English, Gosia Meder, Marcus Reid, Gustavo Sapina.

DENIS BYRNE ARCHITECTS
26 Nth Great George's St, Dublin 1 – T 01-8788535 / E info@denisbyrnearchitects.ie / W info@denisbyrnearchitects.ie

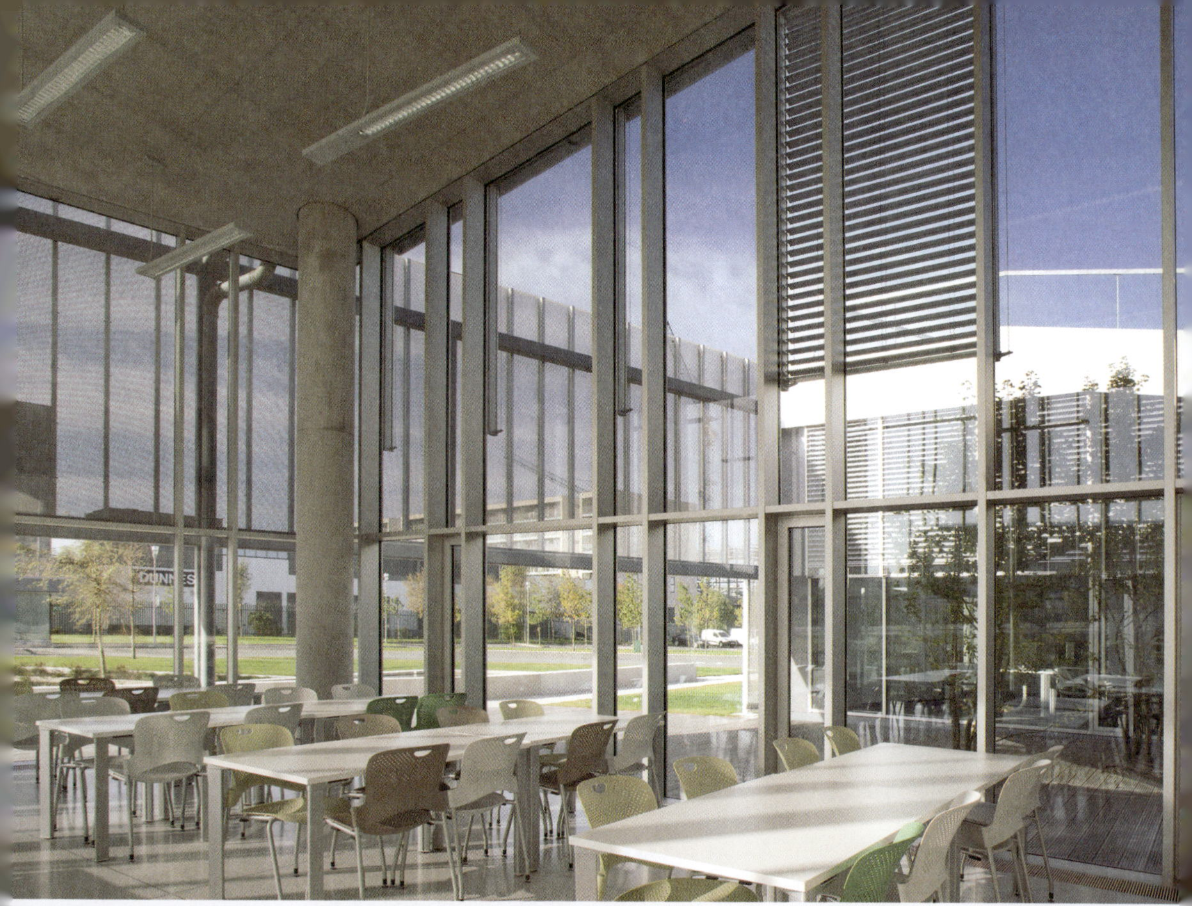
DUNNES

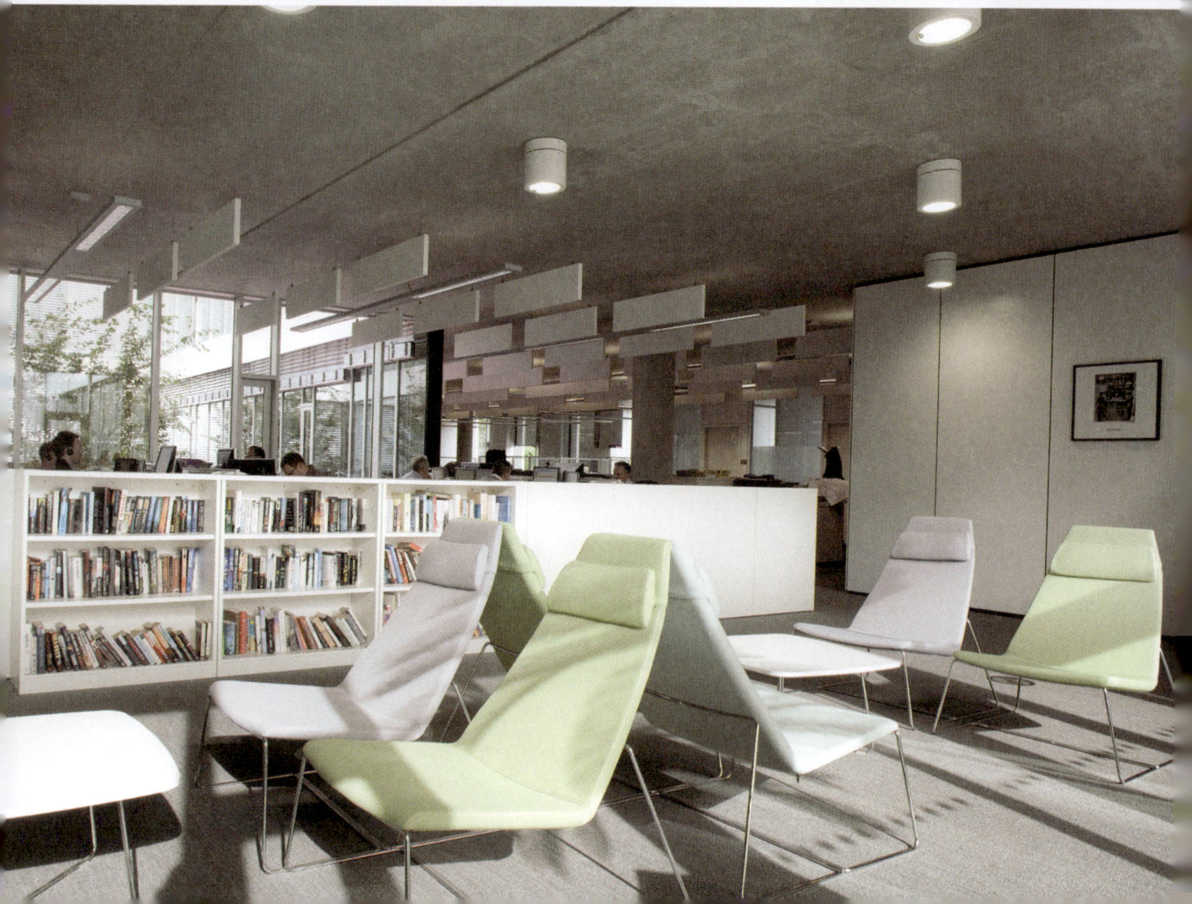

Special Mention

THE GARAGE, Co Fermanagh

JOHN MAGUIRE ARCHITECT

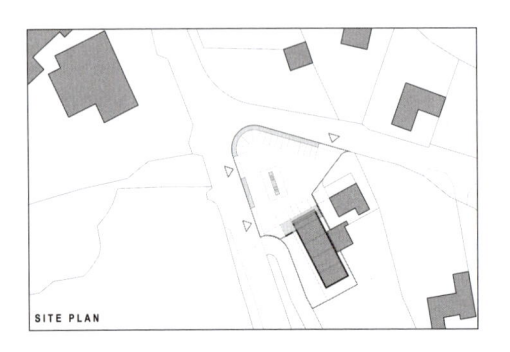

SITE PLAN

This project involved the construction of a new shop and the reconfiguration of an existing forecourt of a previously abandoned service station on the outskirts of a small town in Co Fermanagh. The client wished to recommission the existing fuel tanks and canopy structure, and construct a convenience store on the site.

Adequate commercial parking is key to the success of this type of retail premises, and therefore the shop building is located far back into the site in order to maximise the size of the forecourt. As the budget for the project was extremely low, a cost-effective building structure was required, but one which would create a strong visual impact in order to attract consumers. What was implemented was a building of two parts – a simply constructed main shop enclosure and a visually strong front entrance element. The main shop is a simple portal steel-frame structure, clad in a metallic insulated roof and wall panel. The front structure, formed in steel and blockwork, and finished in sand cement render, is the opposite of the shop enclosure, and provides the strong presence which is attractive to clients. This is similar to the traditional Irish garage which consisted of a shed building with a pitched or barrel-vaulted roof, agricultural in nature, with a false stone front. The project relates to this typology, but forms a more three-dimensional front structure. It provides for a sheltered entrance area, integrated storage for external products, fixed picture window to form a connection between the forecourt and the shop interior, and integrated lighting to enhance its visual impact.

address – Glenwood Filling Station, Mossfield Road, Irvinestown, Co Fermanagh
client – Peter Maguire
photography – Aidan Monaghan

design to completion – 2011-2012
site area – 2,500m^2 / *floor area* – 260m^2
budget – £285,000stg (approx €370,000)

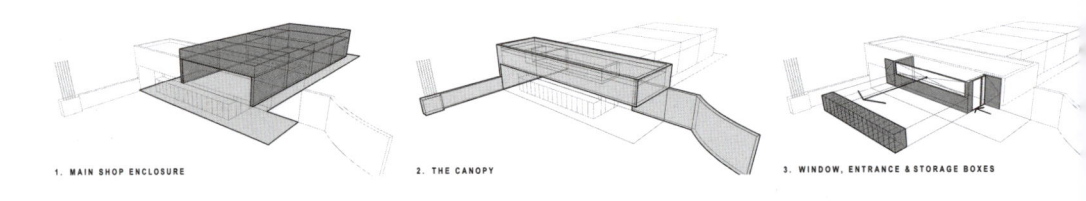

1. MAIN SHOP ENCLOSURE
2. THE CANOPY
3. WINDOW, ENTRANCE & STORAGE BOXES

GROUND FLOOR PLAN

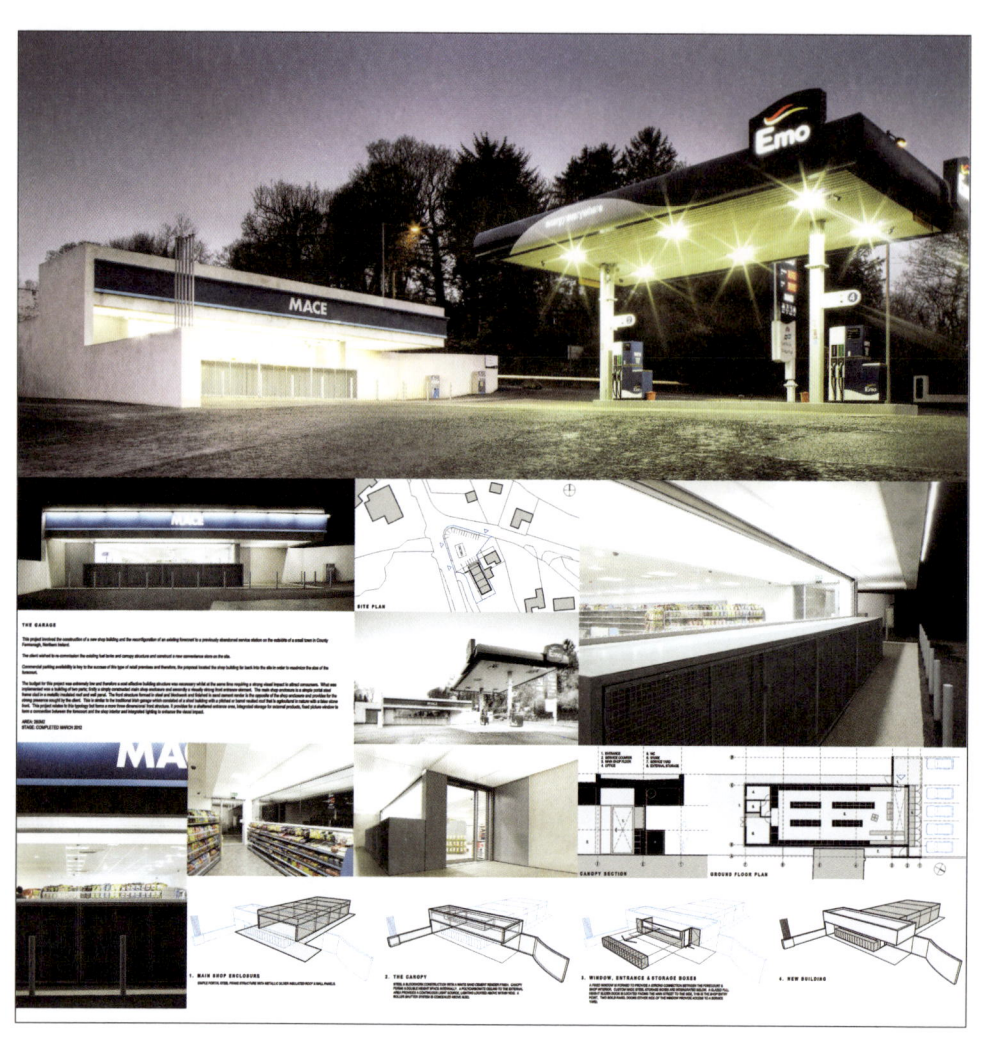

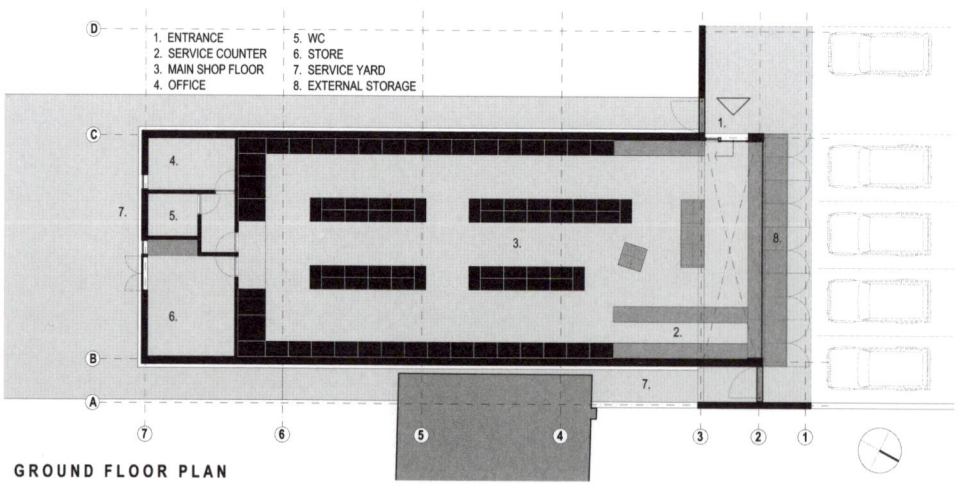

1. ENTRANCE
2. SERVICE COUNTER
3. MAIN SHOP FLOOR
4. OFFICE
5. WC
6. STORE
7. SERVICE YARD
8. EXTERNAL STORAGE

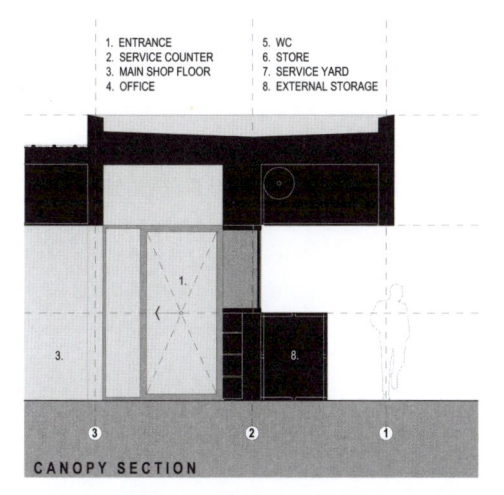

1. ENTRANCE
2. SERVICE COUNTER
3. MAIN SHOP FLOOR
4. OFFICE
5. WC
6. STORE
7. SERVICE YARD
8. EXTERNAL STORAGE

CANOPY SECTION

ASSESSORS' COMMENTS

ROSBOTTOM – I think if you're going to do heroic petrol stations, the canopy is critical. I just wish the architect had been allowed to design the canopy. You know those amazing modernist petrol stations where they did incredible things, like those paintings by Ed Ruscha?

HATZ – But the project was about leaving the existing petrol station and adding a shop. And I think that's fine, because why redesign it when it's there. I think it's quite humorous actually – it has an obliqueness that I like.

COTTER – I was interested in it as a project, but I need another bit of fantasy. It is a sculptural field that it's setting up between these two objects.

ROSBOTTOM – But don't you think it's quite weird that we don't get a view from the car? What do you see when you drive down the road?

HICKEY – Yes, that is bizarre. It's a bit like those sheds that they put those architectural things onto the face of – you know, dance halls and all those kind of things.

HATZ – It made me look a second time. It's something that's all around us, and I just like that someone is handling this. And doing it without making any kind of drama. It's about seeing, and it's not about what things look like. I think it's interesting.

HICKEY – It's not rarified either.

DE BLACAM – I'm not going to stand in the way of it.

HATZ – It's actually about contributing to architecture, and I do think that this does. It contributes in terms of finding ways of being creative with the existing, by reinterpreting what is there and by adding, giving it another sense, reusing.

ROSBOTTOM – Here is someone taking notice of a very contingent, very ordinary building type. That someone actually thinks about that context, considers how to make a 24-hour convenience store in a way that has an architectural intention. Most of the world that we engage with, that we drive or walk past, once you get out of the centres of cities, is full of this stuff. For people to take notice of it and think about it and make the best of it is commendable. I think this is a commendable piece of work.

HATZ – Yes. It's commendable. It contributes.

COTTER – I appreciate the dynamic that says even with this type of building, if good judgement is brought to bear on it, then it can become aesthetically charged. I think it's important to commend ideas that we think are relevant.

ROSBOTTOM – This is trying to elevate a building type that has some kind of civic or cultural presence.

HICKEY – It's trying to make background foreground.

ROSBOTTOM – Well, I think it's just trying to be background quite well. I don't think it's trying to be foreground. It's just trying to give some kind of dignity to the everyday.

JOHN MAGUIRE graduated from Queen's University Belfast in 2004, obtained a Masters of Architecture at the Mackintosh School of Architecture, Glasgow, in 2008, and gained his professional qualification at UCD in 2010. He previously worked with Keys & Monaghan Architects in Fermanagh, Michael Hopkins in London, and Boyd Cody Architects in Dublin, and is currently a senior architect with DTA Architects, Dublin.

JOHN MAGUIRE ARCHITECT – E maguirejohn@mac.com

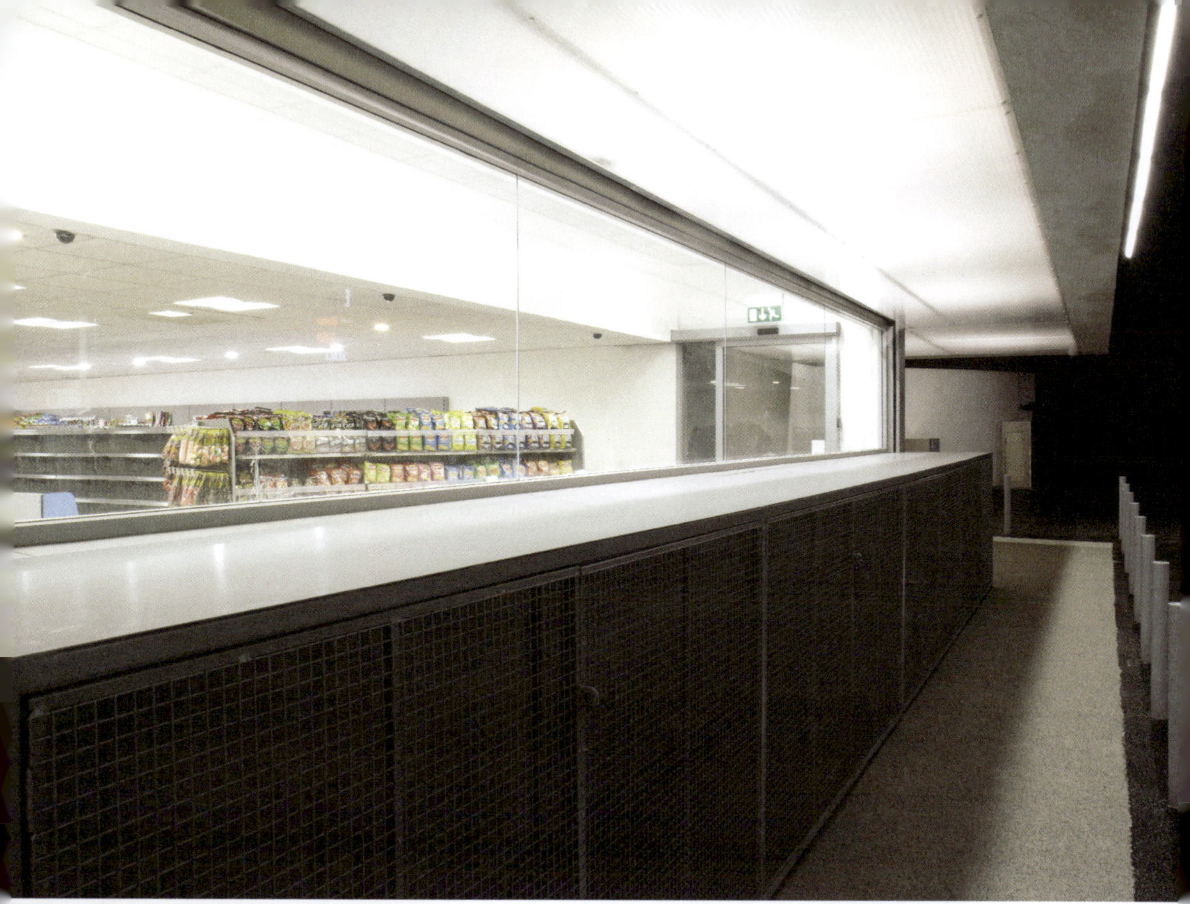

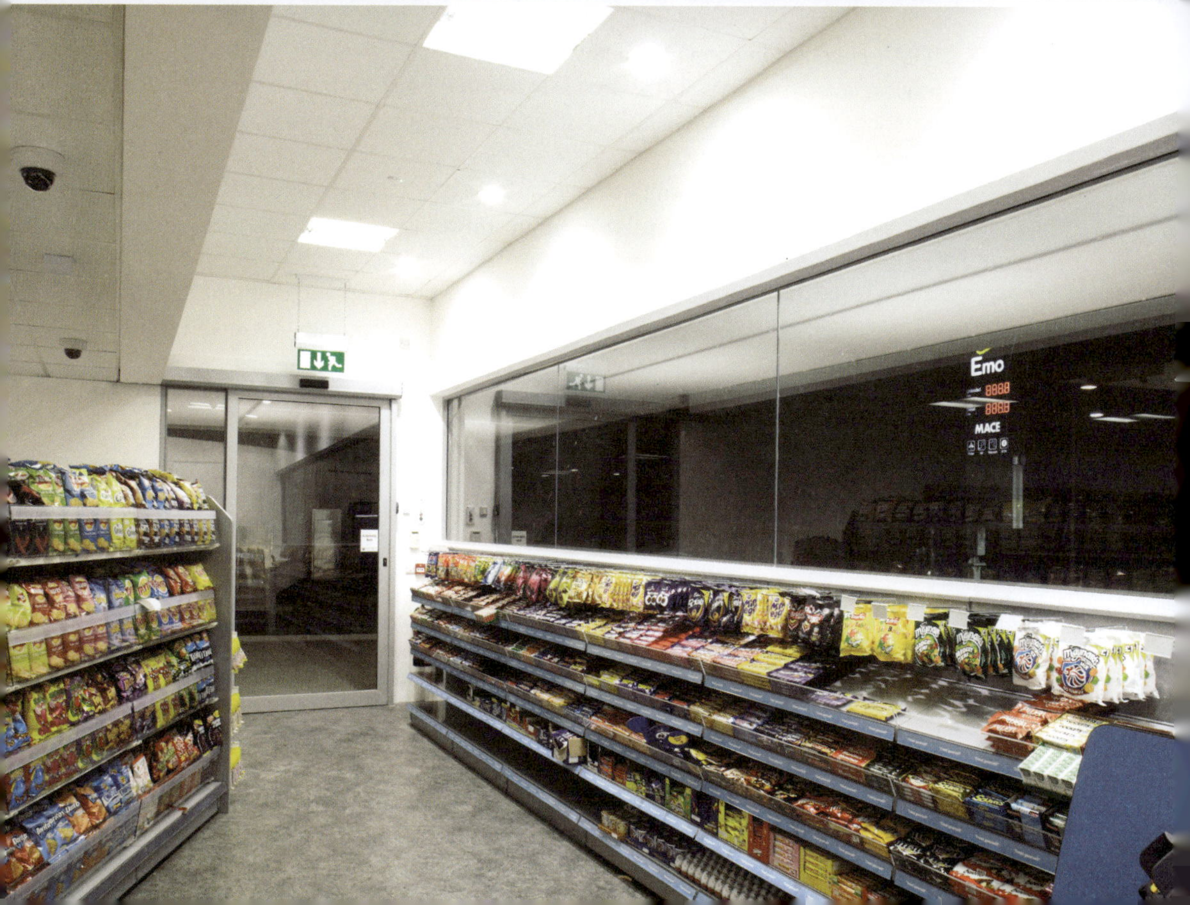
Emo
MACE

Special Mention

VESSEL – La Biennale di Venezia

O'DONNELL + TUOMEY ARCHITECTS

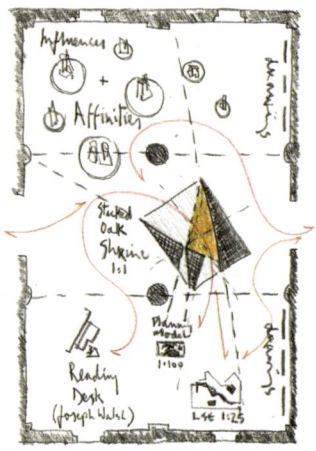

The word "vessel" is suggestive of embodiment, enshrinement and containment. It carries associations of craft and circulation. Airship, boat, blood vessel, utensil. *Vessel* is a site-specific response to the 2012 Venice Biennale theme of "Common Ground", a plank-stacked structure in conversation with the layered brick construction of the Corderie. *Vessel* is a contemplative space hollowed out of solid matter, a light funnel, a lantern chamber, and a passage leading towards our common ground.

Literary and artistic affinities constitute our common ground. Architecture's deeper resonance is related to its wider culture. The work of other architects, artists, poets and performers sustains us. Their work provides inspiration for us to make our own work. Such affinities are part of our cultural context. We have invoked precedent and invited practitioners to contribute to our installation. We have remembered inspirational works and reflected on projects that run parallel to our own pursuits.

Bricks are cast from a mould. Each special brick has to be hand-thrown from its own wooden casing. Clods of clay are dug out from the forest floor and the wood for the mould is cut from the trees. Brick and timber, the raw materials of archaic construction, have not changed much since the shipbuilders built their vessels between the brick columns of the Arsenale.

Common Ground, 13th International Architecture Exhibition of La Biennale di Venezia, Italy

address – Arsenale, Venice, Italy
client – La Biennale di Venezia
photography – Alice Clancy

design to completion – 2012
site area – n/a / floor area – 100m^2
budget – n/a

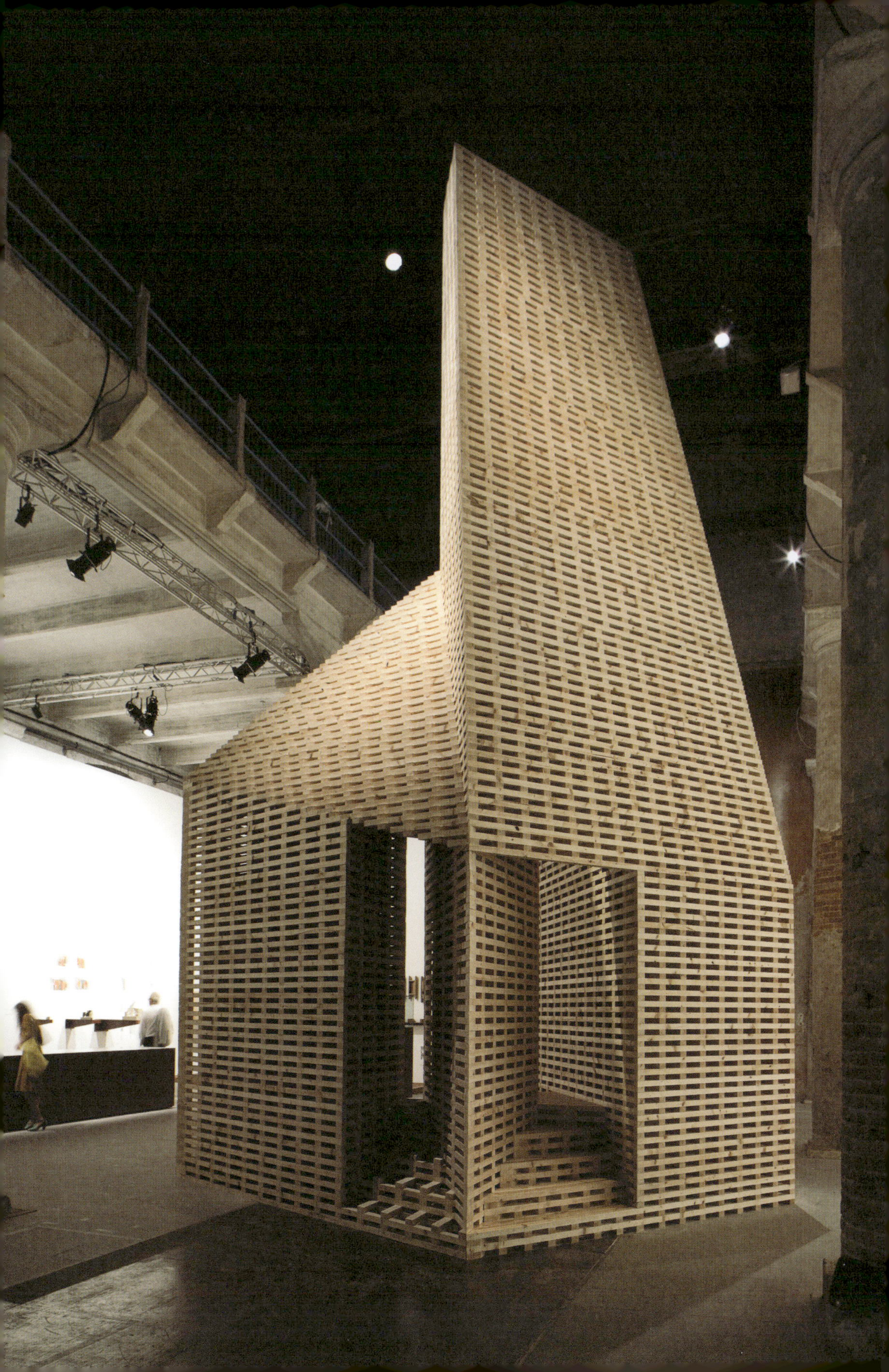

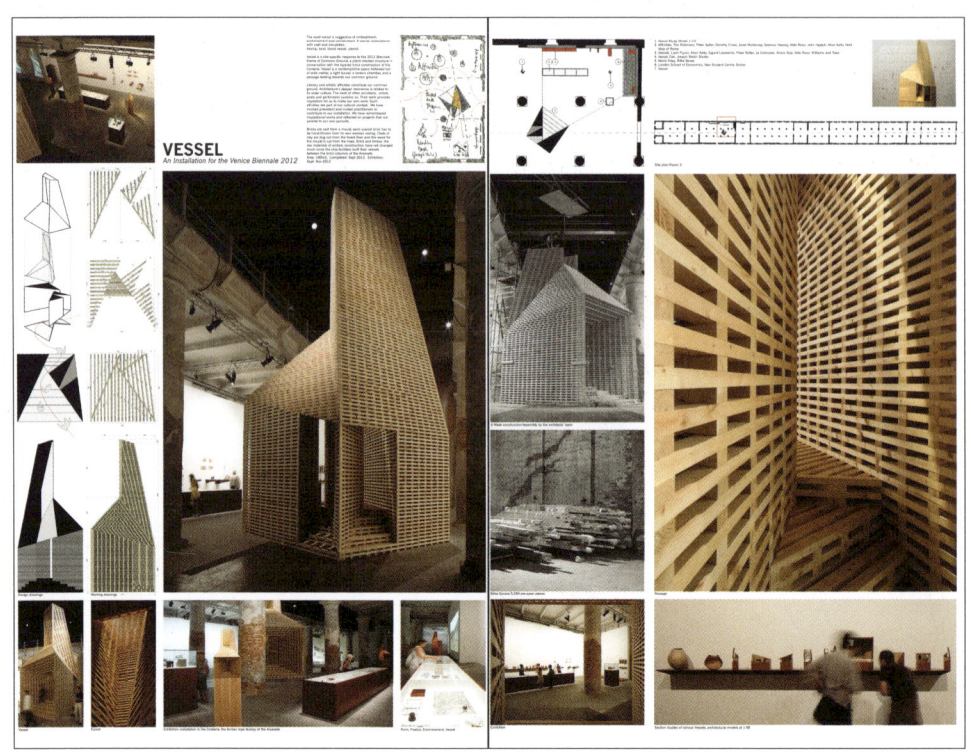

VESSEL

AAI Awards entry panels
Plan of exhibition layout
Exploded axonometric with plan of Vessel

opposite – Construction plans 1, 2, 3 / Section / Elevation

page 156 – Concept sketch / Plan of Corderie

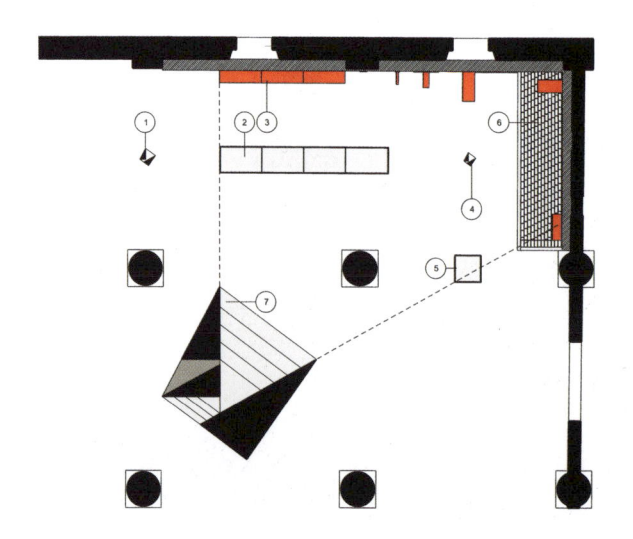

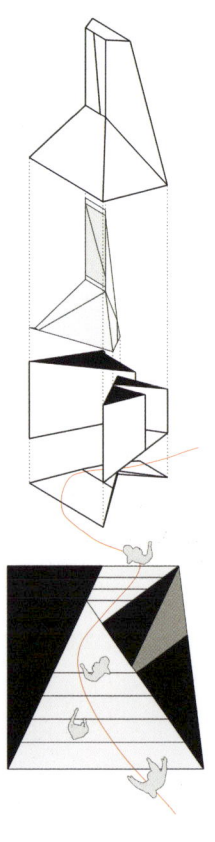

159

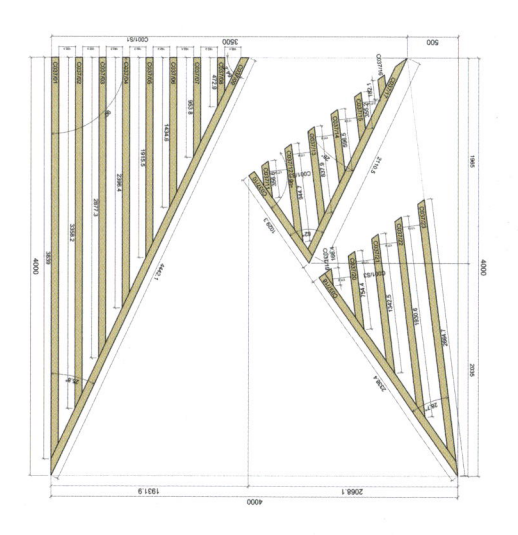

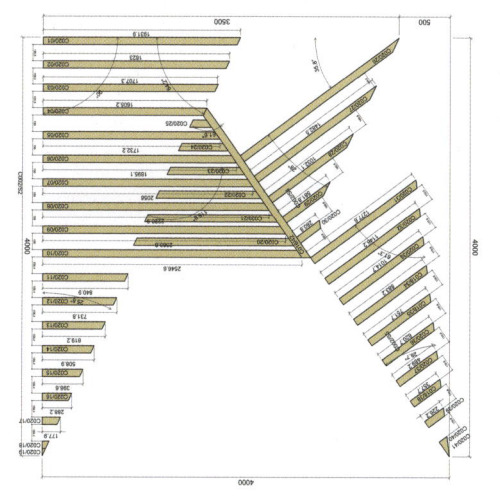

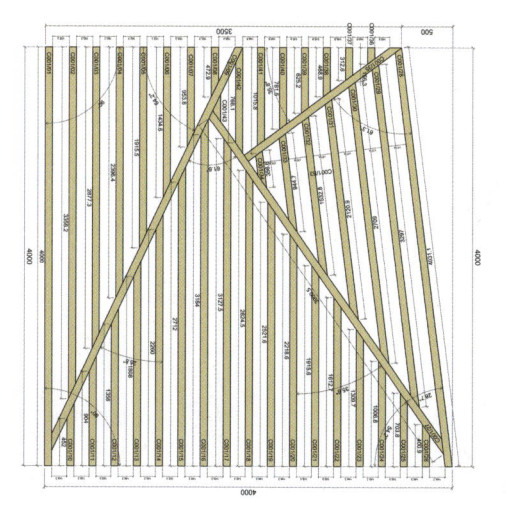

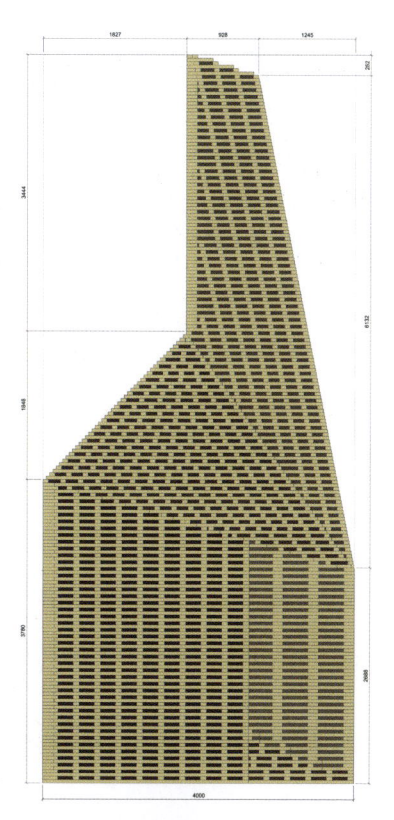

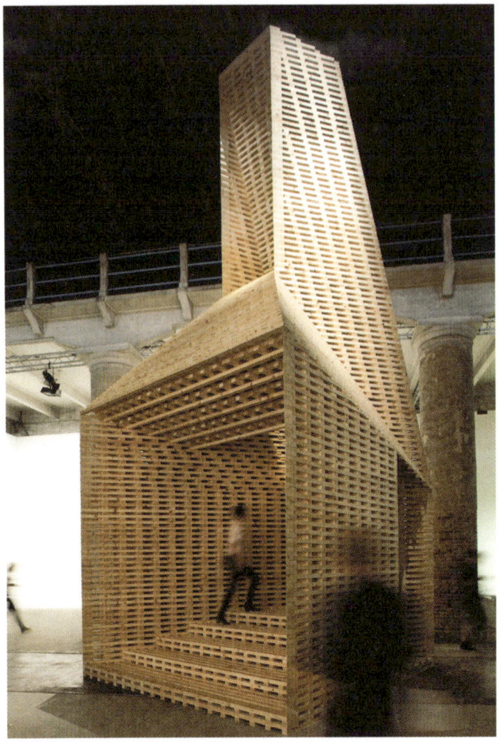

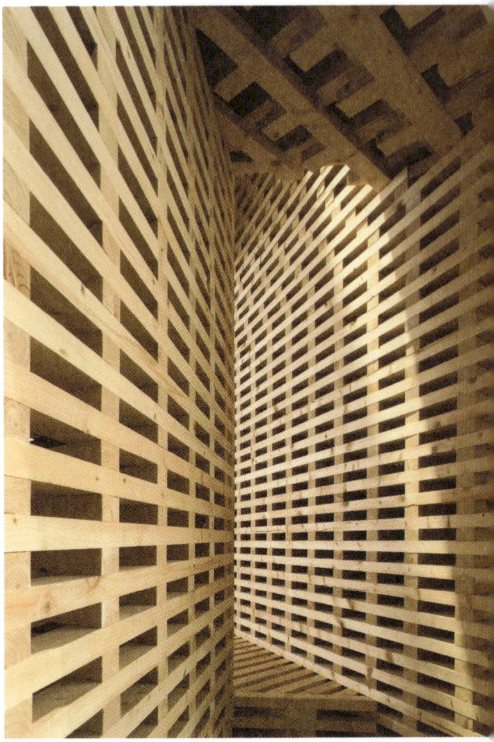

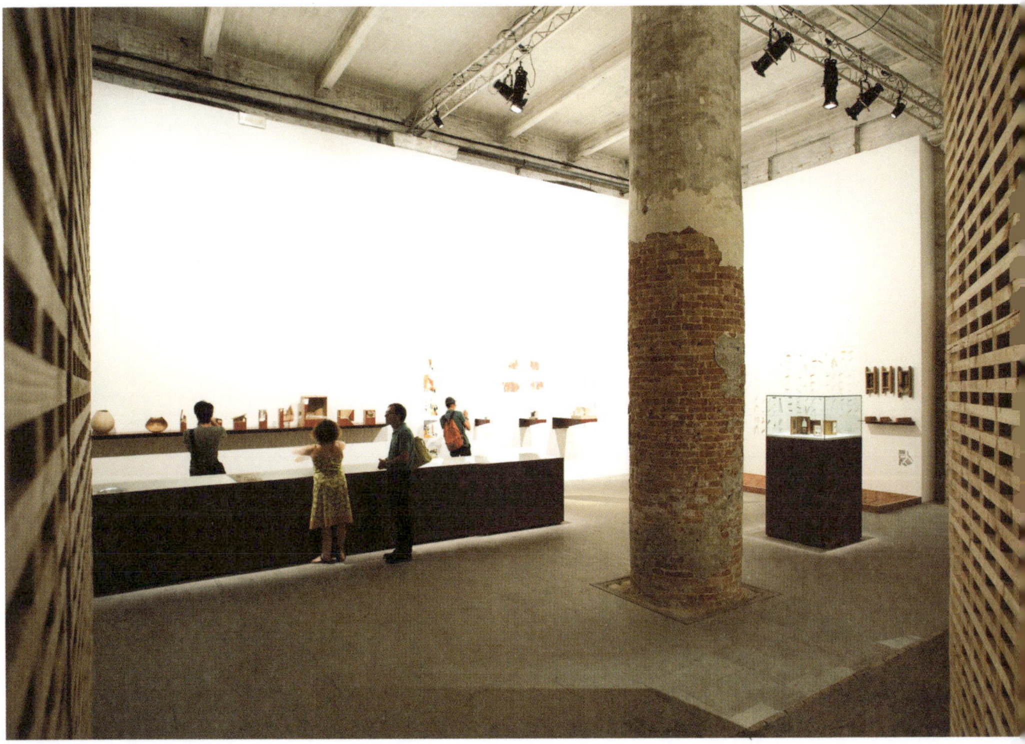

ASSESSORS' COMMENTS

ROSBOTTOM – I've seen this, and I enjoyed it in the context of that place. And I like some of the games it plays. As an exhibition, it did some interesting things, where it was constantly juxtaposing these models with the actuality. So I enjoyed the exhibition, which I guess is what we are judging. This was a really interesting set of pieces.

HATZ – I really find it beautiful, really beautiful. I'm very puzzled by the theme of vessels, because to me a vessel is something you descend into rather than ascend up to. To me this is reminiscent of some vernacular kiln or chimney.

HICKEY – It's not a vessel. I think it misses the point to be honest. It sets out in the text what it's trying to do, and I don't think it does what it's saying it's doing. And that's disappointing. I recognise that it's a very nice thing. It may well have looked like a beautiful piece of furniture where it was, but I don't think it does what it says it's setting out to do, unfortunately.

COTTER – I like how the rhythm in the timber picks up the rhythm in the brick. I really like that aspect of it.

HICKEY – It's timber, but it wants to be brick, doesn't it?

COTTER – I don't know. It's filigree. It's very crafted. I like the passage of air through it. I don't know if you go in there, is there an interior chamber or are you just going right through?

HATZ – It's a passage. But then here you have the upward shift, a kind of mental space.

HICKEY – It's like that old cottage up in the Ulster Folk Museum where the chimney is the space where they smoked fish. But I just don't like it.

HATZ – I would commend it for the beauty of the sculptural effect and the text alone. I am very puzzled by the theme though, and I wonder whether it really works as a kind of contemplative piece.

ROSBOTTOM – It's not. I don't think it was contemplative. I don't think that's what it does.

DE BLACAM – I think it's very lightweight. There's a lot of that stuff in the Biennale, and it actually appeals to the most shallow of motives, I think. But more seriously, the architectural content in it is subjected to a sculptural purpose. I would be very unhappy with it. I think this is very shallow stuff.

HICKEY – I have to agree with you. There's a series of steps that actually don't go anywhere. It looks as if they have all the bits, but they need to take it apart and do it again because it's not doing the things that they say it's doing. Maybe it's really appropriate for Venice, because in Venice you just walk through. And if that's what it's doing, maybe that's okay. Venice is littered with projects like this.

DE BLACAM – We're asked to love it, you see, because of its shape, and that's what's really the most base and the most shallow motive in architecture.

COTTER – But there is one aspect that I like in terms of the context of the Arsenale. When you go through that space, it's very dry and very solid, and it's nice to come across something that's light. So contextually I could understand it, it works, and I like it.

DE BLACAM – But there are a dozen of those in the Biennale, and there's now one up in the Mater hospital on the North Circular Road. I actually don't think it's a pavilion at all. It's a work of art.

HICKEY – And then it has no responsibility. But we're not talking about art here.

HATZ – I don't understand the vessel thing. I try to relate it to a whole set of other kind of beacons in Irish architecture, which has this mental space, which is upwards. In Synge's Cottage on Inis Meáin you sit right next to the fireplace, feeling drawn up into its dark chimney. You seem to have nowhere to dwell here. It looks a bit awkward to me to walk on this. But maybe the mental space is enough.

COTTER – The question about the art or the sculpture or the building… For me, if it had a slightly closed skin and if you had that moirée translucence through the thing, and if it created the mystique of potential going but not going, I think then it would come close to being a work of art.

HICKEY – But that's not why it's here.

ROSBOTTOM – I thought it was an interesting exhibition in the context of Venice. It was one of the things that made me stop. And in the freneticness of the Arsenale, there was a holistic-ness about a series of pieces that spoke to each other, which I enjoyed.

COTTER – For me, it's critical that I understand the way the object closes off and opens, how it offers and closes itself. And it suggests to me that it does that when you walk around it.

ROSBOTTOM – I agree. It's about form. It's a formal piece. I think that's absolutely true.

HICKEY – It's not a vessel then. That's what they said.

COTTER – It doesn't have to be a totally literal description just because the title's "Vessel". It can be suggestive of the notion of containment.

HATZ – But a vessel is an amazing thing, and also, potentially, very architectural. But this doesn't quite seem to explore that, does it?

ROSBOTTOM – It's an intriguing question, that. If what you're saying is does it fulfil its own intention, then you might, perhaps, say no, it doesn't. However I think as an object and as a piece of construction, it's skilful and interesting, and I enjoyed it.

COTTER – It's an installation of engagement with an evolved language of its own, and there's a real sense of judgement in how things are placed, and how that's articulated, but I would need to experience that in its totality. My feelings towards it are positive. I wouldn't put it down just because it's called "Vessel" – my understanding of a vessel is something that allows something to pass through it also.

ROSBOTTOM – And those are the things that I enjoyed in it, these moments where it was playing scale games, so as a constellation of things I thought it was strong.

O'DONNELL + TUOMEY ARCHITECTS was established by Sheila O'Donnell and John Tuomey in 1988. Winners of more than 80 national and international awards, including 7-time winner of the AAI Downes Bronze Medal, 5-time finalist for the Mies Van der Rohe Award for European Architecture, shortlisted 5 times for the Stirling Prize and twice for the Lubetkin Prize. Also winners of the RIAI Gold Medal in 2005 and the 2015 RIBA Royal Gold Medal. Their work has been exhibited in architecture galleries in London, Ljubljana, New York, Paris and Tokyo. Currently working on a master plan for the Central European University, Budapest, with the first phase due for completion in 2016. DESIGN TEAM – John Tuomey, Sheila O'Donnell, Brian Barber, Laura Harty, Jonathan Janssens, Donn Holohan, Gary Watkin.

O'DONNELL + TUOMEY ARCHITECTS
20a Camden Row, Dublin 8 – T 01-4752500 / F 01-4751479 / E info@odonnell-tuomey.ie / W www.odonnell-tuomey.ie

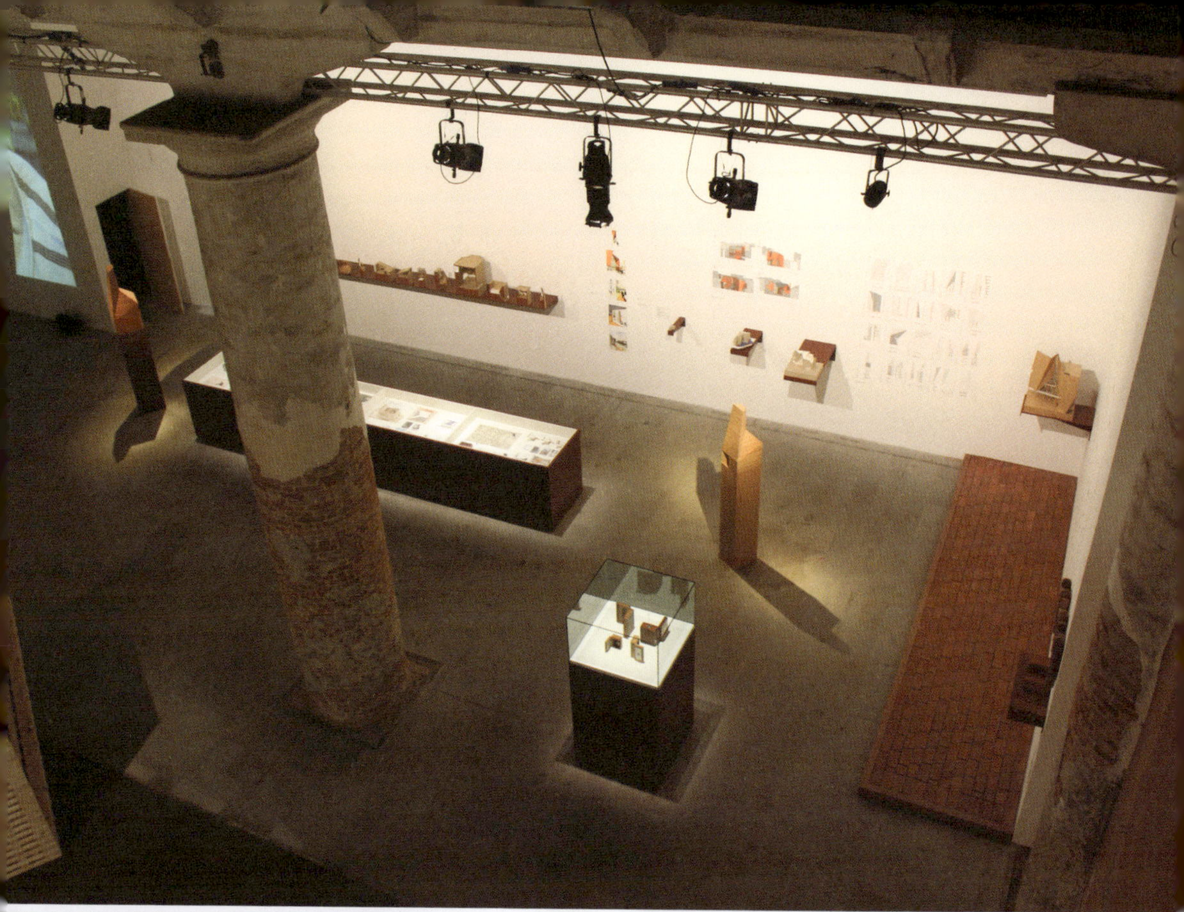

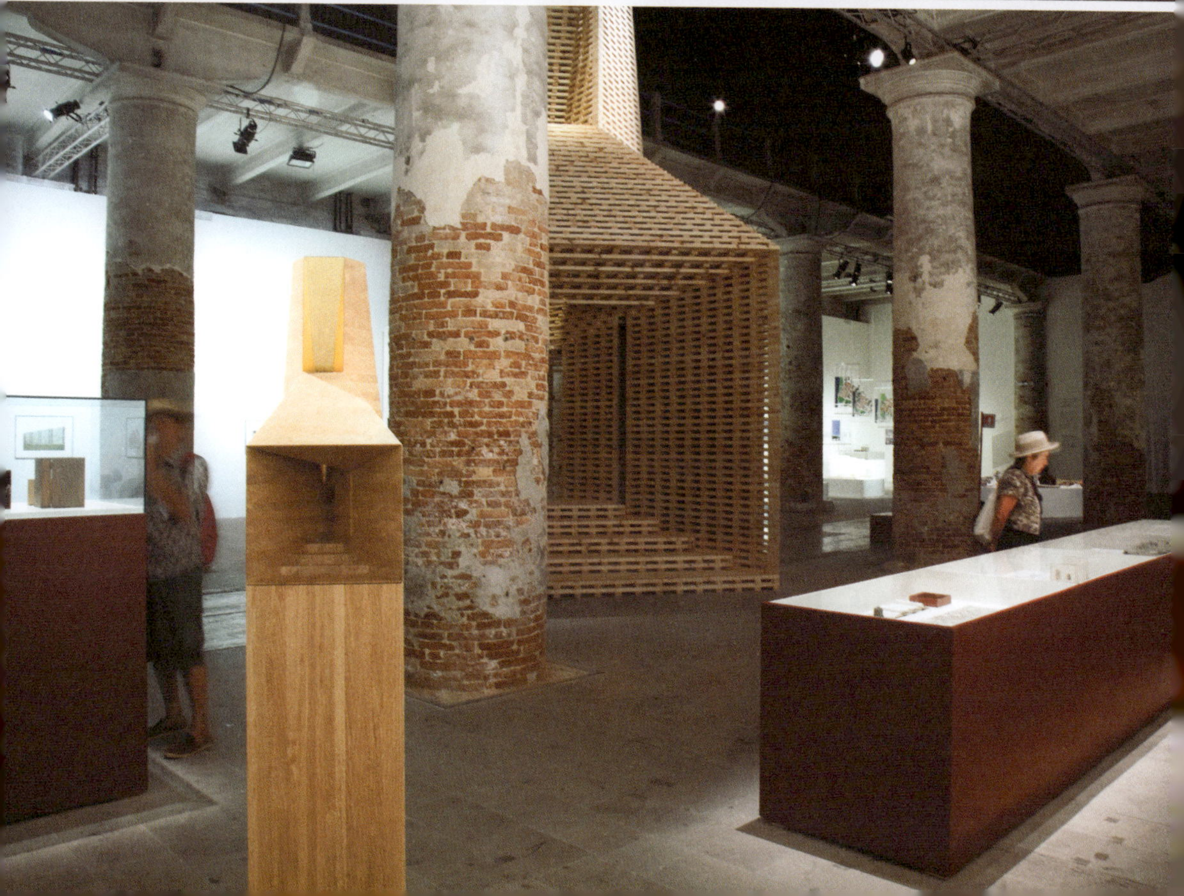

ARCHITECTURAL ASSOCIATION OF IRELAND

SPONSORS & SUPPORTERS, 2016-17

- AAI FRIEND – €350
Architectural Farm
Aughey O'Flaherty Architects
Broadstone Architects
Bucholz McEvoy Architects
DMVF Architects
FKL Architects
GKMP Architects
Grafton Architects
McCullough Mulvin Architects
McGarry Ní Éanaigh Architects
O'Connell Mahon Architects
O'Donnell + Tuomey Architects
O'Mahony Pike Architects
RKD Architects
Robin Mandal Architects
Scott Tallon Walker Architects
Taylor Architects
Urban Agency

- AAI EDUCATION PARTNER – €500
Department of History of Art and Architecture, Trinity College Dublin
Dublin School of Architecture DIT
School of Architecture, University of Limerick
Queen's University Belfast

- AAI PATRON – €1,500
darc space
Embassy of Portugal in Ireland
Embassy of France in Ireland
Embassy of Switzerland in Ireland
Gandon Editions
Irish Architecture Foundation
Irish Concrete Society
Irish Landscape Institute
Royal Institute of the Architects of Ireland

Continued thanks to Denis Byrne Architects

ARCHITECTURAL ASSOCIATION OF IRELAND

The AAI was founded in 1896 "to promote and afford facilities for the study of architecture and the allied sciences and arts and to provide a medium of friendly communication between members and others interested in the progress of architecture."

MEMBERSHIP

Membership of the AAI is open to architects, architectural students, and anyone interested in architecture.
Under our new membership structure, standard AAI membership is now free, and entry to AAI lectures and site visits will be charged at €5 per event, unless stated otherwise in the events programme. There will be an additional charge of €5 for those who wish to avail of CPD certificates for these events. The AAI Annual Pass entitles members to free entry to all AAI events and the free issuing of CPD certificates, if required. Practices entering the AAI Awards must hold at least one AAI Annual Pass. The membership fee structure is as follows:
– membership – free
– Annual Pass (standard) – €80
– Annual Pass (student, retired or unemployed) – €20
– Annual Pass (other approved organisation) – €20
Membership runs from September-August.
Applications for membership can be made through www.architecturalassociation.ie.

ARCHITECTURAL ASSOCIATION OF IRELAND
26 Nth Great George's Street, Dublin 1
E contact@architecturalassociation.ie
W www.architecturalassociation.ie

MAURICE CRAIG AWARD

AAI COMMITTEE 2012-13

Fergus Naughton, *president*
Colm Moore, *vice-president / programme officer*
Mike O'Dell, *treasurer*
Robert Bourke, *sponsorship officer*
Colm Dunbar, *membership officer*
Donal Colfer, *mentoring forum*
Douglas Carson, *ex-officio*

Noreile Breen	Rae Moore
Alice Clancy	Cormac Nolan
Antoin Doyle	Amy O'Connor
Kate Gannon	Ellen Rowley
Ronan McCann	Michael Stack
Conor McGowan	Ian Tracy

AAI COMMITTEE 2016-17

Ronan McCann, *president / programme officer*
Michael Hayes, *vice-president / publications officer*
Deirdre Spring, *vice-president / secretary*
Amelie Conway, *treasurer*
Elaine Hanna, *Awards officer*
Alanah Doyle, *publicity officer*
Aisling Kehoe, *membership officer*
Helen McCormack, *competitions / workshops officer*
Katie Browne, *website officer*
Aprar Elawad, *podcast officer*
Louise Clavin, *exhibitions officer*
Ailish Walker, *publications officer*

Darragh Breathnach	Oana Miculas
John Flynn	Claudia Murray
Banbha McCann	Michael Stack

The Maurice Craig Award for final year thesis projects was created by the Architectural Association of Ireland in 2011 as an additional category within its annual awards scheme. This award, and any further commendations, is bestowed at the discretion of the jury, with the results published alongside the main awards.

Established in honour of the Belfast-born architectural historian, conservation advocate, model-shipbuilder and poet, Maurice Craig (1919-2011), this award is supported by all the schools of architecture in Ireland, to whom the AAI is grateful.

The assessors for the Maurice Craig Award 2013 were: Elizabeth Hatz, Daniel Rosbottom, Shane de Blacam, Donal Hickey and Maud Cotter.

Maurice Craig Award

MEDIATING GEOGRAPHY: THRESHOLD PLACES

ALAN HILLIARD (School of Architecture, University of Limerick)

The investigations in this project are based on ideas of threshold and mediation in architecture. Movement or mediation between distinct places implies thresholds – skin, walls, doors, bridges etc. This mediating geography describes the physical conditions of the elements that enclose, separate and negotiate between us and the surrounding world. These elements have a duration and an intensity of experience as we pass through them or a power as they enfold. Exploring mediations at various scales, from the city to the house, and the door to the skin, furthers the ideas of an architecture of reconciliation (reconciling between two or more specific places). This is about finding an architecture based on the meeting place between conditions – light and dark, public and private, fast and slow – which might become more than an object building, to be a geography of mediation which meaningfully describes the spaces, structures, programmes and experiences of inhabitation.

Following my investigations in mediation and the space between conditions, the programme for the project developed as a place of performance, including making, movement and learning as part of performance. The traditional thresholds between actor and spectator are questioned and spaces of circulation (procession) mix with programmed spaces (ritual), creating experiential relationships between active and passive users. Along with performances, events, rehearsal and teaching spaces, the programme extends to costume and stage set making as well as the making of stage boats which move up river to interact with the city, making the river part of the public space of the city and testing the boundaries/thresholds of inhabitation along the river edge.

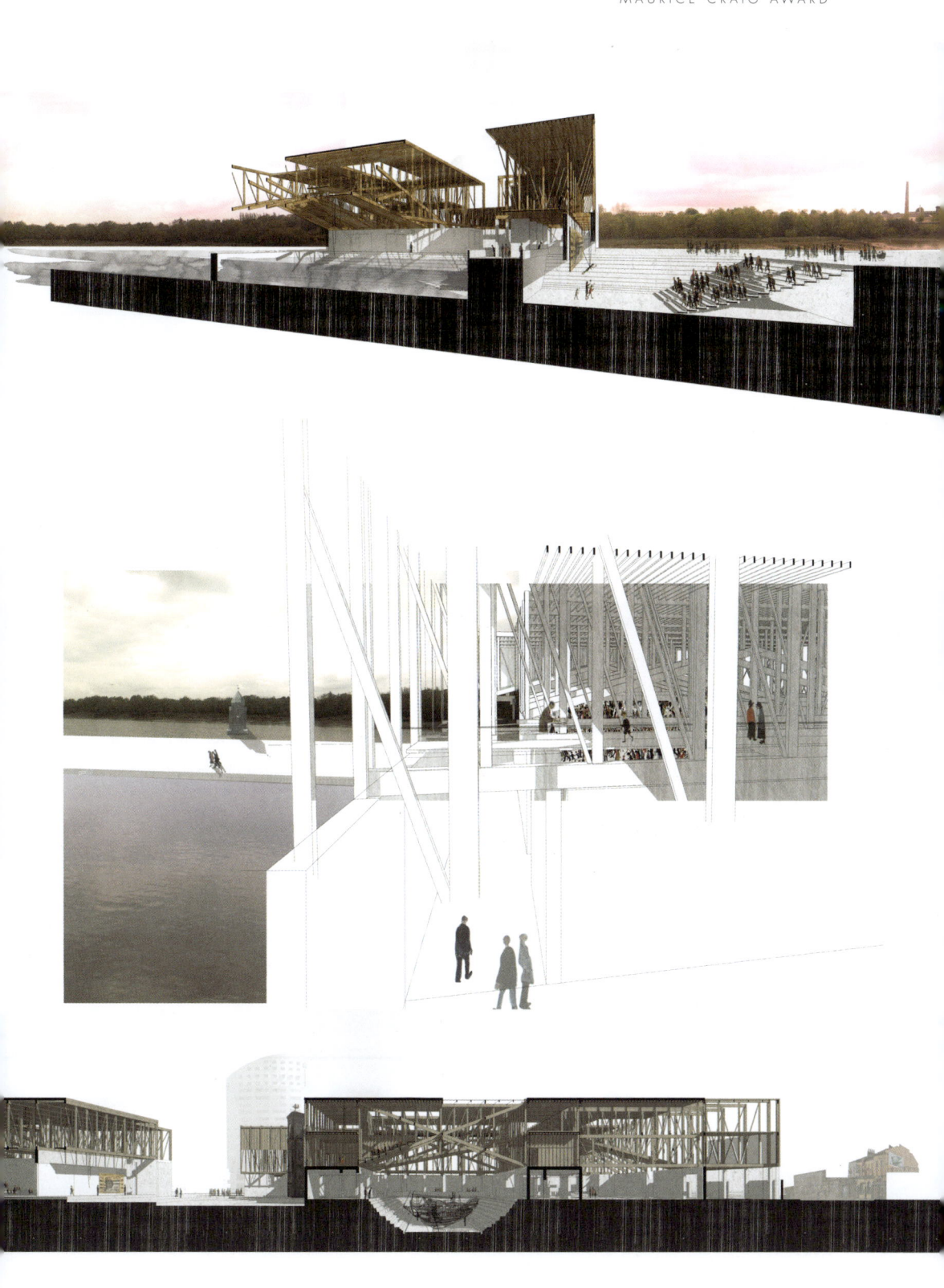

MAURICE CRAIG AWARD

MAURICE CRAIG AWARD

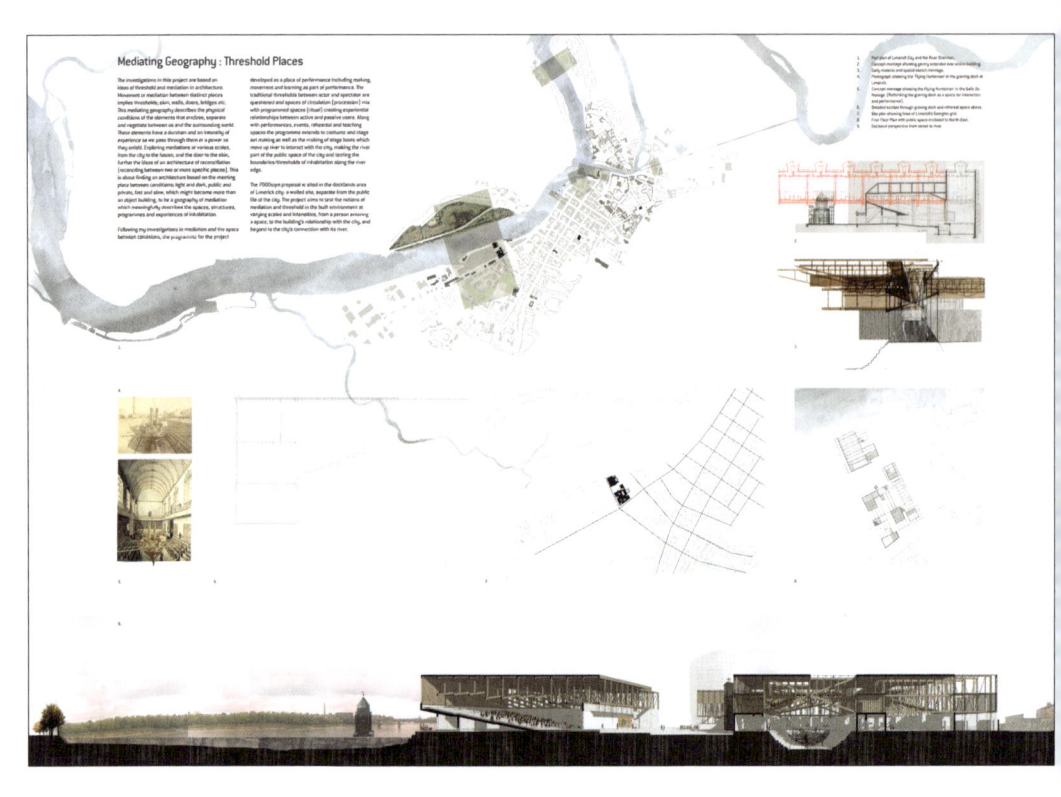

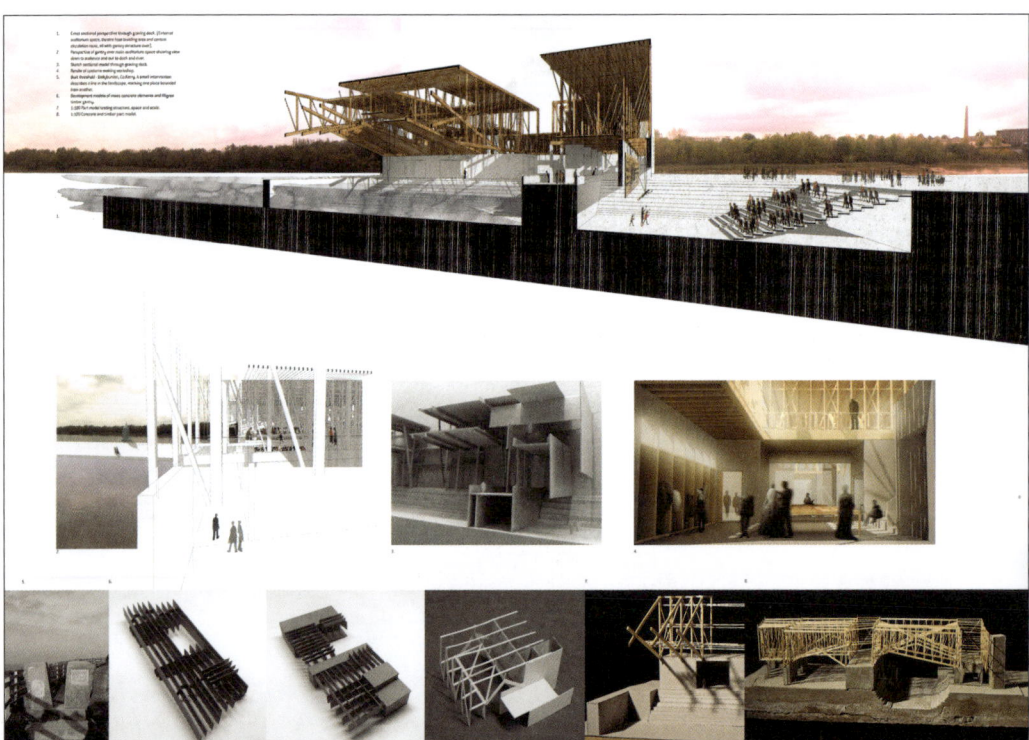

Mediating Geography : Threshold Places

MAURICE CRAIG AWARD

MEDIATING GEOGRAPHY:
THRESHOLD PLACES

Study models

opposite – Maurice Craig Award entry panels

The traditional gantry over the stage extends over the entire programme allowing for its use and experience in all parts of the project. Moving up into this traditionally private space of the theatre becomes part of the structure and daily public use of the space.

The proposal is sited in the docklands area of Limerick city – a walled site, separate from the public life of the city. The continuous wall surrounding the docks makes it hidden from view and inaccessible. Once a thriving dock, it has more recently been in decline, and its main income now comes from the storage and export of scrap metal, as well as importing fertilizer. It is relatively underused and there have been calls in recent years for its redevelopment, with mixed-use housing and retail.

The project aims to test the notions of mediation and threshold in the built environment at varying scales and intensities, from a person entering a space, to the building's relationship with the city and beyond, to the city's connection with its river. The bias towards form-making and programmed 'rooms' which we move between as quickly as possible shifts to highlight the importance of the geography of the space between and the way in which we traverse it. In the inhabitation of and protection from the surrounding elements, every opening (door, window, vent, etc), circulation space or enclosing envelope, everything which describes a point of mediation/transition in the built environment, takes on a significance beyond physical necessity, becoming social and psychological expressions.

INHABITED THRESHOLD, Schaerbeek, Brussels

EIMEAR MURPHY (Queen's University, Belfast)

Schaerbeek in Brussels is characterised by meandering streets meeting at staggered junctions. Where the streets meet, a 'room' within the city is created, around which micro-economies are centred. At each street corner, bordering the room, sits a shared building – for instance, a launderette, a barber shop, a grocery store. This thesis grew from a series of sketches of the 'room' conditions along a route in Schaerbeek.

A distinct sense of occupancy can be observed in the room. In the morning, old men sit on the windowsills of the corner shop where they have just bought their local paper; in the afternoon, the doorways play host to a huddle of women, stopping to chat as they pick up their groceries.

The proposed language and literacy centre will sit on the corner of Rue l'Olivier and Rue Jospaphat, providing spaces to learn and live in. It must not only preserve the transience of the 'room' which it borders, but should also contribute. The threshold between user and dweller thus becomes important and must facilitate cohabitation.

The centre greets the street corner with an open loggia, offering a solid but permeable block. The concrete structure of the loggia breaks, bends and folds to allow staircases to penetrate and to provide seating in the form of concrete benches. In order to translate the monolithic concrete structure into a more human scale, everything to be touched, tread upon, or sat upon will be lined in warm brick.

Within the entrance space there is a main staircase which draws you up to the first room of assembly. Beyond this space, the building becomes an open extension of the street and continues the loggia to the upper floors. Like Schaerbeek, the building is characterised by walkways and routes creating shared rooms at intervals, where people sit, or hang their washing from the concrete structure overhead.

MAURICE CRAIG AWARD

Ground Floor Entrance

Shared walkway outside apartments

Shared walkway outside apartments

171

HILL WALKERS' SHELTER
AAI DESIGN COMPETITION FOR SECOND YEAR STUDENTS 2013

Facilities required

You are required to design a hill walkers' shelter along a walking route over a mountain in Connemara. Your design is to be part of a Rural Environment Protection Scheme (REPS) where nine farmers will build and maintain the shelter and any access gates/styles along the walking route through their lands.

This basic project for a small shelter, just 10m^2 in size, is intended to challenge the designer to find meaning and clarity in their work, and demonstrate to themselves and others that their skills are needed in society. Designers are asked to consider not just the physical environment of the site but also broader cultural and economic environments.

Brief and Judging   by Paul Dillon

There were 120 entries for the competition where it seemed the scale and basic nature of the hikers' shelter allowed the second year students an opportunity to present their individual skill at this stage of their education. A variety of presentation techniques were displayed, which presumably reflected the emphasis the different schools placed on presentation. Regardless of presentation ability, each of the entries was reviewed in detail to assess how well the students understood the brief and fulfilled their roll in the process of building the hill walkers shelter.

Most of the proposals showed a clear respect for the environment and unspoilt landscape, in the selection of the site and use of building materials. However, there was much less respect shown to the needs of the commissioning group; for example, many proposed very innovative interior spaces with elevated sleeping lofts or hammocks and large windows with views over a beautiful landscape, when the brief called for a place to seek shelter when stranded on the mountain in an emergency. Several proposals presented buildings which were pre-fabricated by others and easily and quickly assembled on site by the farmers. These types of proposals missed to point of the REPS Scheme, which was to protect and support rural environments and livelihoods by providing ongoing employment to the farmers over a number of years. There were also a number of proposals which wrongly assumed a low level of skill among the farmers and proposed almost primitive methods of construction. In reality, some of the hill farmers might already be the most skilled in local building methods, either from their families' building traditions or from previous government training schemes.

First
Lindsay Roughneen DIT, Bolton Street

Building Concept – The building is split into two volumes of 2.2m x 2.5m to maximise heat gains; these two forms are connected by the central hearth. The entrance is sheltered from south-westerly winds. The first volume is a preparation area and allows for the shedding of wet clothes. It provides storage for bags and a shelving unit for supplies like candles, matches, fuel and shovel. The central fireplace is based on a Kang bed-stove design, providing heat to the beds and quick drying facilities for the first volume. There are two thresholds to access the beds, for increased warmth. Close sleeping quarters utilise body heat – beneficial in case of acute hypothermia. A trough is located at the split roof for water harvesting.

Materials and Construction – The main body is constructed of concrete, using a timber and corrugated-sheet shuttering system and the materials that are found on the site – aggregate, quartzite, sand,

SECOND YEAR COMPETITION

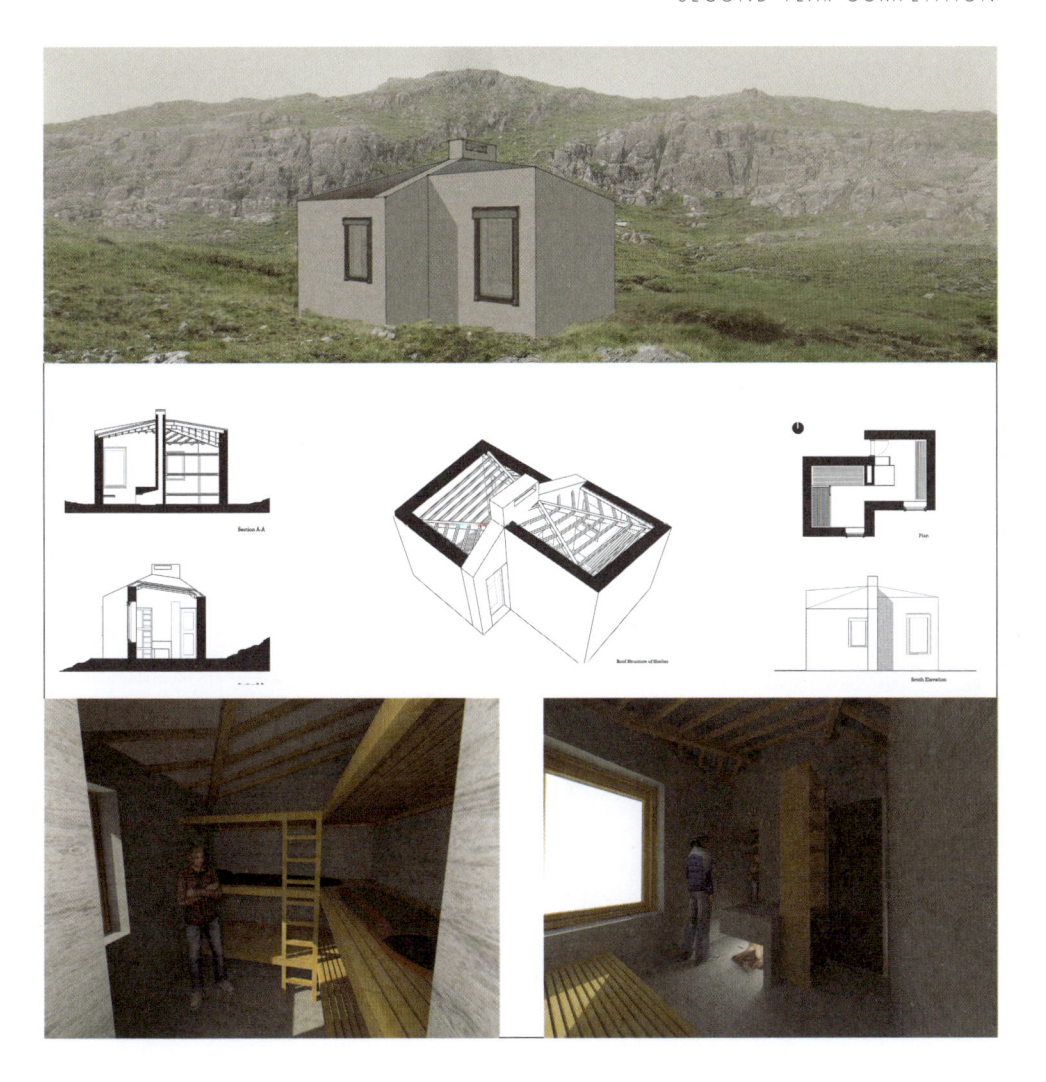

water from a local source. Cement would need to be brought. Timber used for shuttering will then be reused in the internal warm roof structure and corrugated iron sheet will be the external roof envelope – a shiny beacon when new, then oxidising over time, turning burnt orange (easily visible). Standard Velux windows used, for ease of transport. Window area is 25% of the facade and orientated south facing. The envelope of the building is 350mm, with a U-value of 0.2.

Assessors' comments

This proposal had a level of skill in responding to the brief not seen in any of the other proposals. The decision to split such a small building into two distinct volumes, entry and sleeping, showed courage and the development of this idea in every detail showed competence. The details revealed that the designer had researched this particular building type beyond what was outlined in the brief. The thinking was clear and critical, like positioning the door away from the prevailing wind, the two windows to maximise light and solar gain, or the position of the stove between the entry and the sleeping to create a warm sleeping area. The construction methods were traditional but very challenging and inventive. It would be easy to imagine the designer on site explaining, discussing, inspecting and making a livelihood as part of a sustainable rural community. However there were weaknesses in the proposal. The way the building was placed on the site was not convincing and the overall A1 presentation needed more work. Nevertheless, this designer has met the challenge of this brief by demonstrating that their skills are needed in society.

SECOND YEAR COMPETITION

Second – **Niall Murphy** QUB   *(above)*

Reclaim. A cube of stone, the shelter merges with the mountain. Alone it sits in a dormant state, part of the whole. With a walker's grasp and pull, the structure wakes. Timber and tin emerge from within. A simple act, it lays temporary claim to the space for oneself.

Assessors' comments – *This was a simply composed and presented concept, with the stone cube set against the raw landscape. This was a demonstration of the skill only a good designer can bring to a simple project like this. However there were doubts about whether the constructed reality could match the simplicity of the concept as conveyed in the drawings. There were also some concerns whether an injured hill walker would be able to safely use the shelter in stormy weather conditions.*

Third – **James Kipling** QUB   *(opposite)*

Assessors' comments – *This was a clear and original response to the brief. Flawless graphics were used to show the designer's complete understanding of the environment, the exact environment a hill walker would want to escape from – cold driving rain close to dark on the peak of the mountain. However, the design does not explain the choice of timber-frame construction for such an exposed location, when maybe more solid and local method of construction would have been more suitable for the farmers to build and maintain.*

SECOND YEAR COMPETITION

MORALE is the focus of the design.

The shelter aims to provide a space that feels completely SEPARATED from the mountain.

The outer skin is dark, burnt timber, pierced by a warm plywood entrance.

Contrast in materials exaggerates the THRESHOLD between inside and out.

The first step not touching the ground breaks the user's PHYSICAL connection to the mountain.

The lack of windows breaks the user's VISUAL connection to the mountain.

A Simple timber frame sits on four timber columns, that in turn sit on four concrete pads.

The structure is insulated and damproofed, built with lightweight plywood beams.

Commended – **Stephen Gotting** UCD
Assessors' comments – This was a very well-drawn and developed idea about site and material. The construction methods required a high level of skill, but there was enough information on the drawings to suggest the farmers could build it over a longer period of time. The shelter would have been a very welcome resting place for a hill walker but the finished building didn't quite meet the full requirements of the brief to provide emergency shelter in extreme weather conditions.

Commended – **Lee Kennedy** UCD
Assessors' comments – This is a memorable project. The building meets the basic requirements of emergency shelter but then goes much further in providing a navigational landmark above the local villages. The presentation shows a nice balance of hand sketches and computer graphics but the plans and section were very basic. The presentation was weak on construction detail. Other than stating the structure was based on timber post-and-beam construction, there was not enough information to show how the 9m high structure might be built and maintained on top of the mountain.

Commended – **Niall Quinn** QUB
Assessors' comments – A very sensitive and well-presented proposal, with text that clearly demonstrated the designer's thought process. Externally the straightforward reasoning behind the construction makes for a very convincing and compelling building to the passers-by. Internally, the decision-making is less clear and the layout of the bunks seems in conflict with the plan.

the 28 volumes of *New Irish Architecture* feature:

5,500+ illus
3,500+ pages
450+ projects by
100+ Irish architects

NIA °1 (1986)   NIA °28 (2017)

BACK-ISSUES	pages 177-179
LISTINGS	pages 180-199
ARCHITECTS	pages 200-212
BUILDING TYPE	pages 213-224

Back-Issues

NEW IRISH ARCHITECTURE °1-28 – AAI Awards 1986-2013

For twenty-eight years, the *New Irish Architecture* series has comprehensively documented the best of contemporary Irish architecture through the buildings and projects featured in the annual AAI Awards for Excellence in Architectural Design. Entries are judged by a panel of five Irish and international assessors, offering a unique critical appraisal of contemporary Irish architecture.

Each volume of *New Irish Architecture* carries copious drawings and photographs, architects' descriptions and assessors' comments on every awarded and commended scheme. It also carries a keynote essay by the international critic on that year's jury.

The *New Irish Architecture* series was established for the AAI by Gandon Editions in 1986, and is edited by John O'Regan and Nicola Dearey.

All of the more recent book-like volumes – from NIA °16 onwards – are still in print. These books can be ordered from any good bookshop at home or abroad, or direct from Gandon Editions (see overleaf).

———

Coming from the UK, I was really taken with the examples of public infrastructure being built here. Some of the educational projects feel like they have a real sense of purpose and quality and care, which I think is symptomatic of a fundamentally strong profession, but also a strong social sensibility in a country. I think there's a sense of care and an understanding here that these things are pivotal for a community.
— Daniel Rosbottom (NIA °28)

This year's assessors had to consider many projects of a very high standard. And surely it is the case that the tradition of the AAI Awards has certainly contributed to this situation. — Jo Taillieu (NIA °26)

The Irish architecture we saw in the AAI Awards was of a very high standard, especially in terms of urbanism, and that is a cause for celebration. — Charles Jencks (NIA °25)

One would be hard-pressed to find this density and level of architectural quality being produced in a year in any federal state in Germany with Ireland's population (Berlin, Saxony, or Rhineland-Palatinate). More than that: the depth and the breadth of conceptual and detailing precision visible in the work contained in this publication would not be seen in Germany. — Wilfried Wang (NIA °24)

As seen in the projects presented for this year's AAI Awards, the Irish architectural stage exudes effort and tenacity, attention to urban context and attachment to rural landscape, professional craftsmanship in the details and tactile sensibility in the materials. – Luis Fernández-Galiano (NIA °22)

BACK-ISSUES

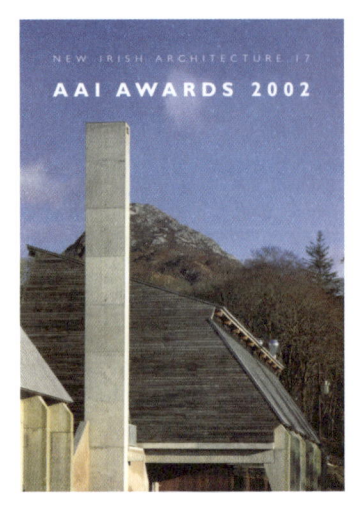

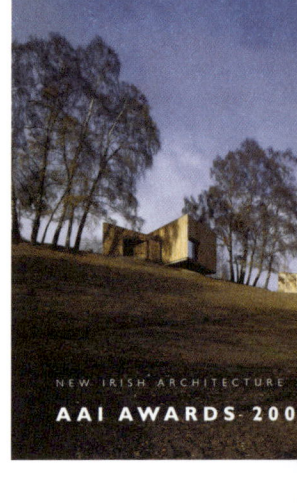

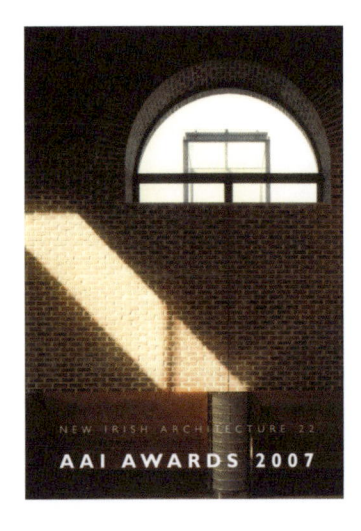

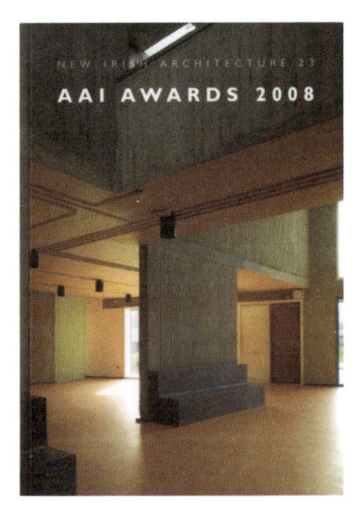

AAI AWARDS 2001
AAI AWARDS 2002
AAI AWARDS 2003

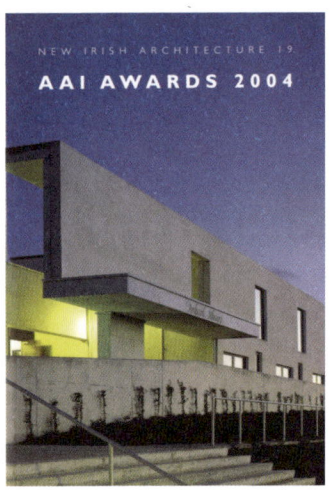

AAI AWARDS 2004
AAI AWARDS 2005
AAI AWARDS 2006

AAI AWARDS 2007
AAI AWARDS 2008
AAI AWARDS 2009

BACK-ISSUES

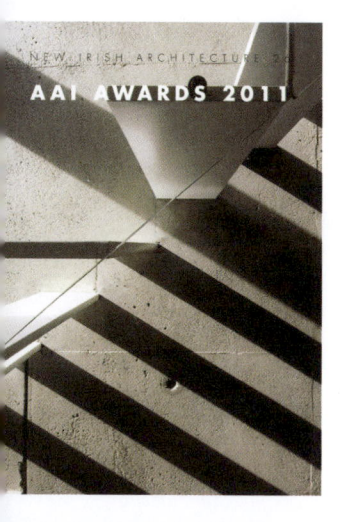

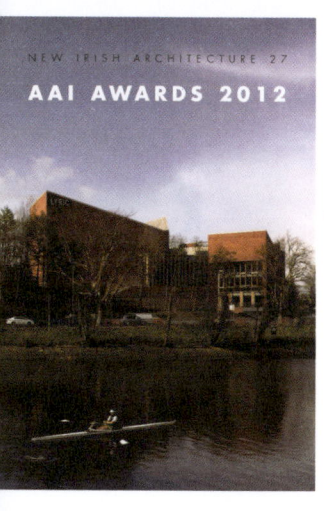

Order Form

The *New Irish Architecture – AAI Awards* series can be ordered from any good bookshop or direct from Gandon (same-day dispatch; postage free in Ireland, elsewhere at cost).

full-colour, octavo books:

___ NIA °16 – AAI Awards 2001 €20
___ NIA °17 – AAI Awards 2002 €20
___ NIA °18 – AAI Awards 2003 €20
___ NIA °19 – AAI Awards 2004 €20
___ NIA °20 – AAI Awards 2005 €20
___ NIA °21 – AAI Awards 2006 €20
___ NIA °22 – AAI Awards 2007 €20
___ NIA °23 – AAI Awards 2008 €20
___ NIA °24 – AAI Awards 2009 €25
___ NIA °25 – AAI Awards 2010 €25
___ NIA °26 – AAI Awards 2011 €20
___ NIA °27 – AAI Awards 2012 €20
___ NIA °28 – AAI Awards 2013 €20

small quantity of these catalogues available:

___ NIA °8 – AAI Awards 1993 €10
___ NIA °12 – AAI Awards 1997 €10
___ NIA °13 – AAI Awards 1998 €10
___ NIA °15 – AAI Awards 2000 €10

❏ cheque enclosed for euro € / stg £ / US $ _____
❏ charge € _____ to my
   Maestro / Mastercard / Visa account

account no. ___ ___ ___ ___   ___ ___ ___ ___   ___ ___ ___ ___
___ ___ ___ ___ expires ___ ___ / ___ ___ security code ___ ___ ___

name _____ date _____

address _____

_____

TRADE: order # _____ contact _____ S/R

GANDON EDITIONS – Oysterhaven, Kinsale, Co Cork
T +353 (0)21-4770830 / E gandon@eircom.net   2/17

Listings

NEW IRISH ARCHITECTURE °1-28 – AAI Awards 1986-2013

NEW IRISH ARCHITECTURE °1 — AAI Awards 1986
ISBN 0902345 109, 40 pages, 30 x 21 cm, b/w illus – o/p

assessors   John Miller (UK), *foreign assessor*
               Arthur Gibney, John Meagher, *Irish assessors*

contents   Introduction by John Mitchell, AAI President   4
               Assessors' Report by Arthur Gibney   5
               AAI Awards 1986 – featured buildings and projects   6-37
               Architectural Association of Ireland (an outline history)   39

Awards
APARTMENTS IN CARLOW	Derek Tynan Architects	6-7
WORK IN PROGRESS, 1985	Quilligan & Twamley Architects	8-9
IRISH FILM CENTRE, Trinity Street, Dublin 2	Sheila O'Donnell Architect	10-11
SPORTS HALL, Mount Anville, Dublin	Moloney O'Beirne, Guy + Hutchison Locke & Monk Architects	12-13
ZANUSSI KITCHEN DESIGN	James Horan and Anne Harper Architects	14-15

Selected for Exhibition
HOUSING AT RUTLAND ST, Dublin 1	Cathal Crimmins, Housing Architect's Dept., Dublin Corporation	16-17
MORIARTY HOUSE, Howth, Co Dublin	Edmund Fitzgerald Selby, Fitzgerald Selby & Sugars Architects	18-19
FAMILY HOUSE, Co Kildare	Liam Hennessy Architect	20-21
FAMILY HOUSE, Co Wexford	Liam Hennessy Architect	22-23
KITCHEN, Booterstown, Co Dublin	James Horan and Anne Harper Architects	24-25
'THE ARGO'	James Horan and Anne Harper Architects	26-27
HOUSE AT LOUGH ENNELL	Paul Keogh Architects	28-29
MAUSOLEUM, Co Carlow	Shane O'Toole, Lynch O'Toole Walsh Architects	30-31
KILLYKEEN FOREST PARK, Co Cavan	Ciaran O'Connor, Office of Public Works	32-33
LABORATORY AT ABBOTSTOWN, Co Dublin	John Tuomey, Office of Public Works	34-35
LEISURE CENTRE, Greystones, Co Wicklow	Danuta Kornaus-Wejchert, A+D Wejchert Architects	36-37

NEW IRISH ARCHITECTURE °2 — AAI Awards 1987
ISBN 0902345 125, 44 pages, 30 x 21 cm, b/w illus – o/p

assessors :   Edward Cullinan (UK), *foreign assessor*
                Yvonne Farrell, Derek Tynan (1986 award-winner), *Irish assessors*

contents   Assessors' Report by Derek Tynan   4-5
               AAI Awards 1987 – featured buildings and projects   6-35
               Update (AAI Awards 1986)   39-41

Downes Bronze Medal
HARP BREWHOUSE, Dundalk	Mitchell Ó Muire Smyth Architects	6-7

LISTINGS

Awards

THE DINING HALL AND ATRIUM, Trinity College Dublin	de Blacam & Meagher Architects	8-9
COURTHOUSE AT SMITHFIELD, Dublin	John Tuomey, Office of Public Works	10-11
DONNINGTON BATH HOUSES, London	David Naessens and Christopher Stead, Architects	12-13

Selected for Exhibition

RUSH CHURCH COMPETITION	Gallagher & Mullen Architects	14-15
YORK RIVERSIDE COMPETITION	Gibney & Van Dijk Architects	16-17
PUPPET TRAILER	Derek Heavey and Sheila McCarthy, Architects	18-19
HOUSE IN A COURTYARD, Co Dublin	McCullough Mulvin Architects	20-21
A SMALL COUNTRY HOUSE, Co Louth	Michael McGarry and Siobhán Ní Éanaigh, Architects	22-23
4 HOUSES AT DONNYBROOK, Dublin 4	Mitchell Ó Muire Smyth Architects	24-25
PSYCHIATRIC / GERIATRIC UNITS, St James's Hospital	Moloney O'Beirne Guy + Hutchison Locke & Monk	26-27
ALSAA SPORTS COMPLEX, Dublin Airport	Declan O'Dwyer and Sheila Jones, Architects	28-29
EMPLOYMENT EXCHANGE, Ballyfermot, Dublin	Mary MacKenna, Michael Haugh, Office of Public Works	30-31
CASTLE HALL, Dublin Castle	Angela Rolfe, Klaus Unger, Office of Public Works	32-33
DEVELOPMENT AT NORTH WALL QUAY, Dublin	Quilligan & Twamley Architects	34-35

NEW IRISH ARCHITECTURE °3 — AAI Awards 1988
ISBN 0902345 141, 56 pages, 29 x 21.5 cm, b/w illus – o/p

assessors Michael Gold (UK), *foreign assessor*
Neil Hegarty, Gerry Mitchell (1987 award-winner), *Irish assessors*

contents   Assessors' Report by Michael Gold   2, 4
           AAI Awards 1988 – featured buildings and projects   5-49
           Update (AAI Awards 1987)   53-55

Downes Bronze Medal

IRISH FILM CENTRE, Eustace Street, Dublin 2	Sheila O'Donnell Architect	5-7

Awards

A RURAL HOUSE	Ross Cahill O'Brien Architect	8-9
SHOWROOM AND OFFICES	Shay Cleary Architects	10-11
PROTOTYPE DESIGN FOR A PSYCHOGERIATRIC HOSPITAL	de Blacam & Meagher Architects	12-13
BRUNSWICK STREET IMPROVEMENT SCHEME	Desmond FitzGerald Architects	14-15
HOUSE AT RATH, Dundalk	Gibney & Van Dijk Architects	16-17
EXTENSION TO COLLEGE OF TECHNOLOGY, Bolton Street	Des McMahon, Gilroy McMahon Architects	18-20
HOUSE IN THE BARROW VALLEY	Derek Tynan Architects	21-23

Selected for Exhibition

RTE TV RECEPTION AREA	de Blacam & Meagher Architects	24-25
RUSSELL STREET HOUSING	Bernard Grimes, Housing Architect's Dept., Dublin Corporation	26-27
BYRNE HOUSE	Duffy + Mitchell Architects	28-29
MILLENNIUM TOWER, Dublin	M J Kinsella, Keane Murphy Duff Architects	30-31
HOUSE AT MODEL FARM ROAD, CORK	John E Keating & Associates, Architects	32-33
PAVILION AT DUBLIN ZOO	Paul Keogh Architects	34-35
THE CITY ARTS CENTRE	McCullough Mulvin Architects	36-37
EXTENSION TO C18TH HOUSE IN LEINSTER	Michael McGarry and Siobhán Ní Éanaigh, Architects	38-39
A GARDEN EXTENSION TO THE FULLAM RESIDENCE	O'Dea Skehan & Associates, Architects	40-41
GARDEN AT ROYAL HOSPITAL KILMAINHAM	Elizabeth Morgan, Office of Public Works	42-43
PARK CENTRE BUILDING, Glenveagh National Park	Anthony & Barbara O'Neill Architects	44-45
EXTENSION TO CROSS & PASSION COLLEGE	RP McCaffrey, Robinson Keefe Devane Architects	46-47
CHAPEL AT ST ANGELA'S SCHOOL, Stevenage, Herts	Niall Scott, Scott Tallon Walker Architects	48-49

LISTINGS

NEW IRISH ARCHITECTURE °4 — AAI Awards 1989
ISBN 0902345 168, 40 pages, 29 x 21.5 cm, b/w illus – o/p

assessors   David Chipperfield (UK), *foreign assessor*
            Des McMahon, Sheila O'Donnell (1988 award-winner), *Irish assessors*

contents   Assessors' Reports   2-3
            AAI Awards 1989 – featured buildings and projects   4-37
            Update (AAI Awards 1988)   38-40

Downes Bronze Medal
ENTRANCE HALL, BAR & RESTAURANT, POINT DEPOT, Dublin	Shay Cleary Architects	4-8

Awards
A HOUSE IN PORTARLINGTON	Gerard Carty Architect	9-11
RESIDENTIAL DEVELOPMENT, Ailesbury Road, Dublin 4	de Blacam & Meagher Architects	12-14
GARDEN ROOMS, Leeson Park and Percy Place, Dublin	Paul Keogh Architects	15-17
THE O'REILLY INSTITUTE, Trinity College Dublin	Ronald Tallon, Scott Tallon Walker Architects	18-21

Selected for Exhibition
DEVELOPMENT AT CHASE ROAD, Acton, London	Delany MacVeigh & Pike Architects	22-23
A BOOKSHOP ON COLLEGE GREEN	Desmond FitzGerald Architects	24-25
CANOE CLUB ON THE RIVER LIFFEY	Yvonne Farrell, Shelley McNamara, Grafton Architects	26-27
COMMERCIAL INFILL, Ormond Quay, Dublin 1	Shelley McNamara, Tony Murphy, Grafton Architects	28-29
HOUSE IN NORTH COUNTY DUBLIN	Derek Byrne, Henry J Lyons & Partners, Architects	30-31
HOUSE ON A DRUMLIN, Co Monaghan	Michael McGarry and Siobhán Ní Éanaigh Architects	32-33
LUTTRELLSTOWN FARM	O'Dowd O'Herlihy Horan Architects	34-35
A GARDA STATION IN CAVAN	Kevin Wolohan, Office of Public Works	36-37

NEW IRISH ARCHITECTURE °5 — AAI Awards 1990
ISBN 0902345 175, 60 pages, 29 x 21.5 cm, b/w illus – o/p

assessors   Esteve Bonell (Spain), *foreign assessor*
            Peter Doyle, Shay Cleary (1989 award-winner), *Irish assessors*

contents   Assessors' Reports   2-3
            AAI Awards 1990 – featured buildings and projects   4-55
            Update (AAI Awards 1989) / Invitation to Enter   56-58

Downes Bronze Medal
LIVING IN THE CITY	O'Donnell + Tuomey Architects	4-7

Awards
NEWHALL MILL WORKSHOPS, Birmingham	David Naessens and Louise Cotter, Architects	8-11
CHAPEL OF RECONCILIATION, Knock, Co Mayo	de Blacam & Meagher Architects	12-13
THREE TICKET SALES OFFICES FOR AER LINGUS	de Blacam & Meagher Architects	14-16
LECTURE HALL AND ARCHIVE	McCullough Mulvin Architects	17-19
DEANS OF RESIDENCE (Chaplaincy), University College Dublin	Prof Cathal O'Neill & Partners, Architects	20-22
BRADAN MARA TEO, Land-Based Salmon Hatchery, Derryclare, Co Galway	Ronald Tallon, Scott Tallon Walker Architects	23-25

Selected for Exhibition
A YOUTH HOSTEL IN LEITRIM	Bingham & Kelly Architects	26-27

LISTINGS

CAFÉ KLARA, Dawson Street, Dublin 2	de Blacam & Meagher Architects	28-29
RAVENSBURY MILL, Morden, London	James Pike, DSMP Architects	30-31
HOUSE AND STUDIO RECONVERSION IN Co DOWN	Desmond FitzGerald Architect	32-33
RE-DEVELOPMENT OF Nos. 27-29 CLARE STREET, Dublin 2	Des McMahon, Gilroy McMahon Architects	34-35
TWO MEWS HOUSES AT CLYDE LANE, Dublin 4	Yvonne Farrell, Grafton Architects	36-37
DIFFNEY MANSHOP, Stephen's Green, Dublin 2	Paul Keogh Architects	38-39
HOUSE IN A CHURCH	McCullough Mulvin Architects	40-41
RENOVATION OF STONE COTTAGE, Co Meath	McGarry Ní Éanaigh Architects	42-43
A SUITE OF PRIVATE MEDICAL CONSULTING ROOMS	McGarry Ní Éanaigh Architects	44-45
HARP BREWERY VISITOR CENTRE, Dundalk	Mitchell Ó Muire Smyth Architects	46-47
RESTAURANT AT CASTLEKNOCK	Timothy Kane, Murphy Kenny Architects	48-49
CHAPEL OF RECONCILIATION, Knock, Co Mayo	O'Donnell + Tuomey Architects	50-51
SCHOOL OF ENGINEERING (Phase 1), University College Dublin	Ronald Tallon, Scott Tallon Walker Architects	52-53
DOUBLE HOUSE, Belgrave Square, Monkstown, Co Dublin	Derek Tynan Architects	54-55

NEW IRISH ARCHITECTURE °6 — AAI Awards 1991
ISBN 0902345 187, 64 pages, 29 x 21.5 cm, b/w illus – o/p

assessors	Rafael Moneo (Spain), *foreign assessor*
	David Naessens, Ronald Tallon, John Tuomey (1990), *Irish assessors*
	Richard Kearney (philosopher), *distinguished non-architect*

contents		
	Invitation to Enter / Registrar's Report	2-3
	Assessors' Reports	4-5
	AAI Awards 1991 – featured buildings and projects	6-35
	Update (AAI Awards 1990)	36-37
	• THE GREEN BOOK, 1975-1990	41-64
	– contents include: Calendar of events / AAI Committee	
	– *'AAI History'* by Shane O'Toole	
	– *'AAI Constitution'* by Shane O'Toole	
	– AAI Constitution and Rules, 1984	
	– AAI Members 1990-1991	

Awards

A ROOM WITH A VIEW	Paul Kelly, Bingham Kelly Architects	6-7
HOUSE AT BOFARA, Westport, Co Mayo	Ross Cahill-O'Brien Architect	8-10
RECONSTRUCTION OF TROPICAL FRUITS BUILDING	Felim Dunne in assoc. with Beardsmore Yauner Byrne Architects	11-13
MEDICAL CENTRE, DROGHEDA	McGarry Ní Éanaigh Architects	14-17

Special Mentions

MIGRANT ACCESS CENTRE, Camden, London	Brady Mallalieu Architects	18-19
MEWS, Blackrock, Co Dublin	Cathal Crimmins Architect	20-21
HOUSE EXTENSION WALTHAM TERRACE, Blackrock, Co Dublin	Cathal Crimmins Architect	22-23
REFURBISHMENT OF QUAYSIDE HOUSE AND SHOP	Richard Wentges, DAC Architects	24-25
HOLIDAY HOUSES AT VELVET STRAND, Portmarnock	Paul Keogh Architects	26-27
ABBEY THEATRE PORTICO	McCullough Mulvin Architects	28-29
SOCIAL WELFARE SERVICES OFFICE, BALLYFERMOT, Dublin	Mary McKenna, Office of Public Works	30-31
MEWS AT 26 WATERLOO ROAD, Dublin 4	Cathal O'Neill Architects	32-33
MONTESSORI SCHOOL, Howth Road, Co Dublin	Neil Sholdice Architect	34-35

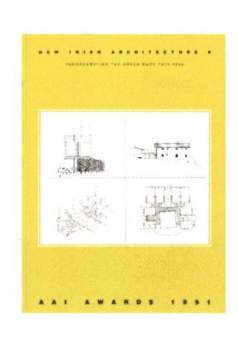

LISTINGS

NEW IRISH ARCHITECTURE °7 — AAI Awards 1992
ISSN 0780-0578, 44 pages, 29 x 21.5 cm, b/w illus – o/p

assessors:	Peter Wilson (UK), *foreign assessor*	
	Gerard Carty, James Horan, Ross Cahill-O'Brien (1991), *Irish assessors*	
	Dorothy Walker (art writer), *distinguished non-architect*	
contents	Registrar's Report / Assessors' Reports / Invitation to Enter	2-3, 42
	AAI Awards 1992 – featured buildings and projects	4-41
	Update (AAI Awards 1991)	43
	AAI Student Measured Drawing Competition 1991	46-47

Downes Bronze Medal
THE IRISH PAVILION	O'Donnell + Tuomey Architects	4-7

Awards
IRISH MUSEUM OF MODERN ART	Shay Cleary Architects	8-10
EXIT CONTROL BUILDING, DUBLIN AIRPORT	Noel Dowley Architect	11-13
VISITORS CENTRE, VALENTIA	Doyle Architects	14-16
29 SOUTH PARK, Foxrock, Co Dublin	Michelle Fagan, Newenham Mulligan & Associates, Architects	17-19

Special Mentions
HOUSE A	Alan deLacy, The Bacon Group, Architects	20-21
THEATRE ROYAL FOYER, WEXFORD	de Blacam & Meagher Architects	22-23
RETAIL BANK	Duffy Mitchell Architects	24-25
DUBLIN 2 DELIVERY OFFICE	Kavanagh Architects	26-27
HOUSE IN A CHURCH	McCullough Mulvin Architects	28-29
HOUSE ON A RIVER	McGarry Ní Éanaigh Architects	30-31
THE COCOON, MULLET PENNINSULA	Patricia Mangan and Rory Murphy, Architects	32-33
VISITORS CENTRE, KING JOHN'S CASTLE, Limerick	Murray Ó Laoire Associates, Architects	34-35
LIMERICK INFORMATION OFFICE	Murray Ó Laoire Associates, Architects	36-37
WATERWAYS VISITORS CENTRE, Grand Canal Dock	C O'Connor, G O'Sullivan, Office of Public Works	38-39
LIMERICK SOCIAL WELFARE OFFICES	Elizabeth Morgan, Office of Public Works	40-41

NEW IRISH ARCHITECTURE °8 — AAI Awards 1993
ISBN 0946641 072 (ISBN-13: 978 0946641 079), 44 pages, 21 x 21 cm, 53 illus (16 col)

assessors	Peter Cook (UK), foreign assessor	
	Seán Ó Laoire, Mary Donohoe, Noel Dowley (1992), *Irish assessors*	
	Fintan O'Toole (journalist), *distinguished non-architect*	
contents	Registrar's Report / Assessors' Reports	2-6
	AAI Awards 1993 – featured buildings and projects	7-27
	Update (AAI Awards 1992)	28-29
	• THE GREEN BOOK, 1990-1992	37-43
	– contents include: Calendar of events / AAI Committee	
	– *'AAI Awards 1992'*, opening address by Nicholas Robinson	42-43

Downes Bronze Medal
BECKETT THEATRE, Trinity College Dublin	de Blacam & Meagher Architects	7-11

Awards
VISITOR BUILDING, Royal Gunpowder Mills, Ballincollig, Co Cork	dpon Architects	12-15

LISTINGS

| 6 APARTMENTS, 2 Crosthwaite Park South, Dun Laoghaire | Ken Edmondson Architect | 16-19 |
| MEWS HOUSES AT CLYDE LANE, Dublin 4 | Grafton Architects | 20-23 |

Special Mention

| ST PAUL'S SECONDARY SCHOOL, Oughterard, Co Galway | Grafton Architects | 24-27 |

NEW IRISH ARCHITECTURE °9 — AAI Awards 1994
ISBN 0946641 080, 48 pages, 21 x 21 cm, 63 illus (8 col) – o/p

assessors	John Hejduk (USA), *foreign assessor*
	Tom de Paor, Joan O'Connor, Shane de Blacam (1993), *Irish assessors*
	Vivienne Roche (artist), *distinguished non-architect*

| contents | Assessors' Reports / Registrar's Report | 3-5 |
| | AAI Awards 1994 – featured buildings and projects | 6-33 |

• THE GREEN BOOK, 1992-1993   41-48
– contents include: Calendar of events / AAI Committee / AAI Members
– *'The Irish in London: an appreciation of Jim Stirling'* by Ed Jones   44-45
– *'Markers on the Land'* by Peter Smithson   46-47

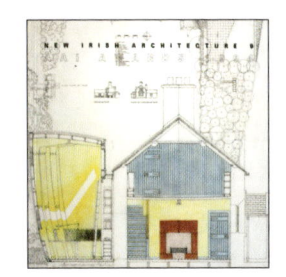

Awards

EXTENSION AND RENOVATION OF A RECTORY	McGarry Ní Éanaigh Architects	6-9
CÉIDE FIELDS VISITOR CENTRE	Mary MacKenna, Office of Public Works	10-13
PLAN FOR THE GARDEN OF A MODERN MOVEMENT HOUSE	Donohoe & FitzGerald Architects	14-17
RESIDENTIAL QUARTER AT ST PETER'S PORT, ATHLONE	MV Cullinan, National Building Agency	18-21

Special Mentions

STUDENT FACILITIES CENTRE, Aston Place, Dublin	Tim Kane, Frank Kenny Associates, Architects	22-23
WATERWAYS VISITOR CENTRE, Dublin	Ciaran O'Connor, Gerard O'Sullivan, Office of Public Works	24-25
GOLF CLUB AT LUTTRELLSTOWN	James Horan, Peter McGovern, O'Dowd O'Herlihy Horan Architects	26-27
CLIFFS OF MOHER VISITOR CENTRE	O'Riordan Staehli Architects	28-29
HOUSING AT BROOKWOOD	Fionnuala Rogerson Architect	30-31
BIOTECHNOLOGY RESEARCH BUILDING, UCD	Scott Tallon Walker Architects	32-33

NEW IRISH ARCHITECTURE °10 — AAI Awards 1995
ISSN 0780-0578, 96 pages, 21 x 21 cm, 160 illus (19 col) – o/p

assessors	Willem Jan Neutelings (Netherlands), *foreign assessor*
	James Barrett, Kevin Woods, Michael Cullinan (1994), *Irish assessors*
	Felim Egan (artist), *distinguished non-architect*

| contents | Assessors' Reports / Registrar's Report / Invitation to Enter | 3-5, 83-84 |
| | AAI Awards 1995 – featured buildings and projects | 6-63 |

• AAI AWARDS 1986-1995 – 10-YEAR RETROSPECTIVE   73-84
– *'Beautiful pictures of fine buildings
will not change public perceptions'* by Shane O'Toole   74-77

• THE GREEN BOOK, 1993-1994   85-95
– contents include: Calendar of events / AAI Committee / AAI Members
– review: *'Michel W Kagan – Selected Projects'* by Sam Mays   88-89
– *'Sentences on the house and other sentences'* by John Hejduk   90-93

LISTINGS

Downes Bronze Medal
THE PRINTWORKS, Temple Bar, Dublin 2   Group 91 / Derek Tynan Architects   6-11

Awards
NEW LIBRARY, Cork Regional Technical College	de Blacam & Meagher / Boyd Barrett Murphy-O'Connor	12-15
SOCIAL HOUSING, New Street, Dublin 8	Gerry Cahill Architects	16-19
HOUSE IN DOOLIN, Co Clare	Grafton Architects	20-23
THE COUNTDOWN 2000 PROJECT	Hassett Ducatez Architects	24-27
TEMPLE BAR GALLERY AND STUDIOS, Dublin 2	McCullough Mulvin Architects	28-31
MOTORWAY BRIDGE, Killarney Road, Co Wicklow	Roughan & O'Donovan / Grafton Architects	32-35

Special Mentions
NEW TERMINAL DEVELOPMENT, Kerry Airport	Aer Rianta Technical Consultants	36-37
THE KITCHEN NIGHTCLUB, Temple Bar, Dublin 2	Cahill-O'Brien Associates, Architects	38-39
NEW FOYER ETC, DEPT OF AGRICULTURE	Shay Cleary Architects	40-41
CASHEL SECOND-LEVEL SCHOOL	Doyle Architects	42-43
DESIGNYARD, Applied Arts Centre, Temple Bar	Felim Dunne & Associates / Robinson Keefe Devane	44-45
IRISH ENERGY CENTRE	Energy Research Group, UCD	46-47
FAMINE MUSEUM, Strokestown Park House, Co Roscommon	Orna Hanly Architect	48-49
TWO APARTMENTS, Haddington Road, Dublin 4	Paul Keogh Architects	50-51
THE GREEN BUILDING, Temple Bar, Dublin 2	Murray Ó Laoire Associates, Architects	52-53
'THE YOKE ON THE OAK', Dame Street, Dublin 2	Murray Ó Laoire Associates, Architects	54-55
A CONSTRUCTED LANDSCAPE – Blackwood Golf Centre, Co Down	O'Donnell + Tuomey Architects	56-57
HOUSE IN WEST CORK	James Horan, O'Dowd O'Herlihy Horan Associates	58-59
RHK / IMMA ARTISTS' STUDIOS	Elizabeth Morgan, Office of Public Works	60-61
A HOUSE IN GIFU, JAPAN	Deirdre Whelan and Paul Kelly, Architects	62-63

NEW IRISH ARCHITECTURE °11 — AAI Awards 1996
ISBN 0946641 706, 76 pages, 22.5 x 22.5 cm, 125 illus (28 col) – o/p

assessors	Wiel Arets (Netherlands), *foreign assessor*
	Michelle Fagan, Prof Cathal O'Neill, Gerry Cahill (1995), *Irish assessors*
	Ciarán Benson (psychologist; chair, The Arts Council), *dist. non-architect*

contents	Assessors' Reports	4-6
	Registrar's Report / Invitation to Enter / Assessors	7-9
	AAI Awards 1996 – featured buildings and projects	10-65
	• THE GREEN BOOK, 1994-1995	71-76
	– contents include: Calendar of events / AAI Committee / AAI Members	

Downes Bronze Medal (joint medal)
THE ARK – A Cultural Centre for Children, Temple Bar	Group 91 / Shane O'Toole and Michael Kelly	10-17
BLACK CHURCH PRINT STUDIOS, Temple Bar, Dublin 2	McCullough Mulvin Architects	18-25

Awards
NATIONAL MUSEUM AT COLLINS BARRACKS (Phase 1), Dublin	Gilroy McMahon / Office of Public Works	26-31
JOHN ROCHA DESIGN STUDIO, Temple Lane, Dublin 2	Group 91 / Derek Tynan Architects	32-36
DUNDALK FREIGHT DEPOT – Check-In Office	David Hughes, Iarnród Éireann Architects	37-41
CIVIC OFFICES AT WOOD QUAY, Dublin	Scott Tallon Walker Architects	42-47

Special Mentions
FAMILY APARTMENT IN THE LIBERTIES, Dublin 8	MV Cullinan Architect	48-49
GARDEN IN CORK	de Paor Architects	60-61
A FOOTBRIDGE AT KELLS, Co Kilkenny	Desmond FitzGerald Architect	50-51

LISTINGS

MUSEUM AT MELLIFONT ABBEY, Co Louth	McGarry Ní Éanaigh Architects	52-53
FOUR HOUSES AT TULACH ARD, Rahoon, Galway	MV Cullinan, National Building Agency	54-55
HOUSE IN NORTH COUNTY DUBLIN	O'Donnell + Tuomey Architects	56-57
HOUSE TO LET	Ó Muire Smyth Architects	58-59
PRIVATE RESIDENCE, Roebuck, Dublin 14	Derek Tynan Architects	62-63
SOLICITORS OFFICES, Francis Street, Dublin 8	Derek Tynan Architects	64-65

NEW IRISH ARCHITECTURE °12 — AAI Awards 1997
ISBN 0946641 781 (ISBN-13: 978 0946641 789), 96 pages, 22.5 x 22.5 cm, 205 illus (32 col)

assessors	Kenneth Frampton (US), *foreign assessor*	
	Michael Hussey, Sam Stephenson, David Hughes (1996), *Irish assessors*	
	Dorothy Cross (artist), *distinguished non-architect*	
contents	Assessors' Reports	4-6
	Registrar's Report / Invitation to Enter / Assessors	7-9
	AAI Awards 1997 – featured buildings and projects	10-84

Downes Bronze Medal

GALLERY OF PHOTOGRAPHY, Temple Bar, Dublin 2	Group 91 / O'Donnell + Tuomey Architects	10-19

Awards

WALLPAPER HOUSE, CORK	de Paor Architects	38-41
DEPT OF MECHANICAL ENGINEERING, Trinity College Dublin	Grafton Architects	20-25
NATIONAL PHOTOGRAPHY ARCHIVE / DIT SCHOOL OF PHOTOGRAPHY	Group 91 / O'Donnell + Tuomey	32-37
MEWS DWELLING, DUBLIN 6	Derek Tynan Architects	26-31

Special Mentions

NEW SCHOOL OF ARCHITECTURE & INTERIOR DESIGN, UNL, London	Brady + Mallalieu Architects	44-46
ESB TRAINING CENTRE, Portlaoise	Vincent Coleman, Building Consultancy Group	47-49
CO-OPERATIVE HOUSING, Allingham Street, Dublin	Gerry Cahill Architects	50-52
BLACKROCK EDUCATION CENTRE, Co Dublin	Shay Cleary Architects	53-55
A13 FENCE, England	de Paor Architects	80-81
MoS BUILDING, Abbeyfeale, Co Limerick	Alan de Lacy, Conor Dennison, 5F Architects	56-58
THREE URBAN SPACES, Temple Bar, Dublin 2	Group 91 Architects	59-61
ARTHOUSE, Temple Bar, Dublin 2	Group 91 / Shay Cleary Architects	62-64
TEMPLE BAR SQUARE, DUBLIN	Group 91 / Grafton Architects	65-67
MIXED USE BUILDING, MEETING HOUSE SQUARE, Temple Bar, Dublin	Group 91 / Paul Keogh Architects	68-70
MUSIC CENTRE, Temple Bar, Dublin 2	Group 91 / McCullough Mulvin Architects	71-73
REFURBISHMENT OF 42 ARRAN QUAY, Dublin 7	James Kelly, Gabrielle Dempsey, James Kelly Architect	74-76
ENVIRONMENTAL PROTECTION AGENCY HQ	Derek Byrne, Finghín Curraoin, Henry J Lyons Architects	77-79
PIZZA HUT RESTAURANT, Blanchardstown, Co Dublin	Colin Conn, Gavin Buggy, Studio Architects	82-84

NEW IRISH ARCHITECTURE °13 — AAI Awards 1998
ISBN 0946641 951 (ISBN-13: 978 0946641 956), 84 pages, 22.5 x 22.5 cm, 190 illus (32 col)

assessors	Alberto Campo-Baeza (Spain), *foreign assessor*	
	Kevin Kieran, Esmonde O'Briain, Sheila O'Donnell (1997), *Irish assessors*	
	Edward McParland (architectural historian), *distinguished non-architect*	
contents	Assessors' Reports	4-6
	Registrar's Report / Invitation to Enter / Assessors	7-10
	AAI Awards 1998 – featured buildings and projects	11-67

LISTINGS

    • THE GREEN BOOK, 1995-1997   69-75
    – contents include: Calendar of events / AAI Committee / AAI Members

Awards
BAY WINDOW & STAIRCASE INSERTION, Windsor Terrace, Dublin 4	Gerard Carty Architect	12-17
MEWS HOUSE TO HEYTESBURY LANE, Dublin 4	de Blacam & Meagher Architects	18-23
GARDEN ROOM FOR LITTLE BIRD, rear 13 Merrion Square, Dublin 2	Grafton Architects	24-29
SOFTWARE DESIGN BUILDING, Leopardstown, Co Dublin	McGarry Ní Eanaigh Architects	30-35

Special Mentions
EXPERIMENTAL SOLAR HOUSE & STUDIO, West Cork	Akiboye Conolly Architects	36-39
MAIN ENTRANCE, UNIVERSITY OF LIMERICK	de Blacam & Meagher Architects	40-43
EDEN RESTAURANT, Temple Bar, Dublin 2	de Paor Architects	44-47
BALLINA CREDIT UNION	John Dorman Architects	48-51
ISOLDE'S TOWER, Essex Quay, Dublin 2	Gilroy McMahon Architects	52-55
PARALLEL HOUSE, Kingscourt, Co Cavan	McGarry Ní Eanaigh Architects	56-59
HERBARIUM AND LIBRARY, Botanic Gardens, Dublin	Ciarán O'Connor, Gerard O'Sullivan, Sheila Foley, Office of Public Works	60-63
GRAPHIC DESIGN STUDIO, North Lotts, Dublin 1	Dominic Stevens Architect	64-67

NEW IRISH ARCHITECTURE °14 — AAI Awards 1999
ISBN 0946846 219, 132 pages, 22.5 x 22.5 cm, 220 illus (53 col) – o/p

assessors   Yves Lion (France), *foreign assessor*
               Mary Doyle, Peter Tansey, Shelley McNamara (1998), *Irish assessors*
               Theo Dorgan (poet), *distinguished non-architect*

contents   Assessors' Reports   5-8
               Registrar's Report / Invitation to Enter / Assessors   9-12
               AAI Awards 1999 – featured buildings and projects   13-107

    • THE GREEN BOOK, 1997-1998   108-120
    – contents include: Calendar of events / AAI Committee / AAI Members
    – 'A Grounding in Fragments' by Peter Cody   112-118

Downes Bronze Medal
RANELAGH MULTI-DENOMINATIONAL SCHOOL, Dublin 6	O'Donnell + Tuomey Architects	14-23

Special Award
11 EUSTACE STREET, Temple Bar, Dublin 2	Group 91 / Shane O'Toole, Michael Kelly and Susan Cogan, Architects	24-29

Awards
HOUSE AM ZOO, LEIPZIG	Henchion + Reuter Architects	30-35
MEWS HOUSE, LOUIS LANE, Dublin 6	McCullough Mulvin Architects	36-39
SIENA MONASTERY, Drogheda, Co Louth	McCullough Mulvin Architects	40-45
HOUSE IN A LONG BACK GARDEN, Navan, Co Meath	O'Donnell + Tuomey Architects	46-51
DOMESTIC ACUPUNCTURE	Dominic Stevens Architects	52-57
GATE MULTIPLEX, North Gate, Cork	Derek Tynan Architects	58-63

Special Mentions
DUBLIN DENTAL HOSPITAL, Lincoln Place, Dublin 2	Ahrends Burton & Koralek Architects	64-67
NOHO LOFT, New York	Boyd Cody Architects	68-71
SCHOOL OF ART, GALWAY	de Blacam & Meagher Architects	72-75

LISTINGS

RETURN HOUSE	de Paor Architects	76-79
APARTMENT BUILDING, Amiens Street, Dublin 1	Fagan Kelly Lysaght Architects	83-85
TWO ROOFTOP APARTMENTS, BONN	Henchion + Reuter Architects	80-82
NEW KITCHEN AND BATHROOM IN A HOUSE IN RATHMINES	O'Donnell + Tuomey Architects	86-89
SACRED HEART ORATORY, Dún Laoghaire	Conor Moran, Office of Public Works	90-93
NATIONAL MUSEUM EXHIBITIONS	OPW / McCullough Mulvin Architects	94-95
RESIDENTIAL DEVELOPMENT, Beresford Street, Dublin 1	Ó Muire Smyth Architects	96-99
APARTMENT IN MIXED-USE DEVELOPMENT, Crane Lane, Dublin 2	Derek Tynan Architects	100-103
ROOM: ORGANISER-DIVIDER	Simon Walker Architect	104-106

NEW IRISH ARCHITECTURE °15 — AAI Awards 2000

ISBN 0946846 421 (ISBN-13: 978 0946846 429), 108 pages, 22.5 x 22.5 cm, 185 illus (incl 72 col)

assessors   Beatriz Colomina (Spain/USA), *architectural critic*
Florian Beigel (Germany/UK), *foreign assessor*
Tarla Mac Gabhann, James Pike, *Irish assessors*
Garry Hynes (theatre director), *distinguished non-architect*

contents		
	Assessors' Reports	5-8
	Registrar's Report / Invitation to Enter / Assessors	9-12
	AAI Awards 2000 – featured buildings and projects	13-95
	• THE GREEN BOOK, 1998-1999	96-104
	– contents include: Calendar of events / AAI Committee / AAI Members	
	– Submission to the Arts Council for the Arts Plan 1999-2001	

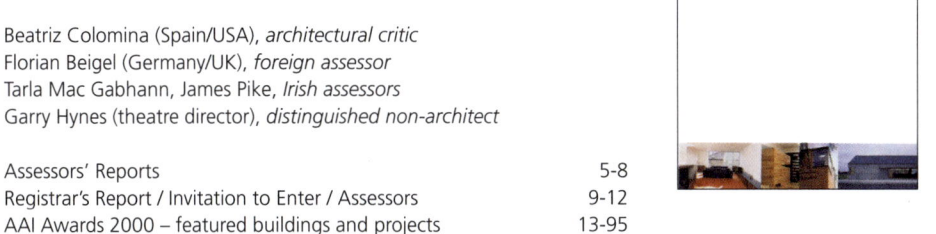

Special Awards

THREE HOUSES IN RATHMINES	Boyd Kelly Whelan Architects	14-19
TWO TIMBER BOXES	Grafton Architects	20-25
COILL DUBH & DISTRICT CREDIT UNION, Co Kildare	Hassett Ducatez Architects	26-31

Awards

URBAN PROTOTYPE	Roland Bosbach, BSPL Architects	32-37
OUR LADY'S SECONDARY SCHOOL, CASTLEBLAYNEY	Grafton Architects	38-43
ADAPTABLE ROOM	Camille O'Sullivan Architect	44-47

Special Mentions

GARAGE CONVERSION, DUN LAOGHAIRE	Box Architecture	48-51
MIXED DEVELOPMENT, 1 Castle St / 24 Werburgh St	de Blacam & Meagher Architects	52-55
ÍOSLACHT	de Paor Architects	56-59
17 PRIORY AVENUE, STILLORGAN, Co DUBLIN	Duffy Mitchell Architects	60-63
THE BOOKEND, TEMPLE BAR	Arthur Gibney & Partners, Architects	64-67
SCREENING ROOM FOR LITTLE BIRD AND CLARENCE PICTURES	Grafton Architects	68-71
DUN LAOGHAIRE DART STATION	Iarnród Éireann Architects	72-75
SOCIAL HOUSING, Rathasker Road, Naas	Kelly & Cogan Architects	76-79
CONVERSION & REFURBISHMENT OF KODAK BUILDING	Paul Keogh Architects	80-83
DESIGN STUDIOS, 47-48 Pearse Street, Dublin 2	Derek Byrne, Henry J Lyons & Partners, Architects	84-87
PINE TREES AND THE SEA	McCullough Mulvin Architects	88-91
BALTINGLASS COURTHOUSE & VISITORS' CENTRE	Newenham Mulligan & Associates, Architects	90-95

note – after New Irish Architecture °7, *the series had changed from A4 to a square format with part-colour printing;
after* New Irish Architecture °15, *it changed to a much-expanded, full-colour, and more book-like octavo format*

LISTINGS

NEW IRISH ARCHITECTURE °16 — AAI Awards 2001
ISBN 0946846 634 (ISBN-13: 978 0946846 634), 176 pages, 24 x 17 cm, 271 illus (incl 153 col)

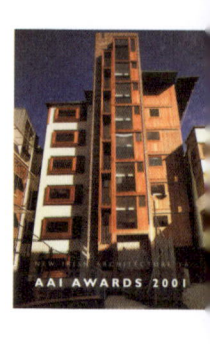

assessors	Jean-Louis Cohen (France), *architectural critic*
	Jonathan Sergison (UK), *foreign assessor*
	Sheila Foley, Michael O'Doherty, *Irish assessors*

contents   keynote essay:

'Ireland's Critical Internationalism' by Jean-Louis Cohen	6-11
Assessors' Reports	12-15
Registrar's Report / Invitation to Enter / Assessors	16-19
AAI Awards 2001 – featured buildings and projects	21-167

Awards

PROJECT ARTS CENTRE, Dublin	Shay Cleary Architects	22-31
No.1 GRAND CANAL QUAY, Dublin	de Blacam & Meagher Architects	32-41
A RESIDENTIAL TOWER IN TEMPLE BAR, Dublin	de Blacam & Meagher Architects	42-51
N³ – THE IRISH PAVILION, Architectural Biennale, Venice	de Paor Architects	52-59
11m² EXTENSION TO FAMILY HOUSE IN CITY-CENTRE VICTORIAN TERRACE, Dublin	Hassett Ducatez Architects	60-65
TOWER, Stranorlar / Ballybofey, Co Donegal	Henchion + Reuter Architects	66-71
MODEL ARTS & NILAND GALLERY, Sligo	McCullough Mulvin Architects	72-81
SMITHFIELD PUBLIC SPACE, Dublin	McGarry Ní Éanaigh Architects	82-89

Special Mentions

A.NON.ARCH	Roland Bosbach, BSPL Architects	90-95
NEW GALLERIES, IRISH MUSEUM OF MODERN ART, Royal Hospital Kilmainham, Dublin	Shay Cleary Architects	96-101
VAN – an insertion to the National Sculpture Factory, Cork	de Paor Architects	102-105
URBAN TRANSFORMATION – Styne House, Hatch Street, Dublin	Coli O'Donoghue, Gilroy McMahon Architects	106-111
FOUR PRIVATE HOUSES	Henchion + Reuter Architects	112-117
TWO HOLIDAY HOUSES, Kinsallagh, Westport	Paul Keogh Architects	118-123
MEWS HOUSE AT RAGLAN LANE, Dublin	P+A Lavin Associates, Architects	124-129
BUNSCOIL PHOBAIL FEIRSTE / Primary School, Belfast	Mackel & Doherty Architects	130-135
CORK SCHOOL PROJECT	Magee Creedon Architects	136-139
TIME TRIALS STARTING RAMP, Tour de France	Mellett Architectes Paris	140-143
BELVEDERE COLLEGE SJ / O'REILLY THEATRE, Dublin	Murray Ó Laoire Architects	144-149
IRISH PAVILION, Expo 2000, Hanover	Murray Ó Laoire Architects	150-155
EXTENSION TO TERRACED HOUSE, Heytesbury Street, Dublin 8	Derek Tynan Architects	156-159
CUT-OUT FURNITURE	Simon Walker Architect	160-163
REGENT, Temple Bar, Dublin 2	Simon Walker Architect	164-167

NEW IRISH ARCHITECTURE °17 — AAI Awards 2002
ISBN- 0946846 812 (ISBN-13: 978 0946846 818), 192 pages, 24 x 17 cm, 273 illus (incl 155 col)

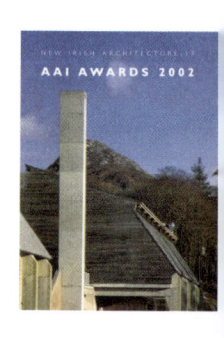

assessors	Dietmar Steiner (Austria), *architectural critic*
	Jan Olav Jensen (Norway), *foreign assessor*
	Róisín Heneghan, Barrie Todd, *Irish assessors*
	John Hutchinson (gallery director), *distinguished non-architect*

contents   keynote essay:

'Storm of Calm – a lecture on a theme' by Dietmar Steiner	6-13
Assessors' Reports	14-18

LISTINGS

Registrar's Report / Invitation to Enter / Assessors	19-23	
AAI Awards 2002 – featured buildings and projects	25-136	
• THE GREEN BOOK, 1999-2001	145-190	
– contents include: Calendar of events / AAI Committee / AAI Members		
– 'Whose city is it? Globalisation and rights to place'		
by Saskia Sassen	152-158	
– AAI Student Award 2000	160-165	
– 'Today's Manners' by Rafael Moneo	170-173	

Downes Bronze Medal

FURNITURE COLLEGE, LETTERFRACK, Co Galway	O'Donnell + Tuomey Architects	26-39

Awards

THE LONG HOUSE, Percy Lane, Dublin 4	Grafton Architects	40-47
URBAN BEEHIVE, North King Street Apartments, Dublin 7	Grafton Architects	48-57
LIFFEY BOARDWALK, Dublin	McGarry Ní Éanaigh Architects	58-67

Special Mentions

ON HOUSING	BSPL Architects	68-77
HOLDING PATTERN, A13, London	de Paor Architects	78-83
TOWN HALL, DUNSHAUGHLIN, Co Meath	Grafton Architects	84-93
OLD BOROUGH SCHOOL & PARISH CENTRE, Swords	Paul Keogh Architects	94-99
GALLERY 2, Douglas Hyde Gallery, Trinity College Dublin	McCullough Mulvin Architects	100-105
URBAN HOUSING, Apartments at 116 Grafton Street, Dublin	McCullough Mulvin Architects	106-111
EXTENSION TO TOM'S BAR, Mountrath, Co Laois	Architecture 53seven	112-117
NATIONAL MUSEUM OF COUNTRY LIFE, Castlebar, Co Mayo	Des Byrne, Office of Public Works	118-125
BUILDING THE HOME, Co Leitrim	Dominic Stevens Architect	126-135

NEW IRISH ARCHITECTURE °18 — AAI Awards 2003

ISBN 0948037 024 (ISBN-13: 978 0948037 023), 144 pages, 24 x 17 cm, 224 illus (incl 116 col)

assessors	Deyan Sudjic (Italy), *architectural critic*	
	Louisa Hutton (Germany), *foreign assessor*	
	Angela Brady, Mark Turpin, *Irish assessors*	
	Corban Walker (artist), *distinguished non-architect*	
contents	keynote essay:	
	'Building by Numbers – Political aspects of architecture'	
	by Deyan Sudjic	6-9
	Assessors' Reports	10-14
	Registrar's Report / Invitation to Enter / Assessors	15-19
	AAI Awards 2003 – featured buildings and projects	21-143

Downes Bronze Medal

USSHER LIBRARY, Trinity College Dublin	McCullough Mulvin Architects and KMD Architecture	22-37

Awards

BALDOYLE LIBRARY & PUBLIC AREA OFFICE, Co Dublin	FKL Architects	38-47
URBAN INSTITUTE IRELAND, University College Dublin	Grafton Architects	48-59
SQUARE HOUSE, South County Dublin	McCullough Mulvin Architects	60-67
LETTERKENNY AREA OFFICE, Co Donegal	Antoin Mac Gabhann Architects	68-77
LEINSTER HOUSE PRESS RECEPTION ROOM	O'Donnell + Tuomey Architects	78-85
SOCIAL HOUSING, GALBALLY, Co Limerick	O'Donnell + Tuomey Architects	86-93

LISTINGS

Special Mentions

3 (INTERVENTIONS) MODIFICATIONS	Boyd Cody Architects	94-101
ON HOUSING 2	Roland Bosbach, BSPL Architects	102-107
ARDOYNE MEWS, Ballsbridge, Dublin 4	Design Strategies	108-113
LUMEN GENTIBUS – Landscape projects for Cashel	Desmond FitzGerald Architect / LRS	114-119
MIND THE GAP, The Mall, Dublin City University	Grafton Architects	120-125
MONAGHAN EDUCATION CENTRE	McGarry Ní Éanaigh Architects	126-131
PRECAST LINES	Dominic Stevens Architect (in collaboration with John Graham)	132-137
URBAN SPACE / PRIVATE PLACE, Clarion Quay, Dublin 1	Urban Projects	138-143

NEW IRISH ARCHITECTURE °19 — AAI Awards 2004
ISBN 0948037 075 (ISBN-13: 978 0948037 078), 200 pages, 24 x 17 cm, 335 illus (incl 214 col)

assessors   Aaron Betsky (Netherlands), *architectural critic*
            Paul Robbrecht (Belgium), *foreign assessor*
            Eddie Conroy, Antoinette O'Neill, *Irish assessors*
            Marian Finucane (broadcaster), *distinguished non-architect*

contents   keynote essay:
            'Dublin From a Bird's-Eye View' by Aaron Betsky   6-9
            Assessors' Reports   10-15
            Registrar's Report / Invitation to Enter / Assessors   16-19
            AAI Awards 2004 – featured buildings and projects   21-198

Downes Bronze Medal

A WAY TO SCHOOL – Ardscoil Mhuire, Ballinasloe, and North Kildare Educate Together Project, Celbridge	Grafton Architects	22-47

Awards

CIGAR BOX, 26 North Great Georges St, Dublin 1	Denis Byrne Architects	48-59
UTILITY BUILDING, Vernon Avenue, Clontarf, Dublin 3	de Paor Architects	60-69
BRICK HOUSE, Milltown Path, Dublin 6	FKL Architects	70-79
DOUBLE GLASS HOUSE, Dublin	Hassett Ducatez Architects	80-87
TUBBERCURRY LIBRARY AND CIVIC OFFICES	McCullough Mulvin Architects	88-99
EXTENSION TO VIRUS REFERENCE LABORATORY, UCD	McCullough Mulvin Architects	100-107
MEDICAL RESEARCH LABORATORIES, UCD	O'Donnell + Tuomey Architects	108-117

Special Mentions

BRICK COURTS HOUSE, 37 Daniel Street, Dublin 8	Architects Bates Maher	118-121
3, 4, 5 TEMPLE COTTAGES, Dublin 7	Boyd Cody Architects	122-127
ON HOUSING 3	Roland Bosbach, BSPL Architects	128-135
LIMERICK COUNTY COUNCIL HEADQUARTERS	Bucholz McEvoy Architects	136-139
PERISCOPE, Pembroke Lane, Dublin 4	Gerard Carty Architect	140-145
ALLINETT'S LANE APARTMENTS, Blackpool, Cork	MV Cullinan Architects	146-151
LIFFEY HOUSE, Tara Street, Dublin 2	Donnelly Turpin Architects	152-159
SPORTS AND YOUTH SERVICES CENTRE, Cabra, Dublin 7	Henchion + Reuter Architects	160-165
OFFICE FOR A COFFEE IMPORTER, Dargan Road, Belfast	Alan Jones Architect	166-171
MORTUARY CHAPELS & POSTMORTEM SUITE, St James's Hospital, Dublin 8	Henry J Lyons & Partners, Architects	172-179
HOWTH HOUSE, Co Dublin	O'Donnell + Tuomey Architects	180-187
AIRPORT BRIDGES Northern Motorway / Airport-Balbriggan Bypass	Roughan & O'Donovan / Grafton Architects	188-191
IN-BETWEEN HOUSE, Ballinamore, Co Leitrim	Dominic Stevens Architect	192-197

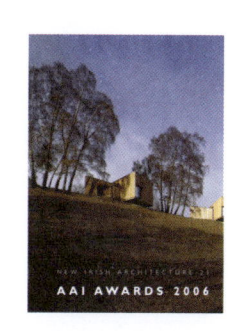

LISTINGS

NEW IRISH ARCHITECTURE °20 — AAI Awards 2005
ISBN 0946846 561 (ISBN-13: 978 0946846 566), 224 pages, 24 x 17 cm, 362 illus (255 col)

assessors   Terence Riley (USA), *architectural critic*
               Kees Kaan (Netherlands), Manuel Aires Mateus (Portugal), *foreign assessors*
               Denis Byrne, *Irish assessor*
               Patrick T Murphy (gallery director), *distinguished non-architect*

contents   keynote essay:

'This Will Kill That – A brief history of seven centuries of architecture and the media' by Terence Riley	6-23
Assessors' Reports	24-29
Registrar's Report / Statistics / Invitation to Enter / Assessors	30-35
AAI Awards 2005 – featured buildings and projects	37-157
• THE GREEN BOOK, 2001-2005	161-176
– contents include: Calendar of events / AAI Committee	
• AAI AWARDS XX – 20th ANNIVERSARY, 1986-2005	
– annual results lists (with award-winning projects illustrated)	177-217
– award-winning projects listed by architect	218-223

Downes Bronze Medal

ALMA LANE, Monkstown, Co Dublin	Boyd Cody Architects	38-51

Awards

WELLINGTON ROAD, Dublin 4	Boyd Cody Architects	52-61
YOUTH AND COMMUNITY CENTRE, Donore Avenue, Dublin 8	Henchion + Reuter Architects	62-75
PEABODY HOUSING, Silvertown, London E16	Níall McLaughlin Architects	76-87

Special Mentions

REFURBISHMENT OF CAR PARK, Drury Street, Dublin 2	Cullen Payne Architects	88-93
CONNEMARA BOATHOUSE, Moyard, Co Galway	MV Cullinan Architects	94-97
DUBCO CREDIT UNION, Little Green Street, Dublin 1	Donnelly Turpin Architects	98-105
FINGLAS SWIMMING POOL AND LEISURE CENTRE, Mellowes Park, Dublin 11	Donnelly Turpin Architects	106-113
HOUSE AT DIRK COVE, Clonakilty, Co Cork	Níall McLaughlin Architects	114-123
HOUSEBOAT	Níall McLaughlin Architects	124-129
VEHICULAR AND PEDESTRIAN BRIDGE, University of Limerick	Murray Ó Laoire Architects / Arup	130-135
LEWIS GLUCKSMAN GALLERY, University College Cork	O'Donnell + Tuomey Architects	136-147
IRELAND'S PAVILION AT THE VENICE BIENNALE	O'Donnell + Tuomey Architects	148-157

NEW IRISH ARCHITECTURE °21 — AAI Awards 2006
ISBN 0946846 901 (ISBN-13: 978 0946846 900), 176 pages, 24 x 17 cm, 310 illus (186 col)

assessors   Andrej Hrausky (Slovenia), *architectural critic*
               Carmé Piños (Spain), *foreign assessor*
               Dominic Stevens, *Irish assessor*
               Ciarán Benson (psychologist), *distinguished non-architect*

contents   keynote essay:

'Joze Plecnik (1872-1957), Ljubljana' by Andrej Hrausky	6-20
Assessors' Reports	22-25
Registrar's Report / Statistics / Assessors	26-29
AAI Awards 2006 – featured buildings and projects	31-173

LISTINGS

Downes Bronze Medal

POUSTINIA, Glencomeragh House of Prayer, Clonmel, Co Tipperary	Architects Bates Maher	32-45

Awards

SORRENTO HEIGHTS, Dalkey, Co Dublin	Boyd Cody Architects	46-55
CITY HOUSE AND WORKPLACE, 41 Francis Street, Dublin 8	Donaghy + Dimond Architects	56-63
MME – Extension to Dept of Mechanical & Manufacturing Engineering, Trinity College Dublin	Grafton Architects	64-75
ENGINEERS IRELAND, 20 Clyde Road, Dublin 4	McCullough Mulvin Architects	76-83
HOUSE AT CROUCH END, London	Níall McLaughlin Architects	84-93
BROOKE HEUSSAFF LIBRARY, South Circular Road, Dublin 8	NJBA Architects	94-101
13a THOR PLACE, Stoneybatter, Dublin 7	ODOS Architects	102-111

Special Mentions

HOUSE, RICHMOND PLACE, Rathmines, Dublin 6	Boyd Cody Architects	112-119
TWO TWO UP TWO DOWN, John Dillon Street, Dublin 8	de Paor Architects	120-129
KITCHEN-GARDEN-PARTY-WALL, Arran Road, Dublin 9	Donaghy + Dimond Architects	130-137
MARTIN VALLEY SCULPTURE PARK, Cork	FKL Architects	138-145
REUBEN STREET APARTMENTS, Dublin 8	FKL Architects	146-151
IJBURG BLOK 4, Amsterdam	Maccreanor Lavington Architects	152-159
No.33 ST KEVIN'S ROAD, Portobello, Dublin 8	ODOS Architects	160-165
ATHLONE CIVIC CENTRE, LIBRARY AND TOWN SQUARE	Keith Williams Architects	166-171

NEW IRISH ARCHITECTURE °22 — AAI Awards 2007

ISBN 978 0948037 467, 176 pages, 24 x 17 cm, 240 illus (incl 162 col)

assessors   Luis Fernández-Galiano (Spain), *architectural critic*
Jonathan Woolf (UK), *foreign assessor*
Peter McGovern, Robert Payne, *Irish assessors*
Mary McCarthy (arts administrator), *distinguished non-architect*

contents   keynote essay:

'Dublin Duet – Landscape with Figures / The Celtic Tiger' by Luis Fernández-Galiano	6-12
Assessors' Reports	14-17
Registrar's Report / Statistics / Invitation to Enter / Assessors	18-23
AAI Awards 2007 – featured buildings and projects	25-152
• THE GREEN BOOK, 2004-2007	161-176
– contents include: Calendar of events / AAI Committee	
– 'A brief history of the AAI' by Shane O'Toole	174

Awards

MEETING PLACE, North Campus Development, Cork Institute of Technology	de Blacam & Meagher Boyd Barrett Murphy-O'Connor Architects	26-41
HOUSE AT AILL BREAC, Baile Uí Chonaola, Contae na Gaillimhe	de Paor Architects	42-49
SOLSTICE ARTS CENTRE, Navan, Co Meath	Grafton Architects	50-63
SOURCE ARTS CENTRE & LIBRARY, Thurles, Co Tipperary	McCullough Mulvin Architects	64-77
RIVERSIDE ONE, Sir John Rogerson's Quay, Dublin 2	Scott Tallon Walker Architects	78-89
MIMETIC HOUSE, Dromaheir, Co Leitrim	Dominic Stevens Architect	90-99

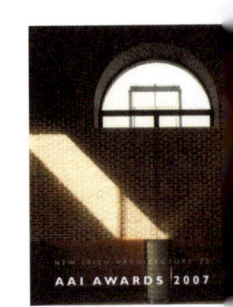

Special Mentions

BRICK THICKNESS, 11 Cowper Drive, Dublin 6	A2 Architects	100-107
ST JUDE'S RESIDENCE, Glengowla, Co Galway	Boyer Kennihan Architects	108-115
REDEVELOPMENT OF CORK COUNTY HALL	Shay Cleary Architects	116-127

LISTINGS

SOCIAL HOUSING, BALLYMUN | FKL Architects | 128-135
CAVAN INSTITUTE, Cathedral Road, Cavan | McCullough Mulvin Architects | 136-143
KNOCKTOPHER FRIARY, Co Kilkenny | ODOS Architects / O'Shea Design Partners | 144-152

NEW IRISH ARCHITECTURE °23 — AAI Awards 2008
ISBN 978 0948037 573, 176 pages, 24 x 17 cm, 255 illus (incl 136 col)

assessors   Francis Rambert (France), *architectural critic*
            Julien de Smedt (Denmark), *foreign assessor*
            Martin Henchion, Angela Rolfe, *Irish assessors* /
            John Gerrard (artist / photographer), *distinguished non-architect*

contents   keynote essay:
            'New Landscapes and Fresh Attitudes' by Francis Rambert   6-18
            Assessors' Reports   20-24
            Registrar's Report / Statistics / Invitation to Enter / Assessors   25-30
            AAI Awards 2008 – featured buildings and projects   31-161

            • THE GREEN BOOK, 2007-2008   171-175
            – contents include: Calendar of events / AAI Committee

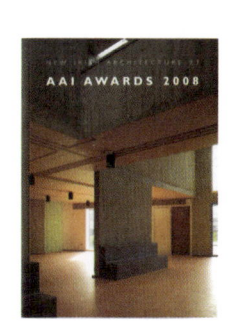

Downes Bronze Medal
BROOKFIELD COMMUNITY YOUTH CENTRE & CRÈCHE, Tallaght, Dublin 24 | Hassett Ducatez Architects | 32-49

Special Awards
EGAN'S JUICE BAR & ROOF TERRACE, Main Street, Portlaoise | Architecture 53 seven | 50-61
34 PALMERSTON ROAD, Rathmines, Dublin 6 | Boyd Cody Architects | 62-75

Awards
ONE UP, ONE DOWN, ONE DEEP, Portobello, Dublin 6 | A2 Architects | 76-83
CORK CITY COUNCIL – NEW CIVIC OFFICES | ABK Architects | 84-99
SITE 7, BRIARHILL BUSINESS PARK, Galway | Paul Dillon Architect | 100-107

Special Mentions
THE NARROW HOUSE, 3 Northumberland Road, Dun Laoghaire | Architecture Republic | 108-115
ST JAMES, Clontarf, Dublin 3 | Boyd Cody Architects | 116-123
GROUNDWORKS, Clontarf, Dublin 3 | de Paor Architects | 124-131
HOUSING AT PEARSE SQUARE, Dublin 2 | GKMP Architects, in assoc. with O'Mahony Pike | 132-139
ARC BUILDING, Built Environment Centre, Hull, England | Níall McLaughlin Architects | 140-147
TAILTEANN, Mary Immaculate College, Limerick | Murray Ó Laoire Architects | 148-155
TRINITY IRISH ART RESEARCH CENTRE, Trinity College Dublin | O'Donnell + Tuomey Architects | 156-161

NEW IRISH ARCHITECTURE °24 — AAI Awards 2009
ISBN 978 0948037 719, 272 pages, 24 x 17 cm, 460 illus (243 ph + 217 drgs)

assessors   Wilfried Wang (UK / Germany), *architectural critic*
            Eero Koivisto (Sweden), Dominic Papa (UK), *foreign assessors*
            Gráinne Hassett, *Irish assessor*
            Tim Robinson (artist / writer), *distinguished non-architect*

contents   keynote essay:
            'Quality Matters' by Wilfried Wang   6-21

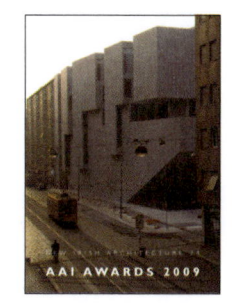

LISTINGS

Assessors' Reports — 24-30
Registrar's Report / Statistics / Invitation to Enter / Assessors — 31-36
First Impressions (assessment day) — 38-39
AAI Awards 2009 – featured buildings and projects — 40-271

Downes Bronze Medal
UNIVERSITÀ LUIGI BOCCONI, Milan — Grafton Architects — 40-59

Special Awards
7-9 MERRION ROW + THE BILLETS, Dublin 2 — Grafton Architects — 60-75
SEÁN O'CASEY COMMUNITY CENTRE, East Wall, Dublin 3 — O'Donnell + Tuomey Architects — 76-89

Awards
HOUSE IN GRAIGUENAMANAGH, Co Kilkenny — Boyd Cody Architects — 90-99
LIGHT HOUSE CINEMA, Smithfield, Dublin 7 — DTA Architects — 100-109
JIG-SAW, Leeson Park, Dublin 6 — McCullough Mulvin Architects — 110-117
LINCOLN PLACE, Dublin 2 — McCullough Mulvin Architects — 118-125
THE SLEEPING GIANT, KILLINEY, Co Dublin — O'Donnell + Tuomey Architects — 126-135

Special Mentions
EUROCAMPUS, Roebuck Road, Dublin 14 — A2 Architects — 136-145
MATILDE, Rathgar, Dublin 6 — Ailtireacht — 146-153
3 HOUSES, CONG, Co Galway — Aughey O'Flaherty Architects — 154-161
STUDIO, PALMERSTON ROAD, Dublin 6 — Boyd Cody Architects — 162-167
SIOPA PAVILION, Kildare Street, Dublin 2 — Bucholz McEvoy Architects — 168-173
ADDITIONAL ACCOMMODATION, SS GEORGE & THOMAS CHURCH,
    Cathal Brugha Street, Dublin 1 — Clancy Moore Architects — 174-179
ALTO VETRO RESIDENTIAL TOWER, Grand Canal Quay, Dublin 2 — Shay Cleary Architects — 180-187
JOYCE'S COURT PEDESTRIAN STREET, Dublin 1 — Dermot Foley Landscape Architects — 188-191
DWELLING SPACE, Eglinton Road, Dublin 4 — GKMP Architects — 192-199
EASA TIMBER PAVILION, Letterfrack, Co Galway — Happy Architecture — 200-203
REGIONAL CULTURAL CENTRE, Letterkenny, Co Donegal — Mac Gabhann Architects — 204-213
TUATH NA MARA, Lough Swilly, Co Donegal — Mac Gabhann Architects — 214-219
BALLYFERMOT LEISURE AND YOUTH CENTRE, Dublin 10 — McGarry Ní Éanaigh Architects — 220-227
BUSH SPORTS HALL, Cooley, Co Louth — McGarry Ní Éanaigh Architects — 228-233
HOUSE AT PIPER'S END, Letty Green, Herts, England — Níall McLaughlin Architects — 234-241
PEDESTRIAN BRIDGE, BRISTOL — Níall McLaughlin Architects — 242-247
DWELLING AT ST PATRICK'S COTTAGES,
    Rathfarnham, Dublin 16 — ODOS Architects — 248-255
10A LOWER GRANGEGORMAN, Dublin 7 — ODOS Architects — 256-263
304 SPRING STREET, New York — Zakrzewski + Hyde Architects — 264-271

NEW IRISH ARCHITECTURE °25 — AAI Awards 2010
ISBN 978 0948037 764, 240 pages, 24 x 17 cm, 429 illus (233 ph + 196 drgs)

assessors — Charles Jencks (USA / UK), *architectural critic*
Andrea Deplazes (Switzerland), *foreign assessor*
Yvonne Farrell, John McLaughlin, *Irish assessors*
Raymond Keaveney (gallery director), *distinguished non-architect*

contents — keynote essay:
'Critical Modernism: The Movement' by Charles Jencks — 6-21
Assessors' Reports — 26-31
Registrar's Report / Statistics / Invitation to Enter / Assessors — 32-37

LISTINGS

First Impressions (assessment day)		40-47
AAI Awards 2010 – featured buildings and projects		48-237

Downes Bronze Medal

TIMBERYARD SOCIAL HOUSING, Coombe Bypass, Dublin 8	O'Donnell + Tuomey Architects	48-63

Special Awards

ALZHEIMER'S RESPITE CENTRE, Blackrock, Co Dublin	Niall McLaughlin Architects	64-77
AN GAELÁRAS, Derry	O'Donnell + Tuomey Architects	78-93

Awards

NEW ORDER, Stoneybatter, Dublin 7	Peter Carroll, Caomhán Murphy, A2 Architects	94-103
LAKE HOUSE EXTENSION + RENOVATION, Co Kerry	Clancy Moore Architects	104-113
HOUSE – GARDEN – GRAFT, Ranelagh, Dublin 6	Donaghy + Dimond Architects	114-123
HOUSE 1 + HOUSE 2, Morehampton Road, Dublin 4	Taka Architects	124-133

Special Mentions

THE PLASTIC HOUSE, Dublin 3	Maxim Laroussi, Jean Baptiste Astruc, Architecture Republic	134-141
Y = 3 HOUSES, North Circular Road, Dublin 1	Maxim Laroussi, Javier Burón García, Architecture Republic	142-147
SLATE-STOREY EXTENSION, Chapelizod, Dublin 20	Tom Maher, ArchitectsTM	148-155
DARTMOUTH SQUARE, Dublin 6	Max O'Flaherty, Aughey O'Flaherty Architects	156-163
EXTENSION TO A PROTECTED STRUCTURE, Rathgar, Dublin 6	Garbhann Doran Architects	164-171
SLIABH BÁN HOUSING, Galway	DTA Architects	172-179
COMMON GROUND: Urban Landscape in Kilkenny	GKMP Architects	180-187
LANDSCAPE ROOM, Glencar, Sligo	LID Architecture	188-193
PLUG-IN PATH AT WOODVALE PARK, Shankill, Belfast	LID Architecture, with Building Initiative	194-201
SCHOOL OF ENGINEERING, Athlone Institute of Technology	McCullough Mulvin Architects	202-209
ARCHITECT'S OFFICE, Letterkenny, Co Donegal	Mac Gabhann Architects	210-215
FATHER COLLINS PARK, Donaghmede, Dublin 13	MCO Projects / ARARQ Ireland	216-221
3 MEWS DWELLINGS, Portobello, Dublin 8	ODOS Architects	222-229
31 CARYSFORT ROAD, Dalkey, Co Dublin	ODOS Architects	230-237

NEW IRISH ARCHITECTURE °26 — AAI Awards 2011

ISBN 978 0948037 870, 176 pages, 24 x 17 cm, 375 illus (229 ph + 146 drgs)

assessors	William JR Curtis (UK), *architectural critic*
	Jo Taillieu (Belgium), Tony Fretton (UK) *foreign assessors*
	Merritt Bucholz, *Irish assessor*
	Ivana Bacik (professor of law), *distinguished non-architect*

contents	keynote essay:	
	'*The Time of Life, The Time of Architecture*' by William JR Curtis	6-13
	Assessors' Reports	16-19
	Registrar's Report	20-21
	First Impressions (assessment day)	22-25
	AAI Awards 2011 – featured buildings and projects	26-171
	• AAI 2nd Year Competition – '*A Smallest Room for the City*'	174-175

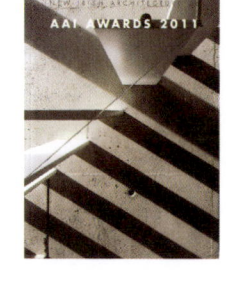

Special Awards

RATHMINES SQUARE – Leisure Centre + Apartments, Dublin 6	Mark Turpin, Donnelly Turpin Architects	26-37
SOCIAL & AFFORDABLE HOUSING, SANTRY DEMESNE	Niall Rowan, DTA Architects	38-49
A-HOUSE, Rathmines, Dublin 6	FKL Architects	50-59
HOUSE IN WOODS, Co Kildare	Hassett Ducatez Architects	60-69

LISTINGS

Awards
'Flow', BORD GÁIS ABOVE-GROUND INSTALLATION, North Wall Quay, Dublin 1	John McLaughlin, DDDA and Martin Richman, artist	70-75
AVIVA STADIUM, Lansdowne Road, Dublin 4	Scott Tallon Walker Architects and Populous	76-85
E25,000 HOUSE, Cloone, Co Leitrim	Dominic Stevens Architects	86-93

Special Mentions
ARTIST'S PRODUCTION SPACE, Vienna	A2 Architects	94-97
BRICK A BACK, Gordon Street, Dublin 4	Maxim Laroussi, Architecture Republic	98-101
LOGGIA – STUDENT WORKSHOP, Angone, Italy	Attley Donnellan Kelly O'Brien Architects	102-105
BALLYROAN PARISH CENTRE, Rathfarnham, Dublin 14	Gary Mongey, Ashlene Ross, Box Architecture	106-111
HOUSE REFURBISHMENT & EXTENSION, Dartry, Dublin 6	Carson and Crushell Architects	112-115
FLITCH, Ranelagh, Dublin 6	Donaghy + Dimond Architects	116-119
A DOMESTIC EVOLUTION, Sandymount, Dublin 4	David Flynn Architects	120-125
HOUSE FOR A PRESIDENT, University of Limerick	Grafton Architects	126-131
SALLYMOUNT TERRACE, Ranelagh, Dublin 6	Ryan W Kennihan Architects	132-135
Z SQUARE HOUSE, Temple Gardens, Dublin 6	McCullough Mulvin Architects	136-141
DUNSHAUGHLIN PASTORAL CENTRE, Co Meath	McGarry Ní Éanaigh Architects	142-147
TWO OF EVERYTHING, Sandymount, Dublin 4	Robin Mandal Architects / Fitzpatrick & Mays Architects	148-153
CHILD & ADOLESCENT MENTAL HEALTH UNIT, Merlin Park, Galway	Mícheál de Siún, Moloney O'Beirne Architects	154-159
JESUIT COMMUNITY, Milltown Park, Dublin 6	Scott Tallon Walker Architects	160-165
GLASNEVIN NATIONAL HERITAGE PROJECT + GLASNEVIN TRUST MUSEUM	Andrzej Wejchert, Hugh Maguire, A&D Wejchert & Partners	166-171

NEW IRISH ARCHITECTURE °27 — AAI Awards 2012
ISBN 978 0946641 864, 160 pages, 24 x 17 cm, 255 illus (135 ph + 120 drgs)

assessors   Joseph Rykwert (UK), *architectural critic*
Keith Williams (UK), *foreign assessor*
Noel Brady, Merritt Bucholz, *Irish assessors*
Rúairí Ó Cuív (arts consultant), *distinguished non-architect*

contents   keynote essay:
'Refuse and the Body Politic' by Joseph Rykwert	8-19
Assessors' Reports	22-26
Registrar's Report / Assessors / Statistics	27-29, 35
First Impressions (assessment day)	30-34
AAI Awards 2012 – featured buildings and projects	36-133
• Maurice Craig Award (final year thesis projects) – winner: Patrick Phelan (UCD); commended: Catherine Blaney (QUB), Sinéad MacMahon (SAUL), Claire McMenamin (UCD)	135-151
• AAI 2nd Year Competition – 'A Boat-Building Facility'	156-159

Special Award
LYRIC THEATRE, Belfast	O'Donnell + Tuomey Architects	36-51

Awards
HOUSE ON MOUNT ANVILLE, Dublin 14	Aughey O'Flaherty Architects	52-61
LANEWAY WALL GARDEN HOUSE	Donaghy + Dimond Architects	62-69
HOUSE IN BOGWEST, Co Wexford	Steve Larkin Architects	70-79
BUTTERFLY HOUSE, Co Leitrim	LiD Architecture	80-87

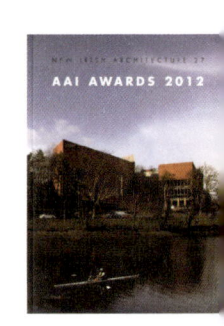

Special Mentions

SHELTERED SPACES	A2 Architects	88-95
FORMWORK	Architecture Republic	96-103
BACKYARD, John Dillon Street, Dublin 8	Boyd Cody Architects	104-109
EXTENSION AND RENOVATION IN PORTOBELLO	Donal Colfer Architect	110-117
EDGE OF TOWN – Local Area Offices, Claremorris	SImon J Kelly + Partners Architects	118-125
LONG ROOM HUB, Trinity College Dublin	McCullough Mulvin Architects	126-133

NEW IRISH ARCHITECTURE °28 — AAI Awards 2013

ISBN 978-1-910140-00-0, 224 pages, 24 x 17 cm, 300 illus (163 ph + 137 drgs)

assessors   Elizabeth Hatz (Sweden), *architectural critic*
                Daniel Rosbottom (UK), *foreign assessor*
                Shane de Blacam, Donal Hickey, *Irish assessors*
                Maud Cotter (artist), *distinguished non-architect*

contents   keynote essay:

'Between Permanance and Transience' by Elizabeth Hatz	8-19
Assessors' Reports	22-24
Registrar's Report / Statistics / Assessors	25-28
First Impressions (assessment day)	29-33
AAI Awards 2013 – featured buildings and projects	34-163
• Maurice Craig Award (final year thesis projects)	165-171
– winner: Alan Hilliard (SAUL); highly commended: Eimear Murphy (QUB)	
• AAI 2nd Year Competition – 'Hill Walkers' Shelter'	172-175
• Index to all 28 volumes of *New Irish Architecture – AAI Awards*	
– back-issues / order form	176-179
– listings (contents, volume by volume)	180-199
– architects index	200-212
– building type index	213-224

Downes Bronze Medal

SLIEVEBAWNOGUE (double-house)	Clancy Moore Architects	34-49

Awards

RECASTING	Donaghy + Dimond Architects	50-61
MEDICAL SCHOOL, STUDENT RESIDENCES & BUS SHELTER, University of Limerick	Grafton Architects	62-77
ARCHITECTURE AS NEW GEOGRAPHY (Venice Biennale 2012)	Grafton Architects	78-87
SCOIL MHUIRE ÓGH, Crumlin, Dublin	Mary Laheen Architects	88-101
HOUSE IN CO CARLOW	Steve Larkin Architect	102-113
HOUSE 4, Firhouse, Dublin	Taka Architects	114-125

Special Mentions

CARNIVAN HOUSE, Fethard-on-Sea, Co Wexford	Aughey O'Flaherty Architects	126-133
HOUSE ON CHESTNUT LANE	Boyd Cody Architects	134-141
BORD GÁIS NETWORKS SERVICES CENTRE	Denis Byrne Architects	142-149
THE GARAGE, Co Fermanagh	John Maguire Architect	150-155
VESSEL: an installation for the Venice Biennale 2012	O'Donnell + Tuomey Architects	156-163

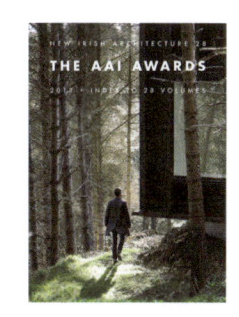

---

note – to order back-issues of New Irish Architecture, *see order form on page 179*

Architects

NEW IRISH ARCHITECTURE °1-28 — AAI Awards 1986-2013

architects index covering the 455 projects featured in the AAI Awards 1986-2013 and the 28 volumes of *New Irish Architecture* (with projects listed chronologically by architect)

awards   M = Downes Bronze Medal / *M = Joint Medal / SA = Special Award / A = Award
SM = Special Mention / SE = Selected for Exhibition (AAI Awards 1986-1990)

note   only the main illustrated project-spreads are listed; projects may also be referred to in the Assessors' Reports (NIA °1–28), Update section (NIA °2–8), and First Impressions (NIA °24–28)

architect	project	award	volume / year	pages
5F Architects	MoS BUILDING, Abbeyfeale, Co Limerick	SM 1997	NIA–12	56-58
A2 Architects	BRICK THICKNESS, 11 Cowper Drive, Dublin 6	SM 2007	NIA–22	100-107
	ONE UP, ONE DOWN, ONE DEEP, Portobello, Dublin 6	A 2008	NIA–23	76-83
	EUROCAMPUS, Roebuck Road, Dublin 14	SM 2009	NIA–24	136-145
	NEW ORDER, Stoneybatter, Dublin 7	A 2010	NIA–25	94-103
	ARTIST'S PRODUCTION SPACE, Vienna	SM 2011	NIA–26	94-97
	SHELTERED SPACES	SM 2012	NIA–27	88-95
ABK Architects	CORK CITY COUNCIL – NEW CIVIC OFFICES	A 2008	NIA–23	84-99
	• see also: Ahrends Burton & Koralek Architects			
Aer Rianta Technical Consultants	NEW TERMINAL DEVELOPMENT, Kerry Airport	SM 1995	NIA–10	36-37
Ahrends Burton & Koralek Architects	DUBLIN DENTAL HOSPITAL, Lincoln Place	SM 1999	NIA–14	64-67
	• see also: ABK Architects			
Ailtireacht	MATILDE, Rathgar, Dublin 6	SM 2009	NIA–24	146-153
Akiboye Conolly Architects	EXPERIMENTAL SOLAR HOUSE & STUDIO, West Cork	SM 1998	NIA–13	36-39
ARARQ Ireland / MCO Projects	FR COLLINS PARK, Donaghmede, Dublin 13	SM 2010	NIA–25	216-221
Architects Bates Maher	BRICK COURTS HOUSE, 37 Daniel Street, Dublin 8	SM 2004	NIA–19	118-121
	POUSTINIA, Glencomeragh House of Prayer, Co Tipperary	M 2006	NIA–21	32-45
	• see also: ArchitectsTM			
Architecture 53seven	EXTENSION TO TOM'S BAR, Mountrath, Co Laois	SM 2002	NIA–17	112-117
	EGAN'S JUICE BAR & ROOF TERRACE, Main Street, Portlaoise	SA 2008	NIA–23	50-61
Architecture Republic	NARROW HOUSE, Northumberland Road, Dun Laoghaire	SM 2008	NIA–23	108-115
	THE PLASTIC HOUSE, Dublin 3	SM 2010	NIA–25	134-141
	Y = 3 HOUSES, North Circular Road, Dublin 1	SM 2010	NIA–25	142-147

ARCHITECTS

	BRICK A BACK, Gordon Street, Dublin 4	SM 2011	NIA–26	98-101
	FORMWORK	SM 2012	NIA–27	96-103
ArchitectsTM	SLATE-STOREY EXTENSION, Chapelizod, Dublin 20	SM 2010	NIA–25	148-155
	• see also: Architects Bates Maher			
Attley Donnellan Kelly O'Brien Architects	LOGGIA, Angone, Italy	SM 2011	NIA–26	102-105
Aughey O'Flaherty Architects	3 HOUSES, CONG, Co Galway	SM 2009	NIA–24	154-161
	DARTMOUTH SQUARE, Dublin 6	SM 2010	NIA–25	156-163
	HOUSE ON MOUNT ANVILLE, Dublin 14	A 2012	NIA–27	42-61
	CARNIVAN HOUSE, Fethard-on-Sea	SM 2013	NIA–28	126-133
The Bacon Group, Architects	HOUSE A	SM 1992	NIA–7	20-21
Beardsmore Yauner Byrne Architects / Felim Dunne & Associates	RECONSTRUCTION OF TROPICAL FRUITS BUILDING	A 1991	NIA–6	11-13
Bingham & Kelly Architects	A YOUTH HOSTEL IN LEITRIM	SE 1990	NIA–5	26-27
	A ROOM WITH A VIEW	A 1991	NIA–6	6-7
Box Architecture	GARAGE CONVERSION, DUN LAOGHAIRE	SM 2000	NIA–15	48-51
	BALLYROAN PASTORAL CENTRE, Rathfarnham, Dublin 14	SM 2011	NIA–26	106-111
Boyd Barrett Murphy-O'Connor Architects	• see: de Blacam & Meagher			
Boyd Cody Architects	NOHO LOFT, New York	SM 1999	NIA–14	68-71
	3 (INTERVENTIONS) MODIFICATIONS	SM 2003	NIA–18	94-101
	3, 4, 5 TEMPLE COTTAGES, Dublin 7	SM 2004	NIA–19	122-127
	ALMA LANE, Monkstown, Co Dublin	M 2005	NIA–20	38-51
	WELLINGTON ROAD, Dublin 4	A 2005	NIA–20	52-61
	SORRENTO HEIGHTS, Dalkey, Co Dublin	A 2006	NIA–21	46-55
	HOUSE, RICHMOND PLACE, Rathmines, Dublin 6	SM 2006	NIA–21	112-119
	34 PALMERSTON ROAD, Rathmines, Dublin 6	SA 2008	NIA–23	62-75
	ST JAMES, Clontarf, Dublin 3	SM 2008	NIA–23	116-123
	HOUSE IN GRAIGUENAMANAGH, Co Kilkenny	A 2009	NIA–24	90-99
	STUDIO, PALMERSTON ROAD, Dublin 6	SM 2009	NIA–24	162-167
	BACKYARD, JOHN DILLON STREET, Dublin 8	SM 2012	NIA–27	104-109
	HOUSE ON CHESTNUT LANE	SM 2013	NIA–28	134-141
Boyd Kelly Whelan Architects	THREE HOUSES IN RATHMINES, Dublin 6	SA 2000	NIA–15	14-19
Boyer Kennihan Architects	ST JUDE'S RESIDENCE, Glengowla, Co Galway	SM 2007	NIA–22	108-115
Brady + Mallalieu Architects	MIGRANT ACCESS CENTRE, Camden, London	SM 1991	NIA–6	18-19
	NEW SCHOOL OF ARCHITECTURE & INTERIOR DESIGN, University of North London	SM 1997	NIA–12	44-46
BSPL Architects	URBAN PROTOTYPE	A 2000	NIA–15	32-37
	A.NON.ARCH	SM 2001	NIA–16	90-95
	ON HOUSING	SM 2002	NIA–17	68-77
	ON HOUSING 2	SM 2003	NIA–18	102-107
	ON HOUSING 3	SM 2004	NIA–19	128-135
Bucholz McEvoy Architects	LIMERICK COUNTY COUNCIL HEADQUARTERS	SM 2004	NIA–19	136-139
	SIOPA PAVILION, Kildare Street, Dublin 2	SM 2009	NIA–24	168-173

ARCHITECTS

architect	project	award	volume / year	pages
Building Consultancy Group	ESB TRAINING CENTRE, Portlaoise	SM 1997	NIA–12	47-49
Denis Byrne Architects	CIGAR BOX, 26 North Great Georges St, Dublin 1	A 2004	NIA–19	48-59
	BORD GÁIS NETWORKS SERVICES CENTRE	SM 2013	NIA–28	142-149
Gerry Cahill Architects	CO-OPERATIVE HOUSING, Allingham Street, Dublin 1	SM 1997	NIA–12	50-52
	SOCIAL HOUSING, New Street, Dublin 8	A 1995	NIA–10	16-19
	• see also: Urban Projects			
Ross Cahill-O'Brien Architect	A RURAL HOUSE	A 1988	NIA–3	8-9
	HOUSE AT BOFARA, Westport	A 1991	NIA–6	8-10
	THE KITCHEN NIGHTCLUB, Temple Bar, Dublin 2	SM 1995	NIA–10	38-39
Carson and Crushell Architects	HOUSE REFURBISHMENT & EXTENSION, Dartry, Dublin 6	SM 2011	NIA–26	112-115
Gerard Carty Architect	A HOUSE IN PORTARLINGTON	A 1989	NIA–4	9-11
	BAY WINDOW & STAIRCASE INSERTION, Windsor Terrace, Dublin 4	A 1998	NIA–13	12-17
	PERISCOPE, Pembroke Lane, Dublin 4	SM 2004	NIA–19	140-145
Clancy Moore Architects	ADDITIONAL ACCOMMODATION, SS GEORGE & THOMAS CHURCH, Cathal Brugha Street, Dublin 1	SM 2009	NIA–24	174-179
	LAKE HOUSE EXTENSION + RENOVATION, Co Kerry	A 2010	NIA–25	104-113
	SLIEVEBAWNOGUE (double-house)	M 2013	NIA–28	34-49
Shay Cleary Architects	SHOWROOM AND OFFICES	A 1988	NIA–3	10-11
	ENTRANCE HALL, BAR & RESTAURANT, POINT DEPOT, Dublin	M 1989	NIA–4	4-8
	IRISH MUSEUM OF MODERN ART	A 1992	NIA–7	8-10
	NEW FOYER ETC, DEPT OF AGRICULTURE	SM 1995	NIA–10	40-41
	BLACKROCK EDUCATION CENTRE, Co Dublin	SM 1997	NIA–12	53-55
	PROJECT ARTS CENTRE, Dublin	A 2001	NIA–16	22-31
	NEW GALLERIES, IMMA, Royal Hospital Kilmainham, Dublin	SM 2001	NIA–16	96-101
	REDEVELOPMENT OF CORK COUNTY HALL	SM 2007	NIA–22	116-127
	ALTO VETRO RESIDENTIAL TOWER, Grand Canal Quay, Dublin 2	SM 2009	NIA–24	180-187
	• see also: Group 91			
Donal Colfer Architect	EXTENSION AND RENOVATION IN PORTOBELLO	SM 2012	NIA–27	110-117
Cathal Crimmins Architect	MEWS, Blackrock, Co Dublin	SM 1991	NIA–6	20-21
	HOUSE EXTENSION WALTHAM TERRACE, Blackrock, Co Dublin	SM 1991	NIA–6	22-23
Cullen Payne Architects	REFURBISHMENT OF CAR PARK, Drury Street, Dublin 2	SM 2005	NIA–20	88-93
MV Cullinan Architects	FAMILY APARTMENT IN THE LIBERTIES, Dublin 8	SM 1996	NIA–11	48-49
	ALLINETT'S LANE APARTMENTS, Blackpool, Cork	SM 2004	NIA–19	146-151
	CONNEMARA BOATHOUSE, Moyard, Co Galway	SM 2005	NIA–20	94-97
	• see also: National Building Agency			
DAC Architects	REFURBISHMENT OF QUAYSIDE HOUSE AND SHOP	SM 1991	NIA–6	24-25
DDDA Architects and Martin Richman, artist	'FLOW', BORD GÁIS INSTALLATION, North Wall Quay, Dublin 1	A 2011	NIA–26	70-75

ARCHITECTS

de Blacam & Meagher Architects	DINING HALL AND ATRIUM, Trinity College	A 1987	NIA–2	8-9
	PROTOTYPE DESIGN FOR A PSYCHOGERIATRIC HOSPITAL	A 1988	NIA–3	12-13
	RTE TV RECEPTION AREA	SE 1988	NIA–3	24-25
	RESIDENTIAL DEVELOPMENT, Ailesbury Road, Dublin 4	A 1989	NIA–4	12-14
	CHAPEL OF RECONCILIATION, Knock, Co Mayo	A 1990	NIA–5	12-13
	THREE TICKET SALES OFFICES FOR AER LINGUS	A 1990	NIA–5	14-16
	CAFÉ KLARA, Dawson Street, Dublin 2	SE 1990	NIA–5	28-29
	THEATRE ROYAL FOYER, WEXFORD	SM 1992	NIA–7	22-23
	BECKETT THEATRE, Trinity College Dublin	M 1993	NIA–8	7-11
	MEWS HOUSE TO HEYTESBURY LANE, Dublin 4	A 1998	NIA–13	18-23
	MAIN ENTRANCE, UNIVERSITY OF LIMERICK	SM 1998	NIA–13	40-43
	SCHOOL OF ART, GALWAY	SM 1999	NIA–14	72-75
	MIXED DEVELOPMENT, 1 Castle St / 24 Werburgh St, Dublin 8	SM 2000	NIA–15	52-55
	No.1 GRAND CANAL QUAY, Dublin	A 2001	NIA–16	32-41
	A RESIDENTIAL TOWER IN TEMPLE BAR, Dublin	A 2001	NIA–16	42-51
de Blacam & Meagher / Boyd Barrett Murphy-O'Connor	NEW LIBRARY, Cork Regional Technical College	A 1995	NIA–10	12-15
	MEETING PLACE, North Campus Development, Cork Institute of Technology	A 2007	NIA–22	26-41
de Paor Architects	GARDEN IN CORK	SM 1996	NIA–11	60-61
	WALLPAPER HOUSE, Cork	A 1997	NIA–12	38-41
	A13 FENCE, England	SM 1997	NIA–12	80-81
	EDEN RESTAURANT, Temple Bar, Dublin 2	SM 1998	NIA–13	44-47
	RETURN HOUSE	SM 1999	NIA–14	76-79
	ÍOSLACHT	SM 2000	NIA–15	56-59
	N³ – THE IRISH PAVILION, Architectural Biennale, Venice	A 2001	NIA–16	52-59
	VAN – An Insertion to the National Sculpture Factory, Cork	SM 2001	NIA–16	102-105
	HOLDING PATTERN, A13, London	SM 2002	NIA–17	78-83
	UTILITY BUILDING, Vernon Avenue, Clontarf, Dublin 3	A 2004	NIA–19	60-69
	TWO TWO UP TWO DOWN, John Dillon Street, Dublin 8	SM 2006	NIA–21	120-129
	HOUSE AT AILL BREAC, Baile Uí Chonaola, Contae na Gaillimhe	A 2007	NIA–22	42-49
	GROUNDWORKS, Clontarf, Dublin 3	SM 2008	NIA–23	124-131
	• see also: dpon Architects			
Delany MacVeigh & Pike Architects	DEVELOPMENT AT CHASE ROAD, Acton, London	SE 1989	NIA–4	22-23
Design Strategies	ARDOYNE MEWS, Ballsbridge, Dublin 4	SM 2003	NIA–18	108-113
	• see also: James Horan / O'Dowd O'Herlihy Horan			
Paul Dillon Architect	SITE 7, BRIARHILL BUSINESS PARK, Galway	A 2008	NIA–23	100-107
Donaghy + Dimond Architects	CITY HOUSE AND WORKPLACE, 41 Francis Street, Dublin 8	A 2006	NIA–21	56-63
	KITCHEN-GARDEN-PARTY-WALL, Arran Road, Dublin 9	SM 2006	NIA–21	130-137
	HOUSE – GARDEN – GRAFT, Ranelagh, Dublin 6	A 2010	NIA–25	114-123
	FLITCH, Ranelagh, Dublin 6	SM 2011	NIA–26	116-119
	LANEWAY WALL GARDEN HOUSE	A 2012	NIA–27	62-69
	RECASTING	A 2013	NIA–28	50-61
Donnelly Turpin Architects	LIFFEY HOUSE, Tara Street, Dublin 2	SM 2004	NIA–19	152-159
	DUBCO CREDIT UNION, Little Green Street, Dublin 1	SM 2005	NIA–20	98-105
	FINGLAS SWIMMING POOL & LEISURE CENTRE, Mellowes Park, Dublin 11	SM 2005	NIA–20	106-113
	RATHMINES SQUARE – LEISURE CENTRE + APARTMENTS, Dublin 6	SA 2011	NIA–26	26-37

ARCHITECTS

architect	project	award	volume / year	pages
Donohoe & FitzGerald Architects	PLAN FOR THE GARDEN OF A MODERN MOVEMENT HOUSE	A 1994	NIA–9	14-17
Garbhann Doran Architects	EXTENSION TO A PROTECTED STRUCTURE, Rathgar, Dublin 6	SM 2010	NIA–25	164-171
John Dorman Architects	BALLINA CREDIT UNION, Ballina, Co Westport	SM 1998	NIA–13	48-51
DTA Architects	LIGHT HOUSE CINEMA, Smithfield, Dublin 7	A 2009	NIA–24	100-109
	SLIABH BÁN HOUSING, Galway	SM 2010	NIA–25	172-179
	SOCIAL & AFFORDABLE HOUSING, SANTRY DEMESNE	SA 2011	NIA–26	38-49
	• see also: Derek Tynan Architects / Group 91 / Urban Projects			
Noel Dowley Architect	EXIT CONTROL BUILDING, DUBLIN AIRPORT	A 1992	NIA–7	11-13
Doyle Architects	VISITORS CENTRE, VALENTIA	A 1992	NIA–7	14-16
	CASHEL SECOND-LEVEL SCHOOL	SM 1995	NIA–10	42-43
dpon Architects	VISITOR BUILDING, Royal Gunpowder Mills, Ballincollig	A 1993	NIA–8	12-15
	• see also: dePaor Architects			
Dublin Corporation, Housing Architect's Dept.	HOUSING AT RUTLAND STREET, Dublin 1	SE 1986	NIA–1	16-17
	RUSSELL STREET HOUSING	SE 1988	NIA–3	26-27
Duffy Mitchell Architects	BYRNE HOUSE	SE 1988	NIA–3	28-29
	RETAIL BANK	SM 1992	NIA–7	24-25
	17 PRIORY AVENUE, STILLORGAN, Co Dublin	SM 2000	NIA–15	60-63
DSMP Architects	RAVENSBURY MILL, London	SE 1990	NIA–5	30-31
Felim Dunne & Associates / Beardsmore Yauner Byrne Architects	RECONSTRUCTION OF TROPICAL FRUITS BUILDING	A 1991	NIA–6	11-13
Felim Dunne & Associates / Robinson Keefe Devane	DESIGNYARD, Applied Arts Centre, Temple Bar	SM 1995	NIA–10	44-45
Ken Edmondson	6 APARTMENTS, 2 Crosthwaite Park South, Dun Laoghaire	A 1993	NIA–8	16-19
Energy Research Group, UCD	IRISH ENERGY CENTRE	SM 1995	NIA–10	46-47
Fagan Kelly Lysaght Architects	APARTMENT BUILDING, Amiens St, Dublin 1	SM 1999	NIA–14	83-85
	• see also: FKL Architects			
Desmond FitzGerald Architects	BRUNSWICK STREET IMPROVEMENT SCHEME	A 1988	NIA–3	14-15
	A BOOKSHOP ON COLLEGE GREEN	SE 1989	NIA–4	24-25
	HOUSE AND STUDIO RECONVERSION IN Co DOWN	SE 1990	NIA–5	32-33
	A FOOTBRIDGE AT KELLS, Co Kilkenny	SM 1996	NIA–11	50-51
Desmond FitzGerald Architect / LRS	LUMEN GENTIBUS, Cashel	SM 2003	NIA–18	114-119
Fitzgerald Selby & Sugars Architects	MORIARTY HOUSE, Howth, Co Dublin	SE 1986	NIA–1	18-19
Fitzpatrick & Mays Architects / Robin Mandal Architects	TWO OF EVERYTHING, Sandymount, Dublin 4	SM 2011	NIA–26	148-153

ARCHITECTS

FKL Architects	BALDOYLE LIBRARY & PUBLIC AREA OFFICE, Co Dublin	A 2003	NIA–18	38-47
	BRICK HOUSE, Milltown Path, Dublin 6	A 2004	NIA–19	70-79
	MARTIN VALLEY SCULPTURE PARK, Cork	SM 2006	NIA–21	138-145
	REUBEN STREET APARTMENTS, Dublin 8	SM 2006	NIA–21	146-151
	SOCIAL HOUSING, BALLYMUN	SM 2007	NIA–22	128-135
	A-HOUSE, Rathmines, Dublin 6	SA 2011	NIA–26	50-59
	• see also: Fagan Kelly Lysaght Architects			
Dermot Foley Landscape Architects	JOYCE'S COURT Pedestrian Street, Dublin 1	SM 2009	NIA–24	188-191
David Flynn Architect	A DOMESTIC EVOLUTION, Sandymount, Dublin 4	SM 2011	NIA–26	120-125
Gallagher & Mullen Architects	RUSH CHURCH COMPETITION	SE 1987	NIA–2	14-15
Arthur Gibney & Partners	THE BOOKEND, TEMPLE BAR, Dublin 2	SM 2000	NIA–15	64-67
Gibney & Van Dijk Architects	YORK RIVERSIDE COMPETITION	SE 1987	NIA–2	16-17
	HOUSE AT RATH, Dundalk	A 1988	NIA–3	16-17
Gilroy McMahon Architects	EXTENSION TO COLLEGE OF TECHNOLOGY, Bolton Street, Dublin	A 1988	NIA–3	18-20
	RE-DEVELOPMENT OF 27-29 CLARE STREET, Dublin 2	SE 1990	NIA–5	34-35
	ISOLDE'S TOWER, Essex Quay, Dublin 2	SM 1998	NIA–13	52-55
	URBAN TRANSFORMATION, Hatch Street, Dublin	SM 2001	NIA–16	106-111
Gilroy McMahon Architects / OPW	NATIONAL MUSEUM AT COLLINS BARRACKS (Phase 1), Dublin	A 1996	NIA–11	26-31
GKMP Architects	COMMON GROUND: Urban Landscape in Kilkenny	SM 2010	NIA–25	180-187
	DWELLING SPACE, Eglinton Road, Dublin 4	SM 2009	NIA–24	192-199
GKMP Architects, in assoc. with O'Mahony Pike	HOUSING AT PEARSE SQUARE, Dublin 2	SM 2008	NIA–23	132-139
Grafton Architects	CANOE CLUB ON THE RIVER LIFFEY	SE 1989	NIA–4	26-27
	COMMERCIAL INFILL, Ormond Quay, Dublin 1	SE 1989	NIA–4	28-29
	MEWS HOUSES AT CLYDE LANE	SE 1990	NIA–5	36-37
	MEWS HOUSES AT CLYDE LANE, Dublin 4	A 1993	NIA–8	20-23
	ST PAUL'S SECONDARY SCHOOL, Oughterard, Co Galway	SM 1993	NIA–8	24-27
	HOUSE IN DOOLIN, Co Clare	A 1995	NIA–10	20-23
	DEPT OF MECHANICAL ENGINEERING, Trinity College Dublin	A 1997	NIA–12	20-25
	GARDEN ROOM FOR LITTLE BIRD, rear 13 Merrion Square, Dublin 2	A 1998	NIA–13	24-29
	TWO TIMBER BOXES	SA 2000	NIA–15	20-25
	OUR LADY'S SECONDARY SCHOOL, CASTLEBLAYNEY, Co Monaghan	A 2000	NIA–15	38-43
	SCREENING ROOM FOR LITTLE BIRD & CLARENCE PICTURES, Dublin 2	SM 2000	NIA–15	68-71
	THE LONG HOUSE, Percy Lane, Dublin 4	A 2002	NIA–17	40-47
	URBAN BEEHIVE, North King Street Apartments, Dublin 7	A 2002	NIA–17	48-57
	TOWN HALL, DUNSHAUGHLIN, Co Meath	SM 2002	NIA–17	84-93
	URBAN INSTITUTE IRELAND, University College Dublin	A 2003	NIA–18	48-59
	MIND THE GAP, The Mall, Dublin City University	SM 2003	NIA–18	120-125
	A WAY TO SCHOOL – Ardscoil Mhuire, Ballinasloe, and North Kildare Educate Together Project, Celbridge	M 2004	NIA–19	22-47
	MME – Extension to Dept of Mechanical & Manufacturing Engineering, Trinity College Dublin	A 2006	NIA–21	64-75
	SOLSTICE ARTS CENTRE, Navan, Co Meath	A 2007	NIA–22	50-63
	7-9 MERRION ROW + THE BILLETS, Dublin 2	SA 2009	NIA–24	60-75

ARCHITECTS

architect	project	award	volume / year	pages
	UNIVERSITÀ LUIGI BOCCONI, Milan	M 2009	NIA–24	40-59
	HOUSE FOR A PRESIDENT, University of Limerick	SM 2011	NIA–26	126-131
	MEDICAL SCHOOL, STUDENT RESIDENCES & BUS SHELTER, University of Limerick	A 2013	NIA–28	62-77
	ARCHITECTURE AS NEW GEOGRAPHY (Venice Biennale)	A 2013	NIA–28	78-87
	• see also Group 91			
Grafton Architects / Roughan & O'Donovan	MOTORWAY BRIDGE, Killarney Road, Co Wicklow	A 1995	NIA–10	32-35
	AIRPORT BRIDGES, Northern Motorway / Airport-Balbriggan Bypass	SM 2004	NIA–19	188-191
Group 91 Architects	Temple Bar, Dublin 2			
Group 91 / Derek Tynan Architects	THE PRINTWORKS	M 1995	NIA–10	6-11
	JOHN ROCHA DESIGN STUDIO, Temple Lane	A 1996	NIA–11	32-36
Group 91 / Shane O'Toole and Michael Kelly	THE ARK – A Cultural Centre for Children	*M 1996	NIA–11	10-17
Group 91 / Shay Cleary Architects	ARTHOUSE	SM 1997	NIA–12	62-64
Group 91 Architects	THREE URBAN SPACES	SM 1997	NIA–12	59-61
Group 91 / Grafton Architects	TEMPLE BAR SQUARE	SM 1997	NIA–12	65-67
Group 91 / Paul Keogh Architects	MIXED USE BUILDING, MEETING HOUSE SQUARE	SM 1997	NIA–12	68-70
Group 91 / McCullough Mulvin Architects	MUSIC CENTRE	SM 1997	NIA–12	71-73
Group 91 / O'Donnell + Tuomey Architects	GALLERY OF PHOTOGRAPHY	M 1997	NIA–12	10-19
	NATIONAL PHOTOGRAPHY ARCHIVE / DIT SCHOOL OF PHOTOGRAPHY	A 1997	NIA–12	32-37
Group 91 / Shane O'Toole, Michael Kelly and Susan Cogan	11 EUSTACE STREET	SA 1999	NIA–14	24-29
Orna Hanly Architect	FAMINE MUSEUM, Strokestown, Co Roscommon	SM 1995	NIA–10	48-49
Happy Architecture	EASA TIMBER PAVILION, Letterfrack, Co Galway	SM 2009	NIA–24	200-203
Hassett Ducatez Architects	THE COUNTDOWN 2000 PROJECT	A 1995	NIA–10	24-27
	COILL DUBH & DISTRICT CREDIT UNION, Co Kildare	SA 2000	NIA–15	26-31
	11m^2 EXTENSION TO FAMILY HOUSE in Victorian terrace, Dublin	A 2001	NIA–16	60-65
	DOUBLE GLASS HOUSE, Dublin	A 2004	NIA–19	80-87
	BROOKFIELD COMMUNITY YOUTH CENTRE & CRÈCHE, Tallaght, Dublin 24	M 2008	NIA–23	32-49
	HOUSE IN WOODS, Co Kildare	SA 2011	NIA–26	60-69
Derek Heavey and Sheila McCarthy, Architects	PUPPET TRAILER	SE 1987	NIA–2	18-19
Henchion + Reuter Architects	HOUSE AM ZOO, LEIPZIG	A 1999	NIA–14	30-35
	TWO ROOFTOP APARTMENTS, BONN	SM 1999	NIA–14	80-82
	TOWER, Stranorlar / Ballybofey, Co Donegal	A 2001	NIA–16	66-71
	FOUR PRIVATE HOUSES	SM 2001	NIA–16	112-117
	SPORTS AND YOUTH SERVICES CENTRE, Cabra, Dublin 7	SM 2004	NIA–19	160-165
	YOUTH AND COMMUNITY CENTRE, Donore Avenue, Dublin 8	A 2005	NIA–20	62-75
Liam Hennessy Architect	FAMILY HOUSE, Co Kildare	SE 1986	NIA–1	20-21
	FAMILY HOUSE, Co Wexford	SE 1986	NIA–1	22-23
James Horan and Anne Harper Architects	KITCHEN, Booterstown, Co Dublin	SE 1986	NIA–1	24-25
	'THE ARGO'	SE 1986	NIA–1	26-27
	ZANUSSI KITCHEN DESIGN	A 1986	NIA–1	14-15
	• see also Design Strategies / O'Dowd O'Herlihy Horan			

ARCHITECTS

arnród Éireann Architects	DUNDALK FREIGHT DEPOT – Check-In Office	A 1996	NIA–11	37-41
	DUN LAOGHAIRE DART STATION	SM 2000	NIA–15	72-75
Alan Jones Architect	OFFICE FOR A COFFEE IMPORTER, Dargan Road, Belfast	SM 2004	NIA–19	166-171
Kavanagh Architects	DUBLIN 2 DELIVERY OFFICE	SM 1992	NIA–7	26-27
Keane Murphy Duff Architects	MILLENNIUM TOWER, Dublin	SE 1988	NIA–3	30-31
	• see also: KMD Architecture			
John E Keating & Associates	HOUSE AT MODEL FARM ROAD, CORK	SE 1988	NIA–3	32-33
Kelly & Cogan Architects	SOCIAL HOUSING, Rathasker Road, Naas	SM 2000	NIA–15	76-79
James Kelly Architect	REFURBISHMENT OF 42 ARRAN QUAY, Dublin 7	SM 1997	NIA–12	74-76
Simon K Kelly + Partners	EDGE OF TOWN – Local Area Offices, Claremorris	SM 2012	NIA–27	118-125
Ryan W Kennihan Architects	SALLYMOUNT TERRACE, Ranelagh, Dublin 6	SM 2011	NIA–26	132-135
Frank Kenny Associates	STUDENT FACILITIES CENTRE, Aston Place, Dublin	SM 1994	NIA–9	22-23
Paul Keogh Architects	HOUSE AT LOUGH ENNELL	SE 1986	NIA–1	28-29
	PAVILION AT DUBLIN ZOO	SE 1988	NIA–3	34-35
	GARDEN ROOMS, Leeson Park and Percy Place, Dublin	A 1989	NIA–4	15-17
	DIFFNEY MANSHOP, St Stephen's Green, Dublin	SE 1990	NIA–5	38-39
	HOLIDAY HOUSES AT VELVET STRAND, PORTMARNOCK	SM 1991	NIA–6	26-27
	TWO APARTMENTS, Haddington Road, Dublin 4	SM 1995	NIA–10	50-51
	CONVERSION & REFURBISHMENT OF KODAK BUILDING, Dublin 6	SM 2000	NIA–15	80-83
	TWO HOLIDAY HOUSES, Kinsallagh, Westport	SM 2001	NIA–16	118-123
	OLD BOROUGH SCHOOL & PARISH CENTRE, Swords	SM 2002	NIA–17	94-99
	• see also Group 91			
KMD Architecture	• see McCullough Mulvin Architects and KMD Architecture			
Mary Laheen Architects	SCOIL MHUIRE ÓGH, Crumlin	A 2013	NIA–28	88-101
Steve Larkin Architects	HOUSE IN BOGWEST, Co Wexford	A 2012	NIA–27	70-79
	HOUSE IN Co CARLOW	A 2013	NIA–28	102-113
P+A Lavin Associates	MEWS HOUSE AT RAGLAN LANE, Dublin	SM 2001	NIA–16	124-129
LID Architecture	LANDSCAPE ROOM, Glencar, Sligo	SM 2010	NIA–25	188-193
	BUTTERFLY HOUSE, Co Leitrim	A 2012	NIA–27	80-87
LID Architecture, with Building Initiative	PLUG-IN PATH AT WOODVALE PARK, Shankill, Belfast	SM 2010	NIA–25	194-201
Lynch O'Toole Walsh Architects (Shane O'Toole)	MAUSOLEUM, Co Carlow	SE 1986	NIA–1	30-31
	• see also Group 91			
Henry J Lyons & Partners (Derek Byrne)	HOUSE IN NORTH COUNTY DUBLIN	SE 1989	NIA–4	30-31
	ENVIRONMENTAL PROTECTION AGENCY HQ, Johnstown Castle, Co Wexford	SM 1997	NIA–12	77-79
	DESIGN STUDIOS, 47-48 Pearse Street, Dublin 2	SM 2000	NIA–15	84-87
	MORTUARY CHAPELS & POSTMORTEM SUITE, St James's Hospital, Dublin 8	SM 2004	NIA–19	172-179

ARCHITECTS

architect	project	award	volume / year	page
McCullough Mulvin Architects	HOUSE IN A COURTYARD, Co Dublin	SE 1987	NIA–2	20-21
	THE CITY ARTS CENTRE	SE 1988	NIA–3	36-37
	LECTURE HALL AND ARCHIVE	A 1990	NIA–5	17-19
	HOUSE IN A CHURCH	SE 1990	NIA–5	40-41
	ABBEY THEATRE PORTICO	SM 1991	NIA–6	28-29
	HOUSE IN A CHURCH	SM 1992	NIA–7	28-29
	TEMPLE BAR GALLERY AND STUDIOS, Dublin 2	A 1995	NIA–10	28-31
	BLACK CHURCH PRINT STUDIOS, Temple Bar, Dublin 2	*M 1996	NIA–11	18-25
	MEWS HOUSE, LOUIS LANE, Dublin 6	A 1999	NIA–14	36-39
	SIENA MONASTERY, Drogheda, Co Louth	A 1999	NIA–14	40-45
	PINE TREES AND THE SEA	SM 2000	NIA–15	88-91
	MODEL ARTS & NILAND GALLERY, Sligo	A 2001	NIA–16	72-81
	GALLERY 2, Douglas Hyde Gallery, Trinity College Dublin	SM 2002	NIA–17	100-105
	URBAN HOUSING, Apartments at 116 Grafton St, Dublin	SM 2002	NIA–17	106-111
	SQUARE HOUSE, South County Dublin	A 2003	NIA–18	60-67
	TUBBERCURRY LIBRARY AND CIVIC OFFICES	A 2004	NIA–19	88-99
	EXTENSION TO VIRUS REFERENCE LABORATORY, UCD	A 2004	NIA–19	100-107
	ENGINEERS IRELAND, 20 Clyde Road, Dublin 4	A 2006	NIA–21	76-83
	SOURCE ARTS CENTRE & LIBRARY, Thurles, Co Tipperary	A 2007	NIA–22	64-77
	CAVAN INSTITUTE, Cathedral Road, Cavan	SM 2007	NIA–22	136-143
	JIG-SAW, Leeson Park, Dublin 6	A 2009	NIA–24	110-117
	LINCOLN PLACE, Dublin 2	A 2009	NIA–24	118-125
	SCHOOL OF ENGINEERING, Athlone Institute of Technology	SM 2010	NIA–25	202-209
	Z SQUARE HOUSE, Temple Gardens, Dublin 6	SM 2011	NIA–26	136-141
	LONG ROOM HUB, Trinity College Dublin	SM 2012	NIA–27	126-133
	• see also Group 91			
McCullough Mulvin Architects and KMD Architecture	USSHER LIBRARY, Trinity College Dublin	M 2003	NIA–18	22-37
McCullough Mulvin Architects / OPW	NATIONAL MUSEUM EXHIBITIONS	SM 1999	NIA–14	94-95
Antoin Mac Gabhann Architects	LETTERKENNY AREA OFFICE, Co Donegal	A 2003	NIA–18	68-77
	• see also Mac Gabhann Architects			
Mac Gabhann Architects	REGIONAL CULTURAL CENTRE, Letterkenny,	SM 2009	NIA–24	204-213
	TUATH NA MARA, Lough Swilly, Co Donegal	SM 2009	NIA–24	214-219
	ARCHITECT'S OFFICE, Letterkenny, Co Donegal	SM 2010	NIA–25	210-215
	• see also Antoin Mac Gabhann Architects			
McGarry Ní Éanaigh Architects	A SMALL COUNTRY HOUSE, Co Louth	SE 1987	NIA–2	22-23
	EXTENSION TO C18TH HOUSE IN LEINSTER	SE 1988	NIA–3	38-39
	HOUSE ON A DRUMLIN, Co Monaghan	SE 1989	NIA–4	32-33
	RENOVATION OF STONE COTTAGE, Co Meath	SE 1990	NIA–5	42-43
	A SUITE OF PRIVATE MEDICAL CONSULTING ROOMS	SE 1990	NIA–5	44-45
	MEDICAL CENTRE, DROGHEDA	A 1991	NIA–6	14-17
	HOUSE ON A RIVER	SM 1992	NIA–7	30-31
	EXTENSION AND RENOVATION OF A RECTORY	A 1994	NIA–9	6-9
	MUSEUM AT MELLIFONT ABBEY, Co Louth	SM 1996	NIA–11	52-53
	SOFTWARE DESIGN BUILDING, Leopardstown, Co Dublin	A 1998	NIA–13	30-35
	PARALLEL HOUSE, Kingscourt, Co Cavan	SM 1998	NIA–13	56-59
	SMITHFIELD PUBLIC SPACE, Dublin	A 2001	NIA–16	82-89
	LIFFEY BOARDWALK, Dublin	A 2002	NIA–17	58-67
	MONAGHAN EDUCATION CENTRE	SM 2003	NIA–18	126-131

ARCHITECTS

	BALLYFERMOT LEISURE AND YOUTH CENTRE, Dublin 10	SM	2009	NIA–24	220-227
	BUSH SPORTS HALL, Cooley, Co Louth	SM	2009	NIA–24	228-233
	DUNSHAUGHLIN PASTORAL CENTRE, Co Meath	SM	2011	NIA–26	142-147
	• see also Group 91 / Urban Projects				
Níall McLaughlin Architects	PEABODY HOUSING, Silvertown, London E16	A	2005	NIA–20	76-87
	HOUSE AT DIRK COVE, Clonakilty, Co Cork	SM	2005	NIA–20	114-123
	HOUSEBOAT	SM	2005	NIA–20	124-129
	HOUSE AT CROUCH END, London	A	2006	NIA–21	84-93
	ARC BUILDING, Built Environment Centre, Hull, England	SM	2008	NIA–23	140-147
	HOUSE AT PIPER'S END, Letty Green, Herts, England	SM	2009	NIA–24	234-241
	PEDESTRIAN BRIDGE, BRISTOL	SM	2009	NIA–24	242-247
	ALZHEIMER'S RESPITE CENTRE, Blackrock, Co Dublin	SA	2010	NIA–25	64-77
Maccreanor Lavington Architects	IJBURG BLOK 4, Amsterdam	SM	2006	NIA–21	152-159
Mackel & Doherty Architects	BUNSCOIL PHOBAIL FEIRSTE, Belfast	SM	2001	NIA–16	130-135
Magee Creedon Architects	CORK SCHOOL PROJECT	SM	2001	NIA–16	136-139
John Maguire Architect	THE GARAGE, Co Fermanagh	SM	2013	NIA–28	150-155
Robin Mandal Architects / Fitzpatrick & Mays Architects	TWO OF EVERYTHING, Sandymount, Dublin 4	SM	2011	NIA–26	148-153
Patricia Mangan and Rory Murphy, Architects	THE COCOON, Mullet Penninsula	SM	1992	NIA–7	32-33
MCO Projects / ARARQ Ireland	FR COLLINS PARK, Donaghmede, Dublin 13	SM	2010	NIA–25	216-221
Mellett Architectes Paris	TIME TRIALS STARTING RAMP, Tour de France	SM	2001	NIA–16	140-143
Mitchell Ó Muire Smyth Architects	HARP BREWHOUSE, Dundalk	M	1987	NIA–2	1, 6-7
	4 HOUSES AT DONNYBROOK, Dublin 4	SE	1987	NIA–2	24-25
	HARP BREWERY VISITOR CENTRE, Dundalk	SE	1990	NIA–5	46-47
Moloney O'Beirne Architects	CHILD & ADOLESCENT MENTAL HEALTH UNIT, Merlin Park, Galway	SM	2011	NIA–26	154-159
Moloney O'Beirne Guy + Hutchison Locke & Monk	SPORTS HALL, Mount Anville, Dublin	A	1986	NIA–1	12-13
	PSYCHIATRIC / GERIATRIC UNITS, St James's Hospital, Dublin 8	SE	1987	NIA–2	26-27
Murphy Kenny Architects	RESTAURANT AT CASTLEKNOCK	SE	1990	NIA–5	48-49
Murray Ó Laoire Associates	VISITORS CENTRE, KING JOHN'S CASTLE, Limerick	SM	1992	NIA–7	34-35
	LIMERICK INFORMATION OFFICE	SM	1992	NIA–7	36-37
	THE GREEN BUILDING, Temple Bar, Dublin 2	SM	1995	NIA–10	52-53
	'THE YOKE ON THE OAK', Dame Street, Dublin 2	SM	1995	NIA–10	54-55
	BELVEDERE COLLEGE SJ / O'REILLY THEATRE, Dublin	SM	2001	NIA–16	144-149
	IRISH PAVILION, Expo 2000, Hanover	SM	2001	NIA–16	150-155
	TAILTEANN, Mary Immaculate College, Limerick	SM	2008	NIA–23	148-155
Murray Ó Laoire Associates / Arup	VEHICULAR AND PEDESTRIAN BRIDGE, University of Limerick	SM	2005	NIA–20	130-135
David Naessens and Louise Cotter	NEWHALL MILL WORKSHOPS, Birmingham	A	1990	NIA–5	8-11

ARCHITECTS

architect	project	award	volume / year	pages
David Naessens and Christopher Stead	DONNINGTON BATH HOUSES, London	A 1987	NIA–2	12-13
National Building Agency (MV Cullinan)	RESIDENTIAL QUARTER AT ST PETER'S PORT, ATHLONE	A 1994	NIA–9	18-21
	FOUR HOUSES AT TULACH ARD, Rahoon, Galway	SM 1996	NIA–11	54-55
Newenham Mulligan & Associates	29 SOUTH PARK, Foxrock, Co Dublin	A 1992	NIA–7	17-19
	BALTINGLASS COURTHOUSE & VISITORS' CENTRE, Co Wicklow	SM 2000	NIA–15	90-95
NJBA Architects	BROOKE HEUSSAFF LIBRARY, South Circular Road, Dublin 8	A 2006	NIA–21	94-101
O'Dea Skehan & Associates	A GARDEN EXTENSION TO THE FULLAM RESIDENCE	SE 1988	NIA–3	40-41
O'Donnell + Tuomey Architects	LIVING IN THE CITY	M 1990	NIA–5	4-7
	CHAPEL OF RECONCILIATION, Knock, Co Mayo	SE 1990	NIA–5	50-51
	THE IRISH PAVILION	M 1992	NIA–7	4-7
	A CONSTRUCTED LANDSCAPE – Blackwood Golf Centre, Co Down	SM 1995	NIA–10	56-57
	HOUSE IN NORTH COUNTY DUBLIN	SM 1996	NIA–11	56-57
	RANELAGH MULTI-DENOMINATIONAL SCHOOL, Ranelagh, Dublin 6	M 1999	NIA–14	14-23
	HOUSE IN A LONG BACK GARDEN, Navan, Co Meath	A 1999	NIA–14	46-51
	NEW KITCHEN AND BATHROOM IN A HOUSE IN RATHMINES, Dublin 6	SM 1999	NIA–14	86-89
	FURNITURE COLLEGE, LETTERFRACK, Co Galway	M 2002	NIA–17	26-39
	LEINSTER HOUSE PRESS RECEPTION ROOM	A 2003	NIA–18	78-85
	SOCIAL HOUSING, GALBALLY, Co Limerick	A 2003	NIA–18	86-93
	MEDICAL RESEARCH LABORATORIES, UCD	A 2004	NIA–19	108-117
	HOWTH HOUSE, Co Dublin	SM 2004	NIA–19	180-187
	LEWIS GLUCKSMAN GALLERY, University College Cork	SM 2005	NIA–20	136-147
	IRELAND'S PAVILION AT THE VENICE BIENNALE	SM 2005	NIA–20	148-157
	TRINITY IRISH ART RESEARCH CENTRE, Trinity College Dublin	SM 2008	NIA–23	156-161
	SEÁN O'CASEY COMMUNITY CENTRE, East Wall, Dublin 3	SA 2009	NIA–24	76-89
	THE SLEEPING GIANT, KILLINEY, Co Dublin	A 2009	NIA–24	126-135
	TIMBERYARD SOCIAL HOUSING, Coombe Bypass, Dublin 8	M 2010	NIA–25	48-63
	AN GAELÁRAS, Derry	SA 2010	NIA–25	78-93
	VESSEL: an installation for the Venice Biennale 2012	SM 2013	NIA–28	156-163
	• see also Group 91 / Sheila O'Donnell Architect / OPW (John Tuomey)			
Sheila O'Donnell Architect	IRISH FILM CENTRE, Trinity Street, Dublin 2	A 1986	NIA–1	10-11
	IRISH FILM CENTRE, Eustace Street, Dublin 2	M 1988	NIA–3	5-7
	• see also O'Donnell + Tuomey Architects			
ODOS Architects	No.33 ST KEVIN'S ROAD, Portobello, Dublin 8	SM 2006	NIA–21	160-165
	13a THOR PLACE, Stoneybatter, Dublin 7	A 2006	NIA–21	102-111
	DWELLING AT ST PATRICK'S COTTAGES, Rathfarnham, Dublin 16	SM 2009	NIA–24	248-255
	10A LOWER GRANGEGORMAN, Dublin 7	SM 2009	NIA–24	256-263
	3 MEWS DWELLINGS, Portobello, Dublin 8	SM 2010	NIA–25	222-229
	31 CARYSFORT ROAD, Dalkey, Co Dublin	SM 2010	NIA–25	230-237
ODOS Architects / O'Shea Design	KNOCKTOPHER FRIARY, Co Kilkenny	SM 2007	NIA–22	144-152
O'Dowd O'Herlihy Horan Architects	LUTTRELLSTOWN FARM	SE 1989	NIA–4	34-35
	GOLF CLUB AT LUTTRELLSTOWN	SM 1994	NIA–9	26-27
	HOUSE IN WEST CORK	SM 1995	NIA–10	58-59
	• see also James Horan / Design Strategies			

ARCHITECTS

Declan O'Dwyer and Sheila Jones	ALSAA SPORTS COMPLEX, Dublin Airport	SE 1987	NIA–2	28-29
Office of Public Works				
OPW (Ciaran O'Connor)	KILLYKEEN FOREST PARK, Co Cavan	SE 1986	NIA–1	32-33
OPW (John Tuomey)	LABORATORY AT ABBOTSTOWN, Co Dublin	SE 1986	NIA–1	34-35
	COURTHOUSE AT SMITHFIELD, Dublin	A 1987	NIA–2	10-11
OPW (M MacKenna, M Haugh)	EMPLOYMENT EXCHANGE, Ballyfermot	SE 1987	NIA–2	30-31
OPW (A Rolfe, K Unger)	CASTLE HALL, Dublin Castle	SE 1987	NIA–2	32-33
OPW (Elizabeth Morgan)	GARDEN AT ROYAL HOSPITAL KILMAINHAM	SE 1988	NIA–3	42-43
	LIMERICK SOCIAL WELFARE OFFICES	SM 1992	NIA–7	40-41
	RHK / IMMA ARTISTS' STUDIOS	SM 1995	NIA–10	60-61
OPW (Kevin Wolohan)	A GARDA STATION IN CAVAN	SE 1989	NIA–4	36-37
OPW (Mary McKenna)	SOCIAL WELFARE SERVICES OFFICE, BALLYFERMOT	SM 1991	NIA–6	30-31
	CÉIDE FIELDS VISITOR CENTRE	A 1994	NIA–9	10-13
OPW (C O'Connor, G O'Sullivan)	WATERWAYS VISITORS CENTRE	SM 1992	NIA–7	38-39
	WATERWAYS VISITOR CENTRE, Grand Canal Dock	SM 1994	NIA–9	24-25
OPW (C O'Connor, G O'Sullivan, S Foley)	HERBARIUM AND LIBRARY, Botanic Gardens, Dublin 1	SM 1998	NIA–12	60-63
OPW (Conor Moran)	SACRED HEART ORATORY, Dún Laoghaire	SM 1999	NIA–14	90-93
OPW (Des Byrne)	NATIONAL MUSEUM OF COUNTRY LIFE, Castlebar, Co Mayo	SM 2002	NIA–17	118-125
• see also Gilroy McMahon + OPW / McCullough Mulvin + OPW				
O'Mahony Pike Architects	• see GKMP Architects, in assoc. with OMP			
Ó Muire Smyth Architects	HOUSE TO LET	SM 1996	NIA–11	58-59
	RESIDENTIAL DEVELOPMENT, Beresford Street, Dublin 1	SM 1999	NIA–14	96-99
Anthony & Barbara O'Neill Architects	PARK CENTRE BUILDING, Glenveagh	SE 1988	NIA–3	44-45
Prof Cathal O'Neill & Partners, Architects	DEANS OF RESIDENCE, UCD	A 1990	NIA–5	20-22
	MEWS AT 26 WATERLOO ROAD, Dublin 4	SM 1991	NIA–6	32-33
O'Riordan Staehli Architects	CLIFFS OF MOHER VISITOR CENTRE	SM 1994	NIA–9	28-29
Camille O'Sullivan Architect	ADAPTABLE ROOM	A 2000	NIA–15	44-47
Populous / Scott Tallon Walker Architects	AVIVA STADIUM, Lansdowne Road, Dublin 4	A 2011	NIA–26	76-85
Quilligan & Twamley Architects	WORK IN PROGRESS, 1985	A 1986	NIA–1	8-9
	DEVELOPMENT AT NORTH WALL QUAY, Dublin	SE 1987	NIA–2	34-35
Robinson Keefe Devane Architects	EXTENSION TO CROSS & PASSION COLLEGE	SE 1988	NIA–3	46-47
• see also: Felim Dunne & Associates				
Fionnuala Rogerson Architect	HOUSING AT BROOKWOOD	SM 1994	NIA–9	30-31
Roughan & O'Donovan / Grafton Architects	MOTORWAY BRIDGE, Killarney Road, Co Wicklow	A 1995	NIA–10	32-35
	AIRPORT BRIDGES Northern Motorway / Airport-Balbriggan Bypass	SM 2004	NIA–19	188-191
Scott Tallon Walker Architects	CHAPEL AT ST ANGELA'S SCHOOL, Stevenage, Herts, England	SE 1988	NIA–3	48-49
	THE O'REILLY INSTITUTE, Trinity College Dublin	A 1989	NIA–4	18-21
	BRADAN MARA TEO, Land-Based Salmon Hatchery	A 1990	NIA–5	23-25

ARCHITECTS

architect	project	award	volume / year	pages
	SCHOOL OF ENGINEERING (Phase 1), University College Dublin	SE 1990	NIA–5	52-53
	BIOTECHNOLOGY RESEARCH BUILDING, University College Dublin	SM 1994	NIA–9	32-33
	CIVIC OFFICES AT WOOD QUAY, Dublin	A 1996	NIA–11	42-47
	RIVERSIDE ONE, Sir John Rogerson's Quay, Dublin 2	A 2007	NIA–22	78-89
	JESUIT COMMUNITY, Milltown Park, Dublin 6	SM 2011	NIA–26	160-165
Scott Tallon Walker / Populous	AVIVA STADIUM, Lansdowne Road, Dublin 4	A 2011	NIA–26	76-85
Neil Sholdice Architect	MONTESSORI SCHOOL, Howth Road, Co Dublin	SM 1991	NIA–6	34-35
Dominic Stevens Architects	GRAPHIC DESIGN STUDIO, North Lotts, Dublin 1	SM 1998	NIA–12	64-67
	DOMESTIC ACUPUNCTURE	A 1999	NIA–14	52-57
	BUILDING THE HOME, Co Leitrim	SM 2002	NIA–17	126-135
	IN-BETWEEN HOUSE, Ballinamore, Co Leitrim	SM 2004	NIA–19	192-197
	MIMETIC HOUSE, Dromaheir, Co Leitrim	A 2007	NIA–22	90-99
	E25,000 HOUSE, Cloone, Co Leitrim	A 2011	NIA–26	86-93
Dominic Stevens Architect, in collaboration with John Graham	PRECAST LINES	SM 2003	NIA–18	132-137
Studio Architects	PIZZA HUT RESTAURANT, Blanchardstown, Co Dublin	SM 1997	NIA–12	82-84
Taka Architects	HOUSE 1 + HOUSE 2, Morehampton Road, Dublin 4	A 2010	NIA–25	124-133
	HOUSE 4, Firhouse, Dublin	A 2013	NIA–28	114-125
Derek Tynan Architects	APARTMENTS IN CARLOW	A 1986	NIA–1	6-7
	HOUSE IN THE BARROW VALLEY	A 1988	NIA–3	21-23
	DOUBLE HOUSE, Belgrave Square, Monkstown, Co Dublin	SE 1990	NIA–5	54-55
	PRIVATE RESIDENCE, Roebuck, Dublin 14	SM 1996	NIA–11	62-63
	SOLICITORS OFFICES, Francis Street, Dublin 8	SM 1996	NIA–11	64-65
	MEWS DWELLING, DUBLIN 6	A 1997	NIA–12	26-31
	GATE MULTIPLEX, North Gate, Cork	A 1999	NIA–14	58-63
	APARTMENT IN MIXED-USE DEVELOPMENT, Crane Lane, Dublin 2	SM 1999	NIA–14	100-103
	EXTENSION TO TERRACED HOUSE, Heytesbury Street, Dublin 8	SM 2001	NIA–16	156-159
	• see also: DTA Architects / Group 91 / Urban Projects			
Urban Projects	URBAN SPACE / PRIVATE PLACE, Clarion Quay, Dublin 1	SM 2003	NIA–18	138-143
Simon Walker Architect	ROOM: ORGANISER-DIVIDER	SM 1999	NIA–14	104-106
	CUT-OUT FURNITURE	SM 2001	NIA–16	160-163
	REGENT, Temple Bar, Dublin 2	SM 2001	NIA–16	164-167
A&D Wejchert Architects	LEISURE CENTRE, Greystones, Co Wicklow	SE 1986	NIA–1	36-37
	GLASNEVIN NATIONAL HERITAGE PROJECT + GLASNEVIN TRUST MUSEUM	SM 2011	NIA–26	166-171
Deirdre Whelan and Paul Kelly, Architects	A HOUSE IN GIFU, JAPAN	SM 1995	NIA–10	62-63
	• see also: Boyd Kelly Whelan / FKL Architects			
Keith Williams Architects	ATHLONE CIVIC CENTRE, LIBRARY & TOWN SQUARE	SM 2006	NIA–21	166-171
Zakrzewski + Hyde Architects	304 SPRING STREET, New York	SM 2009	NIA–24	264-271

Building Type

NEW IRISH ARCHITECTURE °1-28 — AAI Awards 1986-2013

building type index covering the 455 projects featured in the AAI Awards 1986-2013 and the 28 volumes of *New Irish Architecture* (with projects listed chronologically by type)

type   apartment / artist's studio / bridge / commercial / community / cultural / education / education –
            3rd level / health / house – new build / house – conversion, extension, refurbishment / houses – up to 4 /
            housing / international exhibitions / mixed-use / monument / office / public / public space /
            religious / sport & leisure / transport / utility / uncategorised

awards   M = Downes Bronze Medal / *M = Joint Medal / SA = Special Award / A = Award
            SM = Special Mention / SE = Selected for Exhibition (AAI Awards 1986-1990)

note   only the main illustrated project-spreads are listed; projects may also be referred to in the Assessors' Reports
            (NIA °1–28), Update section (NIA °2–8), and First Impressions (NIA °24–28)

project	architect	award / year	volume	pages
apartment				
6 APARTMENTS, 2 Crosthwaite Park South, Dun Laoghaire	Ken Edmondson	A 1993	NIA–8	16-19
TWO APARTMENTS, Haddington Road, Dublin	Paul Keogh Architects	SM 1995	NIA–10	50-51
'THE YOKE ON THE OAK', Dame Street, Dublin	Murray Ó Laoire Architects	SM 1995	NIA–10	54-55
FAMILY APARTMENT IN THE LIBERTIES, Dublin	MV Cullinan Architects	SM 1996	NIA–11	48-49
NOHO LOFT, New York	Boyd Cody Architects	SM 1999	NIA–14	68-71
TWO ROOFTOP APARTMENTS, BONN	Henchion + Reuter Architects	SM 1999	NIA–14	80-82
APARTMENT IN MIXED-USE DEVELOPMENT, Crane Lane, Dublin	Derek Tynan Architects	SM 1999	NIA–14	100-103
URBAN HOUSING, Apartments at 116 Grafton Street, Dublin	McCullough Mulvin Architects	SM 2002	NIA–17	106-111
• see also Mixed Use / Housing for larger-scale developments				
artist's studio				
HOUSE & STUDIO RECONVERSION, Co DOWN	Desmond FitzGerald Architects	SE 1990	NIA–5	32-33
RHK / IMMA ARTISTS' STUDIOS	OPW (Elizabeth Morgan)	SM 1995	NIA–10	60-61
JOHN ROCHA DESIGN STUDIO, Temple Lane, Temple Bar	Group 91 / Derek Tynan Architects	A 1996	NIA–11	32-36
GRAPHIC DESIGN STUDIO, North Lotts, Dublin	Dominic Stevens Architects	SM 1998	NIA–12	64-67
11 EUSTACE STREET, Temple Bar	Group 91 / Shane O'Toole, Michael Kelly and Susan Cogan	SA 1999	NIA–14	24-29
CITY HOUSE AND WORKPLACE, 41 Francis Street, Dublin	Donaghy + Dimond Architects	A 2006	NIA–21	56-63
STUDIO, PALMERSTON ROAD, Dublin	Boyd Cody Architects	SM 2009	NIA–24	162-167
ARCHITECT'S OFFICE, Letterkenny, Co Donegal	Mac Gabhann Architects	SM 2010	NIA–25	210-215
ARTIST'S PRODUCTION SPACE, Vienna	A2 Architects	SM 2011	NIA–26	94-97
FORMWORK	Architecture Republic	SM 2012	NIA–27	96-103
• see also Cultural for larger-scale developments				

213

BUILDING TYPE

project	architect	award / year	volume	pages
bridge				
MOTORWAY BRIDGE, Killarney Road, Co Wicklow	Grafton Architects / Roughan & O'Donovan	A 1995	NIA–10	32-35
A FOOTBRIDGE AT KELLS, Co Kilkenny	Desmond FitzGerald Architects	SM 1996	NIA–11	50-51
AIRPORT BRIDGES Northern Motorway / Airport-Balbriggan Bypass	Grafton Architects / Roughan & O'Donovan	SM 2004	NIA–19	188-191
VEHICULAR AND PEDESTRIAN BRIDGE, University of Limerick	Murray Ó Laoire Architects / Arup	SM 2005	NIA–20	130-135
PEDESTRIAN BRIDGE, BRISTOL	Níall McLaughlin Architects	SM 2009	NIA–24	242-247
commercial				
HARP BREWHOUSE, Dundalk	Mitchell Ó Muire Smyth Architects	M 1987	NIA–2	1?, 6-7
SHOWROOM AND OFFICES	Shay Cleary Architects	A 1988	NIA–3	10-11
ENTRANCE HALL, BAR & RESTAURANT, POINT DEPOT, Dublin	Shay Cleary Architects	M 1989	NIA–4	4-8
DEVELOPMENT AT CHASE ROAD, Acton, London	Delany MacVeigh & Pike Architects	SE 1989	NIA–4	22-23
A BOOKSHOP ON COLLEGE GREEN	Desmond FitzGerald Architects	SE 1989	NIA–4	24-25
NEWHALL MILL WORKSHOPS, Birmingham	David Naessens and Louise Cotter	A 1990	NIA–5	8-11
3 TICKET SALES OFFICES FOR AER LINGUS	de Blacam & Meagher Architects	A 1990	NIA–5	14-16
BRADAN MARA TEO, Land-Based Salmon Hatchery, Co Galway	Scott Tallon Walker Architects	A 1990	NIA–5	23-25
A YOUTH HOSTEL IN LEITRIM	Bingham & Kelly Architects	SE 1990	NIA–5	26-27
CAFÉ KLARA, Dawson Street, Dublin	de Blacam & Meagher Architects	SE 1990	NIA–5	28-29
RAVENSBURY MILL, Morden, London	James Pike, DSMP Architects	SE 1990	NIA–5	30-31
DIFFNEY MANSHOP	Paul Keogh Architects	SE 1990	NIA–5	38-39
HARP BREWERY VISITOR CENTRE, Dundalk	Mitchell Ó Muire Smyth Architects	SE 1990	NIA–5	46-47
RESTAURANT AT CASTLEKNOCK	Murphy Kenny Architects	SE 1990	NIA–5	48-49
RETAIL BANK	Duffy Mitchell Architects	SM 1992	NIA–7	24-25
THE KITCHEN NIGHTCLUB, Temple Bar, Dublin	Cahill-O'Brien Associates	SM 1995	NIA–10	38-39
PIZZA HUT RESTAURANT, Blanchardstown, Co Dublin	Studio Architects	SM 1997	NIA–12	82-84
GARDEN ROOM FOR LITTLE BIRD, Merrion Square, Dublin	Grafton Architects	A 1998	NIA–13	24-29
EDEN RESTAURANT, Temple Bar, Dublin	de Paor Architects	SM 1998	NIA–13	44-47
BALLINA CREDIT UNION, Ballina, Co Westport	John Dorman Architects	SM 1998	NIA–13	48-51
COILL DUBH & DISTRICT CREDIT UNION, Co Kildare	Hassett Ducatez Architects	SA 2000	NIA–15	26-31
SCREENING ROOM FOR LITTLE BIRD, Dublin	Grafton Architects	SM 2000	NIA–15	68-71
REGENT, Temple Bar, Dublin	Simon Walker Architect	SM 2001	NIA–16	164-167
EXTENSION TO TOM'S BAR, Mountrath, Co Laois	Architecture 53seven	SM 2002	NIA–17	112-117
OFFICE FOR A COFFEE IMPORTER, Dargan Road, Belfast	Alan Jones Architect	SM 2004	NIA–19	166-171
REFURBISHMENT OF CAR PARK, Drury Street, Dublin	Cullen Payne Architects	SM 2005	NIA–20	88-93
DUBCO CREDIT UNION, Little Green Street, Dublin	Donnelly Turpin Architects	SM 2005	NIA–20	98-105
EGAN'S JUICE BAR & ROOF TERRACE, Main Street, Portlaoise	Architecture 53seven	SA 2008	NIA–23	50-61
SITE 7, BRIARHILL BUSINESS PARK, Galway	Paul Dillon Architect	A 2008	NIA–23	100-107
THE GARAGE, Co Fermanagh	John Maguire Architect	SM 2013	NIA–28	150-155

• see also Mixed Use / Office

project	architect	award / year	volume	pages
community				
HOUSE IN A CHURCH	McCullough Mulvin Architects	SE 1990	NIA–5	40-41
MIGRANT ACCESS CENTRE, Camden, London	Brady + Mallalieu Architects	SM 1991	NIA–6	18-19
HOUSE IN A CHURCH	McCullough Mulvin Architects	SM 1992	NIA–7	28-29
OLD BOROUGH SCHOOL & PARISH CENTRE, Swords	Paul Keogh Architects	SM 2002	NIA–17	94-99
SPORTS AND YOUTH SERVICES CENTRE, Cabra, Dublin	Henchion + Reuter Architects	SM 2004	NIA–19	160-165

BUILDING TYPE

YOUTH AND COMMUNITY CENTRE,					
Donore Avenue, Dublin	Henchion + Reuter Architects	A	2005	NIA–20	62-75
BROOKFIELD COMMUNITY YOUTH CENTRE					
& CRÈCHE, Tallaght, Dublin	Hassett Ducatez Architects	M	2008	NIA–23	32-49
ARC BUILDING, Built Environment Centre, Hull	Níall McLaughlin Architects	SM	2008	NIA–23	140-147
SEÁN O'CASEY COMMUNITY CENTRE,					
East Wall, Dublin	O'Donnell + Tuomey Architects	SA	2009	NIA–24	76-89
BALLYFERMOT LEISURE AND YOUTH CENTRE,					
Dublin	McGarry Ní Éanaigh Architects	SM	2009	NIA–24	220-227
BALLYROAN PASTORAL CENTRE,					
Rathfarnham, Dublin	Box Architecture	SM	2011	NIA–26	106-111
DUNSHAUGHLIN PASTORAL CENTRE, Co Meath	McGarry Ní Éanaigh Architects	SM	2011	NIA–26	142-147

cultural

IRISH FILM CENTRE, Trinity Street, Dublin	Sheila O'Donnell Architect	A	1986	NIA–1	10-11
PUPPET TRAILER	Derek Heavey and Sheila McCarthy	SE	1987	NIA–2	18-19
IRISH FILM CENTRE, Eustace Street, Dublin	Sheila O'Donnell Architect	M	1988	NIA–3	5-7
THE CITY ARTS CENTRE	McCullough Mulvin Architects	SE	1988	NIA–3	36-37
ABBEY THEATRE PORTICO	McCullough Mulvin Architects	SM	1991	NIA–6	28-29
IRISH MUSEUM OF MODERN ART	Shay Cleary Architects	A	1992	NIA–7	8-10
THEATRE ROYAL FOYER, WEXFORD	de Blacam & Meagher Architects	SM	1992	NIA–7	22-23
BECKETT THEATRE, Trinity College Dublin	de Blacam & Meagher Architects	M	1993	NIA–8	7-11
TEMPLE BAR GALLERY & STUDIOS, Dublin	McCullough Mulvin Architects	A	1995	NIA–10	28-31
DESIGNYARD, Applied Arts Centre,	Felim Dunne & Associates				
Temple Bar, Dublin	/ Robinson Keefe Devane	SM	1995	NIA–10	44-45
THE ARK – A Cultural Centre for Children,					
Temple Bar, Dublin	Group 91 / Shane O'Toole and Michael Kelly	*M	1996	NIA–11	10-17
BLACK CHURCH PRINT STUDIOS,					
Temple Bar, Dublin	McCullough Mulvin Architects	*M	1996	NIA–11	18-25
NATIONAL MUSEUM AT COLLINS BARRACKS					
(Phase 1), Dublin 8	Gilroy McMahon Architects / OPW	A	1996	NIA–11	26-31
GATE MULTIPLEX, North Gate, Cork	Derek Tynan Architects	A	1999	NIA–14	58-63
GALLERY OF PHOTOGRAPHY,					
Temple Bar, Dublin	Group 91 / O'Donnell + Tuomey Architects	M	1997	NIA–12	10-19
NATIONAL PHOTOGRAPHY ARCHIVE					
/ DIT SCHOOL OF PHOTOGRAPHY,					
Temple Bar, Dublin	Group 91 / O'Donnell + Tuomey Architects	A	1997	NIA–12	32-37
ARTHOUSE, Temple Bar, Dublin	Group 91 / Shay Cleary Architects	SM	1997	NIA–12	62-64
MUSIC CENTRE, Temple Bar, Dublin	Group 91 / McCullough Mulvin Architects	SM	1997	NIA–12	71-73
ÍOSLACHT	de Paor Architects	SM	2000	NIA–15	56-59
PROJECT ARTS CENTRE, Dublin	Shay Cleary Architects	A	2001	NIA–16	22-31
MODEL ARTS & NILAND GALLERY, Sligo	McCullough Mulvin Architects	A	2001	NIA–16	72-81
NEW GALLERIES, IMMA,					
Royal Hospital Kilmainham, Dublin	Shay Cleary Architects	SM	2001	NIA–16	96-101
VAN – an insertion to the National Sculpture Factory, Cork	de Paor Architects	SM	2001	NIA–16	102-105
GALLERY 2, Douglas Hyde Gallery, TCD	McCullough Mulvin Architects	SM	2002	NIA–17	100-105
LEWIS GLUCKSMAN GALLERY,					
University College Cork	O'Donnell + Tuomey Architects	SM	2005	NIA–20	136-147
MARTIN VALLEY SCULPTURE PARK, Cork	FKL Architects	SM	2006	NIA–21	138-145
SOLSTICE ARTS CENTRE, Navan	Grafton Architects	A	2007	NIA–22	50-63
SOURCE ARTS CENTRE & LIBRARY, Thurles	McCullough Mulvin Architects	A	2007	NIA–22	64-77
TRINITY IRISH ART RESEARCH CENTRE, TCD	O'Donnell + Tuomey Architects	SM	2008	NIA–23	156-161
LIGHT HOUSE CINEMA, Smithfield, Dublin	DTA Architects	A	2009	NIA–24	100-109
REGIONAL CULTURAL CENTRE, Letterkenny	Mac Gabhann Architects	SM	2009	NIA–24	204-213
AN GAELÁRAS, Derry	O'Donnell + Tuomey Architects	SA	2010	NIA–25	78-93

• see also Artist's Studio

BUILDING TYPE

project	architect	award / year	volume	pages

education

SPORTS HALL, Mount Anville, Dublin	Moloney O'Beirne Guy + HLM Architects	A 1986	NIA–1	12-13
EXTENSION TO CROSS & PASSION COLLEGE,				
Kilcullen, Co Kildare	Robinson Keefe Devane Architects	SE 1988	NIA–3	46-47
MONTESSORI SCHOOL, Howth Road, Co Dublin	Neil Sholdice Architect	SM 1991	NIA–6	34-35
ST PAUL'S SECONDARY SCHOOL,				
Oughterard, Co Galway	Grafton Architects	SM 1993	NIA–8	24-27
CASHEL SECOND-LEVEL SCHOOL	Doyle Architects	SM 1995	NIA–10	42-43
BLACKROCK EDUCATION CENTRE, Co Dublin	Shay Cleary Architects	SM 1997	NIA–12	53-55
RANELAGH MULTI-DENOMINATIONAL SCHOOL,				
Ranelagh, Dublin	O'Donnell + Tuomey Architects	M 1999	NIA–14	14-23
OUR LADY'S SECONDARY SCHOOL,				
Castleblayney, Co Monaghan	Grafton Architects	A 2000	NIA–15	38-43
BUNSCOIL PHOBAIL FEIRSTE, Belfast	Mackel & Doherty Architects	SM 2001	NIA–16	130-135
CORK SCHOOL PROJECT	Magee Creedon Architects	SM 2001	NIA–16	136-139
BELVEDERE COLLEGE SJ / O'REILLY THEATRE, Dublin	Murray Ó Laoire Architects	SM 2001	NIA–16	144-149
OLD BOROUGH SCHOOL & PARISH CENTRE, Swords	Paul Keogh Architects	SM 2002	NIA–17	94-99
MONAGHAN EDUCATION CENTRE	McGarry Ní Éanaigh Architects	SM 2003	NIA–18	126-131
A WAY TO SCHOOL				
– Ardscoil Mhuire, Ballinasloe, and				
North Kildare Educate Together Project, Celbridge	Grafton Architects	M 2004	NIA–19	22-47
EUROCAMPUS, Roebuck Road, Dublin 14	A2 Architects	SM 2009	NIA–24	136-145
SCOIL MHUIRE ÓGH, Crumlin	Mary Laheen Architects	A 2013	NIA–28	88-101

education – 3rd level

THE DINING HALL AND ATRIUM,				
Trinity College Dublin	de Blacam & Meagher Architects	A 1987	NIA–2	8-9
EXTENSION TO COLLEGE OF TECHNOLOGY,				
Bolton Street, Dublin	Gilroy McMahon Architects	A 1988	NIA–3	18-20
THE O'REILLY INSTITUTE, Trinity College Dublin	Scott Tallon Walker Architects	A 1989	NIA–4	18-21
DEANS OF RESIDENCE (Chaplaincy),				
University College Dublin	Prof Cathal O'Neill & Partners	A 1990	NIA–5	20-22
SCHOOL OF ENGINEERING (Phase 1),				
University College Dublin	Scott Tallon Walker Architects	SE 1990	NIA–5	52-53
BECKETT THEATRE, Trinity College Dublin	de Blacam & Meagher Architects	M 1993	NIA–8	7-11
BIOTECHNOLOGY RESEARCH BUILDING,				
University College Dublin	Scott Tallon Walker Architects	SM 1994	NIA–9	32-33
NEW LIBRARY,	de Blacam & Meagher			
Cork Regional Technical College	/ Boyd Barrett Murphy-O'Connor	A 1995	NIA–10	12-15
DEPT OF MECHANICAL ENGINEERING,				
Trinity College Dublin	Grafton Architects	A 1997	NIA–12	20-25
NEW SCHOOL OF ARCHITECTURE & INTERIOR DESIGN,				
University of North London	Brady + Mallalieu Architects	SM 1997	NIA–12	44-46
MAIN ENTRANCE, UNIVERSITY OF LIMERICK	de Blacam & Meagher Architects	SM 1998	NIA–13	40-43
SCHOOL OF ART, GALWAY	de Blacam & Meagher Architects	SM 1999	NIA–14	72-75
FURNITURE COLLEGE, LETTERFRACK, Co Galway	O'Donnell + Tuomey Architects	M 2002	NIA–17	26-39
USSHER LIBRARY,	McCullough Mulvin Architects			
Trinity College Dublin	and KMD Architecture	M 2003	NIA–18	22-37
URBAN INSTITUTE IRELAND, University College Dublin	Grafton Architects	A 2003	NIA–18	48-59
MIND THE GAP, The Mall, Dublin City University	Grafton Architects	SM 2003	NIA–18	120-125
EXTENSION TO VIRUS REFERENCE LABORATORY				
University College Dublin	McCullough Mulvin Architects	A 2004	NIA–19	100-107
MEDICAL RESEARCH LABORATORIES,				
University College Dublin	O'Donnell + Tuomey Architects	A 2004	NIA–19	108-117

BUILDING TYPE

MME – Extension to Dept of Mechanical & Manufacturing Engineering, Trinity College Dublin	Grafton Architects	A	2006	NIA–21	64-75
LEWIS GLUCKSMAN GALLERY, University College Cork	O'Donnell + Tuomey Architects	SM	2005	NIA–20	136-147
MEETING PLACE, North Campus Development, Cork Institute of Technology	de Blacam & Meagher / Boyd Barrett Murphy-O'Connor	A	2007	NIA–22	26-41
CAVAN INSTITUTE, Cathedral Road, Cavan	McCullough Mulvin Architects	SM	2007	NIA–22	136-143
TAILTEANN, Mary Immaculate College, Limerick	Murray Ó Laoire Architects	SM	2008	NIA–23	148-155
UNIVERSITÀ LUIGI BOCCONI, Milan	Grafton Architects	M	2009	NIA–24	40-59
SCHOOL OF ENGINEERING, Athlone Institute of Technology	McCullough Mulvin Architects	SM	2010	NIA–25	202-209
HOUSE FOR A PRESIDENT, University of Limerick	Grafton Architects	SM	2011	NIA–26	126-131
LONG ROOM HUB, Trinity College Dublin	McCullough Mulvin Architects	SM	2012	NIA–27	126-133
MEDICAL SCHOOL, STUDENT RESIDENCES & BUS SHELTER, University of Limerick	Grafton Architects	A	2013	NIA–28	62-77

health

PSYCHIATRIC / GERIATRIC UNITS, St James's Hospital, Dublin	Moloney O'Beirne Guy + Hutchison Locke & Monk Architects	SE	1987	NIA–2	26-27
PROTOTYPE DESIGN FOR A PSYCHOGERIATRIC HOSPITAL	de Blacam & Meagher Architects	A	1988	NIA–3	12-13
A SUITE OF PRIVATE MEDICAL CONSULTING ROOMS	McGarry Ní Éanaigh Architects	SE	1990	NIA–5	44-45
MEDICAL CENTRE, DROGHEDA	McGarry Ní Éanaigh Architects	A	1991	NIA–6	14-17
DUBLIN DENTAL HOSPITAL, Lincoln Place	Ahrends Burton & Koralek Architects	SM	1999	NIA–14	64-67
MORTUARY CHAPELS & POSTMORTEM SUITE, St James's Hospital, Dublin	Henry J Lyons & Partners	SM	2004	NIA–19	172-179
ALZHEIMER'S RESPITE CENTRE, Blackrock, Co Dublin	Níall McLaughlin Architects	SA	2010	NIA–25	64-77
CHILD & ADOLESCENT MENTAL HEALTH UNIT, Merlin Park, Galway	Moloney O'Beirne Architects	SM	2011	NIA–26	154-159

house – new build

MORIARTY HOUSE, Howth, Co Dublin	Fitzgerald Selby & Sugars Architects	SE	1986	NIA–1	18-19
FAMILY HOUSE, Co Kildare	Liam Hennessy Architect	SE	1986	NIA–1	20-21
FAMILY HOUSE, Co Wexford	Liam Hennessy Architect	SE	1986	NIA–1	22-23
HOUSE AT LOUGH ENNELL	Paul Keogh Architects	SE	1986	NIA–1	28-29
A SMALL COUNTRY HOUSE, Co Louth	McGarry Ní Éanaigh Architects	SE	1987	NIA–2	22-23
A RURAL HOUSE	Ross Cahill-O'Brien Architect	A	1988	NIA–3	8-9
HOUSE AT RATH, Dundalk	Gibney & Van Dijk Architects	A	1988	NIA–3	16-17
HOUSE IN THE BARROW VALLEY	Derek Tynan Architects	A	1988	NIA–3	21-23
BYRNE HOUSE	Duffy Mitchell Architects	SE	1988	NIA–3	28-29
HOUSE AT MODEL FARM ROAD, CORK	John E Keating & Associates	SE	1988	NIA–3	32-33
A HOUSE IN PORTARLINGTON	Gerard Carty Architect	A	1989	NIA–4	9-11
HOUSE IN NORTH COUNTY DUBLIN	Henry J Lyons & Partners	SE	1989	NIA–4	30-31
HOUSE ON A DRUMLIN, Co Monaghan	McGarry Ní Éanaigh Architects	SE	1989	NIA–4	32-33
HOUSE AT BOFARA, Westport	Ross Cahill-O'Brien Architect	A	1991	NIA–6	8-10
MEWS, Blackrock, Co Dublin	Cathal Crimmins Architect	SM	1991	NIA–6	20-21
MEWS AT 26 WATERLOO ROAD, Dublin	Prof Cathal O'Neill & Partners	SM	1991	NIA–6	32-33
29 SOUTH PARK, Foxrock, Co Dublin	Newenham Mulligan & Associates	A	1992	NIA–7	17-19
HOUSE A	The Bacon Group	SM	1992	NIA–7	20-21
HOUSE ON A RIVER	McGarry Ní Éanaigh Architects	SM	1992	NIA–7	30-31
THE COCOON, MULLET PENNINSULA	Patricia Mangan and Rory Murphy	SM	1992	NIA–7	32-33
HOUSE IN WEST CORK	O'Dowd O'Herlihy Horan Architects	SM	1995	NIA–10	58-59
A HOUSE IN GIFU, JAPAN	Deirdre Whelan and Paul Kelly	SM	1995	NIA–10	62-63
HOUSE IN DOOLIN, Co Clare	Grafton Architects	A	1995	NIA–10	20-23
HOUSE IN NORTH COUNTY DUBLIN	O'Donnell + Tuomey Architects	SM	1996	NIA–11	56-57

BUILDING TYPE

project	architect	award / year	volume	pages
MEWS DWELLING, DUBLIN 6	Derek Tynan Architects	A 1997	NIA–12	26-31
WALLPAPER HOUSE, Cork	de Paor Architects	A 1997	NIA–12	38-41
MEWS HOUSE TO HEYTESBURY LANE, Dublin	de Blacam & Meagher Architects	A 1998	NIA–13	18-23
EXPERIMENTAL SOLAR HOUSE & STUDIO, West Cork	Akiboye Conolly Architects	SM 1998	NIA–13	36-39
PARALLEL HOUSE, Kingscourt, Co Cavan	McGarry Ní Éanaigh Architects	SM 1998	NIA–13	56-59
MEWS HOUSE, LOUIS LANE, Dublin	McCullough Mulvin Architects	A 1999	NIA–14	36-39
HOUSE IN A LONG BACK GARDEN, Navan	O'Donnell + Tuomey Architects	A 1999	NIA–14	46-51
A.NON.ARCH	BSPL Architects	SM 2001	NIA–16	90-95
FOUR PRIVATE HOUSES	Henchion + Reuter Architects	SM 2001	NIA–16	112-117
MEWS HOUSE AT RAGLAN LANE, Dublin	P+A Lavin Associates	SM 2001	NIA–16	124-129
THE LONG HOUSE, Percy Lane, Dublin	Grafton Architects	A 2002	NIA–17	40-47
BUILDING THE HOME, Co Leitrim	Dominic Stevens Architects	SM 2002	NIA–17	126-135
SQUARE HOUSE, South County Dublin	McCullough Mulvin Architects	A 2003	NIA–18	60-67
BRICK HOUSE, Milltown Path, Dublin	FKL Architects	A 2004	NIA–19	70-79
HOWTH HOUSE, Co Dublin	O'Donnell + Tuomey Architects	SM 2004	NIA–19	180-187
IN-BETWEEN HOUSE, Ballinamore, Co Leitrim	Dominic Stevens Architects	SM 2004	NIA–19	192-197
ALMA LANE, Monkstown, Co Dublin	Boyd Cody Architects	M 2005	NIA–20	38-51
HOUSE AT DIRK COVE, Clonakilty, Co Cork	Níall McLaughlin Architects	SM 2005	NIA–20	114-123
SORRENTO HEIGHTS, Dalkey, Co Dublin	Boyd Cody Architects	A 2006	NIA–21	46-55
13a THOR PLACE, Stoneybatter, Dublin	ODOS Architects	A 2006	NIA–21	102-111
HOUSE, RICHMOND PLACE, Rathmines, Dublin	Boyd Cody Architects	SM 2006	NIA–21	112-119
HOUSE AT AILL BREAC, Baile Uí Chonaola, Contae na Gaillimhe	de Paor Architects	A 2007	NIA–22	42-49
THE NARROW HOUSE, 3 Northumberland Road, Dun Laoghaire	Architecture Republic	SM 2008	NIA–23	108-115
MIMETIC HOUSE, Dromaheir, Co Leitrim	Dominic Stevens Architects	A 2007	NIA–22	90-99
HOUSE IN GRAIGUENAMANAGH, Co Kilkenny	Boyd Cody Architects	A 2009	NIA–24	90-99
THE SLEEPING GIANT, KILLINEY, Co Dublin	O'Donnell + Tuomey Architects	A 2009	NIA–24	126-135
TUATH NA MARA, Lough Swilly, Co Donegal	Mac Gabhann Architects	SM 2009	NIA–24	214-219
HOUSE AT PIPER'S END, Letty Green, Herts, UK	Níall McLaughlin Architects	SM 2009	NIA–24	234-241
DWELLING AT ST PATRICK'S COTTAGES, Rathfarnham, Dublin	ODOS Architects	SM 2009	NIA–24	248-255
10A LOWER GRANGEGORMAN, Dublin	ODOS Architects	SM 2009	NIA–24	256-263
A-HOUSE, Rathmines, Dublin	FKL Architects	SA 2011	NIA–26	50-59
HOUSE IN WOODS, Co Kildare	Hassett Ducatez Architects	SA 2011	NIA–26	60-69
€25,000 HOUSE, Cloone, Co Leitrim	Dominic Stevens Architects	A 2011	NIA–26	86-93
HOUSE FOR A PRESIDENT, University of Limerick	Grafton Architects	SM 2011	NIA–26	126-131
Z SQUARE HOUSE, Temple Gardens, Dublin	McCullough Mulvin Architects	SM 2011	NIA–26	136-141
HOUSE ON MOUNT ANVILLE, Dublin	Aughey O'Flaherty Architects	A 2012	NIA–27	42-61
HOUSE IN BOGWEST, Co Wexford	Steve Larkin Architects	A 2012	NIA–27	70-79
HOUSE IN Co CARLOW	Steve Larkin Architects	A 2013	NIA–28	102-113
HOUSE 4, Firhouse, Dublin	Taka Architects	A 2013	NIA–28	114-125
CARNIVAN HOUSE, Fethard-on-Sea	Aughey O'Flaherty Architects	SM 2013	NIA–28	126-133
HOUSE ON CHESTNUT LANE	Boyd Cody Architects	SM 2013	NIA–28	134-141

house – conversion / extension / refurbishment

ZANUSSI KITCHEN DESIGN	James Horan and Anne Harper Architects	A 1986	NIA–1	14-15
KITCHEN, Booterstown, Co Dublin	James Horan and Anne Harper Architects	SE 1986	NIA–1	24-25
DONNINGTON BATH HOUSES, London	David Naessens and Christopher Stead	A 1987	NIA–2	12-13
HOUSE IN A COURTYARD, Co Dublin	McCullough Mulvin Architects	SE 1987	NIA–2	20-21
EXTENSION TO C18TH HOUSE IN LEINSTER	McGarry Ní Éanaigh Architects	SE 1988	NIA–3	38-39
A GARDEN EXTENSION TO THE FULLAM RESIDENCE	O'Dea Skehan & Associates	SE 1988	NIA–3	40-41
GARDEN ROOMS, Leeson Park / Percy Place, Dublin	Paul Keogh Architects	A 1989	NIA–4	15-17

BUILDING TYPE

HOUSE AND STUDIO RECONVERSION IN Co DOWN	Desmond FitzGerald Architects	SE	1990	NIA–5	32-33
RENOVATION OF STONE COTTAGE, Co Meath	McGarry Ní Éanaigh Architects	SE	1990	NIA–5	42-43
HOUSE EXTENSION WALTHAM TERRACE, Blackrock, Co Dublin	Cathal Crimmins Architect	SM	1991	NIA–6	22-23
EXTENSION AND RENOVATION OF A RECTORY	McGarry Ní Éanaigh Architects	A	1994	NIA–9	6-9
PLAN FOR THE GARDEN OF A MODERN MOVEMENT HOUSE	Donohoe & FitzGerald Architects	A	1994	NIA–9	14-17
HOUSE TO LET	Ó Muire Smyth Architects	SM	1996	NIA–11	58-59
GARDEN IN CORK	de Paor Architects	SM	1996	NIA–11	60-61
PRIVATE RESIDENCE, Roebuck, Dublin	Derek Tynan Architects	SM	1996	NIA–11	62-63
BAY WINDOW & STAIRCASE INSERTION, Windsor Terrace, Dublin	Gerard Carty Architect	A	1998	NIA–13	12-17
DOMESTIC ACUPUNCTURE	Dominic Stevens Architects	A	1999	NIA–14	52-57
RETURN HOUSE	de Paor Architects	SM	1999	NIA–14	76-79
NEW KITCHEN AND BATHROOM IN A HOUSE IN RATHMINES, Dublin	O'Donnell + Tuomey Architects	SM	1999	NIA–14	86-89
URBAN PROTOTYPE	BSPL Architects	A	2000	NIA–15	32-37
ADAPTABLE ROOM	Camille O'Sullivan Architect	A	2000	NIA–15	44-47
GARAGE CONVERSION, DUN LAOGHAIRE	Box Architecture	SM	2000	NIA–15	48-51
17 PRIORY AVENUE, STILLORGAN, Co Dublin	Duffy Mitchell Architects	SM	2000	NIA–15	60-63
PINE TREES AND THE SEA	McCullough Mulvin Architects	SM	2000	NIA–15	88-91
11m^2 EXTENSION TO FAMILY HOUSE in city-centre Victorian terrace, Dublin	Hassett Ducatez Architects	A	2001	NIA–16	60-65
EXTENSION TO TERRACED HOUSE, Heytesbury Street, Dublin	Derek Tynan Architects	SM	2001	NIA–16	156-159
3 (INTERVENTIONS) MODIFICATIONS	Boyd Cody Architects	SM	2003	NIA–18	94-101
ON HOUSING 2	BSPL Architects	SM	2003	NIA–18	102-107
PRECAST LINES	Dominic Stevens Architect, in coll. with John Graham	SM	2003	NIA–18	132-137
DOUBLE GLASS HOUSE, Dublin	Hassett Ducatez Architects	A	2004	NIA–19	80-87
BRICK COURTS HOUSE, Daniel Street, Dublin	Architects Bates Maher	SM	2004	NIA–19	118-121
3, 4, 5 TEMPLE COTTAGES, Dublin	Boyd Cody Architects	SM	2004	NIA–19	122-127
ON HOUSING 3	BSPL Architects	SM	2004	NIA–19	128-135
WELLINGTON ROAD, Dublin	Boyd Cody Architects	A	2005	NIA–20	52-61
CONNEMARA BOATHOUSE, Moyard, Co Galway	MV Cullinan Architects	SM	2005	NIA–20	94-97
CITY HOUSE AND WORKPLACE, 41 Francis Street, Dublin	Donaghy + Dimond Architects	A	2006	NIA–21	56-63
HOUSE AT CROUCH END, London	Níall McLaughlin Architects	A	2006	NIA–21	84-93
BROOKE HEUSSAFF LIBRARY, South Circular Road, Dublin	NJBA Architects	A	2006	NIA–21	94-101
KITCHEN-GARDEN-PARTY-WALL, Arran Road, Dublin	Donaghy + Dimond Architects	SM	2006	NIA–21	130-137
No.33 ST KEVIN'S ROAD, Portobello, Dublin	ODOS Architects	SM	2006	NIA–21	160-165
BRICK THICKNESS, 11 Cowper Drive, Dublin	A2 Architects	SM	2007	NIA–22	100-107
ST JUDE'S RESIDENCE, Glengowla, Co Galway	Boyer Kennihan Architects	SM	2007	NIA–22	108-115
34 PALMERSTON ROAD, Rathmines, Dublin	Boyd Cody Architects	SA	2008	NIA–23	62-75
ONE UP, ONE DOWN, ONE DEEP, Portobello, Dublin	A2 Architects	A	2008	NIA–23	76-83
ST JAMES, Clontarf, Dublin	Boyd Cody Architects	SM	2008	NIA–23	116-123
JIG-SAW, Leeson Park, Dublin	McCullough Mulvin Architects	A	2009	NIA–24	110-117
MATILDE, Rathgar, Dublin	Ailtireacht	SM	2009	NIA–24	146-153
LAKE HOUSE EXTENSION + RENOVATION, Co Kerry	Clancy Moore Architects	A	2010	NIA–25	104-113
HOUSE – GARDEN – GRAFT, Ranelagh, Dublin	Donaghy + Dimond Architects	A	2010	NIA–25	114-123
THE PLASTIC HOUSE, Dublin	Architecture Republic	SM	2010	NIA–25	134-141
SLATE-STOREY EXTENSION, Chapelizod, Dublin	ArchitectsTM	SM	2010	NIA–25	148-155
DARTMOUTH SQUARE, Dublin	Aughey O'Flaherty Architects	SM	2010	NIA–25	156-163
EXTENSION TO A PROTECTED STRUCTURE, Rathgar, Dublin	Garbhann Doran Architects	SM	2010	NIA–25	164-171

BUILDING TYPE

project	architect	award / year	volume	pages
LANDSCAPE ROOM, Glencar, Sligo	LID Architecture	SM 2010	NIA–25	188-193
31 CARYSFORT ROAD, Dalkey, Co Dublin	ODOS Architects	SM 2010	NIA–25	230-237
BRICK A BACK, Gordon Street, Dublin	Architecture Republic	SM 2011	NIA–26	98-101
HOUSE REFURBISHMENT & EXTENSION, Dartry, Dublin	Carson and Crushell Architects	SM 2011	NIA–26	112-115
FLITCH, Ranelagh, Dublin	Donaghy + Dimond Architects	SM 2011	NIA–26	116-119
A DOMESTIC EVOLUTION, Sandymount, Dublin	David Flynn Architect	SM 2011	NIA–26	120-125
SALLYMOUNT TERRACE, Ranelagh, Dublin	Ryan W Kennihan Architects	SM 2011	NIA–26	132-135
LANEWAY WALL GARDEN HOUSE	Donaghy + Dimond Architects	A 2012	NIA–27	62-69
BUTTERFLY HOUSE, Co Leitrim	LID Architecture	A 2012	NIA–27	80-87
SHELTERED SPACES	A2 Architects	SM 2012	NIA–27	88-95
BACKYARD, JOHN DILLON STREET, Dublin	Boyd Cody Architects	SM 2012	NIA–27	104-109
EXTENSION AND RENOVATION IN PORTOBELLO	Donal Colfer Architect	SM 2012	NIA–27	110-117
RECASTING	Donaghy + Dimond Architects	A 2013	NIA–28	50-61

houses – max 4

4 HOUSES AT DONNYBROOK, Dublin	Mitchell Ó Muire Smyth Architects	SE 1987	NIA–2	24-25
MEWS HOUSES AT CLYDE LANE	Grafton Architects	SE 1990	NIA–5	36-37
DOUBLE HOUSE, Belgrave Square, Monkstown	Derek Tynan Architects	SE 1990	NIA–5	54-55
MEWS HOUSES AT CLYDE LANE, Dublin	Grafton Architects	A 1993	NIA–8	20-23
FOUR HOUSES AT TULACH ARD, Rahoon, Galway	National Building Agency (MV Cullinan)	SM 1996	NIA–11	54-55
THREE HOUSES IN RATHMINES, Dublin	Boyd Kelly Whelan Architects	SA 2000	NIA–15	14-19
TWO HOLIDAY HOUSES, Kinsallagh, Westport	Paul Keogh Architects	SM 2001	NIA–16	118-123
PERISCOPE, Pembroke Lane, Dublin	Gerard Carty Architect	SM 2004	NIA–19	140-145
TWO TWO UP TWO DOWN, John Dillon Street, Dublin	de Paor Architects	SM 2006	NIA–21	120-129
3 HOUSES, CONG, Co Galway	Aughey O'Flaherty Architects	SM 2009	NIA–24	154-161
NEW ORDER, Stoneybatter, Dublin	A2 Architects	A 2010	NIA–25	94-103
HOUSE 1 + HOUSE 2, Morehampton Road, Dublin	Taka Architects	A 2010	NIA–25	124-133
Y = 3 HOUSES, North Circular Road, Dublin	Architecture Republic	SM 2010	NIA–25	142-147
3 MEWS DWELLINGS, Portobello, Dublin	ODOS Architects	SM 2010	NIA–25	222-229
TWO OF EVERYTHING, Sandymount, Dublin	Fitzpatrick & Mays Architects / Robin Mandal Architects	SM 2011	NIA–26	148-153
SLIEVEBAWNOGUE (double-house)	Clancy Moore Architects	M 2013	NIA–28	34-49

housing

APARTMENTS IN CARLOW	Derek Tynan Architects	A 1986	NIA–1	6-7
HOUSING AT RUTLAND STREET	Dublin Corporation, Housing Architect's Dept.	SE 1986	NIA–1	16-17
KILLYKEEN FOREST PARK, Co Cavan	OPW (Ciaran O'Connor)	SE 1986	NIA–1	32-33
RUSSELL STREET HOUSING	Dublin Corporation, Housing Architect's Dept.	SE 1988	NIA–3	26-27
MILLENNIUM TOWER, Dublin	Keane Murphy Duff Architects	SE 1988	NIA–3	30-31
RESIDENTIAL DEVELOPMENT, Ailesbury Road, Dublin	de Blacam & Meagher Architects	A 1989	NIA–4	12-14
HOLIDAY HOUSES AT VELVET STRAND, Portmarnock	Paul Keogh Architects	SM 1991	NIA–6	26-27
RESIDENTIAL QUARTER AT ST PETER'S PORT, ATHLONE	National Building Agency (MV Cullinan)	A 1994	NIA–9	18-21
HOUSING AT BROOKWOOD	Fionnuala Rogerson Architect	SM 1994	NIA–9	30-31
THE PRINTWORKS, Temple Bar	Group 91 / Derek Tynan Architects	M 1995	NIA–10	6-11
SOCIAL HOUSING, New Street, Dublin	Gerry Cahill Architects	A 1995	NIA–10	16-19
CO-OPERATIVE HOUSING, Allingham Street, Dublin	Gerry Cahill Architects	SM 1997	NIA–12	50-52
APARTMENT BUILDING, Amiens Street, Dublin	Fagan Kelly Lysaght Architects	SM 1999	NIA–14	83-85
RESIDENTIAL DEVELOPMENT, Beresford Street, Dublin	Ó Muire Smyth Architects	SM 1999	NIA–14	96-99
SOCIAL HOUSING, Rathasker Road, Naas	Kelly & Cogan Architects	SM 2000	NIA–15	76-79

BUILDING TYPE

A RESIDENTIAL TOWER IN TEMPLE BAR, Dublin	de Blacam & Meagher Architects	A 2001	NIA–16	42-51
URBAN BEEHIVE, North King Street Apartments, Dublin	Grafton Architects	A 2002	NIA–17	48-57
ON HOUSING	BSPL Architects	SM 2002	NIA–17	68-77
SOCIAL HOUSING, GALBALLY, Co Limerick	O'Donnell + Tuomey Architects	A 2003	NIA–18	86-93
ARDOYNE MEWS, Ballsbridge, Dublin	Design Strategies	SM 2003	NIA–18	108-113
URBAN SPACE / PRIVATE PLACE, Clarion Quay, Dublin	Urban Projects	SM 2003	NIA–18	138-143
ALLINETT'S LANE APARTMENTS, Blackpool, Cork	MV Cullinan Architects	SM 2004	NIA–19	146-151
PEABODY HOUSING, Silvertown, London	Níall McLaughlin Architects	A 2005	NIA–20	76-87
REUBEN STREET APARTMENTS, Dublin	FKL Architects	SM 2006	NIA–21	146-151
HOUSING, BALLYMUN	FKL Architects	SM 2007	NIA–22	128-135
HOUSING AT PEARSE SQUARE, Pearse Street, Dublin	GKMP Architects, in assoc. with O'Mahony Pike	SM 2008	NIA–23	132-139
ALTO VETRO RESIDENTIAL TOWER, Grand Canal Quay, Dublin	Shay Cleary Architects	SM 2009	NIA–24	180-187
DWELLING SPACE, Eglinton Road, Dublin	GKMP Architects	SM 2009	NIA–24	192-199
304 SPRING STREET, New York	Zakrzewski + Hyde Architects	SM 2009	NIA–24	264-271
TIMBERYARD SOCIAL HOUSING, Coombe Bypass, Dublin	O'Donnell + Tuomey Architects	M 2010	NIA–25	48-63
SLIABH BÁN HOUSING, Galway	DTA Architects	SM 2010	NIA–25	172-179
RATHMINES SQUARE – LEISURE CENTRE + APARTMENTS, Dublin	Donnelly Turpin Architects	SA 2011	NIA–26	26-37
SOCIAL & AFFORDABLE HOUSING, SANTRY DEMESNE	DTA Architects	SA 2011	NIA–26	38-49

• see also Mixed Use

international exhibition

THE IRISH PAVILION	O'Donnell + Tuomey Architects	M 1992	NIA–7	4-7
N³ – THE IRISH PAVILION, Architectural Biennale, Venice	de Paor Architects	A 2001	NIA–16	52-59
IRISH PAVILION, Expo 2000, Hanover	Murray Ó Laoire Architects	SM 2001	NIA–16	150-155
IRELAND'S PAVILION AT THE VENICE BIENNALE	O'Donnell + Tuomey Architects	SM 2005	NIA–20	148-157
EASA TIMBER PAVILION, Letterfrack, Co Galway	Happy Architecture	SM 2009	NIA–24	200-203
LOGGIA – STUDENT WORKSHOP, Angone, Italy	Attley Donnellan Kelly O'Brien Architects	SM 2011	NIA–26	102-105
ARCHITECTURE AS NEW GEOGRAPHY (Venice Biennale)	Grafton Architects	A 2013	NIA–28	78-87
VESSEL: an installation for the Venice Biennale 2012	O'Donnell + Tuomey Architects	SM 2013	NIA–28	156-163

mixed use

YORK RIVERSIDE COMPETITION	Gibney & Van Dijk Architects	SE 1987	NIA–2	16-17
DEVELOPMENT AT NORTH WALL QUAY, Dublin	Quilligan & Twamley Architects	SE 1987	NIA–2	34-35
LIVING IN THE CITY	O'Donnell + Tuomey Architects	M 1990	NIA–5	4-7
LECTURE HALL AND ARCHIVE BUILDING	McCullough Mulvin Architects	A 1990	NIA–5	17-19
RE-DEVELOPMENT OF 27-29 CLARE ST, Dublin	Gilroy McMahon Architects	SE 1990	NIA–5	34-35
REFURBISHMENT OF QUAYSIDE HOUSE AND SHOP	DAC Architects	SM 1991	NIA–6	24-25
STUDENT FACILITIES CENTRE, Aston Place, Dublin	Frank Kenny Associates	SM 1994	NIA–9	22-23
THE GREEN BUILDING, Temple Bar, Dublin	Murray Ó Laoire Architects	SM 1995	NIA–10	52-53
MoS BUILDING, Abbeyfeale, Co Limerick	5F Architects	SM 1997	NIA–12	56-58
TEMPLE BAR SQUARE, Temple Bar, Dublin	Group 91 / Grafton Architects	SM 1997	NIA–12	65-67
MIXED USE BUILDING, MEETING HOUSE SQUARE, Temple Bar, Dublin	Group 91 / Paul Keogh Architects	SM 1997	NIA–12	68-70
REFURBISHMENT OF 42 ARRAN QUAY, Dublin	James Kelly Architect	SM 1997	NIA–12	74-76
ISOLDE'S TOWER, Essex Quay, Dublin	Gilroy McMahon Architects	SM 1998	NIA–13	52-55
HOUSE AM ZOO, LEIPZIG	Henchion + Reuter Architects	A 1999	NIA–14	30-35
MIXED DEVELOPMENT, 1 Castle St / 24 Werburgh St, Dublin	de Blacam & Meagher Architects	SM 2000	NIA–15	52-55
THE BOOKEND, TEMPLE BAR, Dublin	Arthur Gibney & Partners	SM 2000	NIA–15	64-67

BUILDING TYPE

project	architect	award / year	volume	pages
CIGAR BOX, 26 North Great Georges Street, Dublin	Denis Byrne Architects	A 2004	NIA–19	48-59
ENGINEERS IRELAND, 20 Clyde Road, Dublin	McCullough Mulvin Architects	A 2006	NIA–21	76-83
IJBURG BLOK 4, Amsterdam	Maccreanor Lavington Architects	SM 2006	NIA–21	152-159
RATHMINES SQUARE				
– LEISURE CENTRE + APARTMENTS, Dublin	Donnelly Turpin Architects	SA 2011	NIA–26	26-37
• see also: Commercial				

monument

MAUSOLEUM, Co Carlow	Lynch O'Toole Walsh Architects (Shane O'Toole)	SE 1986	NIA–1	30-31
THE COUNTDOWN 2000 PROJECT	Hassett Ducatez Architects	A 1995	NIA–10	24-27
MAIN ENTRANCE, UNIVERSITY OF LIMERICK	de Blacam & Meagher Architects	SM 1998	NIA–13	40-43
N^3 – THE IRISH PAVILION, Architectural Biennale, Venice	de Paor Architects	A 2001	NIA–16	52-59
TOWER, Stranorlar / Ballybofey, Co Donegal	Henchion + Reuter Architects	A 2001	NIA–16	66-71
HOLDING PATTERN, A13, London	de Paor Architects	SM 2002	NIA–17	78-83

office

COMMERCIAL INFILL, Ormond Quay, Dublin	Grafton Architects	SE 1989	NIA–4	28-29
RECONSTRUCTION OF TROPICAL FRUITS BUILDING	Felim Dunne			
Sir John Rogerson's Quay	+ Beardsmore Yauner Byrne	A 1991	NIA–6	11-13
IRISH ENERGY CENTRE	Energy Research Group, UCD	SM 1995	NIA–10	46-47
SOLICITORS OFFICES, Francis Street, Dublin	Derek Tynan Architects	SM 1996	NIA–11	64-65
ENVIRONMENTAL PROTECTION AGENCY HQ,				
Johnstown Castle, Co Wexford	Henry J Lyons & Partners	SM 1997	NIA–12	77-79
SOFTWARE DESIGN BUILDING,				
Leopardstown, Co Dublin	McGarry Ní Éanaigh Architects	A 1998	NIA–13	30-35
CONVERSION & REFURBISHMENT OF				
KODAK BUILDING, Dublin	Paul Keogh Architects	SM 2000	NIA–15	80-83
No.1 GRAND CANAL QUAY, Dublin	de Blacam & Meagher Architects	A 2001	NIA–16	32-41
DESIGN STUDIOS, 47-48 Pearse Street, Dublin	Henry J Lyons & Partners	SM 2000	NIA–15	84-87
URBAN TRANSFORMATION				
– Styne House, Hatch Street, Dublin	Gilroy McMahon Architects	SM 2001	NIA–16	106-111
LIFFEY HOUSE, Tara Street, Dublin	Donnelly Turpin Architects	SM 2004	NIA–19	152-159
RIVERSIDE ONE,				
Sir John Rogerson's Quay, Dublin	Scott Tallon Walker Architects	A 2007	NIA–22	78-89
7-9 MERRION ROW + THE BILLETS, Dublin	Grafton Architects	SA 2009	NIA–24	60-75
LINCOLN PLACE, Dublin	McCullough Mulvin Architects	A 2009	NIA–24	118-125

public

LABORATORY AT ABBOTSTOWN, Co Dublin	OPW (John Tuomey)	SE 1986	NIA–1	34-35
COURTHOUSE AT SMITHFIELD, Dublin	OPW (John Tuomey)	A 1987	NIA–2	10-11
EMPLOYMENT EXCHANGE, Ballyfermot	OPW (M MacKenna, M Haugh)	SE 1987	NIA–2	30-31
CASTLE HALL, Dublin Castle	OPW (A Rolfe, K Unger)	SE 1987	NIA–2	32-33
RTE TV RECEPTION AREA	de Blacam & Meagher Architects	SE 1988	NIA–3	24-25
PAVILION AT DUBLIN ZOO	Paul Keogh Architects	SE 1988	NIA–3	34-35
PARK CENTRE BUILDING, Glenveagh	Anthony & Barbara O'Neill Architects	SE 1988	NIA–3	44-45
A GARDA STATION IN CAVAN	OPW (Kevin Wolohan)	SE 1989	NIA–4	36-37
SOCIAL WELFARE SERVICES OFFICE, BALLYFERMOT	OPW (Mary McKenna)	SM 1991	NIA–6	30-31
VISITORS CENTRE, VALENTIA	Doyle Architects	A 1992	NIA–7	14-16
VISITORS CENTRE, KING JOHN'S CASTLE, Limerick	Murray Ó Laoire Architects	SM 1992	NIA–7	34-35
LIMERICK INFORMATION OFFICE	Murray Ó Laoire Architects	SM 1992	NIA–7	36-37
WATERWAYS VISITORS CENTRE	OPW (C O'Connor, G O'Sullivan)	SM 1992	NIA–7	38-39
LIMERICK SOCIAL WELFARE OFFICES	OPW (Elizabeth Morgan)	SM 1992	NIA–7	40-41
VISITOR BUILDING, Royal Gunpowder Mills, Ballincollig	dpon Architects	A 1993	NIA–8	12-15
CÉIDE FIELDS VISITOR CENTRE	OPW (Mary McKenna)	A 1994	NIA–9	10-13

BUILDING TYPE

WATERWAYS VISITOR CENTRE,				
Grand Canal Dock, Dublin	OPW (C O'Connor, G O'Sullivan)	SM 1994	NIA–9	24-25
CLIFFS OF MOHER VISITOR CENTRE	O'Riordan Staehli Architects	SM 1994	NIA–9	28-29
NEW FOYER ETC, DEPT OF AGRICULTURE	Shay Cleary Architects	SM 1995	NIA–10	40-41
FAMINE MUSEUM,				
Strokestown Park House, Co Roscommon	Orna Hanly Architect	SM 1995	NIA–10	48-49
RHK / IMMA ARTISTS' STUDIOS	OPW (Elizabeth Morgan)	SM 1995	NIA–10	60-61
CIVIC OFFICES AT WOOD QUAY, Dublin	Scott Tallon Walker Architects	A 1996	NIA–11	42-47
MUSEUM AT MELLIFONT ABBEY, Co Louth	McGarry Ní Éanaigh Architects	SM 1996	NIA–11	52-53
HERBARIUM AND LIBRARY,				
Botanic Gardens, Dublin	OPW (C O'Connor, G O'Sullivan, S Foley)	SM 1998	NIA–12	60-63
NATIONAL MUSEUM EXHIBITIONS	McCullough Mulvin Architects / OPW	SM 1999	NIA–14	94-95
BALTINGLASS COURTHOUSE				
& VISITORS' CENTRE, Co Wicklow	Newenham Mulligan & Associates	SM 2000	NIA–15	90-95
TOWN HALL, DUNSHAUGHLIN, Co Meath	Grafton Architects	SM 2002	NIA–17	84-93
NATIONAL MUSEUM OF COUNTRY LIFE, Castlebar	OPW (Des Byrne)	SM 2002	NIA–17	118-125
BALDOYLE LIBRARY & PUBLIC AREA OFFICE, Co Dublin	FKL Architects	A 2003	NIA–18	38-47
LETTERKENNY AREA OFFICE, Co Donegal	Antoin Mac Gabhann Architects	A 2003	NIA–18	68-77
LEINSTER HOUSE PRESS RECEPTION ROOM	O'Donnell + Tuomey Architects	A 2003	NIA–18	78-85
TUBBERCURRY LIBRARY AND CIVIC OFFICES	McCullough Mulvin Architects	A 2004	NIA–19	88-99
LIMERICK COUNTY COUNCIL HEADQUARTERS	Bucholz McEvoy Architects	SM 2004	NIA–19	136-139
ATHLONE CIVIC CENTRE, LIBRARY & TOWN SQUARE	Keith Williams Architects	SM 2006	NIA–21	166-171
REDEVELOPMENT OF CORK COUNTY HALL	Shay Cleary Architects	SM 2007	NIA–22	116-127
CORK CITY COUNCIL – NEW CIVIC OFFICES	ABK Architects	A 2008	NIA–23	84-99
SIOPA PAVILION, Kildare Street, Dublin	Bucholz McEvoy Architects	SM 2009	NIA–24	168-173
GLASNEVIN NATIONAL HERITAGE PROJECT				
+ GLASNEVIN TRUST MUSEUM	A+D Wejchert Architects	SM 2011	NIA–26	166-171
EDGE OF TOWN				
– Local Area Offices, Claremorris	Simon K Kelly + Partners Architects	SM 2012	NIA–27	118-125

public space

BRUNSWICK STREET IMPROVEMENT SCHEME	Desmond FitzGerald Architects	A 1988	NIA–3	14-15
GARDEN AT ROYAL HOSPITAL KILMAINHAM	OPW (Elizabeth Morgan)	SE 1988	NIA–3	42-43
THREE URBAN SPACES, Temple Bar, Dublin	Group 91 Architects	SM 1997	NIA–12	59-61
11 EUSTACE STREET,	Group 91			
Temple Bar, Dublin	/ Shane O'Toole, Michael Kelly and Susan Cogan	SA 1999	NIA–14	24-29
SMITHFIELD PUBLIC SPACE, Dublin	McGarry Ní Éanaigh Architects	A 2001	NIA–16	82-89
LIFFEY BOARDWALK, Dublin	McGarry Ní Éanaigh Architects	A 2002	NIA–17	58-67
LUMEN GENTIBUS				
– Landscape projects for Cashel	Desmond FitzGerald Architect / LRS	SM 2003	NIA–18	114-119
GROUNDWORKS, Clontarf, Dublin	de Paor Architects	SM 2008	NIA–23	124-131
JOYCE'S COURT, Pedestrian Street, Dublin	Dermot Foley Landscape Architects	SM 2009	NIA–24	188-191
COMMON GROUND: Urban Landscape in Kilkenny	GKMP Architects	SM 2010	NIA–25	180-187
PLUG-IN PATH AT WOODVALE PARK,				
Shankill, Belfast	LID Architecture, with Building Initiative	SM 2010	NIA–25	194-201
FR COLLINS PARK, Donaghmede, Dublin	MCO Projects / ARARQ Ireland	SM 2010	NIA–25	216-221

religious

RUSH CHURCH COMPETITION	Gallagher & Mullen Architects	SE 1987	NIA–2	14-15
CHAPEL AT ST ANGELA'S SCHOOL,				
Stevenage, Herts, England	Scott Tallon Walker Architects	SE 1988	NIA–3	48-49
CHAPEL OF RECONCILIATION, Knock, Co Mayo	de Blacam & Meagher Architects	A 1990	NIA–5	12-13
DEANS OF RESIDENCE (CHAPLAINCY), UCD	Prof Cathal O'Neill & Partners	A 1990	NIA–5	20-22
CHAPEL OF RECONCILIATION, Knock, Co Mayo	O'Donnell + Tuomey Architects	SE 1990	NIA–5	50-51
SIENA MONASTERY, Drogheda, Co Louth	McCullough Mulvin Architects	A 1999	NIA–14	40-45
SACRED HEART ORATORY, Dún Laoghaire	OPW (Conor Moran)	SM 1999	NIA–14	90-93

BUILDING TYPE

project	architect	award / year	volume	pages
POUSTINIA, Glencomeragh House of Prayer, Clonmel, Co Tipperary	Architects Bates Maher	M 2006	NIA–21	32-45
KNOCKTOPHER FRIARY, Co Kilkenny	ODOS Architects / O'Shea Design	SM 2007	NIA–22	144-152
ADDITIONAL ACCOMMODATION, SS GEORGE & THOMAS CHURCH, Cathal Brugha Street, Dublin	Clancy Moore Architects	SM 2009	NIA–24	174-179
JESUIT COMMUNITY, Milltown Park, Dublin	Scott Tallon Walker Architects	SM 2011	NIA–26	160-165

sport & leisure

project	architect	award / year	volume	pages
SPORTS HALL, Mount Anville, Dublin	Moloney O'Beirne Guy + HLM Architects	A 1986	NIA–1	12-13
LEISURE CENTRE, Greystones, Co Wicklow	A+D Wejchert Architects	SE 1986	NIA–1	36-37
ALSAA SPORTS COMPLEX, Dublin Airport	Declan O'Dwyer and Sheila Jones	SE 1987	NIA–2	28-29
CANOE CLUB ON THE RIVER LIFFEY	Grafton Architects	SE 1989	NIA–4	26-27
GOLF CLUB AT LUTTRELLSTOWN	O'Dowd O'Herlihy Horan Architects	SM 1994	NIA–9	26-27
A CONSTRUCTED LANDSCAPE – Blackwood Golf Centre, Co Down	O'Donnell + Tuomey Architects	SM 1995	NIA–10	56-57
TIME TRIALS STARTING RAMP, Tour de France	Mellett Architectes Paris	SM 2001	NIA–16	140-143
SPORTS AND YOUTH SERVICES CENTRE, Cabra, Dublin	Henchion + Reuter Architects	SM 2004	NIA–19	160-165
FINGLAS SWIMMING POOL & LEISURE CENTRE, Mellowes Park, Dublin	Donnelly Turpin Architects	SM 2005	NIA–20	106-113
TAILTEANN, Mary Immaculate College, Limerick	Murray Ó Laoire Architects	SM 2008	NIA–23	148-155
BALLYFERMOT LEISURE AND YOUTH CENTRE, Dublin	McGarry Ní Éanaigh Architects	SM 2009	NIA–24	220-227
BUSH SPORTS HALL, Cooley, Co Louth	McGarry Ní Éanaigh Architects	SM 2009	NIA–24	228-233
RATHMINES SQUARE – LEISURE CENTRE + APARTMENTS, Dublin	Donnelly Turpin Architects	SA 2011	NIA–26	26-37
AVIVA STADIUM, Lansdowne Road, Dublin	Scott Tallon Walker / Populous	A 2011	NIA–26	76-85

transport

project	architect	award / year	volume	pages
EXIT CONTROL BUILDING, DUBLIN AIRPORT	Noel Dowley Architect	A 1992	NIA–7	11-13
NEW TERMINAL DEVELOPMENT, Kerry Airport	Aer Rianta Technical Consultants	SM 1995	NIA–10	36-37
DUNDALK FREIGHT DEPOT – Check-In Office	Iarnród Éireann Architects	A 1996	NIA–11	37-41
DUN LAOGHAIRE DART STATION	Iarnród Éireann Architects	SM 2000	NIA–15	72-75

utility

project	architect	award / year	volume	pages
DUBLIN 2 DELIVERY OFFICE	Kavanagh Architects	SM 1992	NIA–7	26-27
ESB TRAINING CENTRE, Portlaoise	Building Consultancy Group	SM 1997	NIA–12	47-49
UTILITY BUILDING, Vernon Avenue, Clontarf, Dublin	de Paor Architects	A 2004	NIA–19	60-69
'FLOW', BORD GÁIS ABOVE-GROUND INSTALLATION, North Wall Quay, Dublin	DDDA Architects and Martin Richman, artist	A 2011	NIA–26	70-75
BORD GÁIS NETWORKS SERVICES CENTRE	Denis Byrne Architects	SM 2013	NIA–28	142-149

uncategorised

project	architect	award / year	volume	pages
WORK IN PROGRESS, 1985	Quilligan & Twamley Architects	A 1986	NIA–1	8-9
'THE ARGO'	James Horan and Anne Harper Architects	SE 1986	NIA–1	26-27
LUTTRELLSTOWN FARM	O'Dowd O'Herlihy Horan Architects	SE 1989	NIA–4	34-35
A ROOM WITH A VIEW	Bingham & Kelly Architects	A 1991	NIA–6	6-7
A13 FENCE, England	de Paor Architects	SM 1997	NIA–12	80-81
ROOM: ORGANISER-DIVIDER	Simon Walker Architect	SM 1999	NIA–14	104-106
TWO TIMBER BOXES	Grafton Architects	SA 2000	NIA–15	20-25
CUT-OUT FURNITURE	Simon Walker Architect	SM 2001	NIA–16	160-163
HOUSEBOAT	Níall McLaughlin Architects	SM 2005	NIA–20	124-129